Irish
TRADITIONAL
Cooking

Irish
TRADITIONAL
Cooking

OVER **300** RECIPES FROM IRELAND'S HERITAGE

Darina Allen

KYLE BOOKS

For Aunt Lil, my mother Elizabeth O'Connell and my mother-in-law Myrtle Allen—all of whom kindled my interest in traditional Irish food.

This edition published in Great Britain in 2012 by Kyle Books
An imprint of Kyle Cathie Ltd
www.kylebooks.com
Distributed by National Book Network
(800) 462-6420

First published in Great Britain in 1995 by Kyle Cathie Limited

ISBN 978-1-906868-76-5

Project editors: Jenny Wheatley and Emma Bastow
Designers: Carl Hodson and Lucy Gowans
Special photography: Kristin Perers (see below)
Home economist: Aya Nishimura
Prop stylist: Lorraine Dawkins
Copy editor: Laura Gladwin
Editorial assistance: Estella Hung
Production: Gemma John and Nic Jones

A Cataloguing in Publication record for this title is available from Library of Congress.
Library of Congress Control Number: 2012931279

Color reproduction by ALTA London
Printed in Spain by Indice Arts Gràfiques—Barcelona

Photographic Acknowledgments
All photographs © Kristin Perers except for the following: pages 4, 70 and 198 © Peter Cassidy; pages 7, 9 and 94 © Michelle Garrett/Kevin Dunne; pages 10, 11 and 12 © Claudia Kinmonth.

Contents

Foreword

I suspect that, in common with most food lovers who did not have the good fortune to be reared in Ireland, the first Irish food name I ever heard was Allen. That was Myrtle Allen, of course, the legendary culinary pioneer of Ballymaloe House in Shanagarry, Co. Cork. She was a pioneer by simple virtue of the fact that, in 1964, she had the then absolutely revolutionary notion of presenting honest Irish raw materials and good homestyle cooking in a restaurant environment. Like Alice Waters in Berkeley about half a dozen years later, she also had the equally radical inspiration of actually basing her menu on ingredients that were in season and at their prime—in effect letting the menu be dictated by the products.

The second Irish food name I ever heard was Allen, too—this time Darina Allen. Née Darina O'Connell, in the ancient village of Cullohill in Co. Laois, Darina had, as she writes, "a magical Irish country childhood." Helping milk cows and harvest fruits and vegetables, she grew up taking the idea of "farm to table"—a recently discovered (or at least rediscovered) concept these days—as a given. The fact that her mother was a wonderful cook added to her appreciation of good food, and she became adept in the kitchen herself.

As a young woman looking for employment, she happened to hear about a farm wife named Myrtle Allen down in County Cork who had recently opened a restaurant serving the kind of food she had grown up with. "You could just about count the good restaurants in Ireland on one hand in those days", Darina once told me, "and even the good ones tended to write the menu the day they opened and it would be exactly the same ten years later. Myrtle wrote her menu every day, which was seen as an amateurish thing to do. It sounded right to me, though."

A letter to Myrtle got Darina a job in the Ballymaloe kitchen. It was the perfect place for her, a serious restaurant expressing and elaborating on the culinary values she had grown up with. She not only thrived as a part of the Ballymaloe team but soon became part of the family too, literally, marrying Myrtle's son Tim. In 1983, as the restaurant became increasingly successful and well-furnished guestrooms were added, turning Ballymaloe House into a gastronome's dream destination, Darina and Tim branched off and established a cooking school at nearby Kinoith farm—today officially known as the Ballymaloe Cookery School and Gardens.

The school is hardly exclusively Irish. Students come from all over the world to study everything from beekeeping and pig butchery to vegetable (and rose) gardening, foraging, and food writing, and to learn the various arts of making tapas, pizza, and sushi, among many other foods. But Darina's passion—her life's work, one could say—remains the cooking of her native country: the great, rich Irish traditions of artisanal food production (revived with great enthusiasm in recent years) and honest, skillful preparation.

As a popular television personality and a leading light in Ireland's fast-growing Slow Food movement, as the founder of the first modern day Irish farmers' market (at Midleton, not far from Shanagarry), and above all—for those of us who know Darina mostly from afar—as a prolific, ardently affectionate author of terrific cookbooks celebrating the best the Irish table has to offer (which is very good indeed), Darina is the most eloquent and credible champion of Irish cooking I can imagine. Writing with the kind of authority that comes from having lived her subject matter, Darina evokes the landscapes, personalities, and above all flavors of the Irish food world, and backs them up with the kind of clearly written, sensible recipes that only the experienced proprietor of a first rate international cooking school could manage.

If you have fond memories of good meals in Ireland, whether at home or out and about, this new edition of Darina's classic *Irish Traditional Cooking* will make your mouth water and your heart ache. If you are new to real Irish food, or are one of those benighted souls who doesn't believe that Ireland offers anything worth eating, I predict that this handsome volume will be a revelation to you, opening your mind and palate to a new world of culinary pleasure.

Colman Andrews, author of *The Country Cooking of Ireland* and editorial director of TheDailyMeal.com

Introduction

I had a magical Irish country childhood. I grew up in a tiny village called Cullohill, in Co. Laois, where all the neighbors helped each other during the busiest times of the farming year. Even as children we lent a hand with the haymaking and then took turns to ride home behind the hay cock on the horse-drawn cart. Threshing was still done with a steam machine, and I have many happy memories of helping to cook the enormous threshing dinner and bringing hot sweet tea and "spotted dog" to the men in the fields.

At home, almost everything we and our neighbors ate was fresh, wholesome food, homegrown or produced in the locality. We even had a house cow and our own hens. Every day, my mother cooked three wonderful meals on the range, which we all tucked into with great relish around the big kitchen table—it needed to be big because there were nine of us. A packet of fig rolls or coconut creams from the shop were a rare treat.

Our summer holidays were spent, not in France or the Caribbean, but on an uncle's farm in Co. Tipperary. For us, as children, it was an absolutely enchanting place—a big working farm on the edge of the bog, where my great-aunt churned butter virtually every day, they killed their own pigs, cured bacon and made black and white pudding, and my great-aunt did all the cooking over a huge open turf fire. The O'Connell family of Noard was virtually self-sufficient up to the early 1960s.

Here I also learned the art of cooking in a bastible and how to make a tender "railway cake," speckled with plump golden raisins. Here I learned how to hand-milk a cow, sitting on a three-legged stool with my forehead leaning against the cow's warm stomach. As I write this I remember the sound of the milk squirting into the pail and the cows contentedly eating their ration of sweet hay. When the milking was finished, the milk destined for the creamery was put into tall churns and a few buckets were taken to the dairy to be run through the separator. The ripened cream of several days was then churned into rich golden butter, washed and salted. Great-aunt Lil painstakingly showed me how to use the timber "butter-hands" to shape the butter into little blocks and tiny pats for the house.

It never occurred to any of us that this way of life, which we took so much for granted, was about to come to an abrupt end. I can remember distinctly the day the first packets of Instant Whip and blancmange came to our village and we couldn't wait to try them. These foods had a glamor and a novelty value which made home cooking seem dull by comparison. All over Ireland, within just a few years, people began to prize fancy shop-bought goods. When the priest came to visit, for instance, he would always be offered white "shop bread" in preference to homemade soda bread. With the rush to embrace a new consumer culture of packet and canned foods in the name of progress, a whole food tradition was jeopardized in an alarmingly short space of time. Through the 1950s and

Nancy Ellis shows Darina how to cook griddle bread, Glin Castle, Co. Limerick.

1960s, rural electrification brought the added temptation of frozen foods to more remote areas. Official agricultural policy encouraged farmers to intensify to produce maximum yields at minimum cost—to the detriment of flavor, texture, and nutritional content.

It was just as the novelty of new synthetic flavors was wearing off, and I was beginning to question the wisdom of this food revolution, that I first arrived at Ballymaloe House, near Shanagarry in Co. Cork. Fresh from hotel school in Dublin, I had heard about a farmer's wife who had recently opened a restaurant in her rambling country house, and was cooking with local produce from her garden and from the sea close by.

It was to be a turning point in my life. In Myrtle Allen I found a cook who believed in following the seasons, growing her own herbs—at a time when this was far from fashionable—and using the bounty of her farm and the Cork countryside to the full. She wrote her menus every day, incorporating fresh produce from the farm and the kitchen garden, and the fresh catch from the fishing boats at Ballycotton. Far from being seduced by convenience foods, she had no time for them at all. I quickly realized she was someone whose philosophy I could identify with. Myrtle was serving parsnips, swede, turnips, carrageen moss, and tender spears of rhubarb at a time when they would have been considered far too humble for most restaurant menus. The confidence she had in her own local produce, used in season at its best, was an inspiration.

Almost 40 years later, I am still at Ballymaloe, in the lush East Cork countryside. I became a member of the Allen family by the simple expedient of marrying the boss's eldest son. Since then, Ballymaloe House—the first country-house hotel in Ireland—has developed in various directions with the interest and involvement of different family members.

I started Ballymaloe Cookery School in 1983 in a small way, in converted farm buildings behind our house. Now it has more than doubled in size, and students from all over the world are attracted to a cookery school set amidst an organic farm, fruit, vegetable, and herb gardens with free-range hens, pigs and even our own Kerry cow and Jersey in the orchard to remind me of my childhood. Other members of the family run the large farm which still provides Ballymaloe with much of its produce; manage a shop selling the best of Irish craft work; or are involved in other enterprises under the Ballymaloe umbrella.

During this time, we have built up a network of dedicated food producers who supply the restaurant and the cookery school with naturally reared meat and poultry, home-smoked fish, and stoneground oatmeal. Our cheeses come from the new generation of Irish farmhouse cheesemakers. I have always felt that these wonderful ingredients are best cooked simply, to preserve their true natural flavors. Both Myrtle Allen and I have always been interested in traditional Irish recipes and we have often found at Ballymaloe that recipes handed down from generation to generation produce the most delicious results. Over the years we gradually built up a small collection. About 15 years ago, however, I saw that there was an urgent need to research more vigorously. With the passing of one more generation, I realized, a whole culinary tradition, with all its fascinating regional variations, was in imminent danger of being lost.

That was the starting point for this book. Writing it has been a labor of salvage, as well as one of love. Early on in my research I wrote to regional newspapers inviting readers to send me old family recipes, and the response was overwhelming. I received wonderful replies which encouraged me to contact people all over the country and set off on a journey of discovery. In Ballyheigue in Co. Kerry I spent a fascinating day with John Guerin and his mother Bridget, learning how to collect bairneachs (limpets) off the rocks for a traditional Good Friday soup. In Co. Monaghan, Granny Toye, well into her eighties, described in vivid detail how to make the boxty pancakes of her youth. Everywhere I met people who were delighted to pass on recipes for dishes that had been an essential part of their lives, along with their recollections.

While traditional Irish cooking stems, in the main, from simple farmers, it also embraces the more sophisticated food served in the grand houses of the Anglo-Irish gentry. The cooks in these households would have been expected to know the rudiments of classic French cooking. They would also have been encouraged to adapt recipes brought back from the Grand Tour, or from India, where the younger sons of many Anglo-Irish families made their career in the army. From the dining rooms of the great houses to the kitchens of the poorest cabins, and from pagan times right up to the present day,

Ireland has had a strong tradition of generous hospitality. The best food was generally for guests, and the warmest hospitality was often to be found in the most humble homes.

In recent years there has been a renaissance on the Irish food scene. Irish chefs have become more adventurous and many have a greater appreciation of quality Irish produce, giving them the confidence to serve Irish food proudly. The most encouraging development has been the emergence of an artisanal food culture—most based in the Cork area, but gradually spreading through other counties. The farmhouse cheesemakers have led the way, but there is also a whole generation of fish smokers, artisan bakers, jam, pickle and preserve makers, artisan brewers, and exciting cured-meat producers.

The Slow Food movement has found an enthusiastic following in Ireland; the Euro-toque Association of chefs, which aims to foster the best traditional products of an area, has led the way in supporting and encouraging the artisan food producers and has highlighted the source of the food on menus; Euro-toques and Good Food Ireland have encouraged restaurant and catering businesses to incorporate local food into their menus, so at last there appears to be a growing appreciation of the value of fresh, naturally produced food in season—the wheel is coming full circle. Even as half the country is living on pre-cooked foods from garage forecourts, there is a deep craving among growing numbers of people for forgotten flavors and fresh local food. This grass-roots movement is particularly evident in the crowds that flock to the farmers' markets which are springing up all over the country.

I am delighted at this revival of interest in Irish traditional food—the sort of wholesome, comforting dishes that nourished our ancestors for generations and are just as delicious today. I hope my own enthusiasm will encourage more young Irish chefs to include such things as Champ, Colcannon, Irish Stew and Bacon and Cabbage in their menus, and to cook them with pride—for simple dishes like these have already begun to appear in fashionable restaurants in London and New York. I believe we can learn a great deal from a tradition based around fresh local ingredients, simply and succulently cooked. That is what this book is all about.

Darina Allen

Lana Pringle shows Darina how to make Barm Brack.

The Story of Food in Ireland

For some time now, Ireland has suffered under the assumption that our traditional foods are few, fading, and limited to dishes such as Irish Stew, Coddle, and Bacon and Cabbage. Wholesome and tasty as these are, nonetheless they are just one aspect of a far more complex and interesting tradition—a tradition that has been shaped by climate and terrain, colonization and economics, fashion and commercial developments, and, of course, the Great Famine. Darina's revised *Irish Traditional Cooking* is a wonderful companion to the story of Irish food and may encourage us to rethink our ideas of tradition.

The story of food in Ireland begins some 9,000 years ago when Ireland's earliest inhabitants found an island of dense woodland covered with pine, birch, and hazel woods broken only by meandering rivers and streams. As hunters, gatherers, and fishers, they relied on wild mammals, birds, fishes, and vegetation for subsistence. From a number of the excavations we see that the early Stone Age diet was one of wild pig, fish (including salmon, eels, and trout) wild birds, and probably eggs, wild vegetables, and fruits like apples and hazelnuts. There is also evidence that fish were preserved by smoking over smudge fires on the riverbank, which could then be stored for winter and spring use. Fish were of great importance at this time, especially for communities living around the coast. Shellfish, in particular young limpets, were much sought after. The remains of fish species such as mullet, wrasse, bass, sole, and tope reflect the common practise of inshore fishing, and sea mammals, in particular seal, and various seabirds, such as guillemots, were also eaten by people at this time.

Some time between 4,000 and 3,000BC the hunter-gatherer way of life was superseded by a lifestyle and economy based predominantly on agriculture. This was a major milestone in the evolution of Irish food. Domestic cattle were introduced into the country, as well as cereal crops such as wheat and barley. Woodland was cleared and houses, enclosures and field-systems built. This revolutionized the nature of Irish society, establishing a farming economy that has characterized Irish food until the present day. The cereals introduced at this time consisted of primitive varieties that were used to prepare porridge and bread. Cattle were important because of their milk, meat, hide and, of course, for ploughing. Sheep and goats were reared for wool and milk. Given the value of their secondary products, they would have been eaten less than pig.

The still heavily-wooded landscape was admirably suited to pig rearing. In fact, pigs greatly assisted Ireland's Neolithic farmers because their nosing and rooting helped to prepare the ground for tillage and pasture. Pigs and indeed meat in general may have become increasingly important in the diet and during the Bronze Age (c.1800BC) and the Iron Age (c.800BC). These times are characterized by clear evidence of different social ranks, all of which have implications for the diet. *Fulachta fiadh* (cooking pits), an outdoor system for boiling meat by means of using heated stones placed in a large water trough, become prevalent at this time. Impressive metal cauldrons for cooking appeared for the first time and given that these, when providenced, are associated with the wealthiest sites suggest that boiled flesh, as opposed to spit-roasted meat, may have been considered superior. Indeed, in the saga literature of early medieval Ireland, roast and particularly boiled flesh is the stuff of elaborate aristocratic feasting. The types of cereals available may have been influenced by contact with Roman Britain in the pre-Christian period. It is believed that oats came to the island while there was also a greater emphasis on bread wheat. Domesticated fowl were probably also introduced from the Roman world.

The early 5th century AD saw the introduction of Christianity to Ireland. Literacy developed from this period onwards and many writings of the time provide an invaluable insight into the range and diversity of early medieval Irish food. Dairy produce and cereals were the everyday staples. The former was consumed in the form of fresh milk, sour milk, thickened milk, colostrum, curds, flavored curd mixtures, butter,. and soft and hard cheeses. The existence of several varieties of named soft and hard cheeses in this period is of particular note. Cereals, most commonly oats and barley, a little rye together with more prestigious and high-ranking wheat, were used in the production of flat breads and it is likely that leavened wheat loaves were also prepared. The palatable quality of wheaten bread, compared to that of barley and oats, rendered it the luxury food of Sundays and

Unknown artist, *Interior of a Kerry Cottage* (probably) from *The Pictoral Times*, 1846.

Unknown artist, *A Potato Dinner at Cahirciveen*, Co. Kerry, from *The Pictoral Times*, 1846.

the first choice of kings and nobles. Porridge, gruel, meal pastes, and pottages, and cereal with milk, fruit, and nuts were also consumed. Additional condiments included hen and goose eggs, honey, fish, butter, curds, seaweeds, apples together with different types of onion, garlic, and kale. A wide range of wild foods, notably watercress and wild garlic, brought additional relish.

Meat and butter were important features of the diet, particularly for the affluent and aristocratic classes. The meats most commonly eaten were fresh and salted pork and, to a lesser extent, beef, mutton, venison, and salted venison. However, the vast majority of the populace made do with pieces of salted bacon and enjoyed fresh meat only on holy days or at times of great festivals. The establishment of Norse towns like Dublin, Wexford, Waterford, Cork, and Limerick from the 10th century onwards not only developed the idea of a market economy and its effect upon food production, but these towns may also have looked more closely at the sea as a food resource.

The 12th century Anglo-Norman invasion and the subsequent Norman settlements brought additional dietary changes and developments in certain social quarters, most particularly in the eastern regions of Norman influence. In addition, the new monastic orders coming to Ireland from the 12th century onwards were most active in diversifying the ingredient base and broadening the range and variety of kitchen garden vegetables, herbs, and orchard fruits. The Anglo Normans also brought innovations to arable agriculture. On the table, these advances were seen in the increased use of wheaten loaves which varied in quality, from heavy wholemeal types to finer loaves of white bolted flour, and the production of these loaves in quantity was made possible by the introduction of the built-up oven.

Changes in cooking styles, types of dishes, and an alignment of the palate to the medieval European norm became prevalent in areas of direct Norman influence. Anglo-Norman cookery was characterized by an emphasis on spices and the tendency to mix sweet and acid ingredients in one dish. The Norman concern with the aesthetic presentation of food saw an emphasis on the use of colorants like saffron, parsley, and sandalwood. Meat and fish pies and pasties were consumed, while both meat and fowl were distinctively flavored with garlic and spices. To facilitate these tastes imported items were important and church, manorial, and trade records testify to the importation and use of luxury goods like almonds, spices, honey and sugar, pepper, figs, verjuice, and rice. This tradition was in marked contrast to the milky, salty, and coarse diet of the Gaelic Irish.

Innovation and change also followed in the wake of the Tudor and Stuart conquests of the 16th and 17th centuries. It is clear that by the 17th century, Ireland was home to a diversity of culinary traditions; with the Gaelic diet of oats and dairy produce co-existing with the acquired Anglo-Norman and English traditions.

On a domestic level, the 17th-century English settlers, most especially at the upper levels of society, brought with them to Ireland new cooking styles and taste preferences and in turn introduced an array of new ingredients. As promoters of gardening and horticulture, landlords and their agents undertook the importation of seed and fruit trees to stock their gardens, especially in the period of relative peace and stability after 1660. Most famously, the new settlers introduced the potato to Ireland as a new world exotic that was grown initially in the gardens of the wealthy for its novelty value. The treatment of these new ingredients, imported or homegrown, is dealt with in detail in the manuscript receipt books of the late 17th and 18th centuries. Collections of recipes routinely call for exotic imported ingredients like rosewater, sugar, almonds, and spices. It is clear that these recipes fit into the mainstream of English cookery of the 17th century. Indeed recipes emanating from the Irish country house, which come on line in a steady stream throughout the 18th century in the form of family manuscript receipt books, reveal a food culture that closely follows English styles and fashions with a substantial body of recipes bearing a close resemblance with those in contemporary English published cookery books. Underpinning the rich and diverse tastes of the Anglo-Irish elite was the emergence and solidification of the estate system from the late 1720s onwards. The demesne lands were not only landscaped for their aesthetic appeal but they were also designed with the concerns of the table in mind.

For those living near the developing and thriving urban centers, what could not be produced domestically was available from the growing number of grocers' shops. By the mid 18th century Dublin, for example, offered a vast variety of everyday and exotic foods and household accounts of the economically secure reveal the healthy business relationship between the customer and the growing number of confectioners, grocers, poulterers, and bakers. In addition, the creation of a canal system and road network allowed for the inland transportation of not only fresh fish but it also brought luxury imported goods like tea, sugar, sweetmeats, pepper, ginger, oranges, and lemons to the homes of those who could afford them in the countryside.

The 18th century was a period of sustained economic growth and the demand for Irish cured beef and butter was maintained. Butter, while still an important part of the diet, now lost is former dominance. In addition, the process of butter-making left behind buttermilk and skimmed milk, both low-fat products that were not only less nutritious than whole milk but which were also less functional and versatile in the production of curds and cheeses. Furthermore, as dairy herds became larger, cattle were drawn out of the households of poorer families in the 18th century thus closing off an important food resource. In addition, the port cities associated with the slaughtering of cattle to furnish export trade made a variety of cheap perishable offal foods readily available to the urban poor giving regional specialties like tripe and drisheen in Cork City. The drawing of foods to the market and their withdrawal from the diet of the poorer sectors of Irish society left room for a substitute non-commercial crop to fill the gap. In the 17th century, oats in the form of bread and porridge replaced butter in the diet but as the 18th century progressed the potato was increasingly adopted to fulfil that role.

Ireland's heavy acidic soils and mild, wet, relatively frost-free conditions proved ideal for the potato. From the 1760s onwards, cereal cultivation expanded in response to growing British markets and the potato, as an excellent cleansing crop in rotation, assumed a high profile not only in facilitating the growth of arable agriculture but also in its increased presence at local markets where prices were competitive.

The potato also supported and encouraged the population boom of the late 18th century (from c.2 million in 1750 to c.4.4 million in 1790). A swelling rural population saw widespread subdivision of holdings together with a settlement spread into previously unsettled areas of poor and marginal lands. The potato responded well to both movements. If well manured, the potato gave excellent returns. Its merits as a reclamation crop brought settlement to hill and mountain and, once established, the potato flourished in these seemingly unfavorable conditions. A mushrooming of small farm holdings was especially associated with the west and southwest coast of Ireland where a particular regional dietary pattern developed amongst the small, poorer farmers based on potatoes supplemented with shore foods.

The second half of the 18th century was the high point for the potato in Ireland with several varieties under cultivation. On the eve of the Great Famine, however, one variety, the Lumper, a prolific cropper, was almost the universal food of the poor whose numbers stood at c.3 million. Their dangerous reliance not simply on one food, but on one variety of potato which was susceptible to potato blight, made inevitable the dire consequences of the arrival of this fungal disease (*Phytophthora infestans*) in 1845.

The impoverished diet of the poor in the years immediately preceding the Great Famine is exemplified by the simple manner of potato cookery. Lumpers, a thick, waxy, creamy potato variety, were simply boiled, drained and eaten communally from a basket, sack, or cloth placed centrally and convenient to family members. Depending on the time of the year, two or three potato meals were eaten each day with a limited variety of foods such as herrings, seaweeds, shellfish, buttermilk, or simply salted water. Salted pig meat was an occasional indulgence. The potato continued to play an important part in the post-Famine diet, although it would not resume its former dominance, except in the most impoverish areas of the west. And while the status of the potato had changed, it still remained an indispensable item in the make-up of meals of all classes, thereby giving a distinctive character to Irish food ways.

The second half of the 19th century was a period of rapid commercialization. Increased number of grocers' outlets offered an alternative to the familiar litany of foods produced at home. Factory bread, or "baker's bread," soon became a constant. The importation of cheap American wheat together with the ready availability of buttermilk and the growing popularity of baking soda as a leaven meant that bread could be made easily and quickly

Francis W. Topham (1808–77), *Irish Peasants in a Cottage*, 1844.

at home on a daily basis. By the end of the 19th century, the food economy of rural Ireland was a system which saw a percentage of home-produced goods hived-off to supply the market with the sales subsidizing further food purchases, rent, household necessities, stock, and seed. The sale of a pig or two, butter, potatoes, eggs, and fowl allowed for the purchase of wheat flour, white "shop" bread, maize/yellow meal, tea, sugar, salt fish, and fatty American bacon.

Throughout the first half of the 20th century the rural diet, although increasingly susceptible to the influence of commercial forces, was one that depended largely on home-produced goods and local produce. Potatoes, oatmeal, imported Indian meal, buttermilk, sour milk, and butter were staples along with home cured meats, and, in particular, pig meat, remained standard. The diet followed seasonal changes with wild foods when accessible—berries, mushrooms, watercress, and rabbits making an occasional presence—while the coastal diet was differentiated by its leanings toward fish and shellfish and, at times, seabirds and their eggs. Festive occasions were upheld with the desire to bring fresh meat or fresh fowl, most especially a goose and shop-bought luxuries, into the pattern, while fast days were strictly adhered to with a concentration on salted fish eaten with potatoes and a simple white sauce.

In urban areas increased commercialization and industrialization of food production brought easier access to a wider variety of goods. In line with rural patterns, the urban poor became increasingly reliant on refined white bread, spread or fried with lard or eaten with cheap, factory-made jams. The establishment and growth of a substantial factory-based bacon curing industry throughout the 19th century saw an increase in the availability of pig offal and inferior meat cuts in the cities strongly engaged in the trade. Even for those of better means in urban settings, cooking styles and taste preferences remained largely conservative and repetitive. However, the second half of the 20th century was a period of sustained dietary change in Ireland, with a slow erosion of a long-lived conservative approach to food and cookery. Increased economic prosperity during the 1960s fuelled consumer demand for a greater variety of foodstuffs and for cooking and kitchen equipment. In addition, increased foreign travel during the 1950s and 60s together with the liberating effects of television from the 1960s onwards encouraged dietary experimentation. Central to making these developments and aspirations a reality was the emergence and rise of the supermarket. Indian and Chinese restaurants became increasingly prevalent. French cuisine was taken to be the epitome of fine dining due, in part, to the high reputation of French food culture but also to the influence of French-trained Irish chefs returning home.

The mid 1970s saw the beginnings of a movement that would redirect critical and popular attention back to home-produced quality foods. In 1976, on a smallholding in west Cork, Veronica Steele began producing cheese with her surplus milk stocks, thus heralding the emergence of the hugely successful farmhouse cheese industry. Myrtle Allen, proprietor and chef at Ballymaloe House, began promoting the merits of quality Irish foods. In time, carefully handcrafted foods found a following, especially amongst those who found the production of cheap industrial-style foods objectionable.

Today, in the face of global agri-food systems, many people feel increasingly distanced from understanding how we farm and how we produce food. In a world of food sameness, we strive to regain something of who we are through an understanding of our traditional foods. As a result, local food production and authentic ways of using ingredients are all the more pertinent. An understanding of our past ways with food is enriching; it encourages us to value what is particular to Ireland and in turn we can feel confident and proud of the island's long and continued association with food production. Here Darina gives color and substance to the story of Irish food, presenting us with a richness of dishes—some simple, some sophisticated, some well known, some forgotten, but all good.

There are many voices in this book. We hear of people's personal and family memories of food, we discover local favorites, we see the hand-written recipes of the country houses and we are armored with the nostalgia of hearing again from food writers of the past. With this book to hand, we may come to a new understanding of the nature of Irish traditional food.

Regina Sexton, food historian

Ireland's Culinary Manuscripts

Cultural policy in the early years of the foundation of the state was directed almost entirely to the rescue, maintenance, and documentation of early Christian and Celtic cultural remains. In those early years there was uneasiness surrounding the legacy of the great Irish houses and landed estates, viewed as they were as reminders of what was seen as an alien and oppressive heritage. This attitude has now shifted to the position where these houses and estates are viewed as an intrinsic part of the heritage of Ireland. How this appreciation has developed owes much to the work of culinary, archeological, economic, and cultural historians and bodies such as the Georgian Society and the Centre for the Study of Historic Irish Houses and Estates at Maynooth University under Terence Dooley.

Public interest in culinary heritage is intense and there is an increasing demand to see not only life in the public spaces of these great houses but also in the hidden private spaces of servants and master alike. Nowhere is the complex hierarchy of the house more exposed then in the domestic arrangements centering on the kitchen.

Conservation architects and historians can piece together the physical structure of the kitchen but the documents supporting cultural and culinary historians are altogether more ephemeral and dispersed. One of the most valuable resources that the culinary historian and interested practitioners have are the manuscript cookbooks that have survived through the years and remain important resources for research both in the public domain and in private hands. These manuscripts are particularly important in piecing together the history of the smaller estates where public and private dining went largely unrecorded.

On May 1st 1807 Maria Edgworth wrote to her mother: "there is no flour, but Hetty thinks you would rather buy bread till this cook goes because she is so wasteful, I don't understand the rationale—but in short say if we are to send to Slane...." Mary Ponsenby tells us how "to make turnip soup by Mr Rigby's famous cook..." using 12 large turnips and two heads of cabbage. They are tantalizing glimpses of the forms of relationship that existed between employer and employee in the Georgian era. It also demonstrates why detailed information about who exactly the cooks and chefs were and who realized the recipes in the manuscript cookbooks of the 17th and 18th centuries is so difficult to piece together. It is only through sideways references that the personalities of the people who toiled in the kitchens of the smaller landed estates of the moderately wealthy emerge.

The manuscript cookbooks are also a window into the level of exchange of ideas that the writers engaged in. In Mary Ponsenby's manuscript we find recipes attributed to numerous people, including Mrs Southwell, Mrs Staples, Mrs Tells, Mrs Mason and, in an example of cross–gender knowledge sharing, we find "Mr Loyds receipt for preventing in wheat which he got from Mrs Newman." Provenance is important in establishing reliability and is also often indicative of status. Mary Ponsenby is equally comfortable acknowledging Lady Charleville in her recipe for apple pudding, or Lord Craven for his recipe for raspberry vinegar, as she is in referencing Mr Cummings for his recipe "to dress calves head like turtle." One has to question whether Lord Craven engaged in the practical aspects of his vinegar making, so again the reader is drawn into the reciprocal nature of the exchange of information between the cook and the employer. Undoubtedly literacy levels and access to writing materials played a role in the employer being the conduit of information. The historian Carol Gold has studied Danish cookbooks and established a close connection between literacy levels and the Protestant tradition of bible study. Literacy and numeracy are features of Danish recipes from as early as 1616. Mary Ponsenby, writing in the mid 1850s, is comfortable using precise measurements like pounds and quarts and in the much earlier Smythe of Barbavilla manuscript (c.1690) the author negotiates ounces, pounds, and pecks with ease. The Smyth family (the 'e' was added in 1810) settled in Ireland c.1630 in Co. Down and Antrim. The founder was the Rt. Rev. William Smyth (1638–1699), successively Dean of Dromore, Bishop of Killala, Bishop of Raphoe, and Bishop of Kilmore. In 1670, two years before his marriage to Mary Povey, he purchased what became the Barbavilla estate in Collinstown, Co. Westmeath. The historian Toby Barnard also mentions the Povey family, in the context of the gradual decline of fortune and status that the Irish ascendancy class often embodied. The Smythe of Barbavilla collection allows the reader several glimpses into the day-to-day life as experienced by the writer with all its social obligations and interruptions. A charming example of this being the reference in a letter with a recipe for quince marmalade, which the writer failed to send it earlier as they were "called to a labor."

A fundamental difference exists between printed and manuscript cookbooks in their relationship to the public and private domain. Printed cookbooks draw oxygen from the very fact of being public. Manuscript cookbooks are of their very essence intimate, relatively unedited, and written with an eye to private circulation. Printed books were still a relatively expensive commodity and not a medium that people felt comfortable editing in their own hand. This was not the case with the manuscript cookbooks. Here the ability of the writers to engage in an open-ended conversation with the reader is part of the inherent charm of the text. Culinary manuscripts closely follow the diurnal and annual tasks of the household. In them one finds recipes for cures and restoratives, recipes for cleansing, products for the house and the body, as well as the expected recipes for preserving and cooking all manners of food. The reader is struck when reading these manuscripts by the sheer physical work and planning that the business of food entailed in the pre-industrialized age. The manuscripts also allow the reader to observe how recipes evolve and become personalized through addendums and commentary. Indeed at times one can almost hear the spoken voice as spelling was largely phonetic and accents and rhythms come through in the text: "To Ruff beef yr best way... take a rib of good beef, let not yr chyne nor sholder or bones be taken out nor yr beef in ye least broak or choped, take an ounce of salt peeter and half a pound of glister sugar, mix it with as much bay salt, or rock and white as will save it, rub it on yr beef very well and let it ly so for 12 days turning and rubbing it every day, yn hang it up where it may dry or be smoaked without much heat when it is dry enough yu may keep it in (possibly malt) if yr kitching be too hott, when yu think fit to boyle it water it first at least 24 hours and when it is almost boyled take it up and put it in yr dripin pan before yr fire then froth it and beast it after flower it and beat it before yu take it up this makes it eat tenderer."

At the upper end of the scale the role of the vice-regal court at Dublin Castle during the reign of the Hanoverian kings in England from 1715 to 1830 was to replicate the standards of St. James's Palace in London, and as such it sat at the center of aristocratic culinary influence. Generous hospitality was the order of the day among the Anglo-Irish gentry class. It has been estimated that a workforce of 168,000 brewers, butchers, bakers, millers, cooks, and dealers were necessary to service the feeding of the upper classes in 1770. One of these cooks was Robert Smith and in his career one can get some idea of the transfer of knowledge that took place at these upper echelons of society. Remembered chiefly for his book titled *Court Cookery, or the Compleat English Cook*, published in 1725, Smith had worked for the dukes of Buckinghamshire and Ormonde, King William III, and the French ambassador, the duc d'Aumont. He had trained under Patrick Lambe (1650–1708) who had served as Master Cook to five reigning monarchs from the time of Charles II to that of Queen Anne. Lamb's cookery book, *Royal Cookery: or the Compleat Royal Cook*, was published posthumously in 1710.

It was after independence that Irish food writers found their way into the printed medium and Ireland is now ably represented on the international food scene through the publication of cookery books. But for that earlier unheard articulation of what was eaten and feasted on at the higher end of the social scale, it is to the manuscripts that we can reliably turn. The historian Barbara Ketchum Wheaten has likened recipes to a "magicians hat" in their ability to reveal much more then they seem to contain. These manuscripts allow access to the intimacies of private life, the networks of shared experience and knowledge. They are one strand in the story of Ireland's culinary heritage.

Dorothy Cashman, food historian

Broths and Soups

Brotchán or broth was an integral part of the diet in early Ireland. The earliest broths were little more than oatmeal boiled with water, milk and herbs. Meat was seldom added as it rarely entered the diet of the poor, but in coastal areas seaweeds such as carrageen, laver, dulse, and sloke would have been included. Apart from simple broths, soup did not feature largely in the diet of the ordinary folk, but it was certainly a much more important item on the menu of the country houses.

When researching this book I sourced many of the soup recipes from country house manuscripts. Sometimes these manuscripts can be clearly ascribed to the lady of the house, other times it is less clear who has compiled them. Country house cookbooks were continuously adapted as new recipes became available. The mistress would exchange recipes with her friends; new wives brought recipes from their family home and new cooks from their previous positions.

The earliest references to making soup I came across were in the 1810 manuscript of Mary Lee Heathfield and the 1823 manuscript of Mary Franks. The soups had an unusually long cooking time and would have been very filling but not very appetizing in many cases, and the long cooking time would certainly have diminished the nutrients.

Serves 2

8oz leeks, washed
2 tablespoons (¼ stick) butter
2½ cups stock or milk or water
4 tablespoons steel-cut oats
salt and freshly ground pepper
pinch of ground mace
1 tablespoon chopped parsley

Serves 6

1lb lean neck mutton
2½ cups diced carrot
1½ cups diced onion
2 leeks, chopped
1 white turnip, diced
1 tablespoon pearl barley
7–8½ cups water
salt and freshly ground pepper
3 tablespoons chopped parsley

Serves 8 (approximately)

2–3 raw or cooked chicken
    carcases, or a mixture of both,
    or 1 × 4lb boiling fowl, jointed
giblets from the chicken, i.e.
    neck, heart, gizzard, and scalded
    feet if available
14⅓ cups approx. cold water
1 or 2 onions, sliced
1 or 2 carrots, sliced
few parsley stalks
sprig of thyme
6 black peppercorns
salt

Brotchán Roy

One of the most famous of these broths was made with leeks and was called
Brotchán Roy, *meaning "A broth fit for a king" (*Roy *derives from* Rí, *the
Irish word for king). Onions, chives and leeks were very popular vegetables in
the early medieval period; possibly the perennial Babington leek, a vegetable
frequently mentioned in old manuscripts.*

Slice the white and pale green part of the leeks finely. Melt the butter in a saucepan, toss
in the leeks, cook for a minute or two, add the liquid, bring to a boil then sprinkle in the
oatmeal. Bring back to a boil, stirring all the time, season with salt, freshly ground pepper,
and a pinch of mace. Cover and simmer for about 45 minutes or until both vegetables and
oatmeal are cooked. Add the parsley, boil for a minute or two, then serve.

Mutton, or Lamb, Broth

*This would have been cooked in a big black pot over the open fire, with bits
of scrawny mutton to give it flavor, and a few fistfuls of pearl barley for extra
nourishment. It doesn't sound promising, but this very traditional soup
tastes delicious.*

Cut up the meat into small cubes. Put all the ingredients except the parsley into a
saucepan, season with salt and freshly ground pepper. Add the water, cover, and bring
to a boil, and then simmer for 1½ to 2 hours.
    Taste and correct the seasoning. Stir in lots of freshly chopped parsley and serve hot.

Chicken Stock or Broth

*Chicken broth was the cure-all in many Irish homes—warm, nourishing,
and soothing when one was cold or under the weather. It was a particularly
valuable remedy for those who were endeavoring to recover from self-inflicted
suffering!*
    *I still find a bowl of broth, with saturated soggy white bread and butter
one of the most comforting things in the whole world.*

Chop up the carcases as much as possible. Put all the ingredients except the salt into a
saucepan and cover with the cold water. Bring to a boil and skim the fat off the top with
a tablespoon. Simmer for 3–4 hours. Strain and remove any remaining fat. If you need a
stronger flavor, boil down the liquid in an open pan to reduce by one-third or one-half the
volume. Add a little salt towards the end of the cooking.
    Broth will keep for several days in the refrigerator. If you want to keep it for longer,
boil it up again for 5–6 minutes every couple of days; let it get cold and refrigerate again.
Broth also freezes perfectly.

Beef Consommé

Serves 4

1½ cups boneless beef shank,
    meticulously trimmed finely of
    any fat and finely chopped
1 medium carrot, very finely
    chopped
green tops of 2 leeks, finely
    chopped
2 stalks of celery, very finely
    chopped
2 ripe tomatoes, quartered and
    seeded and then diced
3 egg whites
7 cups well-flavored beef stock
salt and freshly ground pepper
1–2 tablespoons medium or dry
    sherry (optional)

The country house cook was always immensely proud of a well-flavored consommé. Clear, sparkling consommé needed to be made with care and attention. Well-hung shin of beef would have been used: the bones to make a rich beef stock, and the meat to flavor the broth. Consommé was also made using the same method when game, poultry, or wild mushrooms were in season and plentiful.

Mix the chopped beef, carrots, leeks, celery, tomatoes, and egg whites in a bowl. Pour on the cold stock, whisk well, and season with salt and pepper. Pour into a stainless steel saucepan. Bring slowly to a boil on low heat, whisking constantly. This should take about 10 minutes.

As soon as the mixture looks cloudy and slightly milky, stop whisking. Allow the filter of egg whites to rise slowly to the top of the saucepan. Do not stir the consommé, but let simmer gently for 45 minutes to 1 hour to extract all flavor from the beef and vegetables. Add the sherry, if desired.

Put a filter paper or a jelly bag into a strainer and gently ladle the consommé into it, being careful not to disturb the filter. Do not press the sediment in the filter or the consommé will not be sparkling clear. Strain it through the filter or jelly bag a second time if necessary. If serving the consommé hot, bring it almost to a boil and add any flavorings and garnish just before serving. Do not cook the garnish in the consommé as it will become cloudy. Do not let it boil.

Irish Nettle Soup

Serves 6 (approximately)

3 tablespoons butter
2 cups chopped potatoes
1 cup chopped onion
1½–1¾ cups leeks, chopped
salt and freshly ground pepper
4¼ cups homemade chicken stock
½ cup young nettles, washed
    and chopped
⅔ cup cream or half and half

Nettles made their appearance in Ireland almost 6,000 years ago as the first farmers started to cut down forest trees to clear the ground for their crop cultivation. In the "Saints' Lives" from the Book of Lismore there is a story of how St. Colum Cille came upon a woman cutting nettles to make herself a pottage. She explained that this was her diet until her cow calved, when of course she would have milk, cream, butter, and perhaps some cheese.

Stinging nettles still grow in great profusion throughout the Irish countryside. Use gloves when you are gathering them so as not to sting yourself! Maura Laverty in Kind Cooking *describes how people would draw "old footless black woollen stockings" over their hands for protection. With their high iron content nettles were prominent in Irish folk medicine, and helped in some small measure to alleviate hunger during the famine.*

Melt the butter in a heavy-bottomed saucepan. When it foams, add the potatoes, onions, and leeks and toss them in the butter until well coated. Sprinkle with salt and freshly ground pepper. Cover with a paper lid (to keep in the steam) and the lid of the saucepan, then sweat on gentle heat for approximately 10 minutes, or until the vegetables are soft but not colored. Discard the paper lid. Add the stock and boil until the vegetables are just cooked. Add the chopped nettle leaves. Simmer uncovered for just a few minutes. Be careful not to overcook or the vegetables will discolor and also lose their flavor. Add the cream or half and half and liquefy. Taste and correct seasoning if necessary. Serve hot.

Watercress Soup

Serves 6–8

3 tablespoons (1½oz) butter
1 cup chopped potatoes
1¼ cups chopped onion
salt and freshly ground pepper
2½ cups water or homemade
   chicken stock
2½ cups creamy milk
4 cups chopped watercress
   (remove the coarse stalks)

Watercress is frequently mentioned as a foodstuff in the 12th-century manuscript Agallamh na Seanórach *(The Colloquy of the Old Men). Legend has it that it was watercress that enabled St Brendan to live to the ripe old age of 180! In Birr Castle in Co. Offaly, Lord and Lady Rosse still serve a soup of watercress gathered from around St Brendan's Well, just below the castle walls.*

Melt the butter in a heavy-bottomed saucepan. When it foams, add the potatoes and onions and toss until well coated. Sprinkle with salt and freshly ground pepper. Cover and sweat on a gentle heat for 10 minutes. Heat the water or stock and add to the pan. Bring to a boil, and cook until the potatoes and onions are soft. Add the watercress and boil with the lid off for approximately 4–5 minutes until the watercress is cooked. It will taste soft and tender. Do not overcook or the soup will lose its fresh green color. Purée the soup in a blender or food processor. Taste and add a little more salt and pepper if necessary.

Vegetable Soup

Serves 6

¼ cup (½ stick) butter
1 cup chopped potatoes
1¼ cups peeled diced onions
3–4 cups chopped vegetables of
    your choice, e.g. carrot, parsnip,
    and celery
salt and freshly ground pepper
1 quart homemade chicken stock
⅔ cup half and half (optional)

Most farming households grew a few vegetables in the "garden," which was a functional rather than decorative area close to the dwelling and near the haggard *where the hay and straw ricks were stored. Nothing fancy was grown—usually just essential basics such as cabbage, turnips, carrots, and onions, and a few drills of floury potatoes on the corner of a field near the house. Parsley, some thyme, and perhaps a bay were the only herbs. Country houses, on the other hand, grew a wide variety of vegetables, herbs, and fruit in walled gardens and greenhouses, so the soups would have been more varied, reflecting the wider range of ingredients in season and the availability of labor in the kitchen.*

Melt the butter in a heavy saucepan. When it foams, add the potatoes, onions, and vegetables and turn them until well coated. Sprinkle with salt and freshly ground pepper. Cover and sweat on a gentle heat for 10 minutes. Add the stock. Boil until soft, about 15 minutes. Do not overcook or the vegetables will lose their flavor. Nowadays one can always liquefy the soup and add half and half. Taste and correct seasoning.

Field Mushroom Soup

Serves 8–9

¼ cup (½ stick) butter
1 cup very finely chopped onion
1lb field mushrooms
3 tablespoons flour
salt and freshly ground pepper
2½ cups homemade chicken stock
2½ cups milk
a little light or heavy cream
    (optional)

Despite the fact that Ireland has a rich variety of fungi, the common field mushroom (Agaricus campestris) is virtually the only variety that most people will risk eating. Agaricus campestris are most likely to appear in unfertilized grassland grazed by sheep or horses; sand dunes are also worth a search if the weather turns warm and humid between July and the end of September.

This recipe is wonderfully quick and easy to prepare, with a marvelously intense mushroom flavor. Large flat cultivated mushrooms may be used as an alternative and the result is almost as delicious.

Melt the butter in a saucepan over gentle heat. Toss the onions in it, cover, and sweat until soft and completely cooked. Meanwhile, check over the mushrooms carefully, discard any that are infested by worms, wash both caps and stalks quickly, and chop very finely. Add to the saucepan and cook for 5 or 6 minutes. Now stir in the flour, cook on low heat for 2–3 minutes, season with salt and freshly ground pepper, then add the stock and milk gradually, stirring all the time. Increase the heat and bring to a boil. Taste and add a dash of cream if necessary.

Green Pea Soup

The first reference to soup I came across during my research was Green Pea Soup in an 1810 manuscript of Mary Lee Heathfield. It is interesting that in this soup and the following one, bread was used as a thickening agent.

"Take a quart of old peas shell them and set them in 2 quarts of water, the crumb of a penny loaf a little white pepper mace and ginger, let them boil till quite tender then pulp them through a colander. Cut in thick slices a lettuce and 2 cucumbers with a pint of young peas, put all these in a stew pan with a ¼lb of fresh butter shaken and stewed till quite tender, add the old peas boil it up toast the crumb of a penny roll and put in the soup."

Turnip Soup

This is also from the 1810 Mary Lee Heathfield manuscript, accredited to a Mrs T. Vigne. History doesn't relate who Mrs Vigne was, she may have been a cook in another country house or a friend of the family.

"2 heads of celery, 2 or 3 carrots, 2 or 3 turnips an onion, some white pepper and a leek. Stew all these in 2 quarts of water when nearly done enough put into the saucepan a large slice of crumb of bread then put altogether through a sieve to the water they were boiled, put some turnip in, cut round as for a harrico, ½ pint of cream to be added at last."

Vegetable Soup

This comes from the 1871 Mary Franks manuscript.

"Peel and slice 6 large onions, 6 potatoes, 6 carrots and 4 turnips; fry them in ½lb butter till tender, pour 4 quarts of boiling water, toast a crust, and make it as hard and dry as possible, without burning—put to the above some celery, sweet herbs, salt and pepper. Stew it all gently for 4 hours, then strain it through a common cloth. Have ready, shaved celery and a little turnip to your liking; and stew them tender in the soup, to which some anchovy and a little catsup may be added."

Carrot Soup

This is also from the 1810 Mary Lee Heathfield manuscript, accredited to Mrs T. Vigne.

"Make 3 quarts of plain gravy, not over strong put into a saucepan 4 or 5 large onions with a piece of butter and let fry a light brown shaking them about add the liquor with 4 or 5 carrots and turnips cut in pieces let the whole stew gently for near 2 hours till the roots are quite tender strain off the liquor and rub the roots through a sieve with a wooden spoon then add the liquor and make the soup quite hot."

Lady Piggot's Carrot Soup

This is from the 1871 Mary Franks manuscript.

"Cut the carrots in slices—2 heads of celery cut small—2 or 3 large onions well washed and dried through a colander, put into a stew-pan 1lb butter and when it has done hissing throw in the vegetables, add 1 large spoonful of pepper and salt, stew them till tender, then put them into a soup pot with 5 quarts of boiling water, let it boil till all will wet through a sieve, send it to table about the thickneys of peas soup."

Turnip Soup

This recipe comes from the 1865 Lough Rynn Manuscript. Lord Leitrim owned this estate in Co. Leitrim and others in Co. Donegal.

"Take 12 large turnips and 2 heads of cabbage. Cut the cabbage and slice the turnips small with 4 onions. Fry the turnips and onions in butter and put them down with the cabbage, some more pepper and allspice. A large handful of rice, a bunch of sweet herbs, parsley to stew in 8 quarts of water close covered over a slow fire 'til it comes down to 3 quarts. Add a little vermicelli stewed in other water, the water being poured from them and strain your soup over it. Give it a boil. Season it with a little salt."

Potato, Onion, and Lovage Soup

Serves 6

1–2 tablespoons butter
3 onions, very thinly sliced
3 potatoes, thinly sliced
salt and freshly ground pepper
4½ cups good homemade chicken
 or vegetable stock
a large handful of lovage leaves
lovage and parsley, to garnish

Lucy Madden from Hilton Park in Co. Monaghan, one of Ireland's most charming country house hotels, made this delicious soup for me from the organically grown vegetables in her garden.

Melt the butter in a heavy-bottomed saucepan on low heat, add the onions and potatoes, season with salt and freshly ground pepper, and sweat until soft but not colored. Add the stock and boil for 5 minutes. Snip the lovage leaves into thin strips with scissors. Put 3 tablespoons into the soup and cook for a further 10 minutes. Serve with a sprinkling of snipped lovage and a little chopped fresh parsley.

Potato and Fresh Herb Soup

Serves 6

¼ cup (½ stick) butter
1¼ cups diced onions
3⅔ cups peeled diced potatoes
1 teaspoon salt
freshly ground pepper
1 tablespoon chopped fresh herbs,
   to include parsley, thyme, lemon
   balm, chives, and marjoram
3⅔ cups homemade chicken stock
½ cup half and half

This is one of the most delicious of all soups when made with good Irish potatoes and the bonus of fresh herbs, which would have been found in a monastery garden years ago. According to Dr. Synott of the National Botanic Gardens in Dublin, culinary and medicinal herbs are likely to have been brought from the continent by returning Irish monks during the early Christian period.

Melt the butter in a heavy saucepan. When it foams, add the onions and potatoes and toss them in the butter until well coated. Sprinkle with salt and pepper. Cover and sweat on a gentle heat for 10 minutes. Add the fresh herbs (reserving a little for garnish) and the stock, and cook until the vegetables are soft. Purée the soup in a liquidizer or food processor. Taste and adjust seasoning. Thin with creamy milk to the required consistency. Serve sprinkled with the remaining chopped herbs.

Note: If you don't have any fresh herbs just leave them out; the soup will still be very good. Fresh parsley is always widely available and would be delicious chopped and sprinkled over the top.

Pea Soup

Serves 6–8

8oz dried or frozen peas, soaked
   overnight or longer
1 onion, chopped
1 carrot, chopped
½ turnip, chopped
½ parsnip, chopped
2 tablespoons butter
1 quart water or stock
ham bone or bacon rind
1¼ cups milk
3 tablespoons flour
salt and freshly ground pepper

This soup can be made in winter quite successfully with frozen peas, or with dried split green peas which have been soaked. In the latter case, the cooking time will have to be prolonged to an hour.

If using dried peas, wash them first before steeping (soaking overnight). Next day, prepare and chop the rest of the vegetables and fry in butter for 5 minutes. Add the water (or stock), the soaked or frozen peas and the ham bone. Simmer until all are soft and then remove the bone or bacon rind. Rub the soup through a wire strainer and return to the pan. In a separate bowl, blend the flour with the milk and add to the pan. Bring to the boil, stirring, for 5 minutes. Season and serve.

Green Pea Pod Soup

This recipe came from the Kitchen Book of Clonbrock*:*
   Boil the pods in water till quite tender with a small handful of green onions and a sprig of mint—pound in the mortar and add the remains of any thick soup, or some good white sauce. Put back into the stewpan to heat, then pass through a tammy on fine sieve —if the purée is too thick add some stock. When wanted for table to be made hot, but not boiling a pinch of sugar and a pat of fresh butter stirred in just before serving—a few peas added look well.

¼ cup (½ stick) butter
5 cups chopped onions
9¼ cups scrubbed, peeled, and
    chopped Jerusalem artichokes
salt and freshly ground pepper
4⅔ cups light chicken stock
2½ cups half and half approx

GARNISH
freshly chopped parsley
crisp, golden croûtons

Variation

Crispy Bacon Croûtons

Cut 2oz streaky bacon into
lardons, fry in a little oil until
crisp and golden. Drain on
paper towel, mix with the
croûtons and add to the soup
just before serving.

Jerusalem Artichoke Soup with Mussels

Mussels have a wonderful affinity
with artichoke soup. Add 32–40
cooked mussels to the soup and
garnish with snipped flat leaf
parsley.

Jerusalem Artichoke Soup with Crispy Croûtons

Pheasants have a particular weakness for Jerusalem artichokes, so most country houses with a big shooting estate cultivate a patch, and often treat their shooters to Jerusalem artichoke soup after a morning's sport. Jerusalem artichokes are a sadly neglected winter vegetable. They look like knobbly potatoes and are a nuisance to peel, but if they are very fresh you can sometimes get away with just giving them a good scrub. Not only are they a smashing vegetable but they are also delicious in soups and gratins. They are a real gem from the gardener's point of view because the foliage grows into a hedge and provides shelter and cover for both compost heaps and pheasants! They are also a very important source of inulin which enhances the growth of beneficial bacteria in our systems. Particularly essential after a course of antibiotics.

Melt the butter in a heavy-bottomed saucepan, add the onions and artichokes. Season with salt and freshly ground pepper, cover, and sweat gently for about 10 minutes. Add the stock and cook until the vegetables are soft. Purée in a blender or food processor and return to the heat. Thin to the required flavor and consistency with half and half, and adjust the seasoning.

Serve in soup bowls or in a soup tureen. Garnish with chopped parsley and crisp, golden croûtons.

Note: This soup may need more stock depending on thickness required.

Lobster Soup

I have transcribed this recipe faithfully directly from a receipt book found among the Pakenham Mahon papers at Strokestown Park in Co. Roscommon. It illustrates the extraordinarily sophisticated food that was eaten in the homes of the Anglo-Irish gentry in the late 18th century. The lobster would have been brought specially from the coast by pony and trap over 60 miles on bumpy roads.

Make a good stock of variety of fresh meats a bit of lean bacon and vegetables particularly celery. Have ready the shells of 3 good lobsters their coral and the red part that sticks to the shells pounded together as fine as you can, strain and skim the stock, then put in the lobster, boil it very well for a quart of an hour, strain it through a thick sieve or towel add the crust of a French roll cut in small pieces and let it simmer 'till the bread is soft. You may thicken it with a quart of a pound of fresh butter and a spoonful of flour browned if you chose and some put in the fish of the lobster cut in pieces.

This receit was got from a gentleman who brought it from Germany as the method of making crayfish soop there. We substituted lobster and I think it was the best soop I ever saw.

Bairneachs (limpets)

On Cape Clear bairneachs were regarded as "poor people's food" and there was a *sean fhocal* (old saying) "Avoid the public house or you will end up eating *bairneachs*." There was a special device for getting the bairneachs off the rocks and it was called an *eisitean*. It was a bit like a chisel and was made by the blacksmith.

If there was a weed growing on the bairneach, that was prized. It might be a type of *trapain* or *dulamain* or green shiny stuff, but it was nevertheless left on the shell and it added to the flavor of the soup after boiling. They didn't call it Bairneach Soup on Cape Clear, but *Saile Bairneach*—the word *saile* comes from the Irish word for seawater. Enda Conneely from Inisheer, the most southerly of the Aran Islands off Ireland's west coast, told me that April was considered the time to start eating limpets generally after the harvesting of *Feamainn dhubh* (Fucus serratus) for use as fertilizer on potatoes. When the seaweed was cut it exposed the best limpets and the easiest to pry off the rock.

Bairneach Soup

Serves 6 (approximately)

4½lb bairneachs (limpets)
3⅔ cups cold water (Bridget says you should put in a sup of salt water)
8 teaspoons all-purpose white flour
a large pat of butter

Bairneach is the Gaelic name for limpet. I had never picked bairneachs so I was intrigued to discover how to pry them off the rocks. John Guerin, from Ballyheigue in Co. Kerry, remembered the best spot to find the choicest bairneachs; it was down a long boreen and in July the hedges were full of wild flowers. Suddenly there below us was the mouth of the Shannon harbor. The water sparkled in the morning sun and the flat, sloping rocks were speckled with limpets and seed mussels. Like lightning, John was down on his hands and knees, slicing the bairneachs off the rock with a quick flick of the chisel. I got the hang of it after a few attempts. I soon realized the truth of the expression 'sticks like a limpet'. If you hesitate, the limpet, forewarned, tightens its grip and is simply unmovable, so speed in your attack is of the essence!

Don't wash the bairneachs first. Put them into a saucepan, add the water, bring to a boil, and simmer for about 10 minutes. Pour off the liquid and save.

Put the bairneachs out onto a dish. Pick off the shells and discard. Then de-horn the bairneachs. To do this, catch the 2 small protruding tentacles and draw out the trail—it looks like a long thin string.

Strain the liquid gently back in to the saucepan, keeping back any sand. Add the bairneachs, bring to a boil, and simmer for 30–45 minutes. Whisk the flour into ⅔ cup water; pour into the boiling soup, whisking all the time. Allow to thicken and stir in a big lump of butter.

Cocklety Soup

Serves 6

4 dozen cockles
1–2 tablespoons water
2 tablespoons butter
1 small onion, finely chopped
⅕ cup chopped celery
3 tablespoons flour
2½ cups creamy milk
½ cup heavy cream
1–2 tablespoons chopped parsley
salt and freshly ground pepper

Cockles have formed part of the Irish diet since earliest times. Archaeological remains have been found at early historic sites such as Oughtymore, Co. Derry, Park Cave, Co. Antrim, and Potter's Cave, Co. Antrim. Cockles formed the mainstay of the diet along the coastal regions during the great potato famine of 1845. The Congested District Board Records also tell of how cockle gathering was widespread around Donegal on the eve of the great famine.

Wash and scrub the cockles well in several changes of water, to get rid of the sand and grit. Then put them in a large saucepan with a tablespoon or two of water, cover, and steam for 4–5 minutes until the cockles are open. Discard any that do not open. Strain the cooking liquid and set aside. As soon as they are cool enough to handle, remove the cockles from their shells.

Melt the butter in a saucepan. Add the onion and celery and sweat on gentle heat until soft but not colored. Stir in the flour, then add the strained cockle juice and milk. Cook for a minute or two, stirring all the time, until the soup is smooth and silky. Add the cream and chopped parsley and season with salt and freshly ground pepper. Simmer gently for 10 minutes. Finally add the cockles.

Ballymaloe Mussel Soup

Serves 8

generous 1¾ cups light dry
    white wine
8 tablespoons chopped shallots,
    or scallions or very finely
    chopped onion
1 garlic clove, mashed
8 parsley sprigs
½ bay leaf
¼ teaspoon fresh thyme leaves,
a sprig of fresh fennel
a good pinch of saffron or
    ¼ teaspoon curry powder
    (optional)
⅛ teaspoon ground pepper
8–10lb mussels, scrubbed
a little heavy cream

ROUX
¼ cup (½ stick) butter, softened
½ cup, plus ½ tablespoon flour
2½–3⅔ cups boiling milk

GARNISH
chopped parsley or chervil
croûtons

The mussels I use for this soup come from the clean waters of Kilmackillogue harbor on the Beara Peninsula. Clare Connery, in her excellent book In an Irish Country Kitchen, *maintains that saffron was widely used throughout the 18th century to add color to mussel soup. Mussels are available all year round, but are best and plumpest when there is an "r" in the month.*

Put the wine, shallots, garlic, herbs, saffron or curry powder, and pepper into the saucepan, add the mussels, cover, and steam open in the wine and flavorings. Shell the mussels (remove the beards, if necessary) and place them in a bowl. Discard the shells. Strain the mussel cooking liquor into an enameled or stainless steel saucepan and rapidly boil it down over high heat to concentrate its flavor. Taste it frequently as it boils. You may find that if you reduce it too much, the salt content will be overpowering.

Thicken the mussel liquor with a roux (see page 42) to attain a thickish liquid. Add the boiling milk to thin out the soup to a light consistency. Just before serving, add mussels and a little cream. Decorate with chopped parsley or chervil.

Serve croûtons separately.

Oyster Soup

Serves 6–8

2 large potatoes (about 1lb)
36 fresh oysters
1 tablespoon butter
4oz belly of pork, diced
3⅔ cups milk
1 bouquet garni
salt and freshly ground pepper
2 tablespoons chopped parsley

Oysters are one of the oldest foodstuffs in Ireland: there is archaeological evidence of their use from the Later Mesolithic period (Middle Stone Age from c.5,500BC onwards). Exploration and excavation around Cork harbor has uncovered at least 20 major shell middens, which include substantial quantities of oyster shells.

According to Edward MacLysaght, who edited The Kenmare Manuscripts, *in Dublin in the years 1753–4 it was possible to purchase as many as one hundred oysters for two shillings.*

This old recipe, which came from Ballymoney in Co. Antrim, was obviously made when oysters were cheaper and more plentiful than they are nowadays.

Cook the potatoes in boiling salted water until just tender. Open the oysters into a strainer set over a bowl to catch the juice. Melt a small pat of butter in a pan and fry the diced belly of pork over low heat until just tender. Bring the milk to a boil with a bouquet garni, turn off the heat, and infuse for a few minutes. Peel the cooked potatoes and mash in a saucepan with the milk. Add the pork as soon as it is tender, and season to taste. Bring to a boil, stirring all the time. Add the oysters and their liquid and simmer for a few minutes. Adjust seasoning and stir in the remaining butter. Serve at once sprinkled with chopped parsley.

Serves 4 (approximately)

SOUP
giblets from 1 goose or several
    chickens
1 large onion, chopped
1 carrot, chopped
sprig of parsley
sprig of thyme
cold water

POTATO DUMPLINGS
2 cups cooked mashed potatoes
1¾ cups all-purpose flour
½ teaspoon baking powder
½ teaspoon mixed herbs (optional)
1 small onion, minced finely
salt and freshly ground pepper
a little milk
chopped parsley, to garnish

Serves 6

¼ cup (½ stick) butter
1 medium onion, finely chopped
    into ¼ inch dice
3 celery ribs, finely chopped
1 medium leek, halved and
    finely sliced
2 garlic cloves, crushed
2 teaspoons mild curry powder
2 teaspoons tomato paste
a pinch of salt and freshly
    ground pepper
a pinch of sugar
1 cup red lentils
6 cups chicken stock
1 eating apple, peeled and cut into
    ¼ inch dice
4 tablespoons golden raisins,
    soaked in boiling water for
    10 minutes to plump them up
1–2 tablespoons freshly squeezed
    lemon juice
scant 1 cup cooked basmati rice

Giblet Soup with Dumplings

This recipe would have been used for the giblets of all sorts of fowl in earlier times, when not a scrap of food was ever wasted. This particular recipe came from near Two Mile Borris in Co. Tipperary. The dumplings, simmered in the tasty broth, made a soup substantial enough to sustain a ploughman or a reaper.

Put the giblets (neck, head, flying wings, feet, gizzard, heart) into a pot with the chopped onion, carrot, parsley, and thyme. Cover with cold water, bring to a boil, and simmer for about 2 hours.

While the broth is cooking make the dumplings. Mix all the ingredients together and make into a pliable dough, adding a little milk if the mixture is too dry. Form into a roll and cut into 8 pieces.

Add the dumplings to the broth. Season with salt and freshly ground pepper and simmer for 30 minutes or until the dumplings are tender.

Sprinkle with chopped parsley and serve in old-fashioned soup bowls.

Note: Nowadays it might be advisable to remove the head and feet before serving, unless you want to risk a mutiny!

Mulligatawny Soup

During my research I came across many and varied recipes for Mulligatawny Soup, a legacy introduced into Ireland through the close connection to India. Many Irish soldiers who served in the British Army introduced their families to the spicy dishes they had grown to love. I have tried many, and this amalgam has become my favorite.

Heat the butter in a saucepan. Add the chopped onion, celery, leek, and crushed garlic. Cover and sweat on a gentle heat, until soft but not colored. Add the curry powder, stir, and cook for 1 minute. Add the tomato paste, salt, freshly ground pepper, and sugar, and stir well. Next, add the lentils and stock. Bring to a boil, cover, and simmer for 25–30 minutes, until the lentils are tender. Stir in the diced apple, drained golden raisins, and 1 tablespoon of freshly squeezed lemon juice. Cook for a further 2 minutes. Taste and correct the seasoning; it may need more salt or pepper or lemon juice. Divide the cooked rice between the soup bowls and ladle over the hot soup.

Eggs

There is a popular legend in Irish folklore that hens were introduced into Ireland by the Danes, but it is impossible to ascertain whether this is really so. However, we know from the 7th/8th-century Brehon Laws that hens and geese were a regular sight around most farmsteads. The 9th-century Monastery of Tallaght indicates that in the rigidly sparse diet of the extreme penitent monks, the *Céilí Dé*, "dry eggs" were permitted.

Eggs continued to be a staple food into more recent times. In John Dunton's *Letters from Ireland* in 1698, he recounts a dinner he enjoyed in Dublin of "salt fish and eggs, hen and bacon, and rabbits." Throughout the 19th and early 20th centuries, the poultry trade reached its peak in Ireland. In rural areas, poultry rearing was considered exclusively women's work. Thrifty country women bartered the eggs with the village or town grocers in return for luxuries such as tea, sugar, and tobacco. This domestic industry, dominated by women, was of immense economic importance in contributing to paying the rent and running the household. The egg money was known as "Pin Money," and it saw children through school and college, bought them new shoes, and the occasional fancy hat pin. It was the only money a woman could call her own, along with anything she earned from rearing turkeys for Christmas.

Egg in a Cup

Serves 1

1 fresh free-range egg
1 tablespoon white breadcrumbs
a pat of butter
salt and freshly ground pepper

Eggs have always been popular in the Irish diet; hens' and geese eggs are the main types mentioned in early Irish sources. The 9th-century poem Marbán Gúaire *celebrates them in glowing terms:*

> *... delightful feasts come ...*
> *... A clutch of eggs, honey, mast*
> *... sweet apples ...*

My mother used to make this tasty egg snack for us when we were little, particularly if we were feeling fragile. As far as I can gather it was very common throughout Ireland. Eamonn Mac Thomáis, Dublin's popular social historian, remembers it as Gug-gug.

Bring a small saucepan of water to a boil and slip the egg in gently. Bring the water back to a boil and cook for approximately 4 minutes. Meanwhile warm a teacup. (My mother usually did this with hot water from the kettle kept ever boiling on the side of the Aga.)

Pop the egg into an egg cup as soon as it is cooked. Remove the top and spoon out all the inside into the warm dry teacup. Chop with a spoon and immediately add about 1 tablespoon of soft white breadcrumbs, a lump of butter, and pepper and salt to taste. Eat immediately with a teaspoon.

Mary Harlow's Egg in a Cup

I came across similar egg recipes in my research. Mary Harlow, who has lived in Roscommon for 40 years, but was originally from the Burren in Co. Clare, recalled how her mother-in-law (also Mary Harlow) showed her how to cook an egg like this. She also heard of it being popular in Roscommon.

She would melt a little butter in a kitchen cup, crack a fresh egg into it (or two sometimes for a man). You would leave it to cook slowly on the side of the range until it was set to your taste, add a little pepper and salt, and eat with bread.

Oven-Toasted Cheese

Serves 2

butter
2 slices white bread
1 egg, preferably free-range
1¼ cups grated Irish Cheddar
   cheese
½–1 teaspoon English mustard
salt and freshly ground pepper

When my children were small this superior toasted cheese often saved the day if they were ravenously hungry. Quite similar to Welsh Rarebit, it is made from ingredients that are nearly always on hand. When Lenten fasting was much more rigid and very strictly observed in Ireland in the 1950s and 1960s, people were restricted to eating "one full meal and two collations." This was the sort of dish you could have for tea.

Preheat the oven to 450°F. Butter the bread and place the buttered side down on a baking sheet. Whisk the egg in a bowl with a fork, add the grated cheese and the mustard and season well with salt and freshly ground pepper. Spread this mixture evenly onto both the slices of bread and bake in the oven 450°F for about 15 minutes, or until puffy and golden on the top.

Buttered Eggs

One of the most exciting things I have discovered while working on this book is Buttered Eggs. This traditional way of preserving eggs for the short term is likely to have been a long established practise but may have become more popular in the 19th century. At this time, Ireland was exporting an astonishing number of eggs to Britain, where there was a great demand for eggs. For example, in 1850 Ireland exported eleven million eggs per annum and this figure rose to forty million by 1900.

This practise deserves to be more widely known for the wonderful flavor and texture it produces. Anyone who has their own hens can try it. The crucial thing is that the eggs must be collected from the nest as soon as they are laid, and their shells rubbed with a thin layer of butter while they are still warm. This seals in the freshness, so the albumen stays soft and curdy when boiled or poached. They will keep for at least six months, but it is mainly to enjoy their unique flavor that they are buttered rather than to extend their keeping time. Buttered eggs are a great specialty in Cork and are still sold in the Old English Market in Cork city.

Easter Eggs

Even though Easter is the most important Christian festival, the word Easter is linked to the pagan cult of the Saxon goddess of spring, Eostre. The eggs universally associated with Easter are ancient symbols of spring, rebirth and resurrection. It seems to me likely that the Easter egg tradition is also rooted in the ancient custom of Lenten fasting, which was common to both Eastern and Western Christendom. The last eggs were eaten up in the form of pancakes on Shrove Tuesday, but as the hens didn't know it was Lent, they went on laying! The surplus of eggs which accumulated was enjoyed at Easter in all sorts of different ways. In Ireland, traditionally, some were hard-cooked with natural dyes, such as herbs, flowers, lichen, or onion skins, to color their shells. Eggs laid on Good Friday were considered blessed and these, marked with a cross, were cooked for breakfast on Easter Sunday. Everyone was expected to eat their share of eggs in one form or another, and anyone who couldn't manage at least two or three was considered to be very feeble.

Fried Eggs

In 1732, Mrs Mary Delaney, who was the wife of Patrick Delaney, the Dean of Down, wrote of her husband "the greatest feast to him is fried egg and bacon."

Crispy at the edges and soft in the center, fried eggs are probably the most common way of cooking eggs in Ireland—and they can be utterly delicious if one starts with a perfectly fresh free-range egg. Cook it in sizzling bacon fat, olive oil, or even pure beef dripping, and serve immediately. The same thing is a travesty when a stale battery-produced egg is cooked in cheap oil. Sadly superlative fried eggs, simple as they sound, are "as rare as hen's teeth" nowadays.

Heat a little pure bacon fat, butter, or olive oil in a skillet. When it is just about sizzling, break in the eggs, one at a time, but don't overcrowd the pan. Cook on a low heat if you like the eggs soft underneath, or on a higher heat if you like them crispy. Cook until the white is just set but the yolk soft. Baste with hot fat if you like the top filmed over, or cover the skillet with a lid. Flip them over gently with a spatula if that's your preference. Serve immediately on warm but not hot plates.

Egg in Mashed Potato

Áine de Blacam from Inis Meáin, one of the Aran Islands off the coast of Galway, remembers her mother serving this dish. "People had their own hens and eggs, so the eggs were always very fresh. This was a dish often served to children who weren't too keen on eating eggs any other way. It was very nutritious."

Take some freshly made hot mashed potato, add a really fresh raw egg and mix really well through the potato—it will be almost cooked with the heat of the potato.

Mousse au Parmesan (Parmesan Mousse)

I found smarter versions of oven-toasted cheese in some old manuscripts and cookbooks. This one comes from the the Clonbrock manuscript cookbook, used by successive cooks to the Dillon family of Clonbrock in Co. Galway. It contains the recipes (or receipts) used in the house, both for family meals and for entertaining. The first recipes date from the 1730s.

Whip ½ pint of cream stiff enough to stand. Add ¼lb of Parmesan cheese, a teaspoonful of mixed Mustard, Cayenne and Salt. Mix lightly together, and pile up on toast, sprinkling a little Parmesan over.

Stuffed or French Eggs

This also comes from the Clonbrock manuscript.

Boil the eggs hard—break the shells—clean them off and halve the eggs evenly. Take out the yolks with care and pound them to a smooth paste in a mortar with a little butter, salt, pepper, mustard, anchovy, parsley, grated onion and bread crumbs, mix all together, fill the whites with it, put them in the oven for a few minutes, dish them on fried toast—three eggs make a nice dish.

Irishman's Omelet

**Serves 1 hungry man
or 2 less ravenous diners**

4oz Canadian bacon
2 tablespoons lard or butter
1 cup chopped onion
2 cups diced boiled potatoes
1 tablespoon chopped fresh parsley
2 teaspoons chopped fresh chives
salt and freshly ground pepper
2 eggs, preferably free-range,
    beaten

This recipe comes from Nina Farren from Co. Tyrone, who was taught how to make it by her grandmother. There is an extraordinary similarity between this recipe and dishes from other countries, such as frittata in Italy, tortilla in Spain, kuku in the Middle East, and flat omelets of many different origins. People used whatever seasonal ingredients they had on hand to add to the eggs. There were references to something similar in other parts of Ireland, with the addition of breadcrumbs, fresh herbs, and cream. Colman Andrews, in his book The Country Cooking of Ireland, *gives a similar recipe for Wicklow Omelet.*

Trim the rind from the rashers and cut into tiny pieces. Fry the bacon in the lard or butter until crisp and remove to a plate. Sweat the onion for a few minutes in the bacon fat, add the diced potato, reserved bacon, freshly chopped herbs, and seasoning to the pan. Stir in the well beaten eggs and cook over low heat until the eggs are set.

Flip over onto a hot plate and serve immediately.

Kidney Omelet

Serves 1

1 lamb's kidney
a little butter
1 teaspoon freshly chopped parsley
2 eggs, preferably free-range
2 teaspoons water or milk
salt and freshly ground pepper
2 teaspoons clarified butter or
   olive oil
freshly chopped parsley, to garnish

A trip to Dublin with my father was a stupendous treat when I was a child; the occasion was sometimes a rugby match or a visit to see my mother in the Baggot Street Nursing Home and inspect the latest addition to the family. Absolutely everything was exciting but what I looked forward to more than anything else was a meal 'in a hotel' before our long journey home. Often it was The Clarence *on Wellington Quay where the distinguished looking silver-haired maître d'hôtel, Willie James, led us to our table in his tail coat and starched shirt with butterfly collar. Affable Paddy Gannon invariably served our table with that wonderful old-fashioned courteous service that is almost impossible to find nowadays. I ordered the same menu almost every time, kidney omelet followed by crispy fried plaice. I don't remember what I ate for dessert—I expect it must have been ice cream—but it is the flavor of the tender kidney omelet that remains with me.*

Clean and dice the kidney, cook gently in a little butter, add most of the chopped parsley, and keep warm.

Warm a plate in the oven. Whisk the eggs with the water or milk in a bowl with a fork or whisk, until thoroughly mixed but not too fluffy. Season with salt and freshly ground pepper. Put the plate beside the cooker.

Heat a 9 inch nonstick omelet pan over high heat and add the clarified butter or olive oil. As soon as it sizzles, pour in the egg mixture. It will start to cook immediately, so quickly pull the edges of the omelet towards the center with a metal spoon or spatula, tilting the pan so that the uncooked egg runs to the sides. Continue until most of the egg is set and will not run any more, then leave the omelet to cook for a further 10 seconds to brown the bottom. Spoon the cooked kidney in a line along the center.

To fold the omelet: Flip the edge just below the handle of the pan into the center, then hold the pan almost perpendicular over the plate so that the omelet will flip over again, then half roll, half slide the omelet onto the plate so that it lands with the folds underneath. (It should not take more than 45 seconds in all to make the omelet.)

Serve immediately on the warm plate, garnished with a little parsley.

Sweet Light Omelet

Serves 1

2 eggs
1 tablespoon sugar
1 tablespoon butter
jam or superfine sugar, to serve

I came across this recipe in the scrapbook lent to me by Valerie Kingston from Glenilen Farm in West Cork. The scrapbook had been compiled by her grandmother and great grandmother between 1900 and 1940. A similar style of omelet is served at Ballymaloe House.

Separate the egg yolks from the whites. Beat together the yolks and the sugar for 10–15 minutes then beat the whites until very stiff. Carefully fold the beaten egg yolk mixture into the whites and mix lightly together. Melt the butter in a skillet, pour in the omelet mixture and hold over gentle heat for 2–3 minutes while it rises, then turn over quickly. Turn out onto a hot plate, put jam or sugar in the center and serve immediately.

Winnie Cowhig's Duck Egg Sponge

Serves 8

⅔ cup all-purpose flour, sifted, plus
  2 teaspoons for dusting
3 organic duck eggs
½ cup superfine sugar, plus extra
  for sprinkling
homemade jam or fresh berries and
  whipped cream, to serve

Women quickly observed that duck eggs made a lighter and more yellow sponge and therefore they were very sought after by home bakers. You could also use duck eggs in the traditional sponge recipe, with their weight in superfine sugar and flour, whisking the whole eggs with the sugar.

Preheat the oven to 350°F. Brush the base and sides of 2 x 7 inch round cake pans with melted butter and dust with the 2 teaspoons flour. Separate the egg whites from the yolks. Put the whites and sugar into a bowl and whisk until stiff peaks form, preferably with an electric mixer. Whisk in the yolks one by one and then fold in the sieved flour, making sure not to deflate the mixture. Divide the mixture between the prepared tins. Bake for 20–25 minutes. Turn out carefully and let cool on a wire rack. Sandwich together with cream and homemade jam or fresh berries. Sprinkle a little superfine sugar or confectioner's sugar over the top and enjoy with a cup of tea.

Sea Birds' Eggs

In his writings on the Blasket Islands, Co. Kerry, Malachy McKenna says that sea birds' eggs were an integral part of the Islanders' diet. He refers to Máire Ní Ghuithín, who in her book *Bean an Oileáin* (Women of the Island), mentions that the eggs of guillemots, razor-bills, and gulls were all eaten, and adds that those of the oyster-catcher 'are very good to eat.' When fishing for lobster the islanders would sometimes camp on another island, Inis na Bró, and to supplement the food they brought with them (usually bread and pork meat or mutton) they would eat fish and gulls' eggs, which were abundant in May. The eggs, which were either fried in a pan or boiled in a can of water, were popular with the fishermen, but Muiris Ó'Catháin in *Ar muir is ar tír* (On Sea and Land), 1991, said that eating them for a week caused bad breath. Finding eggs was no problem, but finding ones that were fresh was: a basketful of gulls' eggs might not contain a single one that was edible.

An egg could be tested for freshness by placing it in water: if the egg floated, it was not fit to be eaten, since enough air had already got through the shell to make the egg go bad; if the egg was freshly laid, it would sink to the bottom because there would be very little air in it.

Collecting eggs on the cliffs was highly dangerous, yet the instinct to gather food at every possible opportunity was so strong in the Islanders that even young boys would risk clambering up and down cliffs if they had a chance to collect eggs. Tomás Ó Criomhthainn in *Dinnsheanchas na mBlascaodaí* (The Topography of the Blasket Islands), 1935, relates that falcons and eagles were caught by the Blasket Islanders and sold for cash. These birds nested in extremely inaccessible places and one needed to be a good climber to get to them.

In spite of the difficulties and dangers of getting an egg or a fledgling from such places, each of which could be sold for one pound, some people succeeded in doing so. Malachy McKenna, in an article sent to Myrtle Allen, says that "in these times, when self-sufficiency in food supply and organic life-style are ideals that are strived after, we have much to learn from these island people who had to be perfectly in tune with their Atlantic environment if they were to put food on the table."

George Gossip, a keen shot and an accomplished cook who specializes in game recipes at his guest house, Ballinderry Park in Co. Galway, also mentions that when he and his friends went mayfly fishing around Lough Derg they would bring back lots of gulls' eggs, which would be plentiful in April. They would enjoy them hard-cooked with celery salt. Eating gulls' eggs in this way would have been much more traditional than quails' eggs. Pheasant eggs would not have been disturbed in the nest.

Fish

I now live within sight of the sea, but when I was a child our family used to live in Co. Laois in the midlands, just about as far from the sea as it is possible to be in Ireland. Fish, when we could get it, was eaten on Friday—a fast day. Whatever was available that day was dropped off in our village by the bus traveling from Dublin to Cork. Plaice, our favorite, was not always there. Smoked haddock, or red fish as it was called, was a certainty; we could always see the luminous orange fillets packed in a timber box. Whiting arrived almost every week in season, and although we found it less interesting than plaice, it could be tender and melting, when fried in a coating of flour, egg, and breadcrumbs or steamed in the old-fashioned way between two plates. This was a common way of dealing with whiting before ovens were widespread.

Eileen Ryan (O'Riordan) recalled growing up in Ballycotton, our nearby fishing village, in the 1930s when her father was a full-time fisherman. In the early days the fish would be brought by pony and trap to Midleton, the nearest town, and sold there. In later times it was sent by lorry and train to the market in Cork. At the weekend when there was no market and no way of keeping the fish fresh, her mother would dry the cod or ling on the roof of the galvanized shed.

Baked Cod with Cream and Bay Leaves

**Serves 4–6 as a starter or
main course**

2 tablespoons (¼ stick) butter
1 tablespoon finely chopped onion
6 thick pieces of cod (allow approx.
   4–6oz filleted fish per person)
salt and freshly ground pepper
4–5 fresh or dried bay leaves
light cream (enough to cover the
   fish)
1¼ cups roux (see page 42)

*In the olden days milk was put into skimming bowls in the cold dairy to set
so there was always some rich thick cream that could be spooned off the top
to add a little extra savor to a dish. This lovely old recipe will transform even
the dullest white fish into a feast (don't live on it!). Be generous with the bay
leaves, their perfume should distinctly permeate the sauce.*

Melt the butter in a skillet just wide enough to take the fish. Fry the onion gently for a
few minutes until soft but not colored. Put the cod in the pan and cook on both sides for
1 minute. Season with salt and freshly ground pepper. Add bay leaves. Cover with light
cream and simmer with the lid on for 5–6 minutes, until the fish is cooked. Remove the fish
to a serving dish. Bring the cooking liquid to a boil and lightly thicken with roux. Taste and
correct the seasoning. Coat the fish with sauce and serve immediately. For a whole meal
in one dish, pipe a ruff of fluffy mashed potato around the edge. Pollock (see page 41) is a
good alternative fish.

Note: This dish can be prepared ahead and reheated, and it also freezes well. Reheat
in a moderate oven 350°F, for anything from 10–30 minutes, depending on the size of the
container.

Mashed Potato

Serves 4

2lb unpeeled potatoes, preferably
   Burbank or Yukon Gold
salt and freshly ground pepper
1¼ cups half and half
1–2 egg yolks, or 1 whole egg and
   1 egg yolk
2–4 tablespoons (¼–½ stick) butter

*This is a posher, richer version of mashed potato, and it browns better
around the edge of the dish. If the potatoes are not peeled and mashed while
hot and if the boiling half and half is not added immediately, the mashed
potato will be lumpy and gluey.*

Scrub the potatoes well. Put them into a saucepan of cold water, add a good pinch of salt
and bring to a boil. When the potatoes are about half cooked (about 15 minutes for "old
potatoes"), strain off two-thirds of the water, replace the lid on the saucepan, put onto a
gentle heat and allow the potatoes to steam until they are fully cooked.
   Peel immediately by just pulling off the skins, so you waste as little as possible. Mash
while hot. (If you have a large quantity, put the potatoes into the bowl of a food mixer and
beat with the paddle.)
   While the potatoes are being peeled, bring the milk to a boil. Beat the eggs into the hot
mashed potatoes, and add enough boiling half and half to mix to a soft light consistency
suitable for piping; then beat in the butter, the amount depends on how rich you like your
potatoes. Taste and season with salt and freshly ground pepper.

Note: If you only have egg whites they will be fine and will make a delicious light
mashed potato also.

**Serves 4–6
(depending on size of roe)**

a cod's roe
seasoned flour
beaten egg
fine white breadcrumbs
bacon fat or melted butter,
  for frying

Cod's Roe

Like many old-fashioned foods that have been almost forgotten, cod's roe is cheap and delicious and of course hugely nutritious. It still turns up between January and April in many fish markets and is well worth looking out for. Cod's roe is also sold smoked.

Rinse the cod's roe gently in cold water and then tie it loosely in muslin. Choose a saucepan just large enough to fit. Cook the cod's roe in boiling salted water for 20–30 minutes, depending on the thickness. It should be firm to the touch. Drain, put on a plate and cover with another plate to weigh it down slightly. Cool and refrigerate overnight.

Next day, cut the roe into ¾ inch thick slices. Dip each slice into seasoned flour, then the beaten egg, then the breadcrumbs. Fry the slices in bacon fat or melted butter until crisp and golden on both sides. Serve with some crispy rashers of bacon and a few fried potatoes, or simply bread and butter.

Cod's roe is also good dipped in a batter (see page 63) and deep-fried until crisp.

Serves 1

1 whiting fillet
seasoned flour
a few dabs of butter
milk

2 Pyrex plates

Whiting Steamed Between Two Plates

This was one of our favorite ways to cook fresh fillets of whiting for Friday's dinner. The result was mild and delicious. You could even cook it over the potatoes in a steamer and save fuel.

Bring a saucepan of water to a boil. Dip the fillet of fish in seasoned flour. Rub the base of one plate with butter, place the fish on top. Season with salt, pepper, and add a few dabs of butter. Pour a little milk around the fish, enough to come about one-third of the way up the fillet. Cover with the second plate and place on top of the saucepan. Keep the water boiling underneath. The fish will cook in 8–10 minutes, depending on the thickness of the fillet.

Pollock

"Thim's not company fish," remarked the Irish R.M.'s housekeeper of pollock, "but very good nonetheless." This tribute comes from "The Boat's Share" in *Some Experiences of an Irish R.M.* by E.C. Somerville and M. Ross.

Tommy Sliney was a much loved character from Ballycotton who sold fresh fish from his donkey and cart in the neighboring villages and on the pier in summer. Everyone, including children, loved Tommy and in truth he gave away more fish than he ever sold. He explained to me once why pollock—not known for its distinctive flavor—was so popular, " 'tis because it doesn't taste of fish Missus." Of course! Fish and fasting were inextricable in people's minds because of the obligatory Friday fast. Traditionally pollock was boiled or fried.

Water Grouchy of Perch, Plaice, Flounders or Trout

This is one of Mary Ponsonby's recipes from the 1850 manuscript. The term Grouchy seems to have originated from Water Sokey or Water-souchy, from the Dutch "waterzootje." It's a dish of small fish stewed and served in a little water. Bailey (1736) gave "Soochy" defined as "A water soochy, a dish of perch dressed after the Holland fashion."

"In a stewpan put as much water as will cover the Fish, with two spoonfuls of Salt and some whole Pepper. When boiled and scummed put in your fish (after being well scaled and washed) with roots of Parsley slit the long way, and some of the green tied in a bunch. Let it all boil pretty fast 10 or 12 minutes, or according to the size of the fish, dress them up in a deep dish with all the contents and the liquor, and slices of Bread and Butter on a plate, the slices near as thick as your fingers. N.B. Horse Radish improves this dish. The best sauce is Anchovy or Liver Sauce in a boat."

Serves 4–6

3lb fish
2 tablespoons Anchovy Sauce
2 tablespoons Worcestershire
   Sauce
cayenne and mace, to taste

Scalloped Pike

This recipe, from the Kitchen Book of Clonbrock, was signed by "Charley."

Boil the pike or other fish. Pull it to pieces and take out all the bones. Make a roux sauce (see below). Add the sauces, cayenne, and mace to season the finished sauce. Keep stirring the sauce until it boils. Mix the fish with it and place it in a pie dish, or scallop shells with breadcrumbs. Dab little bits of butter over the top and bake.

ROUX

¼ cup (½ stick) butter
2 tablespoons flour
1¾ cups milk
salt and freshly ground pepper

Roux

Melt the butter over a low heat in a saucepan. When it is quite liquid, add the flour, mixing thoroughly to form a smooth paste. Cook gently for 2 minutes.

Remove from heat and add the milk a little at a time, stirring well to remove all lumps from the mixture.

Mullet

Still to this day mullet is a very undervalued fish, because of its reputation as a coarse feeder. It is a familiar sight under the bridges of the River Liffey in Dublin and Lee in Cork, which doesn't endear it to the public. However, grey sea mullet is a wonderful fish; in Ballymaloe we serve it regularly on our menu. In our opinion it is almost as good as sea bass, similar in texture and a fraction of the price. It can be ccoked in any of the ways used to cook round fish. The only recipe I came across for cooking mullet was that sent by Patricia Murphy from Wexford. It has always been known as a favorite for fishermen, a good sport fish, with a tough mouth so there is a great sense of achievement when they catch one. Mullet has huge scales, almost as large as a thumbnail, it is delicious cooked with the skin on, so one needs to be fastidious about removing the scales before cooking.

Twice Cooked Grey Sea Mullet

Serves 6–8, depending on size

1 fresh grey sea mullet
butter
spring onions, finely chopped
parsley, finely chopped
fresh scones, to serve

Patricia Murphy from Newlands in Wexford sent us this recipe. She relates: "My father used to spear mullet on a Sunday afternoon, his only time spent not working. That fish would be our special Sunday supper."

Cut the mullet into thick cutlets. Place in a saucepan of water and bring to a boil. Remove from the heat and strain.

Using butter, fry the fish cutlets in a hot pan until golden in color. Remove from the pan and keep warm. Using the same pan, fry off the chopped spring onion and parsley in the fish juices for a minute or two. Spoon over the cutlets. Serve with freshly made scones.

Herrings

The herring featured prominently in the diet of the Irish from the medieval period through to the early 20th century. The fish was an indispensable item for two main reasons: Firstly, although it could be eaten fresh, it preserved well and proved a most valuable food item for the long lean winter and early spring seasons. Secondly, it was invariably linked with the numerous Christian days of fast and abstinence. Documentary records indicate that by the 14th century, herring was an integral and prevalent item in the Irish diet. In 1306 Scottish fishing fleets were trading in herring that was destined for sale in the Dublin and Drogheda fish shambles; while in 1403 John Slene of Rush exported as many as 4000 salted herring to England.

Its popularity as a foodstuff endured through the 18th and 19th centuries. Arthur Young, writing in the 1770s, notes that the poor of Wexford ate "herrings and potatoes," while of the Limavady region he writes: "the poor live on potatoes, milk and oatmeal with many herrings and salmon." During the 18th and 19th centuries, the bland Irish diet of potatoes and buttermilk welcomed the salty smoked flavor of herrings. Barrels of pickled herrings were commonplace in wealthy households, while in the homes of the poor a number of gutted and salted herrings were hung from the rafters as "winter kitchen."

Up until the early 20th century, the herring was an important part of the Easter Sunday festivities. In a number of towns the butchers, who had little sale for their meat in the Lenten period, celebrated the arrival of Easter by holding a funeral-like procession of a herring: the staple of the church-abiding community during the 40 days of Lent. Henry Morris describes the custom as it took place in Dundalk in 1902:

"They [the butchers] got big long rods and walked through the town... beating the poor herring until hardly a fin was left. On reaching the bridge they hurled the horrid herring into the water with insult and hung up a quarter of lamb decorated with ribbons and flowers in its place."

Huge bubbling shoals of herring were a common sight off the Irish coast until relatively recently. Women gutted and salted the fish onshore; these were then packed into barrels for sale by fish merchants and "cadgers" who transported the herrings right into the heart of the country. My mother remembers as a child in Johnstown, Co. Kilkenny, in the early 1930s, a man coming round selling herrings from a pony and cart on Thursdays. They'd hear the clip, clop of the pony's feet on the road once he left the neighbors' house. At the sound of "fresh herrings, fresh herrings," they'd run to their mother for money and race out to buy the fish. Many farmers also bought a barrel of salted herrings to see them through Lent.

In earlier times a sort of dip or relish was made from dried and salted fish and this "kitchen" often provided the only condiment when times were bad. There was an old cautionary saying: "Dip in the dip and leave the herring for your father."

Herrings, Mackerel, or Bream Cooked Over an Open Fire

The Cork historian Ted O Súilleabháin told me about a method of cooking mackerel, herring, and bream, which he remembers from his childhood on Bere Island off West Cork. The fish was spread over a pair of tongs and cooked until the skin was crisp on the underside. People said they "never tasted the likes of them cooked any other way."

According to Ted, the islanders would split the mackerel down the back, open it out, and pull out the bones so the two fillets were still attached at the belly. The fish was laid crosswise over the two bars of the tongs, flesh-side down, skin-side upwards. It was then held over the open fire to cook. When the fish appeared to be done on one side it was turned with a knife and seasoned with salt and pepper. It was then held over the fire until the skin side was brown and crispy. This was called "roasting fish" by the locals, but in fact it was really barbecuing before the word was even coined. Puffins were also cooked in the same way on the Great Blaskets (see page 72).

Eileen Ryan (O'Riordan) remembers that they used to eat bream a lot at home in Ballycotton. In a warm summer big plump bream would be plentiful. Her mother would stuff them with a light bread and herb stuffing and bake them whole—meaty and delicious.

Soused Herring or Mackerel

Serves 8

8 herrings or mackerel
1 onion, thinly sliced
1 teaspoon whole black
  peppercorns
6 whole cloves
1 teaspoon salt
1 teaspoon sugar
1¼ cups white wine vinegar
1 bay leaf

It was usually a feast or a famine with herrings or mackerel and this is still often the way nowadays. I came across lots of recipes for soused herring or mackerel as a way of preserving in the short term. Herring and mackerel are very perishable—Tommy Sliney, the legendary fish seller from Ballycotton, used to say "never let the sun set on a mackerel."

Gut, wash, and fillet the herrings or mackerel, making sure there are no bones. Roll up the fillets, skin-side down, and pack tightly into a cast-iron casserole. Sprinkle over the onion slices, peppercorns, cloves, salt, sugar, vinegar, and a bay leaf. Bring to a boil on top of the cooker. Put into a very low oven (275°F) and cook for 30–45 minutes.

Allow to get quite cold. Soused herring or mackerel will keep for 7–10 days in the fridge.

Red Herrings

Red herrings were herrings that had been salted and heavily smoked. They needed to be soaked in several changes of water before being cooked, often over the embers of the turf fire. They were very tasty eaten with lots of potatoes, typically they were washed down with a big mug of buttermilk to quench the thirst.

Fried Whitebait or Sprats

beef dripping or vegetable oil, for deep frying
whitebait or sprats
plain white flour, seasoned with salt and freshly ground pepper
lemon segments, to serve

Every year in late summer the sea suddenly boils with tiny whitebait. They can be caught by the bucketful and are irresistible when they are tossed in seasoned flour and fried until crisp. Sprats make their appearance off our coast just after Christmas for two or three weeks. They are cheap and delicious and are also good soused or smoked. In many parts of the country, specially erected wickerwork head weirs were erected to take the sprat. Estyn Evans, in Irish Folkways, *points out that in Donegal sprats constituted the chief food of the peasantry during three or four months of the year. In late summer they were taken from the water in buckets and strainers and the mackerel that were closely pursuing their prey were caught almost as easily.*

Heat good beef dripping or good-quality oil in a deep fryer until good and hot. Toss the fish, a few at a time, in the seasoned flour and shake off the excess. Cook in small batches until crisp and golden. Drain on absorbent paper towels. Serve immediately with segments of lemon.

Note: Some people dip the fish first into milk and then flour.

To preserve sprats

In the Shapland Carew Papers, which detail the accounts of the wealthy Carew family of Castleboro in Co. Wexford, there is an entry for 18 February 1773 which records that a "kegg of red sprats" was delivered to the estate.

This recipe, which preserves sprats like anchovies, comes from the Mocollop Castle Cookbook *of 1801:*

"To a peck of sprats put 2lb of common salt ½lb of bay salt, 1lb of saltpetre, 2oz of salt prunella, a little bole almoniac, put a layer of this compound in a cag and then a layer of sprats and so on till they are all in, press them down very hard and then cover 'em quite close, let 'em stand six months when they may be used, before you use them let 'em be washed in a strong pickle not to let the smallest amount of pickle remain and then repack them with some fresh compound the same as the first."

Mackerel

In his work *Strong Tea*, John B. Keane eulogizes the splendor of mackerel:

"Years before the advent of chip-shops and snack-bars, they sailed in silver armadas through the blue seas of Munster, celestial in design and remarkable humility, proud indeed to show that when God made mackerel, he made them for poor people and if they did nothing more, they kept many a small boy with curls upon his head away from death's door in the horrendous years of the famine."

Every summer the arrival of the mackerel into Ballycotton, our local fishing village, is eagerly awaited; around late July or early August huge shoals sweep around the coastline. Word goes round the village like wildfire that the mackerel are in, and men, women, and children of all ages race to the pier with fishing rods, lines, and hooks. The water churns with hungry mackerel feeding on the sprats. Anyone can dangle a line over the end of the pier and catch a fish. I once did, but was so horrified to see it wriggling on the end of the line that I couldn't kill it, so I never tried again!

Poached Mackerel with Green Sauce

Serves 6

6 very fresh mackerel
scant 5 cups water
1 teaspoon salt

GREEN SAUCE
2 egg yolks (preferably free-range)
1 teaspoon French mustard
  (we use Maille mustard with
  green herbs)
2 tablespoons finely chopped
  mixed herbs: chives, fennel,
  parsley, and thyme
¾ cup (1½ sticks) butter

My husband Tim remembers going out in the early 1960s with a local fisherman to catch mackerel, which they promptly cooked on the boat's stove, fired with coal they dredged up from the bottom of the sea. He assures me that no mackerel ever tasted better. This poached mackerel recipe is a more sophisticated version, but it uses the same basic cooking technique.

First make the sauce. Whisk the egg yolks in a bowl with the mustard and finely chopped herbs. Bring the butter to a boil and pour it in a steady stream onto the egg yolks, whisking continuously until the sauce thickens to a light coating consistency. Keep warm in a bowl over hot water (not stainless steel).

Cut the heads off the mackerel, gut and clean, but keep whole. Bring the water to a boil and add salt and the mackerel. Bring back to boiling point, cover, and remove from the heat. After about 5–8 minutes, check to see whether the fish are cooked. The flesh should lift off the bone. Remove the mackerel onto a plate, scrape off the skin, and carefully lift the fillets off the bones and onto a serving plate. Coat carefully with warm sauce. Serve with a good green salad and perhaps some new potatoes.

Pan Broiled Mackerel with Parsley Butter

Serves 4

8 fillets of very fresh mackerel
seasoned flour
a small knob of butter

PARSLEY BUTTER
¼ cup (½ stick) butter
4 teaspoons finely chopped parsley
a few drops of freshly squeezed
  lemon juice

GARNISH
4 lemon segments
parsley sprigs

When Coquebert de Montbret traveled to Kinsale in 1790, he described the meal of a fishing family as follows: "on the grill over the live coals, they are allowed to cook their mackerel, some mussels and red potatoes with their white eyes."

Certainly fresh mackerel cooked in this time-honored fashion are utterly delicious.

First make the parsley butter. Cream the butter and stir in the parsley and a few drops of lemon juice. Roll into butter pats or form into a roll and wrap in parchment paper or aluminum foil, screwing each end so that it looks like a cracker. Refrigerate to harden.

Heat the broiler pan. Dip the fish fillets in flour that has been seasoned with salt and freshly ground pepper. Shake off the excess flour and then spread a little butter with a knife on the flesh side, as though you were buttering a slice of bread rather meanly. When the broiler is quite hot, but not smoking, place the fish fillets butter-side down on the broiler pan; the fish fillets should sizzle as soon as they touch the pan. Turn down the heat slightly and let cook for 4–5 minutes on that side before you turn them over. Continue to cook on the other side until crisp and golden. Serve on a hot plate with some slices or pats of parsley butter and a segment of lemon.

Parsley butter may be served directly on the fish, or if you have a pretty shell, place it at the side of the plate as a container for the butter.

Note: Fillets of any small fish are delicious broiled in this way. Fish under 2lb, such as mackerel, herring, and brown trout can also be broiled whole on the pan. Fish over 2lb should be filleted first and then cut across into portions. Large fish weighing 4–6lb can also be broiled whole. Cook them for about 10–15 minutes on each side and then put in a hot oven for a further 15 minutes or so to finish cooking.

Baked Lemon Sole or Plaice with Herb Butter

Serves 4

4 very fresh plaice or lemon sole
  on the bone
salt and freshly ground pepper
½ cup (1 stick) butter
2 tablepoons finely chopped mixed
  herbs: parsley, chives, fennel,
  and thyme

Both lemon sole and plaice are abundant around the coast of Ireland and are sought after for their meltingly tender flesh. A splendid extract from Ulysses *by James Joyce:*

"Wouldn't mind being a waiter in a swell hotel. Tips, evening dress, half naked ladies. May I tempt you to a little more filleted lemon sole, miss Dubedat? Yes, do bedad. And she did bedad. Huguenot name I expect that. A miss Dubedat lived in Killiney I remember. Du, de la, French. Still it's the same fish, perhaps old Micky Hanlon of Moore street ripped the guts out of making money, hand over fist, finger in fishes gills, can't write his name on a cheque, think he was painting the landscape with his mouth twisted."

Turn the fish on its side and remove the head. Wash the fish and clean thoroughly. With a knife, cut through the skin right round the fish, just where the "fringe" meets the flesh.

Sprinkle the fish with salt and pepper and lay it in ¼ inch of water in a shallow baking pan. Bake in a moderately hot oven (375°F) for 20–30 minutes. The water should have just evaporated as the fish is cooked. Check to see whether the fish is cooked by lifting the flesh from the bone at the head end; it should lift off the bone easily and be quite white.

Meanwhile, melt the butter and stir in the freshly chopped herbs. Just before serving, catch the skin down near the tail and pull it off gently (the skin will tear badly if not properly cut). Lift the fish onto hot plates and spoon the herb butter over them. Serve immediately.

How to Dress Turbot, Shad, Plaice, or any Flat FishFish

This comes from the Mary Ponsonby manuscript of 1850:

"Clean your Turbot and cut off the finns, then cut the black side four or five times across to the bone, lay it on the proper side uppermost on the fish plate that fits the Kettle, strew on a good handful of salt, squeeze the juice of two Lemons and let the Turbot lie in this manner half an hour, and having your Kettle three parts filled with boiling water (that's hard) throw into it a pint of cold water and then put the turbot in and let it boil gently twenty minutes."

I was fascinated to see that this recipe is almost exactly the same method that we use when poaching salmon and gives a delicious result.

Sauce for the Above

"Put into your saucepan a quarter of a pound of Butter till it boils, then add a table spoonful of Flour and shake it a moment over the fire then add a pint of good and very rich Gravy, a teaspoonful of anchovy juice, and the size of a walnut of good glaze, a pinchfull of pepper, and a teaspoon of Mustard. Let this boil well together, then add half a tea cup full of small capers, turn your sauce well, and strew it over your turbot on sending up."

To Dress Haddock or Cod

From the Mary Ponsonby manuscript of 1850.

"Cut your Haddock in pieces three inches thick, dry them in a cloth, put near a gill of clarified Butter in a stewpan, a middling Onion cut small, a little Parsley cut small. Boil them up in the Butter, season your fish with Salt, Pepper, Mace beaten fine, half a pint of soft water, stew it slow 'till thoroughly done, beat the yolks of two Eggs with the Juice of a Lemon, just when it is to be taken up pour this in."

1 medium ray (skate) wing,
   weighing 1¼–1½lb
1 onion, thinly sliced
a few sprigs of parsley
a little salt
2 tablespoons white wine vinegar
chopped parsley, to garnish

BLACK BUTTER
¼ cup (½ stick) butter
2 tablespoons white wine vinegar

Ray with Black Butter

This classic recipe was a favorite in Anglo-Irish houses and is one of the most delicious ways of serving a piece of ray wing.

Choose a pan wide enough for the ray wing to lie flat while cooking. Put in the fish, cover completely with cold water, add the onion, parsley, salt, and the wine vinegar. Bring to a boil gently, cover, and barely simmer for 15–20 minutes. If the flesh lifts easily from the cartilage, the skate is cooked. Turn off the heat and transfer the fish onto a large serving plate. Skin and lift the flesh onto hot plates, first from one side of the cartilage, then the other, scraping off the white skin. Cover and keep hot.

    Next make the black butter. Melt the butter immediately in a hot pan, allow it to foam and just as it turns a good rich brown color, add the wine vinegar. Let it to bubble up again and then pour sizzling over the fish. Sprinkle with the chopped parsley and serve immediately.

Ray

Ray (skate) used to be landed in vast quantities in the old Dublin fishing port at Ringsend— so much so that it was known as Raytown. Ray and chips are still much sought after in Dublin chip shops. This was not so everywhere. In 1790 the French scholar and consul in Dublin, Charles Etienne Coquebert de Montbret made a visit to Kinsale, Co. Cork, where he noted "so abundant are the catches that ray salted by the people of Skerries are thrown out by the fisherman here."

Eels

My father and grandfather occasionally cooked eels, and as children we giggled in horror as the eels continued to squirm while they cooked in the skillet. Needless to say we couldn't be persuaded to try them and it wasn't until my late teens that I realized what I'd been missing.

    Eels were far more widely available in ancient times than nowadays. Eel weirs, which have a long history, appear to have been the closely guarded property of individual families, In *The Farm* by Lough Gur, which describes life on a farm in Co. Limerick in the 19th century, Cissie O'Brien describes how the eels were caught and either sent to the Limerick market or sold to Meggy the Eel, an itinerant fish woman from Bruff, who used to peddle them from house to house. Eels are still caught around Lough Neagh, Nun's Island Weir in Galway, in parts of Wexford, and in many other parts of the country.

    Marian Sisk showed me how to prepare eels. Wash and rub with a green scratchy pad to remove the slime. Just below the neck cut from the underside through the spine, but not through the skin at the back. Holding the eel firmly, pull off the skin, then gut from vent to head end. Cut a little further down below the vent and carefully remove the sac and all the blood which, according to Marian, is poisonous. Wash well under cold running water.

Fried Eel

Cut the eels into pieces about 2 inches long. Roll in seasoned flour and fry in butter in the pan. Eat with bread and butter and a little lemon. Simple and exquisite. Allow 8oz eel per person.

The Loughsiders around Lough Neagh often deep-fried the eels rather than shallow-frying them in a pan.

Serves 4

1lb fresh eels
2½ cups milk
2 tablespoons green part of scallions or chives
2 tablespoons chopped fresh parsley
roux (see page 42)
salt and freshly ground pepper

Eels with Scallion and Parsley Sauce

In Never no More, *Maura Laverty gives us a glimpse of life on the edge of the Bog of Allen in the 1920s:*

"Living so far inland our fish dishes were mostly ling or red herrings. Occasionally, however, Mike Brophy took his fishing rod and went down to the mill pond, returning with a few eels or perch. Judy Ryan (the servant girl) would never touch an eel, saying that they were cousins to the serpents. Eels could be fried... A favourite method of cooking eels was to skin the fish, cut them in slices, set them to parboil to take out the grease, then stew them in a creamy white sauce with chopped parsley and scallions."

Skin the eels, wash well to remove any trace of blood inside, cut into 3 inch lengths. Put into a pot, cover with cold water, and bring to a boil. Simmer for a few minutes to remove some of the oil; drain.

Bring the milk to a boil with the scallions and parsley. Whisk in the roux and cook until the sauce has a light coating consistency. Season with salt and freshly ground pepper. Add the eels, cover, and continue to simmer in the sauce until the eels are fully cooked. Taste and correct the seasoning. Serve with boiled potatoes.

Trout

In the late 12th century the writer and historian Giraldus Cambrensis wrote in his Topographia Hibernica:

"This Ireland is also specially remarkable for a great number of beautiful lakes, abounding in fish and surpassing in size those of other countries I have visited. The rivers and lakes are also plentifully stored with the sorts of fish peculiar to these waters and especially three species—salmon, trout and muddy eels."

When I was a child a local man, Eoin O'Neill, lived simply by fishing and hunting. I used to watch out for him in the evenings as he came home from his day in the woods or on the river bank. "Catch anything, Eoin?" I'd inquire hopefully. He would always have a story for me and occasionally he'd pluck a little speckledy brown trout out of the deep pockets of his tweedy jacket and drop it into my eager hands. I would race home to my mother, who would cook it for my tea.

2 × 2lb whole rainbow trout
salt and freshly ground pepper
2–4 tablespoons (¼–½ stick) butter
2 sprigs of fennel

SPINACH BUTTER SAUCE
2 handfuls of spinach leaves
⅔ cup light cream
⅓ cup (¾ stick) butter

Trout with Spinach Butter Sauce

In the diaries of Amhlaoibh Uí Shúileabháin from Callan in Co. Kilkenny, Amhlaoibh visits the home of Arthur James Hennebry on June 20, 1828, where he sits down to a dinner of "two fine fat sweet substantial trout, one of them as big as a small salmon." I like to think he would have enjoyed this rich and delicious sauce, which is also exquisite with salmon, trout, plaice, or monkfish.

We sometimes get large rainbow trout that are about two years old and have a wonderful flavor—very much more delectable than the smaller ones.

Gut the trout and wash well, making sure to remove the line of blood from the inside near the back bone. Dry with paper towels, season inside and out with salt and freshly ground pepper. Put a pat of butter and a sprig of fennel into the center of each trout.

Take a large sheet of foil and smear a little butter on the center. Put one trout onto the foil and fold over to make a parcel. Crimp the edges; seal well to make sure that none of the juices escape. Repeat with another sheet of foil and the other trout. Preheat the oven to 375°F. Put the two foil parcels on a baking sheet, but make sure that they are not touching. Bake for about 30 minutes.

Meanwhile, make the spinach butter sauce. Remove the stalks from the spinach, wash, and cook in 2½ cups boiling water with a pinch of salt. Cook for 4–5 minutes or until soft. Drain, pressing out all the water, and chop finely. Put the cream into a saucepan and simmer on a gentle heat until reduced to about 3 tablespoons, or until it is in danger of burning. Then, on a very low heat, whisk in the butter bit by bit as though you were making a Hollandaise sauce. Stir in the spinach.

When the fish is cooked, open the foil parcels. There will be lots of delicious juices; use some of these to thin out the sauce if necessary. Put the two parcels onto a hot serving dish and bring to the table. Skin the fish and lift the juicy pink flesh onto hot plates. Spoon the spinach butter sauce over the fish and serve immediately.

Salmon

Salmon is mentioned frequently in early Irish literature and in the heroic tales of ancient Ireland.

There is archaeological evidence that salmon was eaten in 7000BC by Ireland's earliest inhabitants from the Mesolithic (Middle Stone Age) site of Mount Sandel, near Coleraine in Co. Derry.

The most famous salmon in Irish mythology, which is mentioned in *Macgnímartha Find* (The Boyhood Deeds of Fionn), was the one that gave boundless knowledge to the young hero, Fionn Mac Cumhaill. He was carefully cooking the magical fish over an applewood fire for his master Finnéigeas when he burst a rising blister on the salmon's skin. He burnt his thumb and spontaneously sucked it to relieve the pain. This meant that, inadvertently, he had the first taste of the salmon of knowledge and so became the wisest of men.

There is a specific season for wild salmon, which varies from one part of the country to another. Farmed salmon, now widely produced around the west and south coast of Ireland, is available all the year round, but it doesn't hold a candle to the wild fish.

Poached Salmon with Irish Butter Sauce

Serves 8

2½lb center cut of fresh salmon
water
salt

IRISH BUTTER SAUCE
2 egg yolks
2 teaspoons cold water
½ cup (1 stick) butter, diced
1 teaspoon approx. lemon juice

GARNISH
sprigs of watercress or flat-leaf
    parsley

For maximum flavor, we cook the salmon in the time-honored way, by poaching it gently in well-salted boiling water. Better still, use sea water if you are close to the coast.

The proportion of salt to water is very important. We use 1 rounded tablespoon salt to every 5 cups water. Although the fish or piece of fish should be just covered with water, the aim is to use the minimum amount of water to preserve the maximum flavor, so therefore one should use a saucepan that will fit the fish exactly. An oval cast-iron saucepan is usually perfect.

Half fill the pan with measured salted water and bring to a boil. Put in the piece of fish, just covering with water, and bring back to a boil. Simmer gently for 20 minutes. Turn off the heat, let the fish sit in the water. Serve within 15–20 minutes.

Meanwhile, make the Irish butter sauce. Put the egg yolks into a heavy-bottomed stainless-steel saucepan on a very low heat. Add the cold water and whisk thoroughly. Add the butter bit by bit, whisking all the time. As soon as one piece melts, add the next. The mixture will gradually thicken, but if it shows signs of becoming too thick or "scrambling" slightly, remove from the heat immediately and add a little cold water if necessary. Do not leave the pan or stop whisking until the sauce is made. Finally, add the lemon juice to taste. Pour into a bowl and keep warm over hot, but not boiling, water.

To serve, lift the cooked salmon carefully from the poaching liquid. Peel off the skin gently. Garnish with sprigs of watercress or parsley. Serve with the Irish butter sauce.

2–2½lb freshly poached salmon
(see opposite)

GARNISH
lettuce leaves
tiny scallions
watercress
lemon segments

Salmon Mayonnaise

This was the traditional second course on wedding menus all over Ireland. If you cook fresh wild Irish salmon in well-salted water and serve it while it is still slightly warm with some freshly made salads, it's absolutely magical.

Poach the salmon; let cool. Meanwhile make a tomato and mint salad. Remove the cores from six tomatoes and quarter. Sprinkle with a little salt, a little white wine vinegar, sugar, and black pepper. Toss immediately in a little French dressing; sprinkle with 1–2 teaspoons chopped mint and basil. Next make a cucumber and fennel salad. Slice a medium cucumber, sprinkle with salt, 2–4 teaspoons wine vinegar, and plenty of sugar. Stir in 2 teaspoons chopped fennel. Finally make a potato salad by combining French dressing, parsley, chives, and mayonnaise with stiff, freshly mashed potato. Season to taste.

To make an egg mayonnaise, hard-cook 4 eggs in boiling salted water, drain and put immediately into a bowl of cold water. When cold, shell the eggs and slice in half lengthwise. Strain the yolks and mix the strained egg yolk with mayonnaise (see below). Add chopped chives and salt and pepper to taste. Fill into a piping bag and pipe into the whites. Garnish with a sprig of parsley or chervil and serve on a bed of lettuce.

To assemble the salmon mayonnaise, put a portion of salmon on each plate when it is just cold. Garnish with a few lettuce leaves, pipe some potato salad onto the lettuce, and put a little tomato and cucumber salad on the plate as well as 1 portion of egg mayonnaise. Garnish with tiny spring onions, watercress, and a segment of lemon. Additional mayonnaise can be served separately or put into a bowl on each plate.

2 free-range egg yolks
pinch of English mustard powder or
¼ teaspoon French mustard
¼ teaspoon salt
2 teaspoons white wine vinegar
1 cup oil (sunflower, or olive oil
or a mixture)

Mayonnaise

Many people aren't aware that mayonnaise can be made in under 5 minutes. The secret is to have all your ingredients at room temperature and to drip the oil very slowly into the egg yolks at the beginning.

Put the egg yolks into a bowl with the mustard, salt and the white wine vinegar. Put the oil into a measuring jug. Take a whisk in one hand and the oil in the other and drip the oil into the egg yolks, drop by drop, whisking at the same time. Within a minute you will notice that the mixture is beginning to thicken. When this happens you can add the oil a little faster, but not too quickly or it will suddenly curdle. Taste and add a little more seasoning and vinegar if necessary.

Pickled Salmon

Salted salmon was exported in large quantities to Italy and France during the 18th century. In Ireland itself, salmon was consumed fresh near rivers and coastal regions and when the fish were spawning and plentiful. However, in the regions distant from the salmon habitats and during the winter and spring months, pickled salmon had to suffice. This was served as a breakfast dish in the late 19th century as described in the 1897 publication *The Sportsman* in Ireland:

"A Sportsman's Breakfast: First, a large bowl of new milk which instantly disappeared; then a liberal allowance of cold salmon soaked in vinegar… and a bottle of port wine."

From the Receipt Book of Mrs Dot Drew of Mocollop Castle, Ballyduff, Co. Waterford, dated 1801:

"Cut up a salmon across into any sized pieces when well wash'd let it be boiled in a strong pickle of salt and water till the fish parts from the bone when quite cold pack it up in a crock [...] throwing a little salt petre finely powdered between every layer of fish, when packed close keep it always covered with the following pickle, take one quart of vinegar and one quart of water, 3oz of lump sugar and 12 drops of the best oyle of cloves, twill be fit for use in 3 or 4 weeks, twill look black at first till the oil and fat comes out."

Bream

One of my most valued sources of traditional recipes is John F. Guerin who has lived all his life beside the sea in Ballyheigue, Co. Kerry.

"The traditional Ballyheigue fish dish is boiled bream. The bream is caught with a line off the high rocks; a local knowledge is important to find the right places."

The bream is usually boiled and eaten when cold. It was a favorite dinner for a day in the bog; cold bream, with slices of yellow-meal bread, and a bottle of cold tea.

Salt Cod or Ling

Salted fish has been a prominent feature of the Irish diet since medieval times, when huge quantities of salted fish (cod and ling) were exported to England. Fresh fish was an expensive luxury for inland Irish communities and salted fish became a necessary and important addition to the diet on Fridays and during the Lenten period, when the consumption of meat was forbidden by the church. John Guerin from Ballyheigue remembers:

"Ling was a favourite fish for Lent in my father's time. The average ling was about 2½ feet long, it was salted and cured and usually hung at the back of the kitchen door. A large slice was cut off when needed and boiled for dinner. The first boil of water was usually thrown away as it was too salty."

A pinch of flour was added to the soup, and it was then served hot with boiled potatoes.

Salted Ling and Mashed Potatoes

In many places in Ireland salted ling was called battleboard, perhaps because the drying and salting process rendered the fish rock hard.

Sometimes the cooked salt ling was deboned and flaked and then mixed into some mashed potato with enough of the cooking liquor to make it soft and juicy. Served hot, with butter melting in the center.

Whiting, ling, and rock cod were dried and hung from the rafters, not only in small cabins but also in prosperous farmhouses, alongside flitches of bacon. Salted, dried, and smoked fish were also widely sold in small village shops all round the country.

The celebrated playwright and novelist John B. Keane, from Listowel in Co. Kerry, writes of salted ling with a deep respect in *Strong Tea*:

"The rafters in the thatched houses of your grandfather's were never without a flitch of it and when your Aunty Mary came back from America, 'twas the first thing she asked for. Bishops and Monsignors were reared on it and it was responsible for the pointing of more fifties than sirloin steak and raw eggs put together. "

1lb salt cod or ling
milk, to cover

WHITE SAUCE
2 tablespoons (¼ stick) butter
1 onion, chopped
1 tablespoon all-purpose flour
2½ cups fresh whole milk
salt and freshly ground pepper
1–2 tablespoons chopped parsley
   (optional)

Variation

Parsley Sauce

parsley stalks
4 tablespoons finely chopped
   parsley
2½ cups whole milk
1–1 ½oz roux (see page 42)
salt and freshly ground pepper

Salt Cod or Ling with White Sauce

Salt cod and ling (also known as stockfish or hardfish) are still on sale in the English Market in Cork city, now made famous by the historic visit of Queen Elizabeth II in May 2011. They are available all the year round and form the traditional Cork supper on Christmas Eve.

Cut the salt fish into medium-sized pieces. Cover with cold water and soak overnight. Next day discard the water, cover with milk, and stew until tender (for about 30 minutes).

   Meanwhile, melt the butter in a saucepan. Add the chopped onion, cover, and cook on a gentle heat until soft. Stir in the flour and cook for 2–3 minutes, then whisk in the milk, bit by bit. Season, bring to a boil, and simmer for a few minutes. A little chopped parsley wouldn't do any harm.

   Drain the fish. Serve with the sauce and some freshly boiled potatoes.

Remove the stalks from the parsley, put the stalks into a saucepan with the cold milk, bring slowly to a boil, then remove the stalks. Whisk the roux into the boiling milk until thickened; add the chopped parsley. Season with salt and freshly ground pepper. Simmer for 5–10 minutes on a very low heat, then taste and correct the seasoning before serving.

Note: For plain white sauce, more correctly called Béchamel, omit the parsley

Limpets (*Bairneachs*)

Limpets (*bairneach* in Irish) are rarely eaten nowadays, but formerly they were part of the Irish diet, not only on the islands but also on the mainland. In *An tOileánach* (The Islandman), his famous account of life on the Blasket Island, Tomás O'Criomhthainn writes "and the food I got was hen's eggs, lumps of butter and bits of fish, limpets and winkles—a bit of everything going from sea or land." There follows an evocative passage where he describes his mother roasting the limpets on an open fire, "throwing them to us one by one like a hen with chickens."

   Limpets were also often cooked in an ingenious way in the rock pools along the shore. A fire was lit to heat the stones, which were then transferred to the rock pool where they heated the water in much the same manner as described in the *Fulachta Fiadh*. The limpets were then cooked in the hot sea water.

   Enda Conneely, who runs the Fisherman's Cottage Restaurant with Cookery and Lifestyle Courses on Inisheer, the most southerly of the Aran Islands, sent me some of his suggestions for using *bairneachs* or limpets: "I find that by bringing just to the boil in sea water or salted water the limpets come apart from the shell. If you keep a close eye on the pot, you can take them off the heat and run under cold water as soon as this happens—this means that they are not too tough and chewy. I take the whole top off the limpet and just keep the foot. This is put in a marinade made up of olive oil, lemon and lime juice, salt and pepper, crushed garlic and chopped fresh coriander and left for a few hours or overnight. It will hold in the fridge for days and improves in flavor and texture."

   I also cook limpets in water to which a heaping teaspoon of baking soda has been added. When it comes to a boil, drain away, and run under cold water. This tenderizes the tough part of the limpet. If you grab the head and pull it off, it brings with it the string-like intestine to be discarded. Toss the prepared limpets in seasoned flour and shallow fry in garlic butter. This is excellent hot or cold as part of a wild tapas spread.

Razorfish

Razorfish (*Ensis ensis*) can be harvested all the year round, but are best around Easter. Along with many other types of shellfish, razorfish would have formed part of the diet in coastal regions, particularly in the springtime when the low tides made it easy to collect shellfish.

The razorfish is a burrowing bivalve. It holds its ground at the bottom of its burrow with a single foot, which protrudes from the end of the shell. Razorfish normally live on sandy ground on the extreme lower shore and in shallow water. The speed with which they can withdraw to the bottom of their burrows makes them difficult to harvest by hand. A pinch of salt dropped into the burrow encourages the razorfish to emerge. But you have to be ready to grab them right away, or they will shoot back down into the sand. We love razorfish and forage for them as often as we can. They are delicious either cooked in a pan like mussels or opened on a griddle over an open fire. Dip in melted butter and eat immediately, garlic and parsley are a delicious addition. If we only manage to catch a few, we slice the cooked razorfish very thinly at an angle, to make them go further, and then toss them in garlic butter. They are delicious piled onto mash, or on a baked potato.

Cockles

Shellfish has certainly formed part of the diet of Irish coastal people since earliest times, from the prehistoric period right through to the recent past. In excavations at the historic sites of Oughtymore, Co. Kerry (Co. Derry), Park Cave, Co. Antrim, and Potters Cave, Co. Antrim, archaeological remains of cockle shells attest that they were very popular in antiquity and also in the Viking period. Traders like the legendary Mollie Malone, the famous Dublin fishwoman celebrated in song and verse, were a common sight, measuring out cockles, mussels, and periwinkles from their tin basins on the stalls around old Dublin.

There are many beautiful cockle strands around our Irish coasts. Years ago it was a common sight during the summer months to see hordes of women and children digging cockles with old spoons, gathering them up in their aprons or into tin cans. Sale of the cockles and "perries" often provided a little extra money to supplement a meager income. Experienced cocklers know exactly where to dig on the sandy strands at low tide.

The Donegan family showed me the secret of how to collect cockles on the spectacular Barrow Strand in Co. Kerry. We used a rake rather than a spoon or trowel. A little air hole gives a clue as to where the cockle hides deep in the sand. Any cockles lying on the surface are invariably dead, so you should avoid these.

Cockles can be eaten both raw and cooked. They should be washed several times in cold water to remove the sand from the shells. Years ago they were cooked in a pot over the turf fire. They are every bit as delicious nowadays even when cooked on a gas ring.

Cockles with Melted Butter

Wash the cockles in several changes of cold water to remove the sand and grit from the shells. Put into a saucepan or skillet, cover, and cook over a medium heat. They open in just a few minutes and are best eaten straight from the shells, just dipped in melted butter. Eat with lots of crusty brown bread. The cockle liquid is also delicious. Cockles are also delectable with a bowl of homemade mayonnaise (see page 53).

Periwinkles

fresh live periwinkles
boiling salted water (about 3 cups
    salt to every 9½ cups water)
homemade mayonnaise (see page
    53) or vinegar (optional), to serve

As with cockles, there is evidence from the early historic sites of Oughtymore, Co. Derry, Park Cave, Co. Antrim, and Potter's cave, Co. Antrim, that winkles were exploited as a foodstuff. In general, spring was the season for gathering shellfish, but Easter and Good Friday in particular were special occasions for visiting the seashore. Winkles were a favorite dish on these days, but there was folk belief that after St. Patrick's Day (March 17th) limpets were better for eating than periwinkles.

Periwinkles are still gathered around our coasts when the tide is out. When I take my grandchildren down to Shanagarry strand to pick the shiny black winkles from between the rocks, I tell them how these little shellfish have nourished Irish people since prehistoric times and helped save fisherfolk from starvation on the south-west coast during the Famine times.

Bring the water to a boil, add the salt, and the periwinkles. Bring the water back to a boil, drain the periwinkles and let cool. Pick the periwinkles out of the shells with a large pin. Eat on their own or with mayonnaise. Some people like to dip them in vinegar or oatmeal.

Estyn Evans points out that in Ireland winkles were boiled in milk, as a foodstuff for children or to give extra nourishment to calves.

Mussels

Street cries of "Cockles and Mussels, alive, alive-o" resounded around the streets of Dublin in former times. In some parts of the country, including Bere Island, mussels as well as other shellfish are still shunned as "famine food." Despite the fact that the Great Famine was over 150 years ago, the horror of it is still very strong in folk memory. Now very much in demand both at home and abroad, plump juicy mussels are being farmed very successfully all around Irish coasts.

Mussels with Garlic Butter

48 mussels, approx. 3¼–4lb,
    all tightly shut
1½–2 cups fresh, white
    breadcrumbs

GARLIC BUTTER
2 large garlic cloves
2 tablespoons chopped parsley
1 tablespoon olive oil
⅓ cup (¾ stick) soft butter

Wash the mussels in several changes of water, but don't soak them or you'll lose some of the sweet juices. Put them into a saucepan or skillet, not too many at a time, cover with a lid or folded dish towel and put on a medium heat. Just as soon as the shells open, take out the mussels, and let cool. The mussel broth can be drunk or used for fish soup.

To make the garlic butter, peel and crush the garlic and pound it in a mortar with the finely chopped parsley and olive oil. Gradually beat in the butter – you can do it in a bowl or a food processor. Spread the soft garlic butter over the mussels in the shells. Dip each one into the breadcrumbs. Arrange into individual serving dishes. Brown under the broiler and serve with white bread to mop up the delicious juices.

Irish Oysters

6–12 native Irish oysters per person

GARNISH
seaweed
1 lemon, cut into segments

Oysters must be tightly shut: if a shell is even slightly open, discard it.

Not long before serving, open the oysters. You will need an oyster knife for this operation, unless you are one of the champion oyster openers! Place the oyster on the worktop, deep shell down. Cover your hand with a folded dish towel and hold the oyster firmly. Put the tip of the oyster knife into the crevice at the hinge of the oyster, push hard, and then quickly twist the knife. You need to exert quite a bit of pressure (hence it is essential that the hand holding the oyster is protected, in case the knife slips!) When you feel that the oyster is opening, change the angle of the knife and, keeping the blade close to the shell, slice the oyster off the top shell in one movement. Then run the knife underneath the oyster in the deep shell and flip it over: be careful not to lose any of the delicious juices.

Put a bed of seaweed on 2 chilled plates; place the oysters on the seaweed, and add a few segments of lemon.

Serve with fresh brown soda bread and butter and a glass of Guinness or Murphy stout.

Native oysters are in season only when there is an "r" in the month. Gigas oysters (pictured above) may be eaten all year round and are now farmed in many places off the coast of Ireland.

Native Irish Oysters

Native Irish oysters, famous the world over, are in season from September to March when there is an "R" in the month. The best way to eat them is raw, just like our earliest ancestors who gathered around the mouths of estuaries to feast on shellfish thousands of years ago. There are numerous substantial mounds of oyster shells or shell middens throughout the country; they date from the prehistoric to the medieval periods. A particularly impressive site, which probably dates from the late 13th/early 14th century was discovered during the construction of the "new school" at Carrigtwohill in Co. Cork. Coincidentally, the famous Rossmore oysters now come from the oyster beds on the shoreline close by.

Although oysters are now very much a luxury, they were cheap and abundant for centuries. The Irish writer Jonathan Swift sang their praises and celebrated the aphrodisiac qualities of plump Irish oysters.

To Stew Oysters

This recipe comes from the manuscript of Marianne Armstrong, Kiltoon Glebe, Northern Ireland, c. 1849. I tried this recipe with a ¼ teaspoon each of mace and cayenne pepper, and served it with crusty bread. It was delicious!

"A pint of oysters simmered in their own liquor. Quarter pint milk or cream seasoned with mace, cayenne pepper and salt, 2oz of butter. A dessertspoon of flour, well blended. Simmer for a short time."

Oyster Catchup

This recipe comes from Mary Ponsonby's manuscript (c.1850). She was very precise with the measurements in her recipes and suggested cooking times, which makes them much easier to reproduce. Other manuscript recipes use a pinch of this and that, but Mary actually describes what size to cut ingredients. Her home, Kilcooley Abbey, is well inland in Co. Tipperary, so this recipe would have been made in large quantities once a season and stored for the year. Plenty of help would have been needed in the kitchen: opening 600 oysters is quite a challenge!

"Wash 600 of Oysters in their own liquors. Boil the liquor, skim them well, chop the Oysters very small, stew in the liquor for half an hour, then strain out the Oysters. Put to the liquor half a Pint of Port, the same quantity of White Mountain or Madeira, a quarter of a Pound of Anchovies, half an Ounce of Pepper, four blades of Mace, Nutmeg, Ginger, of each half an Ounce, 3 or 4 Bay Leaves, mix all together, and boil it well, when cold bottle it, pour the Spice into the bottles."

Dutch Fish Sauce

It was interesting to come across elderflower vinegar in this manuscript recipe also from Mary Ponsonby. Nowadays, when we make it with our students they think it is very exotic and of the moment! We make lots of elderflower cordial and vinegar in the month of June, when the elderflowers are at their best.

"Take three yolks of eggs—two Dutch olives or anchovies, a quarter of a pound of butter, as much flour as will lie upon the point of a knife—three spoonfuls of Elder Vinegar, a small bunch of sweet herbs, a little pepper and salt, stir it all together upon the fire till it comes to be thick but you must not let it boil, then squeeze a little lemon into it if you don't think it sharp enough."

Scallops

Up until the early part of this century, scallops were very plentiful around the Irish coast. Then the invention of the steam dredge led to overfishing in many places, so the numbers have decreased. Many older people who live on the islands or around the coast still eat scallops raw as we do, although there seems to be a stigma attached to this—perhaps a relic of famine times. Thinly sliced they are sweet and unbelievably delicious.

Traditionally, they were cooked in the shell, either in sea water or in fresh water. They were boiled for about 4–5 minutes and then removed from the water. The "white bit and the tongue" were set aside and the rest discarded. Ted Ó Súilleabháin from Bere Island explained, "You'd have a hot pan with butter melting in it and you'd just fry the scallops on both sides in butter, turn them out onto a plate and eat them. They were very sweet and tasty. When sea water was used as the cooking liquid it was used and often saved and drunk. It was considered to be a tremendous tonic."

Cluasin or Queen scallops were cooked in the same way. They are small, but absolutely delicious.

Scallops with Cream and Mushrooms

Serves 12 as a starter, 6 as a main course

12 scallops in their shells
dry white wine and water, to cover
⅔ cup chopped shallot or onion
2 tablespoons (¼ stick) butter
2½ cups sliced mushrooms
2 heaping tablespoons all-purpose flour
1 cup half and half
salt and freshly ground pepper
¾–scant 1 cup Irish Cheddar cheese, grated
1 heaping tablespoon chopped parsley
fluffy mashed potato (see page 40)

A friend who grew up on the shores of Mulroy Bay in Co. Donegal used to go out in a rowing boat with family and friends on scallop expeditions. They would peer down through the clear water and raise the scallops one by one from the stony bottom with their very effective homemade scalloping hook. The scallops were brought home and cooked at once.

In his work The Rosses *in 1753, the Most Reverend A.B. recounts the unorthodox method of scallop collection:*

"Their shellfish they got in the following manner… for scallops and oysters, when the tide was out, the younger women waded into the sea where they knew beds of such fish lay; some of them naked, others having stripped off their petticoats, went with their gowns tucked up about their waists and by armfuls brought ashore whatever number of scallops and oysters they thought requisite. The scallops weighed from two to four pounds each."

Put the scallops in a medium-sized stainless-steel saucepan and cover with a mixture of half white wine and half water. Poach for 3–5 minutes (be careful to simmer and not to overcook). Remove the scallops and reduce the cooking liquid to approximately 1¼–1½ cups.

Sweat the chopped shallot or onions gently in butter until soft (about 5–6 minutes). Add the sliced mushrooms and cook for 3–4 minutes more. Stir in the flour and cook for a further 1 minute. Add the milk to the scallop cooking liquid to make up to 2½ cups and pour, stirring continuously, onto the flour in the saucepan. Cook gently to reduce the sauce until the flavor is really good. Season.

Cut the scallops into 3–4 pieces and add to the sauce with some of the cheese and the parsley. Decorate the scallop shells or serving dish by piping fluffy mashed potato round the edge. Fill the center with the scallop mixture and sprinkle the top with the remaining cheese.

Just before serving, reheat in a moderate oven (350°F) until just bubbling (about 20 minutes).

2 × 2lb live lobsters
½ cup (1 stick) butter
a squeeze of lemon juice

COURT BOUILLON
1 carrot, thinly sliced
1 onion, thinly sliced
2½ cups dry white wine
2½ cups water
bouquet garni
a few peppercorns

GARNISH
sprigs of watercress, flat parsley,
   or fennel
lemon segments

Ballymaloe Hot Buttered Lobster

This simple but exquisite way of serving lobster outsells any other dish at Ballymaloe House.

Cover the lobsters with lukewarm well-salted water in a saucepan; use sea water if available. Put the saucepan on a low heat and bring slowly to simmering point; lobster dies at about 112°F. By this stage the lobsters will be changing color, so remove them and discard all the cooking water.

Slice the carrot and onion and put with the wine, fresh water, bouquet garni, and peppercorns into a stainless-steel saucepan. Bring to a boil. Put in the lobsters and cover with a tight-fitting lid. Steam them until the shells have turned uniformly red, then remove them from the pot. Strain the cooking liquid and reserve for a sauce.

As soon as they are cool enough to handle, split them in half from head to tail, remove the "sac" which is just in the top of the head and crack the large claws. Extract all the meat from the body, tail, and large and small claws. Scrape out all the soft, greenish tomalley (liver) from the part of the shell nearest the head, and put it with the firmer meat into a warm bowl wrapped in a dish towel.

Heat the lobster shells. Cut the meat into chunks and melt half the butter. When it is foaming, toss the meat and tomalley in it until the meat is heated through and the juices turn pink.

Spoon the meat back into the hot shells. Put the remaining butter into the pan, heat, and scrape up any bits. Add a squeeze of lemon juice. Pour the buttery juices into small heated ramekins and serve beside the lobster on hot plates. Garnish with sprigs of watercress, flat parsley, or fennel, and lemon segments. Hot buttered lobster should be eaten immediately.

Lobster

Up to relatively recently lobsters were still a modest luxury in Ireland, but nowadays, with the dwindling numbers and large demand for Irish shellfish from European restaurants, particularly in France, Germany, and Belgium, the price has gone through the roof. Lobsters were traditionally caught in handmade wicker lobster pots. Most are now plastic, but the system remains the same.

Lobster is best bought straight from the fisherman who has hauled in the lobster pots that he set that morning. If lobsters are kept in a tank for any length of time they waste inside the shells, the flesh becomes stringy and they lose flavor.

Live lobsters should be heavy for their size. The only inedible parts of a lobster are the stomach sac, the gills, and the long intestine that runs down the center of the tail. Every other scrap, including the creamy meat in the waistcoat, is edible and if properly cooked, delicious and tender. Lobster is one of Ireland's finest gastronomic treats so save your money for the best!

very fresh Dublin Bay or other jumbo shrimp, peeled
oil, for deep frying
lemon segments and tartare sauce, to serve

BATTER
1 cup plus 1 tablespoon all-purpose flour
1¾ tablespoons olive oil
1–1½ egg whites
sea salt

Scampi with Tartare Sauce

Scampi was the "must have" starter of the '60s and '70s, served in the old hotels with tartare sauc,e and it has remained very popular. It is utterly delicious when made with fresh Dublin Bay shrimp, but sadly nowadays is more often a travesty made with inferior soggy frozen shrimp or worse still, some other fish masquerading as shrimp.

In North Atlantic Seafood, *Alan Davidson explains how these crustaceans first were given their name: "It is not, in fact, an inhabitant of Dublin Bay. The name was bestowed because the fishing boats coming into Dublin often had these prawns [shrimp] on board, having caught them incidentally. Since they were not fish, the fishermen could dispose of them on the side to the Dublin street-vendors, of whom Molly Malone of the well-known song, became the archetype. They are also known as langoustines."*

First make the batter. Sift the flour into a bowl. Make a well in the center and gradually whisk in the olive oil. Allow to stand. Just before frying, whisk the egg whites until stiff peaks form and fold into the batter, adding a good pinch of sea salt.

Preheat the oil in the deep fryer to 350°F. Just before serving, dip the very fresh shrimp in batter and deep-fry in the hot oil until crisp and golden. Drain on kitchen paper. Serve immediately with a little bowl of tartare sauce and a segment of lemon.

Serves 8

12 heads and claws of fresh large shrimp or the cracked claws and body shells of 2–3 lobsters
2 tablespoons olive oil
2 shallots, finely chopped
2 garlic cloves, crushed
1¼ cups fish stock
3 medium (about 1lb) fresh tomatoes or 1 x 14oz tin chopped tomatoes
2 tablespoons finely chopped parsley
2 tablespoons brandy
¾ cup light cream
salt and freshly ground pepper
fresh flat-leaf parsley leaves, to garnish

Shrimp or Lobster Bisque

We can't bear to waste any scrap of the shellfish. Use leftover shrimp or lobster shells to make this delicious bisque—then you get double the value from the shellfish. It's rich, so serve it in small bowls. Shrimp or lobster shells are interchangeable in this recipe.

Use a hammer to crush the shrimp or lobster shells into small pieces. Heat the olive oil in a saucepan, add the shallots and garlic, and sauté for 1–2 minutes. Add the bits of shrimp or lobster shells and the fish stock. Stir and cook for 5 minutes. Add the chopped tomatoes, parsley, and brandy and cook for 5–10 minutes (the bisque should just be simmering).

Take the bisque off the heat, strain off the bits, and liquify. Then strain through a fine-mesh strainer. Return to the saucepan. Stir in the cream, season, and taste. The bisque should be light and smooth in texture. Serve in warm bowls and garnish with a few flat parsley leaves.

Miniature shrimp

When my husband Tim and his brothers and sisters were little, they used to make regular excursions to Ring Strand with their fishing nets to catch miniature shrimp to bring home for supper. It was either a feast or a famine. When there was an abundance, there were huge plates of miniature shrimp with homemade mayonnaise and freshly baked bread for supper. Afterwards little fingers helped to shell the surplus shrimp, while their mother Myrtle Allen infused fresh butter with thyme leaves and a scrap of garlic. Packed into little pots in the fridge, they kept for several days and are delicious served with hot thin toast. Nowadays the fishermen around the coast catch shrimp in large quantities in special shrimp pots, but one can still go shrimping as in times gone by.

How to cook shrimps

Bring 9½ cups water to a boil, add 2 tablespoons of salt and toss in the live or very fresh shrimp. They will change color from gray to pink almost instantly. Bring the water back to a boil and cook for just 2–3 minutes. The shrimp are cooked when there is no trace of black at the back of the head. Drain immediately, and spread out on a large baking sheet to cool.

When cold, serve with homemade mayonnaise (see page 53) and freshly baked brown bread, garnished perhaps with a segment of lemon. Alternatively, peel first and then serve or use for another recipe. To peel, first remove the head, pinch the end of the tail and tug it. This will pull off half the shell. Remove the remainder of the shell with your fingers. Small shrimp are much easier on the fingers than Dublin Bay shrimp!

Serves 4 as a first course

½ garlic clove
salt and freshly ground pepper
¼–⅓ cup (½–¾ stick) clarified
   butter
1 teaspoon fresh thyme leaves
about 22 (4oz) cooked shelled
   small shrimp
1–2 teaspoons lemon juice
extra clarified butter, for top of pot

Potted Ballycotton Small Shrimp

Crush the garlic to a paste with a little salt. Bring the clarified butter to a boil with the thyme leaves and garlic. Add the shelled shrimp and simmer together for 3–5 minutes. Season carefully with the lemon juice. Pack into pots and run more clarified butter over the top. Put into the refrigerator and let set. Serve with Melba toast (see below) or crusty bread.

Note: potted small shrimp will keep in the fridge for 3–4 days. Shrimp and lobster may be potted in the same way and are equally delicious.

Variation

Potted Shrimp or Small Shrimp with Marjoram and Ginger

Substitute 2 teaspoons of freshly chopped marjoram for thyme and add 1 teaspoon of freshly grated ginger.

Serves 4

2 thin slices of white bread

Melba Toast

Toast the bread on both sides. Cut the crusts off immediately and then split the slice in half through the middle. Scrape off any soft crumbs, cut into triangles and put the bread back under the grill, untoasted side up. Leave it for a few seconds until the edges curl up.

Serves 6–8

2½lb cod, hake, pollock, or salmon,
  or a mixture
salt and freshly ground pepper
1 tablespoon butter
2½ cups whole milk
4oz cooked mussels, out of shells
  (see page 58)
6–8 (4oz) cooked and peeled large
  shrimp (see page 64)
2oz roux, approx. (see page 42)
¼ teaspoon mustard, preferably
  Dijon
2 cups grated Cheddar cheese or
  1 cup grated Parmesan cheese
2 tablespoons chopped parsley

BUTTERED CRUMBS
2 tablespoons butter
generous 1 cup soft white
  breadcrumbs

scant 4 cups fluffy mashed potato
  or champ (optional, see page 40)

Ballycotton Fish Pie

Skin the fish and cut into portions: 6oz for a main course, 3oz for a starter. Season with salt and freshly ground pepper. Lay the pieces of fish in a lightly buttered sauté pan and cover with the cold milk. Bring to a boil, simmer for 4–5 minutes, or until the fish has changed color. Remove the fish to a serving dish or dishes with a perforated spoon. Scatter the mussels and shrimp over the top.

Bring the milk back to a boil and thicken with roux to a light coating consistency. Add the mustard, two-thirds of the grated cheese and a couple of tablespoons of chopped parsley. Keep the remainder of the cheese for sprinkling over the top. Season with salt and freshly ground pepper, taste, and correct the seasoning if necessary.

Next make the breadcrumbs. Melt the butter in a pan and stir in the white breadcrumbs. Remove from the heat immediately and let cool.

Coat the fish with the sauce. Mix the remaining grated cheese with the buttered crumbs and sprinkle over the top. Pipe a ruff of fluffy mashed potato or champ around the edge for a more substantial dish.

Cook in a preheated moderate oven (350°F) for 15–20 minutes or until heated through and the top is golden brown and crispy. If necessary, place under the broiler for a minute or two before you serve, to brown the edge of the potato.

Note: This dish may be served in individual dishes, scallop shells are particularly attractive, are completely ovenproof and may be used over and over again.

Freshwater Crayfish

Cullohill, the little village in Co. Laois where I spent a happy and carefree childhood, was about as far as it could be from the sea. An occasional day trip to the beach in Tramore, Co. Waterford, was the highlight of our holidays. Apart from that rare treat, the River Goul to the west of the village was the place to cool off on hot days. As we paddled and splashed in the shallow pools, older and wiser people would lean over the bridge, watch bemused and warn us to be careful in case the crayfish bit our toes. We giggled and squirmed, but didn't quite believe them. However, I now know that there were—and still are—crayfish in those streams.

Traditionally, Lough Derg, Co. Donegal, the lake which surrounds the well-known place of pilgrimage, was noted for its abundant population of crayfish. Similarly, most of the lakes in the limestone regions of the country, such as Lough Sheelin, Lough Leen, and Derravaragh Lake, had a plentiful supply. The rare white-clawed crayfish still lives in the Rye water, under the waterfall on the grounds of Carton House, the former home of the Duke of Leinster, near Maynooth in Co. Kildare.

The crayfish were lifted in old style pots and creels which were circular in shape, with a flat weighted bottom, in much the same style as the lobster and crab creels.

If you are fortunate enough to catch some of these delectable crustaceans (which are now a protected species), cook them quickly in boiling salted water, using 1 tablespoon salt to every scant 5 cups water. Peel them and eat them simply with melted butter or with a homemade mayonnaise (see page 53).

Serves 6 as a substantial
starter

ALL OR MOST OF THESE:
6 sea urchins (*Paracentrotus lividus*)
18 Dublin Bay shrimp (*Nephrops norvegicus*) or 24 large shrimp (*Palaemon serratus*)
periwinkles (*Littorina litterea*)
18 mussels (*Mytilus edulis*)
12 palourdes (*Venerupis pullastra*)
18 roghans (*Venus verrucosa*)
18 cockles (*Cerastoderma edule*)
6 native Irish oysters (*Ostrea edulis*)

GARNISH
homemade mayonnaise (see page 53)
6 lemon segments
sprigs of wild watercress or fennel seaweed (optional)

A Plate of Irish Shellfish

Where shellfish are concerned, Ireland has always had an embarrassment of riches, which we have taken for granted, indeed undervalued, for centuries. At Ballymaloe House this selection of delicious Irish shellfish delights guests from all over the world, and is not difficult to prepare. Note that roghans and palourdes are types of clam; use substitutes outside of Ireland.

Cook the sea urchins in boiling salted water (allow 1 tablespoon salt to a scant 5 cups water) for 4–5 minutes. Remove and let cool.

Next cook the Dublin Bay shrimp (see page 64). Bring the water to a boil and add the salt. Remove the heads of the shrimp and, with the underside of the shrimp uppermost, tug the little fan-shaped tail at either side and carefully draw out the trail. (The trail is the intestine, so it is very important to remove it before cooking regardless of whether the shrimp are to be shelled or not.)

Put the shrimp into the boiling salted water and as soon as the water returns to a boil, test a shrimp to see if it is cooked. When it is, remove the shrimp immediately. Very large ones may take 30 seconds–1 minute more. Allow the shrimp to cool in a single layer and then remove the shells. Do not cook too many shrimp together, or they may overcook before the water even comes back to a boil.

Cook the periwinkles (see page 58).

If the large shrimp are live, cook them in boiling salted water also for 2–3 minutes, or until the shells have changed color from grey to bright orangey pink. If there is any trace of black on the heads, cook them for a little longer. Drain and let cool in a single layer.

Wash the mussels, palourdes, roghans, and cockles and check that all the shells are tightly closed. They can then all be opened in the same manner. Spread the shells in a single layer in a heavy-bottomed saucepan. Cover with a folded dish towel or a lid and put the pan on a low heat for a few minutes. Remove the shellfish as soon a they open (if any refuse to open, discard them). Keep the liquid which will exude from the shellfish as they open: it's wonderful for fish soup or a sauce to be served with shellfish.

Remove the beards from the mussels and discard one shell; loosen the mussel from the remaining shell so that the guests won't have to tussle with their fork. Remove the outer round and "exhaust pipes" (siphons) from the palourdes and roghans and discard one shell. Nothing needs to be removed from the cockles, but discard one shell also.

When the sea urchins are cold, scrape the prickles off the top with a spoon or brush, then tap the center with the bowl of a teaspoon; the shell usually cracks like an egg, so the center can be lifted out. Be careful not to lose any of the precious juices and make sure to remove any splinters of shell from the center. It will be necessary to provide a teaspoon for eating the sea urchins and a fingerbowl should also be provided if the guests are to peel the shrimp themselves.

Not long before serving, open the oysters (see page 59). Arrange the shellfish on a large white plate. Place a tiny bowl of homemade mayonnaise in the center and garnish with the lemon segments and herbs. If you wish to use seaweed, e.g. bladderwrack, for garnish you should plunge the sprigs into boiling water for a few seconds, then remove it immediately, and refresh it in a bowl of iced water. The seaweed will turn bright green and should be used fairly soon, because it begins to get slimy quite quickly.

Crabs

The popularity of crab has waxed and waned in Ireland throughout the years. In some cases it was despised as a foodstuff and, up to relatively recently, most Irish fishermen had no meas on (or regard for) crabs. However, in recent years a large export market and a smaller but nonetheless significant home market has opened up, so crabs are being landed all around the coast. Might I put in a plea here: resist the temptation to buy crab claws alone. It encourages the inhumane practice of pulling the claws off the live crabs and dumping the bodies, so the crab is left to die unable to feed itself. Quite apart from that, the delicious creamy brown meat in the shells shouldn't be missed.

Crabs are best straight from the sea and should, like lobsters, feel heavy for their size. The female with the large "flap" underneath is more delicate than the male and often gives a greater return.

Stanley Mosse's Potted Crab

Serves 8–10 as a starter

about ¾–1 cup mixed brown and white cooked crabmeat.
½ cup (1 stick) softened butter
1–2 teaspoons finely chopped parsley
lemon juice, to taste
salt and freshly ground pepper

Many years ago we dropped in to see our friends the Mosses in Bennettsbridge, Co. Kilkenny—well inland. They had just cooked the box of crabs they had brought fresh up from the boats at Dunmore East.

We were given a great welcome: another pair of hands to extract the juicy white and brown meat. Stanley Mosse then made up lots of this potted crab, which we ate gluttonously on hot buttered toast.

Mix all the ingredients together in a bowl or, better still, whizz them in a food processor. Taste carefully and continue to season until you are happy with the flavor; it may need a little more lemon juice. Press the mixture into a pottery bowl, cover, and refrigerate.

Crab Mayonnaise on Brown Bread

Serves 4–6

about ¾–1 cup cooked crabmeat
¾–1 cup homemade mayonnaise (see page 53)
½ teaspoon finely grated onion

brown bread and butter
small lettuce leaves, garden cress, or watercress, to garnish

This simple but delicious recipe was orginally published in Myrtle Allen's Ballymaloe Cookbook *in 1977 and is still a constant favorite on the menu at Ballymaloe House.*

Mix the crabmeat with the mayonnaise and onion. Heap the mixture onto some buttered slices of brown bread, decorating with plenty of lettuce or cress.

3 cups crabmeat, brown and white
  mixed (2–3 crabs should yield
  this)
1½–1¾ cups soft white
  breadcrumbs
2 teaspoons white wine vinegar
2 tablespoons tomato chutney or
  Ballymaloe Tomato Relish
2 tablespoons (¼ stick) butter
a generous pinch mustard powder
  or 1 level teaspoon French
  mustard
salt and freshly ground pepper
¾ cup white sauce

TOPPING
2 tablespoons (¼ stick) butter
1 cup soft white breadcrumbs

White Sauce

1¼ cups milk
a few slices of carrot
a few slices of onion
3 peppercorns
a small sprig of thyme
a small sprig of parsley
3 tablespoons (1½oz) roux (see
  page 42)
salt and freshly ground pepper

Ivan Allen's Dressed Crab

When I first came to Shanagarry, crabs were considered to be a nuisance by most fishermen because they found their way into the lobster pots and were much less lucrative to sell. Tommy Sliney, the legendary Ballycotton man who sold his fish from a donkey and cart on the pier, occasionally brought us a few, and it was always a cause for celebration. We'd prepare all the other ingredients and then my father-in-law, Ivan Allen, would mix and taste the Dressed Crab. Ballymaloe Tomato Relish is now sold countrywide.

First make the buttered crumbs for the topping. Melt the butter in a pan and stir in the breadcrumbs. Remove from the heat immediately and let the mixture cool. Scrub the crab shells. Mix all the ingredients together, except the topping, taste carefully, and correct the seasoning. The texture should be soft, so add a little more white sauce if necessary. Fill into the shells. Bake in a moderate oven (350°F), until heated through and brown on top (about 15–20 minutes). Flash under the broiler if necessary to crisp the crumbs.

Note: 1lb cooked crab in the shell yields about 6–8oz crabmeat depending on the time of the year.

This is a marvelous way of making white sauce if you already have roux made. Put the cold milk into a saucepan with the carrot, onion, peppercorns, thyme, and parsley. Bring to a boil and simmer for 4–5 minutes. Remove from the heat and let infuse for 10 minutes. Strain out the vegetables, bring the milk back to a boil and thicken with roux to a light coating consistency. Season with salt and freshly ground pepper, taste, and correct the seasoning if necessary.

Fish and Chips

Towards the end of the 19th century some of the poor Italian immigrants, who had brought fish and chips to England and Scotland, made their way to Ireland. The fish and chip business in Dublin is still securely in the hands of the thriving Italian community.

portions of fresh fish, e.g. cod, pollock, or skate
old potatoes, peeled and freshly cut into chips
oil, for deep-frying
lemon segments and malt vinegar, to serve

BEER BATTER
2 cups self-rising flour
a good pinch of salt
⅓ cup plus 1½ tablespoons beer
¾–scant 1 cup cold water
2 egg whites

First make the batter. I sometimes dispense with the water and just use beer when making a batter for fish; it produces a crisp coating. Sift the flour and salt into a bowl. Make a well in the center and gradually whisk in the beer and the water. Let stand for at least 1 hour. Just before frying, whisk the egg whites to a stiff peak and fold into the batter, adding a good pinch of sea salt.

Heat the oil to 350°F. Dip the fish pieces into the batter, one piece at a time, and fry until crispy and golden. Dip the chips in hot oil for a few seconds. Drain both fish and chips well on paper towels. Serve on hot plates (or in parchment paper) with a segment of lemon and a dash of malt vinegar to season.

Twice Laid

This recipe came from a little frayed booklet without a cover sent to me by Mrs Teresa Murray from Clontuskert near Ballinasloe in Co. Galway. Perhaps the name Twice Laid is a reference to the fact that both the potatoes and the fish have been around once before.

Serves 4–6

1½–2 cups cooked potatoes
8oz cooked fish, e.g. cod, hake, or flounder
salt and freshly ground pepper
1 beaten egg, free-range if possible
freshly chopped parsley and chives
2 tablespoons dripping or butter

Mash the potatoes with a fork. Remove the skin and bones from the fish and break the flesh into flakes. Mix the fish with the potatoes and add seasonings. (I took the liberty of adding a beaten egg and some chopped parsley and chives.) Shape into a flat cake and fry in dripping or butter until golden on both sides. It tastes quite delicious.

Kedgeree

Kedgeree immediately conjures up images of country house breakfasts served on a silver dish on a polished sideboard. This recipe was, of course, of Anglo-Indian origin and would have been brought back to Ireland by the many Irishmen who fought in India in the British Army during the Raj.

Serves 6–8

1¼ cups white long-grain rice
3 eggs
1lb wild salmon, freshly cooked, or 8oz cooked salmon and 8oz cooked smoked salmon
⅔ cup light cream
2 tablespoons (¼ stick) butter
3 tablespoons chopped parsley
1½ tablespoons chopped chives
salt and freshly ground pepper
cayenne pepper or curry powder

Cook the rice in boiling salted water for about 8–10 minutes; drain. Hard-boil the eggs, also in boiling salted water, for 10 minutes. Drain off the water. Place under a cold tap to cool and stop cooking. Peel and chop roughly.

Remove the skin and bones from the cooked fish and flake into small pieces.

Heat the cream and butter in a saucepan. Add the parsley and chives. As soon as the cream bubbles, add the rice, flaked fish, and the hard-boiled eggs. Season well with salt and freshly ground pepper and a pinch of cayenne or curry powder. Mix very gently. Taste, correct the seasoning if necessary, pile into a hot dish, and serve with freshly baked bread or with hot buttered toast.

Game

In the past, Ireland's heavily wooded landscape and extensive inland waterways provided the ideal habitat for a variety of wild fowl and other game. Evidence found at the Mesolithic site of Mount Sandel in Co. Derry, dating from 7000BC, suggests that Ireland's earliest inhabitants enjoyed a diet which included duck, pigeon, grouse, goshawk, and capercaille.

Ireland's landscape is dotted with archaeological evidence to illustrate the popularity of venison; specialized sites known as *Fulachta Fiadh*, which means "cooking place or boiling place of deer," indicate the importance of deer in the diet, as far back as the Bronze Age (2000BC).

In more recent times, Arthur Young's observation in Co. Fermanagh, from his *A Tour in Ireland 1776–1779*, also highlights the prevalence of fowl and game in the 18th century. He states:

"… living is exceedingly cheap here; besides common provisions which I have everywhere registered, wild ducks are only 3d, snipes 1½d, teal 2d and widgeon the same…"

Huge game shoots, complete with beaters, were also held on the large country estates of Ireland well into the 20th century. Many large landowners now stock their estates with pheasant and grouse, and operate driven shoots as a business.

Puffins

Puffins are to be found on several islands off the north and west of Ireland. It is therefore probable that puffins were eaten by the earliest settlers in Ireland, who would have learned to trap them on the rocky ledges around the coast. There are many references to eating puffins, particularly during times of want. In Robin Flower's account of life on the Blasket Islands there is a fine description of how some fishermen, who were returning home downhearted without a catch during the Great Famine, suddenly spotted a "company of fine fat birds, puffins, and guillemots on a high cliff on Inishvicillane." They would provide an abundance of food for the hungry islanders, but were almost impossible to reach. Nonetheless, driven by desperation, one of the islanders attempted to scale the sheer cliff face while his companions held their breath in terror. He bravely reached the mouth of the hole in the cliff, lured the birds out, and throttled them. He threw down about 10 dozen birds to his companions, who eagerly picked up the floating birds off the water and put them in their currachs. When they called to him to join them, he was unable to get down so he bid them goodbye saying: "Home with you now in God's name, for I think these are the last birds I shall ever catch." However, the story has a happy ending because next day the fisherman's son managed to rescue his father, who received a hero's welcome from the grateful islanders.

According to Malachy McKenna, Máire Ní Ghuithín wrote in *Bean an Oileáin* (Women of the Island) that sea birds were still being eaten on the Blaskets in her lifetime (she was born in 1909). People ate the young of gannets, guillemots, and puffins, as well as shearwaters. They also ate cormorants, which were very tough. Máire describes how they cooked puffin: the birds were plucked, halved, cleaned out, and washed, and were then wrapped in a cloth to soak up some of their oil. They would be cooked in the pot-oven or simply placed on the tongs and roasted over the embers. Máire suggests the latter method is better because the oil from the birds drains into the fire, whereas it would accumulate in the pot-oven and produce an excessively rich tasting meat. If a puffin was roasted on the tongs, it was turned when one side was done and salt and pepper sprinkled over it. Puffins, which were "as nice as any chicken" in Máire's view, were often eaten at the evening meal.

Ortolans

In her book *The Absentee* (1811), Maria Edgeworth referred to her character Heathcock sitting down to a collation of eel pie and Irish ortolans. The footnote in the book explained the reference to Irish ortolans as being a small bird, "said to be peculiar to the Blasquet Islands, called by the Irish Gourder... somewhat larger then a sparrow; the feathers of the back are dark, and those of the belly are white; the bill is short and thick; and it is web footed; they are almost one lump of fat; when roasted, of a most delicious taste, and reckoned to exceed an ortolan; for which reason the gentry hereabouts call them the Irish Ortolan. These birds are worthy of being transmitted a great way to market; for ortolans it is well known are brought from France to supply the markets of London."

Wild Duck

Duck has been eaten in Ireland since the Mesolithic periods, as evidence from Mount Sandel, in Co. Derry, shows. This site dates to 7000BC and provides the earliest evidence of human habitation in Ireland. Birds in general, and ducks in particular, also had a particular significance in Celtic and early Irish mythology. A good example of their use as an artistic motif comes from a bronze trumpet found at Loughnashade, Co. Antrim and dating from c.200BC. A bronze cup with a duck-shaped handle made between c.100BC and 100AD was found in the River Shannon at Keshcarrigan, Co. Leitrim.

The most common species of wild duck in Ireland are mallard, teal, and widgeon. Other duck which may be legally shot in season and eaten include gadwall, shoveler, goldeneye, pintail, pochard, and tufted duck. However, some of these birds are becoming rare and the laws are changing, so it might be wise to check with the Wildlife Department of the Office of Public Works if you plan to shoot any duck.

Roast Wild Mallard

Serves 2

1 mallard
salt and freshly ground pepper
3–4 juniper berries
sprig of thyme
sprig of marjoram
butter or 4–5 slices rindless
    Canadian bacon
½ cup game or chicken stock
splash of wine or juice of
    1 orange

Mallard, one of the best of the wild duck species, makes a delicious roast for two people. Don't forget to save the bones for stock which will enrich the gravy the next time.

Trim the end off the wing tips at the first joint. Chop the ends off the legs just above the "knee." Remove the wing bone. Make sure that the crop has been removed.

Season the cavity with salt and freshly ground pepper; pop in a few crushed juniper berries along with the thyme and marjoram. Smear the breast with butter or bard it with rindless Canadian bacon and truss with cotton string.

Preheat the oven to 450°F. Roast for about 20 minutes if you like it fairly rare or for 30 minutes if you prefer it better done. Be careful not to overcook or it will be dry. Duck which has been barded with bacon will take up to 10 minutes longer to cook. Just as soon as the duck is cooked, remove to a warm serving dish. Pour the fat from the roasting pan. Add some stock and a splash of red or white wine or the juice of an orange. Boil well, taste, correct the seasoning, and strain. Carve the duck and serve the hot gravy with it.

Interesting variations on this recipe are roast widgeon, pintail, or shoveler—cooking time 13–20 minutes. For roast teal, keep the same cooking temperature, but reduce the time—about 12–15 minutes.

Barnacle Goose

The barnacle goose is referred to as early as the 9th century, when it appears in the poem *Marbán agus Gúaire* (King and Hermit):

Notes of gleaming-breasted pigeons
The song of the pleasant constant thrush above my house
Bees, chafers, barnacle geese, brent geese
Shortly before Samhain.

Right up to the early part of this century it was common folk belief that the wild barnacle goose (*Branta Leucopsis*) was actually fish, not fowl, and so could be eaten on days of fast and abstinence.

There was a theory that the barnacle goose first grew out of a worm in the sea, although Giraldus Cambrensis, in his 12th-century *Topographia Hibernica*, believed that it was hatched from an egg. "They were in shells and already formed. No eggs are laid as is usual as a result of mating. No bird ever sits upon eggs to hatch them… Accordingly, in some parts of Ireland, bishops and religious men eat them without sin during a fasting time, regarding them as not being flesh, since they are not born of flesh."

This folk belief persisted right up to the present century—a hotel in Dingle, Co. Kerry, is reported to have had barnacle goose on the menu it served to the clergy until the abstinence laws were relaxed in 1966.

Roast Pheasant with Game Chips

Serves 2–3

2 young, plump pheasants
3 tablespoons butter, plus extra
    for cooking
¾ cup chopped onion
1½ cups soft white breadcrumbs
1 tablespoon fresh chopped herbs
    e.g. parsley, thyme, chives
    and marjoram
salt and freshly ground pepper

GRAVY
1¼ cups game or chicken stock

GAME CHIPS
see opposite

BREAD SAUCE
see below

The pheasant is a relative latecomer to Ireland, coming to Ireland in the post-Norman period and possibly introduced in greater numbers only in Elizabethan times. However, the introduction was successful. Fynes Moryson, who was secretary to the Lord Deputy, Lord Mountjoy, until Mountjoy's death in 1606, records in his Itinerary *(published in parts between 1617 and 1626) that "Ireland hath plenty of pheasants, as I have known sixtie served at one feast."*

Nowadays large sporting estates are stocked annually with game for the shooting season, so the price of the hand-reared pheasant is within everyone's reach. For those of us who enjoy a rich gamey flavor, wild pheasant are unquestionably superior. Corn-fed birds from large shoots have a covering of yellowish-orange fat and their flavor is less pronounced. Birds reared in captivity are at the bottom of the flavor league as they have never foraged in the wild, but are totally corn-fed. Pheasant can be hung by the neck for anything from 5 days to 3 weeks, depending on the weather and your taste. The pheasant season in Ireland is from November 1st through January 31st. In America, you must check with each state's laws.

Gut the pheasant if necessary and remove the "crop" which is at the neck end; wash and dry well.

To make the stuffing, melt the butter and sweat the onions until soft but not colored, then remove from the heat. Stir in the breadcrumbs and herbs, season with salt and freshly ground pepper, and taste. Unless you are about to cook the bird right away, allow the stuffing to get quite cold before putting it into the bird.

Season the cavity with salt and freshly ground pepper, then stuff the pheasant loosely. Smear the breast and legs generously with butter. Season with salt and freshly ground pepper.

Roast in a preheated moderate oven at 375°F for about 30–35 minutes. Test by pricking the leg at the thickest point; the juices should just run clear. If the pheasant is cooked too long it will be dry and tough, but it ought not to be served rare.

Spoon off any surplus fat from the roasting pan (keep it for roasting or sautéeing potatoes). Pour in the game or chicken stock. Bring to a boil, using a whisk to dislodge the caramelized juices so they can dissolve into the gravy. Season with salt and freshly ground pepper, taste, and boil until you are happy with the flavor. Pour into a hot gravy boat.

Carve the pheasant and serve with all the trimmings—stuffing, gravy, game chips, and bread sauce (below). Watch out for lead shot while you are eating the pheasant.

Bread Sauce

Serves 12

2½ cups milk
2¼ cups breadcrumbs
2 onions, each stuck with 6 cloves
¼ cup (½ stick) butter
salt and freshly ground pepper
⅓–½ cup heavy cream

Bread sauce sounds so dull; if I hadn't been reared on it I might never have tried it. It is another ingenious way of using up stale bread. I even love it cold!

Bring all the ingredients except the cream to a boil in a small, deep saucepan. Season with salt and freshly ground pepper. Cover and simmer gently on very low heat or cook in a low oven at 325°F for 30 minutes. Remove the onions and add the cream to the sauce just before serving. Correct the seasoning. Add a little more milk if the sauce is too thick.

Serve hot, from a warm sauceboat.

Game Chips

Serves 2–3

8oz large, even-sized potatoes
olive oil for deep-frying
salt

Wash and peel the potatoes. For even-sized chips, trim each potato with a swivel-top peeler until smooth. Slice them very finely, preferably on a mandolin. Soak in cold water to remove the excess starch (this will prevent them from discoloring or sticking together). Drain off the water and dry well.

Heat the olive oil to 350°F. Drop in the dry potato slices a few at a time and fry until golden and completely crisp. Drain on paper towels and sprinkle lightly with salt. Repeat until they are all cooked.

If they are not to be served immediately, they may be stored in an airtight container and reheated in a low oven just before serving.

Pigeon Pie

Serves 10–12

breasts from 4–6 pigeons or squabs
half their weight in bacon
their weight in lean beef
bacon fat or olive oil, for frying
8 baby carrots or sticks of carrot
10–12 baby onions
1 garlic clove, crushed
1–2 teaspoons flour
scant 1 cup red wine
scant 1 cup homemade beef stock
½ cup homemade tomato sauce or
 smaller quantity of canned paste:
 use according to concentration
 and make up with extra stock
roux (optional; see page 42)
salt and freshly ground pepper
2 teaspoons chopped thyme
 and parsley
1 quantity Mushrooms in Cream
 (see below)
8oz puff pastry dough (see page
 217)

Wood pigeons have always been very prolific in Ireland. In the country young boys were taught how to shoot by their fathers. Before a big dance or party in Ballymaloe House in the 1950s, my husband Tim and his brother Rory would "bag" enough to make large quantities of pigeon pie—a relatively inexpensive and absolutely delicious way to feed a large number of people for a winter house party. In America, pigeon is commonly referred to as squab.

Cut the bacon into 1-inch cubes. Cut the beef and squab into similar-sized pieces.

Heat some bacon fat or olive oil in a skillet and fry the bacon until crisp and golden. Remove to a 9½ cup casserole. Add the beef and squab pieces, a few at a time, to the skillet and toss until they change color. Add them to the casserole. Add the carrots, onions, and crushed garlic to the pan and turn in the fat before adding them to the meat in the casserole. Stir in the flour into the fat in the pan, cook for a minute or so and then stir or whisk in the wine, stock, and tomato paste. Bring to a boil and thicken with roux if necessary. Pour over the meat and vegetables in the casserole. Season with salt and freshly ground pepper, add the thyme and parsley, and bring to a boil. Cover and cook in a low oven (300°F) for 1–2 hours or until tender (this will depend on the age of the squab). When cooked, add the Mushrooms in Cream and set aside to cool. When the stew is cold, pour it into a deep pie dish. Roll out the puff pastry to cover the dish and bake for 10 minutes at 450°F, then reduce the heat to 375°F and cook for a further 20 minutes. Serve with a green salad.

Mushrooms in Cream

1–2 tablespoons butter
¾ cup finely chopped chopped
 onion
4 cups sliced white button
 mushrooms
salt and freshly ground pepper
squeeze of lemon juice
½ tablespoon chopped parsley
½ tablespoon chopped chives
½ cup cream

Melt the butter in a heavy-based saucepan until it foams. Add the chopped onion, cover and sweat over low heat for 5–10 minutes, or until quite soft but not colored. Remove the onion to a bowl. Increase the heat and cook the sliced mushrooms, in batches if necessary. Season each batch with salt, freshly ground pepper and a tiny squeeze of lemon juice. Add the onions, parsley and chives to the mushrooms in the saucepan, then add the cream and allow to bubble for a few minutes. Taste and adjust the seasoning, then set aside to cool.

Pigeon

Pigeon houses were common on Irish country estates from medieval times. I recently visited the well-preserved dovecote at Downhill on the North Antrim coast; it was built on top of an existing ice-house and could accommodate 200 pairs. The pigeons were valued not only for their meat, but also for their eggs. Each pair would have had about 16 chicks a year. The squabs were culled at about four weeks of age, when the meat was fat and juicy. The pigeon manure was valued as fertilizer for the walled garden nearby. Other pigeon houses that have survived include those at Parke's Castle in Co. Leitrim, Annesbrook in Co. Meath and (a particularly fine example) beside the 13th-century Augustinian Friary at Ballybeg, near Buttevant, in Co. Cork.

To Stew Pigeons White

This is a recipe from the Birr manuscript (mid-17th century). Birr Castle in Co. Offaly is the home of the Parsons family who have lived at Birr since the mid-17th century when the first cookbook was started.

"Make a good gravy of veal and a little bacon, season it with pepper, salt and chives. When your pigeons are stuffed and made close stew them in your gravy till they are enough. Take the pigeons out, and thicken the gravy with butter, flour, cream and the yolk of a raw egg. Serve them up and chop small some green chives and parsley to strew over them."

Roast Squab

Serves 4

4 young squabs
salt and freshly ground pepper
butter
8 slices of Canadian bacon
1¼ cups game or chicken stock

Squab are pigeons that have been reared for the table. They are raised to the age of roughly one month before being killed for eating, by which time they have reached adult size, but have not flown.

It is thought that the practice of raising pigeons for their meat may have come from the Middle East. Historically, squab or pigeons have been consumed in many civilizations, including Ancient Egypt, Rome, and medieval Europe. Texts about raising pigeons for their meat have been dated back to 60 AD in Spain. From the Middle Ages a dovecote (known in French as a 'pigeonnier') was a common outbuilding on an estate that was considered to be self-sufficient. The dovecote or columbarium was considered a living pantry, a source of meat for unexpected guests, and was important as a supplementary source of income from selling the surplus birds.

These days, squab meat almost always comes from domestic pigeons. The meat is dark and the skin is fatty, rather like a duck. The tender, fine-grained meat is lean and easily digestible, with a milder flavor than other game birds.

Preheat the oven to 400°F. Season the cavity of each bird with salt and freshly ground pepper. Smear the breasts and legs with butter, and wrap in a couple of pieces of bacon.

Roast for 30–40 minutes depending on size. Transfer to a serving dish. Spoon off the pan juices. Put the roasting pan back on the stove, add the stock, and let bubble, whisking all the while to dissolve the caramelized meat juices. Boil for a few minutes, taste, and season if necessary. Strain and serve with the tender juicy little squabs.

Medlar Jelly (see page 194) would be a delicious accompaniment.

Woodcock and Snipe

Historically game has always been popular with all classes of society in Ireland. In times of scarcity particularly, hunted wild fowl made a welcome addition to the diet.

Unlike most other countries in Europe, Ireland still has expanses of uncleared woodland which provide the perfect natural habitat for game birds such as woodcock. At Temple House in Co. Sligo, the woods have been deliberately managed since the 1800s to yield some of the best snipe and woodcock shooting in Europe. Ireland also has plenty of bogs and marshes favored by snipe.

Amhlaoibh Uí Shúileabháin from Callan, Co. Kilkenny, comments on the availability of snipe in his diary of 1829. On 22 January he states: "It is easy to find out the snipe now, for the frost has driven it from the hill to the running water or the water without ice."

Both birds are highly regarded, not only for their delicious flesh but also for their innards, with the exception of the gizzard which is removed before the birds are roasted. The brains of woodcock are considered to be a great delicacy. Pluck them carefully, head and all, because woodcock or snipe are traditionally served trussed with their own long beak. They are best hung for 4–5 days.

Woodcock Potted Pie

This recipe comes from the Kitchen Book of Clonbrock:
Serves 4–6
"4 or 5 goose or rabbit livers—2 bay leaves—1 sprig of thyme and a very little parsley tied in a bundle and 3 large onions.

Take 2lb of fat bacon, cut it up small and fry it for a few minutes in a stewpan, then add 2½lb of lean veal or rabbit, cut small and without bone.

Stew the whole lot for about 1 hour, take out the herbs, let the rest get cold, then pound it well in a mortar, pass it through a wire sieve, put it back in the mortar, add and mix well with it some pepper, salt and a very little cayenne, 3 fresh eggs, 1oz of shallot chopped very fine, and sweated in butter, a few mushrooms and truffles cut in small squares. Then take a pie dish and line it with some thin slices of fat bacon, put in some of the potted meat, then put in the centre, which has been nicely boned and cut, fill up with potted meat, tie it down with dough. Bake it in a dish with water for 4 hours in a moderately hot oven, take it out, remove the pastry and press it with some heavy weight till cold, then pour on some melted butter and serve—Snipe, Woodcock, Partridges or Pheasant can be equally used."

Sauce for all Sorts of Wild Fowl

From the 1666 book in a later hand.
"Half a pint of claret and a ladel full of strong Gravy or Broth, an anchovy, a shallot, a little whole spice—let them stew over a chafing dish, then strain the sauce, beat it up with a little fresh butter and pour it thro' the bellies of the wild fowl."

Roast Thrush

There is a wonderfully evocative description of hunting thrushes on the Great Blaskets on Halloween night in *Twenty Years A Growing* by Muiris Ó Súileabháin:

"Now," said he, "this is Hallowe'en, and it is not known who will be living when it comes again, so I am going to propose another plan to make a night till morning of it. We will all go in twos and threes with lanterns through the island hunting thrushes, and when we have made our round let everyone come back here. See you have a good fire down for us, Máire, and there is no fear but we'll have a roast for the night... Off we went, the three of us with our lanterns, west to the Strand. It was a frosty night, the stars twinkling, the Milky Way stretched across the sky to the south and the Plough to the north, a light easterly breeze coming straight from Slea Head, gíog-gíog-gíog from peewits in the glen, a light here and a light there on the hill-side from the others, and we on our way west to the Great Glen, for many thrushes do be sleeping in the bushes there... We made no stop or stay till we reached the house. As soon as we went in, "How many have you?" they all cried with one voice.

"Who of yourselves has the most?" said I. "I have twenty," said Tomás an Phuncháin. "Faith," said Pádraig, "we have twenty-eight." With that there was a great outburst, everyone clapping with us.

They were thrown out on the table, and when everyone had added his share there were a hundred. "Let all begin the plucking now," said Séamus O Duinnlévy. We began plucking the feathers, all except my sisters Máire and Eileen, Kate O'Shea and Kate Peg, who were busy roasting and washing plates. The house was a pleasant sight now, everyone full of bright laughter, Seán O Criomhthain seated by the fire playing his melodium, four out on the floor dancing a reel, others cooking, others eating; and as soon as each four would finish their meal another four would take their places at the table until all were satisfied.

Hare and Rabbit

The hare is thought to be native to Ireland, while the rabbit was introduced by the Anglo-Normans in the 12th century. Both have augmented the Irish diet, particularly that of the poorer people, throughout the ages. John Dunton, an English visitor to Ireland in the 17th century, describes a meal at an inn:

Then enters landlady's daughter… in her hand she brought the hare swimming in a wodden bowl full of oyl of butter. I told my guide that they were verie generous in affording me so much sauce to the drye meate, but he answer'd me that was but the broath for they had boyld it in butter and in another cabin.

There was a common folk belief that hares (and hedgehogs) sucked the milk from the cows as they lay in the field at night. It was said that malicious women would go abroad at night in the form of a hare, to take the neighbor's dairy profit. One folktale tells how a farmer lay in wait for the milk-stealing hare. His dog draws blood from the hare. The farmer sets off in pursuit and meets an old woman. He asks her if she has seen the hare, then notices that she is bleeding and realizes that she was the hare. These folk beliefs are assoicated with the festival of May Day, when the milking season comes into its own and therefore it was important to protect the milk, the dairy and the profit of milk and butter for the forthcoming season.

On the Blasket Islands the rabbit hunting season began around November, when they were plentiful and large numbers were caught, either with snares or using ferrets. They were a welcome change from the usual diet of fish. Malachy McKenna describes how the rabbit was cooked, as outlined by Máire Ní Ghuithín in *Bean an Oileáin* (Women of the Island). The first step in preparing a rabbit for cooking was to gut it, it would then be skinned, and the carcase washed thoroughly in cold water.

Nowadays rabbits and hares run wild all over Ireland but they are rarely eaten, partly because they are still associated in many people's folk memory with famine, poverty, and hard times, and partly because of the myxomatosis epidemic. Nonetheless I love rabbit, and will miss no opportunity to eat it.

Rabbit and Dumplings

Serves 4–6, depending on size

1 rabbit, skinned, paunched, and jointed
flour, plus extra for dusting
2 onions, sliced
salt and freshly ground pepper
5 cups water
2 medium-sized carrots, cut into thick batons

DUMPLINGS

2 cups, plus 2 tablespoons all-purpose flour
a pinch of salt
½ teaspoon baking soda
¼ cup (½ stick) butter
nonfat milk, to mix

This recipe was sent to me by Patricia Murphy from Wexford. She said that the kidneys and liver were left in the rabbit carcass when it was being paunched. They added greatly to the flavor and the children argued over who got them (this would have been in the 1950s). I came across several other rabbit or rabbit and hare pies, people used what game they had, some had a pastry topping. This topping was called Dumplings, not to be confused with most people's perception of dumplings, which would be in little ball shapes.

Coat the rabbit pieces in flour, and brown the meat for a few minutes on each side. Place the meat in a large saucepan. Fry the sliced onion in the same pan until golden brown, then season. Add a tablespoon of flour and stir, then slowly add the water and bring to a boil. Pour over the rabbit pieces. Add the carrot and cover the saucepan. Bring to a boil, then simmer for 1 hour.

To make the dumplings: mix the flour, seasoning, and baking soda. Rub in the butter. Mix to a soft pliable dough with the nonfat milk and knead lightly. Shape into a round the size of the saucepan lid, about 1 inch thick. Place over the rabbit and simmer for 30–40 minutes. Serve with potatoes baked in their jackets. A rabbit stew like this could also be covered with a pastry topping.

Roast Rabbit in Milk

Serves 4

1 young rabbit, cleaned
2 medium onions
generous 1 cup fresh white
    breadcrumbs
1 tablespoon chopped sage
salt and freshly ground pepper
2 tablespoons butter, melted
2 tablespoons dripping
1 tablespoon all-purpose flour
2½ cups milk

This recipe was given to me by Anne Kennedy from Rostrevor, in Co. Down. It seems to me to be a good one, because rabbit can be on the dry side, particularly when it is not in the first flush of youth. The milk helps to keep it moist and tender. A young rabbit was called a grazier.

Soak the rabbit in salted water for 2 hours. Boil the onions until tender, then chop and mix with the breadcrumbs, sage, seasoning, and butter. Stuff the rabbit with this mixture and sew up the opening.

Place the rabbit in a roasting pan. Dot it with dripping and sprinkle with flour, salt, and pepper. Pour the milk around the rabbit and bake in a preheated oven at 325°F for 2 hours, basting often during the cooking period with milk.

Serve with mashed potatoes and a green vegetable.

Fried Rabbit

The simplest way to cook rabbit was to cut it into pieces and fry in butter. Alternatively, the pieces might be cooked in a pot along with a few mugfuls of water, some pieces of bacon, an onion, carrots, and parsnips. All this was brought to a boil and simmered.

Máire Ní Ghuithín stressed the importance of bacon as an ingredient—her mother and her aunt Cáit always added a piece of bacon, which gave a special flavor, not only to rabbit, but also chicken, goose, or turkey. When the rabbit meat was almost cooked, 3 or 4 big spoonfuls of flour mixed in milk could be added to the dish. The thickened juice from the meat was drunk. Máire also described how a rabbit was stuffed with a breadcrumb stuffing, stitched up, and cooked in the pot with a piece of bacon, some onions, and water. They also cooked chickens like this, similar to a pot roast.

Fillets of Rabbit à la Marichale

This recipe from the Clonbrock manuscript is dated December 1875 and is accredited to a Mrs Pugh of Clonbrock. This is of French origin, there is a similar recipe in *The Modern Cook* by Charles Elmé Francatelli, 1859. It would have been very fashionable in country houses to use classical French terms.

"Fillet 4 rabbits, slightly flatten them, make an incision round the interior part of them. Fill this with some d'Uxelles Sauce (see below). Mask them over with a thin coating of thick white sauce, when this has become firmly set by cooling, breadcrumb them twice, once in egg and once in butter. Fry a nice brown. Dish in a close circle, fill the centre with scallops of the kidney and inner fillets, mixed with truffles and mushrooms and topped in a little good brown sauce."

d'Uxelles Sauce

"Chop the following ingredients into equal proportions, mushrooms, truffles, ham, parsley and shallots. Put them in a small stewpan for 5 minutes, then add a little good sauce, the juice of a lemon, nutmeg, pepper, salt, a pinch of sugar, yolks of 4 eggs, stir again on the fire till set, put aside for use (it will do without the mushrooms and truffles and bacon will do instead of ham)."

Jugged Rabbit or Hare

This is from the Clonbrock manuscript.

"Cut in pieces making 2 bits of each shoulder, 2 of the head. Colour in the saucepan some bits of lard—4oz—with nearly as much butter. Add pieces of the meat, cover lightly with a good spoonful of flour, mix, add a glaze of red wine and so much bouillon or water a little red pepper, spices, bouquet (of herbs) a few grains of juniper berries, 2 shallots chopped, when half cooked add 12 small onions coloured in a saucepan with a little butter and sugar, then cook. For hare, save the liver, 5 minutes before serving put it in and take it out again for helping to make same another day."

Lord O'Neill's Rabbit Soup

This is Lord O'Neill's recipe from the Mary Ponsonby manuscript, c.1850.

"Skin the rabbits and cut them in quarters—put them in a stew pan. Add quarter lb lean ham or bacon, 3 good onions whole, & a small sprig of thyme, add 3 quarts of water, and let it simmer 'till the meat falls off the bones—then strain it thro' a tamis. Put half an ounce of butter in the pan, & a tablespoon full of fine flour, mix, then pour back the soup, stir it till it boils, let it boil ten minutes, add one tablespoonful catsup & cream, some onion chopped fine with pepper and salt."

Fricassee 17th century

This recipe dates from 1666 and is credited to Mrs Muschamp.

"Take 4 young rabbits cut them in pieces and 2 young lean pullets & flea them and cut them in pieces, take some fair water and put it into a large frying pan and put in a quarter of a pound of sweet butter and a handful of sweet herbs, time, margerum and savery, strip and minced, and 2 or 3 great oynion and put them in ye pan and put in a pretty deal of larg mace, cloves and nutmegs and let them boyle a little while in the pan then put in yr meat and berhuve the liquid do move then cover it, and when it is 3 quaeter done put in a little more then a pint of white wine and 4 or 5 anchovees then take 4 or 5 yolks of eggs and beat them very well and into them squeeze the juice of 2 or 3 lemons. When your meat is fryed enough take it up and put it into a dish and leave the liquor in the pan and put the eggs into the pan and stir it well for fear of curdling, thicken it a little over the fire and pour it over your meat and garnish it with sliced lemon."

To make Hare Soup

From the Receipt Book of Mrs Dot Drew, Mocollop Castle, Ballyduff, Co. Waterford, dated 1801. It serves about 8–10 people.

"Take a hare, cut it in pieces, get 3 quarts of water and one of cyder, a bit of lean bacon cellery onions pepper salt and a little sweet herbs stew it on a slow fire if the soup be not thick enough mix a little flour and water. Fry some toasts in butter and now stir in your soup."

Venison

Red deer is native to Ireland and important to its myths and early literature. There is evidence that red deer was eaten in Ireland in Mesolithic times—from 7000BC—at the site of Mount Sandel, near Coleraine in Co. Derry. Deer hunting near the royal site of Rath Cruachain, the ancient capital of the province of Connaught, is alluded to in the early Irish medieval tale: *Táin Bó Fraích* (The Cattle Raid of Fraoch). Venison from the area around Naas is demanded as tribute for the King of Ireland in the early medieval tale *Lebor na gCert* (The Book of Rights).

Red deer were hunted and cooked over an open fire by the earliest inhabitants of Ireland. They are mentioned in the legends of the warrior hero, Fionn Mac Cumhaill, and his troop of young warriors, the "Fianna," who roamed the landscape hunting and waging war. There are many stories which tell of their deer-hunting exploits. Fionn's name is etymologically related to the Irish word for deer, *fian*, while his son Oisín's name means "little fawn." These colorful stories appear in Ireland from the early medieval period onwards.

The smaller fallow deer, a relatively recent addition to Irish fauna, were introduced by the Anglo-Normans in the 12th and 13th centuries. They became a common sight in deer parks beside castles and country houses. Bunratty Castle had a deer park in the mid-17th century. In 1646, the Papal Nuncio, Cardinal Rinuccini, wrote: "In Italy there is nothing like its ponds and parks with its three thousand head of deer."

Lord Powerscourt introduced sika deer to his demesne in Co. Wicklow in the 19th century. Venison stew still warms and cheers many a ravenous hunter after a day's shooting on some of Ireland's large estates.

Roast Haunch of Venison with Poivrade Sauce

1 haunch of venison—approx. 6–7lb
    in weight
8oz pork back fat or very fat pork
    or pork caul fat

MARINADE
2 teaspoons mixed fresh herbs,
    thyme, savory, marjoram,
    and sage
4 tablespoons olive oil
½ cup dry white wine

GRAVY
2½ cups beef or venison stock
red wine (optional)
roux (optional; see page 42)
salt and freshly ground pepper

POIVRADE SAUCE *see below*

A haunch of venison makes a splendid dish for a country house party.

First lard the venison. Cut the pork back fat into ¼ inch wide strips. Insert a strip into a larding needle and draw a lardon through the meat to make a stitch; trim the end. Repeat the stitches at 1 inch intervals to make horizontal rows, positioning each row about ½ inch away from the previous row.

Put the haunch into a shallow dish made of stainless steel or cast iron, not tin or aluminium. Sprinkle the venison with the freshly chopped herbs. Pour the olive oil and wine over the meat. Cover the dish or tray and marinate the meat for about 4 hours at room temperature or in the refrigerator overnight, turning the meat occasionally. The liquid from this marinade will be used to baste the meat during cooking.

Preheat the oven to 350°F. Weigh the venison and calculate 10 minutes to the pound. We like our venison slightly pink and still very juicy, so I usually turn off the oven then and leave the meat to relax for 20–30 minutes. While it is cooking, baste the venison every 10 minutes with the oil and wine marinade and turn the joint over halfway through. When the venison is ready, remove to a serving dish while you make the gravy.

Skim the fat from the roasting pan and add the beef or venison stock and perhaps a dash of wine. Bring to a boil, scraping and dissolving the sediment and crusty bits from the pan. Thicken slightly with a little roux, if you wish, then taste and correct the seasoning, and pour into a warm gravy boat.

Serve the haunch of venison on a large serving dish surrounded by roast potatoes. Red cabbage, celeriac purée, or Brussels sprouts would be delicious accompaniments. Carve and serve onto very hot plates.

Note: It is very easy to overcook venison, mainly because it goes on cooking after the oven has been turned off.

Makes quite a large quantity but any spare may be frozen to use another time

3 tablespoons sunflower oil
1½ cups diced carrot
1½ cups diced onion
scant ½ cup flour
3½ cups, plus 2 teaspoons beef
    stock
1 tablespoon tomato paste
bouquet garni
venison bones, if available
⅔ cup vinegar
⅔ cup marinade, made with ⅔ cup
    dry white wine seasoned with
    nutmeg, cinnamon, and ground
    black pepper
8 black peppercorns, crushed
⅔ cup red wine

Poivrade Sauce

George Gossip, from Ballinderry Park in Co. Galway, is a wonderful game cook. He makes this delicious sauce to serve with venison and other game. It is particularly good with roast venison.

Heat the oil in a stainless steel saucepan, add the carrot and onion and cook until browning at the edges. Add the flour and stir until also browned. Stir in the stock and tomato paste. Add the bouquet garni and the venison bones if available, cover, and simmer for 2 hours. Skim off the fat and strain.

Meanwhile, reduce the vinegar and white wine marinade in a small pan with the black peppercorns. When it has reduced to ¾ cup put it into a larger pan and add the strained brown sauce. Simmer for a further 30 minutes and then add the red wine, continue to cook for 5–10 minutes. Taste and correct the seasoning.

3lb shoulder of venison, trimmed
   and cut into 1½ inch cubes
seasoned flour

MARINADE
1¼–1½ cups red wine
1 medium onion, sliced
3 tablespoons brandy
3 tablespoons olive oil
salt and lightly crushed black
   pepper
bouquet garni

SAUCE
2 tablespoons olive oil
8oz fat bacon, diced
2 large onions, chopped
1 large carrot, diced
1 large garlic clove, crushed
scant 2 cups beef or venison stock
bouquet garni
24 small mushrooms, preferably
   white button mushrooms, sliced
a small pat of butter
salt and freshly ground pepper
lemon juice, sugar and/or crab
   apple jelly (see page 193),
   to taste

Variation
Venison Pie

Fill a pie dish with the stew
mixture, cover with puff or flaky pie
dough (see page 217) and bake in a
medium-hot oven (400°F) until the
pastry is golden and fully cooked.

Venison Stew

This type of stew was a way of using the stewing venison, and the basic formula would have been the basis of many game pies. The ingredients would not necessarily have been measured, it was a question of using what one had, what came in the shoot. More adventurous cooks might have added juniper berries, coriander, or perhaps a little pimento.

Mix the ingredients for the marinade. Add the venison and marinate for 24–48 hours. Next day, drain the meat well, pat it dry on paper towels and toss in seasoned flour. Reserve the marinade.

Heat the olive oil in a skillet and add the bacon. Cook it slowly at first to persuade the fat to run, then raise the heat so it crisps on the outside. Transfer to a casserole.

Brown the venison pieces in the bacon fat and add to the bacon in the casserole. Then toss the onions, carrot, and garlic in the remaining bacon fat and add to the casserole. Be careful not to overheat the pan or the fat will burn. Pour off any surplus fat, and strain in the marinade. Stir to dissolve the caramelized juices, bring to a boil and pour over the venison. Add enough stock to almost cover the meat and vegetables. Put in the bouquet garni and bring to a boil. Cover and simmer gently, either on top of the stove or in the oven, preheated to 300°F. Test the venison after an hour, but be aware that it can take up to 2½ hours to cook.

When the meat is tender, sauté the sliced mushrooms in a little butter. Season with salt and freshly ground pepper and add to the stew.

Finally taste the sauce. It will need seasoning and perhaps also a little lemon juice. It sometimes benefits from a pinch of sugar or some crab apple jelly.

Note: For best results, it is wise to cook this kind of dish one day and then reheat it the next. This improves the flavor and gives you a chance to make sure that the venison is tender.

Serves 6

2 cups pickling onions (or sliced large onions)
butter
2 cloves garlic, chopped
1½lb game meat, off the bone and sliced or diced, pheasant, pigeon, hare, venison, or the like
8oz bacon (not rashers), diced
2 teaspoons flour
1 tablespoon oil
bay leaf
⅔ cup game stock made from the bones of a hare for preference
⅔ cup red wine
4 cups button mushrooms
salt and freshly ground pepper
12oz homemade puff pastry dough (see page 217)
1 egg mixed with a splash of milk to form an eggwash

George Gossip's Game Pie

This is an ideal way to use up old or damaged pheasants and the odd pigeon or the like that you cannot think up a good use for. It is really delicious and none the worse for being made from leftovers. Do try to use a number of different types of game for this, as it dramatically improves the flavor. Hare is especially good, but do not use duck.

Fry the onions lightly in butter until golden. Add the garlic and fry for a further minute. Transfer to a large casserole. Sprinkle the meats with seasoned flour and brown them gently in a little oil.

Transfer the browned meat to the casserole, put in the bay leaf and pour in the stock and wine. Bring to a boil and simmer until the meat is tender. Just before the meat is done, add the mushrooms and continue cooking for a further few minutes. If there is too much sauce, strain and return the sauce to the heat and boil down rapidly until sufficiently reduced. Check the seasoning and let cool.

(Note: This stage is best completed a day or so in advance for the flavors to intensify. The stew may also be made up in larger amounts and then frozen in the required portions.)

To assemble the pie, line a small pie dish with puff pastry dough. Fill with the mixture, cover with a pastry lid and decorate with pastry trimmings. Glaze with egg wash.

Bake in a hot oven for 20–25 minutes until golden brown. Serve with baked or mashed potatoes, red cabbage, celery, and redcurrant jelly.

Game Shoots

George also sent me this entertaining account of a typical breakfast before a day's shoot.

"Shooting trips are often an all-male affair, with a distinct lowering of standards. Personal memories involve enormous fried breakfasts, making full use of any leftover potatoes from the previous night; vast numbers of under-done kidneys; fried eggs either runny, or very over-cooked and leathery; a dozen eggs poaching all-together in a saucepan, lots of fried bread, wonderful black puddings, made by the local butcher in a roasting tin and cut in thick slices, like cake, and far, far too many rashers and sausages. Thick slices of bread, thickly buttered. Comparisons between each others wives' marmalade. To drink, strong tea or even stronger coffee, made in a jug and filtered through a sieve with too wide a mesh. Beware the question: 'Would you like a starter?' It probably means a glass of Paddy! Usually the dogs are allowed to lick the frying pans, before they are washed."

Poultry

Domestic fowl were bred in Ireland from the early Christian era; the texts and borders of many medieval Irish manuscripts feature the motif of an entwined cook and hen. *The Book of Kells*, now on view in Trinity College, Dublin, is the most famous example.

Our choice of poultry now seems meager in comparison to that of earlier times. Brid Mahon writes in *Land of Milk and Honey*, that "Giraldus Cambrensis, writing in the 12th century, mentions 'flocks of cranes, geese with prodigious croakings, falcons, wild peacocks, wild hens, snipe, wood-cock pheasants and nightingale' as well as 'clouds of larks singing the praises of God.'"

Poultry has always been associated with festive meals— whether it was the goose for Michaelmas, the turkey for Christmas, or the roast chicken for Sunday. The diarist Amhlaoibh Uí Shúileabháin noted, with great satisfaction, in his entry for Easter Sunday, April 6, 1828:

"Easter Sunday and Christmas Day are the two best days for eating. Today I had chicken and smoked ham for my dinner."

Modern intensive rearing means that chicken and even turkey are no longer eaten solely on religious festivals or holidays. However, the flavor and texture are infinitely better in naturally raised, free-range birds.

1 free-range chicken, 5lb or more
salt and freshly ground pepper
a little soft butter
2–2½lb piece bacon
a handful of toasted breadcrumbs
roux (optional; see page 42)
sprigs of flat-leaf parsley, to garnish

STOCK
giblets and wishbone
1 carrot, sliced
1 onion, sliced
1 celery stalk
a few parsley stalks
a sprig of thyme

STUFFING
1 cup chopped onion
¼ cup (½ stick) butter
generous 2 cups soft white
    breadcrumbs
2 tablespoons finely chopped
    herbs e.g. parsley, lemon thyme,
    chives, and annual marjoram

TO SERVE
Parsley Sauce (see page 55)

Variation
Roast Turkey

Roast turkey is a traditional
Christmas dinner. Make four times
the quantity of the above stuffing.
Stuff the cavity of the bird in the
same way. Weigh the turkey and
calculate the cooking time. Allow
15 minutes per 1lb and 15 minutes
over. Brush the turkey with melted
butter (or smear the breast, legs,
and crop with soft butter), season,
cover loosely with parchment
paper, and roast in a moderate
oven for 3–3½ hours. To test the
turkey, prick the thickest part at
the base of the thigh; when the
juices run clear, the turkey is done.
Remove to a carving dish, keep
warm and let rest for a few minutes
while you make the gravy.

Traditional Roast Stuffed Chicken with Bacon and Parsley Sauce

Roast chicken is everyday food nowadays, but it was a rare treat up to the late 1950s when the intensive rearing of chickens began to bring down the price. Our hens hatched out several clutches of chickens in the ditches every year, so the cocks were fattened up for the table and the pullets kept for laying. Roast chicken was a longed-for treat when I was at boarding school in Wicklow. I shall never forget the ripple of excitement that ran around the refectory when roast chicken was served for Mother Prioress's feast day—and that was in the 60s. Search for a really free-range chicken or, better still, an organic one if you want to recapture the forgotten flavor.

First remove the wishbone from the neck end of the chicken. This isn't at all essential, but it does make carving much easier later on. Tuck the wing tips underneath the chicken for a neat shape. To make the stock, put the wishbone, giblets, carrot, onion, celery, and herbs into a saucepan. Cover with cold water, bring to a boil, skim, and simmer gently while the chicken is roasting. Strain and skim any fat from the surface before using.

Next make the stuffing. Sweat the onions gently in the butter until soft, for about 10 minutes, then stir in the breadcrumbs, herbs, and a little salt and pepper to taste. Leave it to get quite cold before stuffing the bird.

If necessary wash and dry the cavity of the bird, then season, and half fill with cold stuffing. Season the breast and legs, and smear with a little soft butter. Preheat the oven to 350°F. Weigh the chicken and allow about 20 minutes to the pound and 20 minutes over (20 minutes per 1lb plus 20 minutes). Halfway through the cooking, turn the chicken upside down to allow the juices to run into the breast. Baste a couple of times during the cooking with the buttery juices.

Put the bacon piece into a pan of cold water, bring to a boil, cover the saucepan, and simmer until the bacon is tender (about 1 hour). Change the water several times, particularly if the bacon is salty. A skewer should go through the bacon easily when it is cooked and the skin should peel off without resistance. I then sprinkle the fat with a few toasted and sieved dry breadcrumbs.

To test the chicken, prick the thickest part at the base of the thigh and examine the juices: they should be clear. Remove the chicken to a carving dish, keep it warm, and let rest while you make the gravy.

To make the gravy, spoon off the surplus fat from the roasting pan. Pour in the stock from the giblets and bones (you will need 1¾–2½ cups depending on the size of the chicken). Using a whisk, stir and scrape well to dissolve the caramelized meat juices from the roasting pan. Boil it up well, season, and thicken with a little roux if you like. Taste and correct the seasoning. Serve in a hot gravy boat.

If possible, serve the chicken on a nice carving dish surrounded by crispy roast potatoes and some sprigs of flat parsley. Serve each person a slice of bacon, some brown and white meat, gravy, and Parsley Sauce (see page 55).

1 × 4–4½lb free-range chicken
salt and freshly ground pepper
1 large carrot, sliced
1 celery stick
1 large onion, sliced
bouquet garni
5 peppercorns
2½ cups water or water and white
   wine or light chicken stock
1 cup plus 1 tablespoon light cream
2 tablespoons roux (see page 42)
2–3 tablespoons chopped parsley

Poached Chicken

Most farmers' wives kept at least a few hens and sold the eggs for "pin money." The broody hens hatched out a clutch or two of chicks hidden in the hay rick or the back of the haggard in the summer. Birds no longer in the first flush of youth were often poached gently and gave you a nice pot of soup.

Aine de Blacam on Inis Meáin remembers chicken as a special treat, it would be sometimes boiled and they would have the broth as soup, but she doesn't remember having soup otherwise.

Season the chicken and place in a heavy casserole with the carrot, celery, onion, bouquet garni, and peppercorns. Pour in water, water and wine, or stock. Cover and bring to a boil, then simmer either on top of the stove for 1½–3 hours, depending on the age of the bird. When cooked, remove the chicken from the casserole.

Strain the cooking liquid and skim the fat from the surface. Return to the casserole. Discard the vegetables; they have already given their flavor to the cooking liquid. If it tastes a little weak, reduce it by boiling, uncovered, for a few minutes. Add cream and reduce again. Thicken to a light coating consistency with roux. Taste, add salt, and correct the seasoning. Skin the chicken and carve the flesh into 2 inch pieces. Add the meat and the chopped parsley to the sauce and let it heat through and bubble up.

"Wise women dress themselves to suit their age. Wise cooks dress poultry with the same discernment. It is both unbecoming and unnecessary to overdress spring chickens with elaborate cooking. The tender young things need no such adornment. Far better to emphasise their youthful charm with simple styles like roasting, frying and boiling. Keep the beauty treatments and sophisticated styles for the middle-aged and elderly ones, and you'll be rewarded by seeing even the hardiest and scraggiest become soft and yielding and attractive. All this is merely to say that successful poultry-cooking depends on being able to recognise the age of a bird and on treating it according to its age. Young birds can take dry heat and quick cooking. Mature ones need slow cooking in moist heat."
Kind Cooking, *Maura Laverty*

Chicken and Bacon Press

Serves 8–10

1 large boiling fowl or free-range
   chicken (4–4½lb)
2lb lean bacon in one piece
2 onions
2 carrots
1 celery stalk
a few parsley stalks
a few sprigs of thyme and
   maybe a sprig of marjoram
salt
5 peppercorns
2 tablespoons chopped parsley

This recipe was handed down through Myrtle Allen's family, and is still in frequent use. Originally it was a handy way of using up a boiling fowl past its prime, but nowadays it is almost impossible to find a boiling fowl, either before or after its prime! Use a free-range chicken instead.

Put the boiling fowl and bacon into a saucepan with the onions, carrot, celery, herbs, salt, and a few peppercorns.

Add about 2 inches of water. Bring to a boil, cover, and cook in a moderate oven (350°F) for 1½–2 hours, depending on the size and age of the chicken. Discard the vegetables.

When the chicken and bacon are cooked, skin and chop the meat into ¾ inch dice while it is still hot. Add the parsley, taste and correct the seasoning, then press into a bowl. Pour a little of the cooking liquid over the top, cover with a plate, and weight it down. Leave the mixture overnight in the fridge. Cut into slices and serve with a salad.

A more elaborate version can be made by layering the chicken, bacon, and parsley.

Fricassee of Chicken

We came across this startlingly rich recipe in the Lough Rynn manuscript 1865.

"Take three chickens and cut them up as for a fricassee. Put them in a saucepan with a pound of butter with an onion stuck with cloves. There let them stew a while and put to them as much water as will cover them and stew them 'til they are tender. Then beat the yolks of six eggs with a little parsley and so toss them up. Squeeze a lemon over them."

Mary Ponsonby also had a recipe for Fricassy of Chickens

"Wash the chickens well in cold water, when cut up then in warm water, put a lump of Butter as big as a Goose Egg into the stew pan, stir it to prevent oiling 'till all the pieces are greased over, put in warm water to cover the chickens, throw in a little flower during the stewing, when done; put in the following sauce keeping it over the fire about two or three minutes—the yolks of two eggs beat up with half a pint of cream, a little shallot, a little onion, chopped parsley, lemon peel, with pepper and salt. Mix well."

The Letrim Papers (1800–1875) yielded this recipe for Indian Curry

"Take two chickens cut them small and wash them. Cut some onions very small put them into a pan with some butter and fry them brown. Parboil the chickens and drain off the liquor. Mix two spoonfuls of curry powder with the chickens with a little salt, put them in the pan with the onions and fry them a little with as much liquor as will cover them. Add also a little (*poss cayenne pepper… end of page frayed*) and cream keep the pan covered till they are sufficiently done and add the juice of a lemon. A pint of rice must be well boyled and drained quite dry and served up in a bason to eat with the above."

1 free-range duck (about 4lb)
salt and freshly ground pepper

STUFFING
¼ cup (½ stick) butter
¾ cup chopped onion
2 cups soft white breadcrumbs
1 tablespoon finely chopped sage

STOCK
neck and giblets
1 carrot, sliced
1 onion, sliced
bouquet garni
small celery stalk
2–3 peppercorns

TO SERVE
Apple Sauce (see below)

How to render a duck

Remove the remainder of the duck fat from the raw carcase— particularly the pieces near the tail end inside the carcase. Cut into small pieces and put in a roasting pan in a cool oven at 225°F. The liquid fat will render out slowly over several hours.

Serves 4

2–3 Granny Smith apples
  (about 1lb)
2–4 teaspoons water
about ¼ cup sugar
  (depending on tartness
  of apples)

Papie's Roast Duck with Sage and Onion Stuffing

My maternal grandfather, whom we called Papie Tynan, was very fond of his food. He reared ducks, geese, chickens, and guinea hen for the table. The ducks and geese had a happy life, puddling about in the pond and pecking at the windfall apples in the orchard, and they tasted exquisite. Every scrap of the ducks and geese was used, including the blood which was made into a soft pudding and eaten on bread. The feathers were kept for pillows, and the down for quilts.

Put the neck, gizzard, heart, and feet into a saucepan with carrot and onion. Add the bouquet garni and celery stalk. Cover with cold water and add peppercorns, but no salt.

Bring slowly to a boil, skim, and simmer for 2–3 hours. This will make a delicious broth, which will be the basis of the gravy. Meanwhile, singe the duck and make the stuffing: melt the butter on a gentle heat, add the onion, and sweat for 5–10 minutes until soft but not colored. Remove from the heat and add the breadcrumbs and sage. Season to taste. Unless you are cooking the duck immediately, let it get cold.

When the stuffing is quite cold, season the cavity of the duck and stuff. Roast in a moderate oven (350°F) for about 1½ hours. When the duck is cooked, remove to a serving dish, and let rest while you make the gravy.

Skim the fat from the broth (keep the duck fat for roast or fried potatoes). Strain and add to the juices in the roasting pan, bring to a boil, taste, and season if necessary. Strain the gravy into a sauceboat and accompany the duck with some apple sauce (see below).

Apple Sauce

Peel, quarter, and core the apples, cut the pieces into two and put in a stainless-steel or cast-iron saucepan, with sugar and water. Cover and put on a low heat. As soon as the apple has broken down, stir and taste for sweetness. Serve warm.

Goose

Years ago, most farms in Ireland would have reared geese. The fowl were the responsibility of the farmer's wife and there was a tradition of making presents of geese to friends or to poor families.

In many parts of the country the first corn of the year was ground into flour and baked into bread for the Michaelmas feast. The last sheaf of corn was the centerpiece for the table. There were many traditions associated with the last sheaf: in some places, the girl who tied it had the honor of opening the first dance of the evening with the farmer's son. Until recently, "a set of ware" was the most common present given to young Irish couples when they married. The big serving platter from the set would be given pride of place on the dresser, reserved for the rare occasion when a goose or turkey was cooked.

We did learn that they kept geese on the Blasket Islands, off Co. Kerry, although it was difficult to get them to stay put on the island. Peig Sayers said "I once had a fine flock of geese," "but devil the one of them stayed with me." This did not stop the Island women from looking after them, because as well as meat the geese supplied them with down for their mattresses and pillows. There is also evidence that a cure for thrush could be got from the breath of a gander.

Máire Ni Ghuithín in her book *Bean an Oileáin* (Women of the Island) gives a recipe for Stuffed Goose which she got from her aunt. The stuffing consisted of mashed potatoes, to which butter, salt, pepper, and a finely chopped onion were added. When the goose had been stuffed, it was placed in a large pot with a little water and a large piece of bacon. The lid was placed on the pot and covered with embers. According to Máire her aunt "let the goose boil, bake and roast at the same time."

Serves 8–10

1 goose (about 10lb)
sea salt and freshly ground pepper
roux (optional; see page 42)

STOCK
giblets (neck, heart, and gizzard)
1 small onion
1 carrot
bouquet garni consisting of
   1 sprig thyme, 3–4 parsley
   stalks, a small piece of celery,
   6–7 peppercorns

STUFFING
2lb potatoes
¼ cup (½ stick) butter
scant 4 cups chopped onions
3 medium Granny Smith
   apples (about 1lb), peeled
   and chopped
1 tablespoon chopped parsley
1 tablespoon chopped lemon balm

Michaelmas Goose with Traditional Potato and Apple Stuffing

There's an old saying in Ireland that if you eat goose on Michaelmas Day, 29 September, you will not be "in want" for the rest of the year. By this time, the geese that hatched out in spring will be plump and wonderfully juicy and tender.

I have vivid childhood memories of the preparations for the Michaelmas feast in a neighbor's house. The bird was smothered several days ahead and hung by the neck in the outside shed. It was then plucked. The wings were kept (and much sought after for brushing out dusty corners). The large feathers were sometimes made into quills or fishing floats, and the smaller ones and the precious down were collected for stuffing pillows and feather beds. From time to time, as the goose cooked, the fat was poured off. Some of it was used to roast potatoes, but the rest was stored for myriad purposes. It was rubbed into chests to stop wheezing. It was used to shine the kitchen range and even to polish leather shoes. Nothing was wasted.

A goose looks enormous, but it has a large carcase and so looks as if it will serve more people than it does. Allow at least 1lb uncooked weight per person.

Traditionally goose is stuffed with a potato stuffing. There are many variations; this is one I particularly like.

First make the stuffing. Boil the potatoes "in their jackets" in boiling salted water until cooked. Peel and mash. Melt the butter and sweat the onions in a covered saucepan on a gentle heat for about 5 minutes. Add the apples and cook until they break down into a fluff, then stir in the mashed potatoes and herbs. Season with salt and pepper. Let the stuffing get quite cold before stuffing the goose.

To prepare the goose, first gut the goose and singe if necessary. Remove the wishbone for ease of carving. Put it into a saucepan with the giblets, onion, carrot, bouquet garni, and peppercorns. Cover with cold water, bring to a boil and simmer for about 2 hours. (Add the wing tips to the stock if desired.)

Season the cavity of the goose with salt and freshly ground pepper, and fill with the cold stuffing. Sprinkle some sea salt over the breast and rub it into the goose skin. Roast for 2–2½ hours in a preheated moderate oven, 350°F.

Take the roasting pan from the oven 3–4 times during the cooking and pour off the excess fat. (Store this fat in your refrigerator—it keeps for months and is wonderful for roasting or sautéeing potatoes.) To test whether the goose is cooked, prick the thigh at the thickest part. The juices that run out should be clear; if they are pink the goose needs a little longer. When cooked, remove the goose to a large serving dish and put it into a low oven while you make the gravy.

To make the gravy, pour or spoon off the remainder of the fat and save. Add about 3½ cups plus 2 teaspoons of the strained giblet stock to the roasting pan and bring to a boil. Using a small whisk, scrape the pan well to dissolve the meaty deposits which are full of flavor. Taste for seasoning and thicken with a little roux if you like a thickened gravy. If the gravy is weak, boil for a few minutes to concentrate the flavor; if it is too strong, add a little water or stock. Strain and serve in a hot gravy boat.

Carve the goose. Serve with apple sauce (see page 91) and the gravy.

Lamb

Irish lamb is for the most part naturally reared on lush green pastures. Connemara and Kerry lambs have a flavor all their own and are much sought after. No lamb I've tasted from any high-quality restaurant in Europe could equal the flavor of the lamb I used to buy from my local butcher, Michael Cuddigan, who reared his animals on rich old pastures full of wild flowers and herbs. There are still many conscientious butchers around the country who have not forgotten the old ways.

In former times, sheep were kept primarily for their wool. The meat was eaten only when the animal was old or died by accident and when sheep meat was eaten it was primiarily mutton.

In *The Farm by Lough Gur*, which describes rural life in Ireland in the late 19th century, Mary O'Brien recalls that "except when a sheep or lamb fell and had to be killed, we never had mutton."

On Inis Meáin, Aine de Blacam told us that everyone had sheep and lambs and the same was true of the Blasket Islands (see page 96). It was a real treat to have lamb, it would be pot roasted in the bastible with turnips, onion, carrots—delicious.

Mary Harlow who grew up in the Burren, Co. Clare, said that roast kid was a huge delicacy, it was delicious, they had it at Easter—never lamb. The goats were wild on the Burren and there for the taking. You just had to catch them!

The Blasket Islands

Malachy McKenna tells us in his treatise about the Blasket Islands—*Putting food on the Table* that sheep were of crucial importance to the island food-supply system, as well as to the Island economy in general. The same applied on the Mainland. Once a sheep had been acquired there was little other financial outlay, they grazed on the hill on the island and nearby islands and required little attention, except when they got stuck on cliff faces and at lambing time. Sheep were a kind of insurance for the Islanders against hard times: "When they don't have fish, they'll have sheep... one to shear, one to sell and one to eat." Sheep were easy to sell and fetched a good price on the Mainland; in the 1920s, two sheep would fetch between five and six pounds, which was regarded as an "extraordinary" amount of money at the time (from Allager na hInise). "The butchers say that there is no mutton to be had which is sweeter than a good sheep from An Blascaod."

Máire Ní Ghuithín writes in *Bean an Oileain* (Women of the Islands) that people believed that the meat got its good taste from the salt water on the grass. Sheep were milked too. Given the importance of sheep to the Islanders, it is no surprise that those who had no sheep were looked down on: "No-one lacks them," commented one Islander, "except a good-for-nothing."

Some fleeces were sold on the Mainland and those that were kept were washed, dried, and combed before being sent to the carding mill at An Daingean (Dingle). When returned to the Island it was spun by the women and used to make wool. The women used the wool yarn to make socks and ganseys. Some was spun into balls which could be woven by the weaver to make flannel, this was used to make trousers and waistcoats. The cloth was dyed using berries, bar, roots, moss, etc. to color the cloth.

It was the custom to kill sheep on Christmas Eve: "We would go to the hill then" writes Seán Ui Cearnaigh in *An tOileán a tréigeadh* (The Island That Was Abandoned) "and bring back big fat wethers and slaughter them on Christmas Eve. A sheep would be hanging in every house on Christmas Eve and if a man had no sheep the others would give him a share."

When the sheep had been slaughtered and skinned, it was hung up inside the house with the door open to allow air to get at the meat, thus enhancing the flavor. The meat would need to be hung for a couple of days before it could be eaten. Only a certain amount of the fresh mutton was eaten then, the rest being pickled and kept for later use. Before cooking, pickled mutton had to be steeped overnight in lukewarm water to draw out the salt, according to Máire Ní Ghuithín in *Bean an Oileáin* (Women of the Islands).

They cooked it in the following ways: Stuffed Intestines; Grilled Mutton Ribs; Roast Haunch of Mutton; Mutton Pies; and Mutton Stew.

Irish Lamb and Potato Hotpot

Serves 8

8 lamb shoulder or neck chops
(bone in), 1 inch thick
4 lamb kidneys
2 large onions, thinly sliced
1 tablespoon fresh thyme leaves
salt and freshly ground pepper
1–2 large baking potatoes (about
1½lb), peeled and thinly sliced
3 cups plus 1 tablespoon hot lamb
or chicken stock
2 tablespoons (¼ stick) butter

This is a delicious, comforting recipe. It's easy to prepare and doesn't take long to cook. Everything in one pot—great for a winter's evening.

Preheat the oven to 350°F. Trim the excess fat from the lamb and cut into dice. Pull off the skin and remove the central core from the kidneys. Cut each half into large chunks, wash well in cold salted water, then rinse and dry.

Heat the chopped lamb fat in a heavy casserole on a low heat until the lamb fat liquifies. Remove and discard the rendered fat pieces. Cut the lamb chops into 2–3 pieces (ask your butcher to do this) if very large. Add the lamb to the casserole and cook in batches on a high heat for 2–3 minutes until golden on both sides. Remove to a plate, add the kidneys, and toss to seal them on both sides. Set aside with the lamb.

Put the onions into the casserole and fry for 4–5 minutes until golden. Put a layer of lamb chops on top, sprinkle with most of the thyme leaves, then add the kidneys. Season with salt and pepper. Arrange the potato slices on top in a pretty circular pattern. Pour in the hot stock so that the potatoes are almost covered. Dot the top of the potatoes with the butter, and sprinkle over the remaining thyme. Cover the casserole, transfer to the oven, and bake for 1 hour or until the potatoes are crisp and golden, and the meat is falling off the bone.

Shepherd's Pie

Serves 6–8

2 tablespoons (¼ stick) butter
1 cup chopped onion
3 tablespoons flour
scant 2 cups stock and leftover
gravy from the roast
1 teaspoon tomato paste
2 teaspoons chopped parsley
1 teaspoon thyme leaves
salt and freshly ground pepper
2 cups minced cooked lamb
3 medium potatoes (about 1lb),
cooked and mashed
chopped parsley, to garnish

TO SERVE
Garlic Butter (see page 58)

I adore shepherd's pie—so much so that I would almost cook a roast specially to make it! Cooking raw ground lamb simply doesn't give the same flavor. Now that lamb is quite expensive, people seldom allow themselves the luxury of buying a joint large enough to yield the necessary leftovers. However, if one can manage to buy a bigger roast, make extra gravy and a delicious shepherd's pie with the extra meat. You might have to hide the meat, covered, in the back of the fridge in case it's pinched for sandwiches or a late night snack! Traditionally when people bought a bigger roast, they had it cold on Monday (when many women did the weekly wash and therefore didn't have time for much cooking), rissoles on Tuesday and Shepherds' Pie on Wednesday. This was an economical way of stretching a piece of meat—one can, of course, use cooked beef in the same way.

Melt the butter in a skillet and add the onion. Cover with a butter wrapper and cook over a slow heat for 5 minutes until soft but not colored. Add the flour and cook until brown. Pour in the stock, bring to a boil, and skim. Add the tomato paste, chopped parsley, thyme leaves, salt, and pepper and simmer for 5 minutes.

Add the meat to the sauce and bring to a boil. Put in a pie dish, cover with the mashed potatoes and score the top with a fork. Reheat in a moderate oven (350°F) for about 30 minutes. Garnish with parsley and serve with Garlic Butter (see page 58).

Mummy always added a dash of homemade mushroom ketchup to her sheperd's pie. It's a brilliant flavor enhancer.

Potted Meats

Serves 6

¾ cup cooked chopped meat
  (about 4oz)
2–4 tablespoons (¼–½ stick) butter,
  cut into cubes
2½ tablespoons jellied meat juices,
  if available (about 1oz)
salt and freshly ground pepper
spices e.g. freshly ground nutmeg,
  mace, allspice, or juniper berries,
  depending on the meat
clarified butter

Tasty potted meats were another way of using up little scraps of the leftover Sunday roast. In the days of the mortar and pestle this was a labor-intensive business, but nowadays delicious potted meats and fish can be made in seconds using a food processor. Spices were traditionally used for potted meat, but I also find some fresh herbs, for example parsley, chives, and thyme leaves, can be a delicious addition. Chicken, ham, beef, and game all make successful potted meats.

Remove any fat and gristle from the meat. Chop the meat finely and pound to a paste. Alternatively, put into a food processor and whizz for a few seconds. Add the cubed butter, meat juices, salt, freshly ground pepper, and spice. Whizz for a further few seconds, taste, and add seasoning until you are happy with the flavor. Pack the meat into little pots or ramekins and pour a layer of clarified butter over the top to exclude the air. These will keep for 7–10 days in the refrigerator. Serve with hot buttered toast.

2½–3lb lamb chops, not less than 1 inch thick
5 medium or 12 baby onions
5 medium or 12 baby carrots
salt and freshly ground pepper
2½ cups stock (lamb stock if possible) or water
8 potatoes, or more if you like
a sprig of thyme
1 tablespoon roux (optional; see page 42)
2 tablespoons chopped fresh parsley
1 tablespoon chopped fresh chives

Variations
Irish Stew Pie

Irish Stew may also be made into a pie. However, in this case the bones would be removed before covering the pie. You can use suet pastry, hot water crust pastry (see page 102), or even a pie dough which includes potato for the topping (see Mutton Pie à l'Irlandaise, page 100).

Pearl Barley

Pearl barley, nourishing and delicious, is also a traditional addition. Beware: it soaks up lots of stock, so increase the liquid by 1¼ cups.

Ballymaloe Irish Stew

In her Ballymaloe Cookbook *(1977), Myrtle Allen discusses the question of carrots in the Irish Stew—everyone she asked says they did put them in. Her mother did, as did everyone in Shanagarry. It seems to have been common practice in the south and Myrtle noted that they were used as far north as Tipperary. She continues: "Originally, we made Irish Stew by putting alternate layers of onions, carrots, potatoes and meat in a pot. It was seasoned, covered with water and stewed gently for 2 hours. Very simple and enjoyable." Later on when my children were small, a good woman called Madge Dolan came to cook for us and brought us a new and better version, which is the basis of our current recipe.*

Cut the chops in 2–3 pieces, if large, and trim off some of the excess fat. Place the trimmed-off fatty pieces in a heavy pan and cook on a gentle heat so that the fat runs out. Discard the solid bits that remain.

Peel the onions and scrape or thinly peel the carrots (if they are young, you could leave some of the green stalk on the onion and carrot). Cut the carrots into large chunks, or, if they are young, leave them whole. If the onions are large, cut them small; if small, they are best left whole.

Toss the meat in the hot fat in the pan until it is slightly brown. Transfer the meat into a casserole, then quickly toss the onions and carrots in the fat. Build the meat, carrots, and onions up in layers in the casserole, carefully seasoning each layer with pepper and salt. Pour the stock into the pan, stir to dissolve the caramelized deposits and pour into the casserole. Peel the potatoes and lay them on top, so they will steam while the stew cooks. Season the potatoes. Add a sprig of thyme and bring to a boil on top of the stove. Cover and transfer to a moderate oven (350°F) or let simmer on top of the stove until the stew is cooked. This will take about 1–1½ hours, depending on whether the stew is being made with lamb or mutton. The meat should be fork tender and almost falling off the bone.

When the stew is cooked, pour off the cooking liquid and skim off the fat. Reheat the liquid in another saucepan. Slightly thicken it with a little roux if you like. Check the seasoning, then add the chopped parsley and chives and pour it back over the stew. Bring it back up to boiling point and serve direct from the pot or in a large pottery dish.

Serves 6–8

6 lamb chops
salt and freshly ground pepper
4 onions
8 potatoes
1–2 dozen oysters

POTATO PIE DOUGH
6 large potatoes
salt, pepper and nutmeg, to taste
2 egg yolks
2½ tablespoons (¼ stick) butter
eggwash

Mutton Pie *à l'Irlandaise* —Lamb and Oyster Pie

Charles Elmé Francatelli, chef to Queen Victoria, gave a recipe for Mutton Pie à l'Irlandaise *in* The Cook's Guide, *published in 1871. It is interesting to note the inclusion of oysters in this recipe; they were extremely plentiful and in many cases cheaper than meat. They were included in many recipes as already seen and were even used to make sausages. A variation that is a popular dish at Ballymaloe House is beef and oyster pie.*

Cut the meat into pieces about 2 inches square. Season well. Peel the onions and cut into quarters. Peel the potatoes and keep whole. Mix the meat with the onions in a casserole and add water to almost cover. Lay the potatoes on top, bring to a boil, then cover and cook until the meat is tender. This will take about 1–1½ hours, depending on the quality of the meat. Meanwhile make the potato pie dough. Scrub the potatoes and cook in boiling salted water. As soon as they are cooked, peel and mash. Season with salt, pepper, and nutmeg. Mix with the egg yolks and butter, taste, and correct the seasoning.

As soon as the lamb and vegetables are almost cooked, open the oysters, and add to the casserole. Stir and transfer the mixture to a large pie dish. Roll out the potato pie dough on a floured board and use to cover the pie. As you can imagine, the potato mixture is quite soft, so this is easier said than done! You may have to patch it a little. Brush with eggwash and bake in the oven at 350°F for a further 30–40 minutes.

Serves 6–8

1 × 6½lb leg of mutton or hogget
salt
3 onions, halved
4–5 carrots, halved if large
2 celery stalks halved
6 peppercorns
a sprig of thyme
bay leaf

CAPER SAUCE
2 tablespoons (¼ stick) butter
1 tablespoon all-purpose flour
2½ cups whole milk
salt and freshly ground pepper
2 tablespoons chopped capers
1 tablespoon chopped parsley
   (optional)

Note: Mutton is meat from a sheep over two years old, and has a less tender flesh. In general, the darker the color, the older the animal. Baby lamb meat will be pale pink, while regular lamb is pinkish-red.

Boiled Mutton with Caper Sauce

Boiled mutton was very popular and the juice or boiling water would often have been made into a broth or soup maybe with the addition of pearl barley.

The gourmet writer Amhlaoibh Uí Shúileabháin, who kept a record of many of the meals he ate in his diaries, tells us that on September 14, 1828 "four of us dined with Father James Hennebry: we had boiled leg of mutton with carrots and turnips."

Mutton is virtually impossible to find nowadays, but a nice leg of hogget cooked in the same way is very flavorsome—a wonderful dish for a cold winter's evening. Ballymaloe House is one of the few places where hogget is served on the menu—often braised with winter vegetables or wild garlic.

Ask your butcher to cut the leg at the shank end. Weigh the meat and work out the cooking time: for every 1lb allow 30 minutes, then add another 25 minutes to the time. Put the meat into a saucepan just large enough to fit it nicely. Cover with water, add a good sprinkle of salt and bring to a boil. Remove any scum that rises to the surface. Add the vegetables, peppercorns, thyme and bay leaf. Cover the pan; simmer very gently until cooked.

Meanwhile make the sauce. Melt the butter in a saucepan, stir in the flour, and cook for a minute or two. Gradually whisk in the milk, bring to a boil and simmer for 4–5 minutes. Season and put aside until you are ready to serve the meat. Just before serving, add ⅔ cup of the degreased broth from cooking the meat. Bring back to a boil, add the roughly chopped capers, and a tablespoon of chopped parsley, if you like. Taste and correct the seasoning. Carve the meat into slices at the table and serve with the caper sauce.

1 leg of corned mutton—around
  5lb 8oz
2 bay leaves
2 onions, quartered
2 carrots, cut into chunks
2 leeks, cut into chunks
2lb potatoes

Parsley Sauce (see below)

Poached Leg of Mutton with Parsley Sauce

Kay Harte, from the much-loved Farmgate Café upstairs in Cork City's English Market, shared this recipe with us. Kay constantly features local produce on her menu, if possible from the market downstairs. The corned mutton is supplied by Paul and Alan from Coughlan's Butchers in the market. They bone the leg of lamb and open it out, then corn it for about 36 hours and it is absolutely mouthwatering. Any leftovers can be converted, very simply, into a mutton pie the next day.

Put the leg of mutton into a large pot and add enough water to cover.

Add the bay leaves, onions, carrots, and leek (Kay says she just chops the onions into quarters and adds them "skin and all"); these are to flavor the cooking water.

Bring to a boil, then turn down the heat, and simmer very slowly with the lid on for 1½–2 hours—depending on how big the piece of mutton is. When cooked, turn off the heat and let cool in the cooking liquid until ready to carve.

Put well-scrubbed local potatoes into a steamer; they usually take about 30 minutes, depending on size. When cooked, remove the lid and put a damp dish towel on top while you are waiting to serve. This helps the "floury" process!

Make the parsley sauce (below) while the potatoes are cooking. Kay says that either mashed turnip or mashed carrot and parsnip are lovely served with this dish. You can cook the vegetables in the mutton broth for added flavor. Mash them with salt and pepper and a teaspoon of local honey. Creamy mash or scallion champ are good with this too.

4 tablespoons finely chopped
  fresh parsley leaves (retain
  the stalks)
2½ cups fresh whole milk
1–1½oz roux (see page 42)
salt and freshly ground pepper

Parsley Sauce

Put the parsley stalks into a saucepan with the cold milk, bring slowly to a boil, then remove the stalks. Whisk the roux into the boiling milk until thickened and add the chopped parsley. Season with salt and freshly ground pepper. Simmer for 5–10 minutes on a very low heat, then taste and correct the seasoning before serving.

Kerry Pies

Serves 6

1lb boneless lamb (from the
    shoulder or leg—keep the
    bones for stock)
2½ cups chopped onions
2 cups chopped carrots
2 tablespoons flour
1¼ cups lamb stock
1 teaspoon chopped parsley
1 teaspoon thyme leaves
salt and freshly ground pepper

PIE DOUGH
2½ cups all-purpose flour
pinch of salt
¾ cup (1½ sticks) butter, diced
½ cup water
1 egg beaten with a pinch of salt
    to glaze

2 round pie dishes, 6 inches in
    diameter and 1¼ inches deep,
    or 1 round pie dish, 9 inches in
    diameter and 1¼ inches deep

Years ago when my mother-in-law, Myrtle Allen, began to collect old Irish recipes, this was one of the first to arouse her curiosity. Mutton pies, made in Kerry, were served at the famous Puck Fair in Killorglin in August, and taken up the hills when men were herding all day. Traditionally they were cooked in the bastible and reheated in mutton broth, then served in a deep plate with some of the broth over the top. It sounds strange, but the old people who remember them are adamant that they were delicious. Below is our version. The original hot-water crust pie dough was made with mutton fat, but we have substituted butter for a really rich crust.

I've since discovered that these delicious pies were not just found in Killorglin, they also featured in Listowel. Mary Keane, wife of the late playwright John B. Keane, told me that the tradition of pie making in Listowel came about because the women wanted to go to the horse races, so would make "a blast of pies" a few days before the races so as not to be deprived of their fun. I included Mary's recipe in my book, Forgotten Skills of Cooking.

Mutton Pies were also made on the Blasket Islands and Máire Ní Ghuithín writes of these pies in Bean an Oileáin: *"We thought that there was no food in the world as good as them."*

There is a similarity between these pies and Cornish Pasties, it is possible that a link goes back to the 1800s when a community of Cornish miners and their families lived in a valley near Allihies in West Cork and worked the copper mines. These are the mines Daphne du Maurier wrote about in her book Hungry Hill.

Cut all the surplus fat off the meat, then cut the meat into small neat pieces about the size of a small sugar lump. Cook the scraps of fat in a hot, wide saucepan until the fat runs. Discard the pieces. Cut the vegetables into slightly smaller dice and toss them in the fat, leaving them to cook for 3–4 minutes. Remove the vegetables and toss the meat in the remaining fat on a high heat until the color turns. Stir the flour into the meat. Cook gently for 2 minutes and blend in the stock gradually. Bring to a boil, stirring occasionally. Return the vegetables to the pan with the parsley and thyme leaves. Season with salt and freshly ground pepper and let simmer. If using young lamb, 30 minutes will be sufficient; an older animal may take up to 1 hour. When the lamb is cooked, let cool slightly.

Meanwhile make the pie dough. Sift the flour and salt into a mixing bowl and make a well in the center. Put the butter cubes into a saucepan with the water and bring to a boil. Pour the liquid all at once into the flour and mix together quickly; beat until smooth. At first the pie dough will be too soft to handle, but it will become more workable as it cools. Roll out two-thirds of the pastry to ¼ inch thick and use to line the base of your pie dishes.

Fill the pie dough-lined dishes with the slightly cooled meat mixture. Cut lids from the remaining pie dough, brush the edges of the base with water and eggwash and put on the pie dough lid/s, pinching them tightly together. Roll out the trimmings to make pie dough leaves or twirls to decorate the pie tops. Make a hole in the center and brush the pie dough carefully with eggwash.

Bake the pie/s at 400°F for about 40 minutes.

Serve hot or cold.

Serves 4

½ cup almonds
1 cup plus 1 tablespoon light cream
1 inch piece of fresh ginger
1lb boneless lamb or mutton
  (leg or shoulder is perfect)
salt
2 tablespoons ghee or clarified
  butter
2 onions, sliced in rings
2 garlic cloves, crushed
1 teaspoon ground coriander
1 teaspoon black peppercorns
½ teaspoon green cardamom pods
¼ teaspoon ground cloves or
  4 whole cloves
2 teaspoons ground turmeric
1 teaspoon sugar
juice of 1 lime or lemon

Captain Donovan's Mild Madras Curry

Many Irish men who served in the British Army in India in the days of the Raj and developed a taste for curries; the memory of the tantalizingly spiced food remained with them after their return. Many came home armed with little boxes of spice mixtures lovingly blended by their Indian cooks, which they hoped would enable Irish cooks to reproduce the flavors of the Indian curry they had grown to love. This is one of the most delicious curries I've tasted.

Blanch, peel, and chop up the almonds (they should be the texture of nibbed almonds). Put them in a saucepan with the cream and simmer for 5 minutes. Turn off the heat and leave to infuse for 15 minutes.

Peel the ginger thinly with a vegetable peeler, then pound it into a paste in a mortar and pestle or chop finely with a knife. (You need about 2 teaspoons of pounded ginger.) Cut the meat into 1½ inch cubes and mix it with the ginger and a sprinkling of salt. Melt the ghee or clarified butter in a saucepan and cook the onion rings and crushed garlic in it for 5 minutes. Grind the coriander, pepper, cardamom, and cloves in a clean spice or coffee grinder. Add the spices to the onions and cook on a medium heat for 5 minutes. Remove the onions and add the meat to the saucepan. Stir over high heat until the meat browns, then return the onion and spices to the pot. Add the almond cream, turmeric, and sugar. Stir well. Cover and simmer gently on top of the stove, or in a low oven at 325°F, until the meat is cooked (about 1 hour). Finish by adding lemon or lime juice to season, according to taste.

Serve with boiled rice and other curry accompaniments, such as mango or tomato chutney, mint chutney, raita, Indian breads, and poppadoms.

Cooking Pits of the Fianna

All over Ireland, but particularly in Munster and Connaught, can be found the remains of ancient cooking pits known as *Fulachta Fiadh*. They date back to the Bronze Age, but are traditionally associated with Fionn Mac Cumhaill and his heroic band of warriors, the Fianna, who, according to legend, lived in Ireland around the 3rd century AD.

The ancient burnt mounds and cooking pits are usually found near water—rivers, streams, or wells. They consist of a boiling pit, a hearth, and an enclosing mound of burnt stone. The boiling pits seem to have been lined with stone slabs or timber, depending on the area, and then filled with fresh spring water.

Here is a description from G. Keating's *The History of Ireland*:

"... from Bealltaine [1 May] until Samhain [1 November] the Fian were obliged to depend solely on the products of their hunting and of the chase as maintenance and wages from the kings of Ireland... And it was their custom to send their attendants about noon with whatever they had killed in the morning's hunt to an appointed hill, having wood and moorland in the neighbourhood, and to kindle raging fires thereon, and to put into them a large number of emery stones; and to dig two pits in the yellow clay of the moorland, and put some of the meat on spits to roast before the fire; and to bind another portion of it with sugans in dry bundles, and set it to boil in the larger of the two pits and keep plying them with stones that were in the fire, making them seethe often until they were cooked."

Modern-day reconstructions of the cooking pits have demonstrated that meat cooked in this way would have been moist and juicy—cooked to perfection in about the same time as it would take in a moderate oven today.

Beef

The cattle of early Ireland were generally smaller than the modern breeds and were rarely slaughtered for their meat. The size of your herd of cattle was an indication of your wealth and status. Only for special occasions would a cow or bullock be killed and eaten.

Until recent times roast beef was standard Sunday fare in many prosperous Irish households. The leftovers were often turned into shepherd's pie on Monday or Tuesday.

Most butchers would agree that the best beef comes from Polled Angus cattle ("polled" means hornless), a cross between Aberdeen Angus and Shorthorn. With the exception of ground meat, which should be cooked fresh, all other beef cuts benefit from dry-ageing by hanging. We like to hang our beef for up to six or seven weeks, and the resulting flavor is absolutely superb. Unfortunately, many butchers can't afford the inevitable weight loss incurred from hanging meat for such a long period, and customers are not always prepared to pay the premium that this would require when buying their meat. Generally, the flavor depends on the breed of animal, how it is fed, the handling of the meat, and hanging. Local butchers who buy from local farmers know how the animals are reared: this is real traceability and its importance is once again being recognized and valued.

Roast Rib of Beef with Batter Pudding, Horseradish Sauce and Gravy

Serves 10–15

prime rib of beef on the bone, with
    a nice covering of fat (well-hung)
salt and freshly ground pepper

GRAVY
2½ cups stock (preferably
    homemade beef stock)
roux (optional; see page 42)

ROASTING TIMES
15 minutes per 1lb for rare
20 minutes per 1lb for medium
25 minutes per 1lb for well done

A fine roast of beef or lamb with lots of gravy and roast potatoes has long been the traditional Sunday lunch in many Irish homes. In more affluent houses from the 1950s to the mid-1970s there would have been a standard order with the local butcher who delivered it, wrapped in brown paper, and tied with cotton string. Usually a bigger piece of meat than was required for one meal was purchased. Cold leftover meat formed the basis of several other meals—a few slices of the roast cold with salad for Sunday evening supper, or for Monday's lunch. If it stretched a bit further, rissoles or shepherd's pie would have made an enjoyable meal on Tuesday or Wednesday.

Most butchers sold a boned and rolled joint, which suited them because they were able to roll the end piece into the middle. Unfortunately, this was the toughest piece and made the joint difficult to cook successfully, and it made many a cook think that she couldn't cook roast beef. From time immemorial, butchers always blamed the cooks and cooks blame the butcher!

Beef was usually cooked well-done. Serving beef rare is a relatively recent way of doing things in many households and restaurants in Ireland. Roast beef continues to be a popular option on hotel Sunday lunch menus, served with roast potatoes and gravy. In the country houses, a larger joint of meat would have been served with horseradish from the kitchen garden.

Ask your butcher to saw through the upper chine bone of the beef, so that the "feather bones" will be easy to remove before carving. Weigh the roast and calculate the cooking time (see left). Preheat the oven to 475°F.

Score the fat and season with salt and freshly ground pepper. Place the meat in a roasting pan with the fat side uppermost. As the fat renders down in the heat of the oven, it will baste the meat. The bones provide a natural rack to hold the meat clear of the fat in the roasting pan.

Put the meat into the fully preheated oven. After 15 minutes, turn down the heat to a moderate 350°F until the meat is cooked to your taste.

There are various ways of checking if the beef is cooked. I usually put a skewer into the thickest part of the roast, leave it there for about 30–45 seconds and then put it against my wrist. If it still feels cool, the meat is rare; if it is warm, it is medium-rare; if it is hotter, it's medium; and if you can't keep the skewer against your wrist for more than a second, then you know the meat is well-done. Also, if you check the color of the juices you will find they are clear, as opposed to red for rare or pink for medium.

When the meat is cooked it should be allowed to rest on a plate in a warm oven for 15–30 minutes before carving, depending on the size of the roast. The internal temperature of the meat will continue to rise by as much as 5°F, so remove the roast from the oven while it is still slightly underdone.

Meanwhile make the gravy. Spoon the fat off the roasting pan. Pour the stock into the cooking juices remaining in the pan. Boil for a few minutes, stirring and scraping the pan well to dissolve the caramelized meat juices (I find a small whisk ideal for this). Thicken very slightly with a little roux if you like (years ago flour would have been sprinkled over the fat in the pan, but I prefer to use roux). Taste and add salt and freshly ground pepper if necessary. Strain and serve in a warm gravy boat.

Carve the beef at the table and serve with horseradish sauce and batter pudding (see opposite). Accompany with the gravy and lots of crusty roast potatoes.

Batter Pudding

Serves 8–10

¾ cup plus 1½ tablespoons all-
  purpose white flour
2 eggs, preferably free-range
1¼ cups milk
1 tablespoon butter, melted and
  cooled
oil or pure beef dripping, for
  greasing the pans

Sift the flour into a bowl and make a well in the center. Drop in the eggs. Using a small whisk or wooden spoon, stir continuously, gradually drawing in flour from the sides and adding the milk in a steady stream at the same time. When all the flour has been mixed in, whisk in the remainder of the milk and the cool melted butter. Let the batter stand for 1 hour at least. Grease hot deep bun pans with oil or pure beef dripping and fill them half to three-quarters full with batter. Bake in a hot oven (450°F) for about 20 minutes.

Horseradish Sauce

Serves 8–10

3–6 tablespoons grated horseradish
2 teaspoons wine vinegar
1 teaspoon lemon juice
¼ teaspoon mustard powder
¼ teaspoon salt
lots of freshly ground pepper
1 teaspoon sugar
scant 1 cup softly whipped cream

Horseradish grows wild in many parts of Ireland and looks like giant dock leaves. The root has been used for many years to make a punchy sauce.

Put the peeled and grated horseradish root into a bowl with the wine vinegar, lemon juice, mustard, salt, freshly ground pepper, and sugar. Fold in the softly whipped cream, but do not overmix or the sauce will curdle. It keeps for 2–3 days; cover so that it doesn't pick up flavors in the fridge.

Pot-roasted Beef

Serves 6–8

beef dripping
4lb well-hung best top round
  or silverside
salt and freshly ground pepper
thyme leaves (optional)
grainy mustard (optional)
1¼ cups beef stock
roux (optional; see page 42)

It was only from the early part of this century that ranges and cookers (or stoves, as they were frequently called) came into general use. I remember in the 1950s the excitement generated when a new range arrived in a friend's house in my village in Co. Laois. Before that, food was cooked over or beside the open fire.

Pot roasting was a common method, particularly for a rich, flavorsome Sunday joint. The flat-bottomed pot oven or bastible was used, but nowadays a good heavy casserole gives a similar result. This dish can be cooked on top of the stove or in the oven.

Heat a little beef dripping in a heavy casserole, brown the meat on all sides, and season with salt and freshly ground pepper. (I can't resist adding a sprinkling of thyme leaves at this point, or perhaps smearing the beef with grainy mustard.) Cover with the lid and cook on the lowest heat possible for 2½–3 hours. The beef can also be transferred to a preheated low oven, at 275°F.

When the roast is cooked, remove to a serving plate and make a little gravy in the casserole dish. Skim off the fat from the meat juices, add the stock, bring to a boil, and simmer for a few minutes. Taste and add seasoning if necessary; thicken slightly with a little roux if you like.

Serve the pot-roasted beef with the gravy. The traditional accompanying vegetables would have been carrots and potatoes, but in the autumn I love marrow in cheese sauce, buttered mashed swede, or carrots and parsnips.

Beef and Guinness Stew

Serves 6–8

2lb lean stewing beef
3 tablespoons oil or dripping
2 tablespoons all-purpose flour
salt, freshly ground pepper and
    cayenne
2 large onions (about 10oz),
    coarsely chopped
1 large garlic clove, crushed
    (optional)
2 tablespoons tomato paste,
    dissolved in 4 tablespoons water
1¼ cups Guinness
¾ cup carrots, cut into chunks
sprig of thyme

GARNISH
chopped parsley

Guinness, Ireland's famous black stout, has been brewed in Dublin since 1759. It has a very special place in Irish life. Nowadays the "liquid food" is used increasingly in cooking. It is a tasty addition to stews and casseroles, helping to tenderize the meat and imparting its distinctive malty flavor to any dish. This recipe makes a wonderful gutsy stew, which tastes even better a day or two after it is made.

Trim the meat of any fat or gristle, cut into 2-inch cubes and toss them in a bowl with 1 tablespoon oil. Season the flour with salt, freshly ground pepper and a pinch or two of cayenne. Toss the meat in this mixture.

Heat the remaining oil or dripping in a wide skillet on a high heat. Brown the meat on all sides. Add the onions, crushed garlic, and tomato paste to the pan, cover, and cook gently for about 5 minutes. Transfer the contents of the pan to a casserole, and pour some of the Guinness into the skillet. Bring to a boil and stir to dissolve the caramelized meat juices on the pan. Pour onto the meat with the remaining Guinness; add the carrots and the thyme. Stir, taste, and add a little more salt if necessary. Cover with the lid of the casserole and simmer very gently until the meat is tender—2–3 hours. The stew may be cooked on top of the stove or in a low oven at 300°F. Taste and correct the seasoning.

Scatter with lots of chopped parsley and serve with champ (see page 148), colcannon (see page 152) or plain boiled potatoes.

Boiled Beef

Boiled fresh beef was a great standby dinner for farming households—a good piece of tail end or brisket could be left simmering away on top of the range while the woman of the house got on with her chores. Turnips or carrots or cabbage would be added later, and it would be dished up with plenty of potatoes when the men came in with a good appetite.

Beef and Dumplings

Patricia Murphy from Wexford, who sent me several recipes, said: "Dumplings seemed to feature a lot in years gone by. They were hot and filling and made a little food go a long way." Beef shin was usually used, which took hours to cook. Whatever vegetables that were available at the time were used. Dumplings were added in the final 30 minutes of cooking. See page 80 for Patricia's dumpling recipe.

Stewed Beef

This recipe comes from the 1900 manuscript of Annie Irwin.
"Dredge the beef with flour and fry it in butter until brown, then put it in your pan with a bundle of sweet herbs, a few cloves, some peppercorns and an onion. Pour a kettle full of boiling water over it and let it stew three hours then take it out, strain the gravy and skim off the grease. Put it again into the gravy and stew about an hour longer very slowly. Just before you take it off the fire put in your turnips, carrots etc and boil them in the gravy."

Leg or Shin of Beef Stew

Mary Conniffe from Robertstown, Co. Kildare sent me a recipe from her mother's Collins school series Domestic Economy. This stew, which Mary's mother cooked for them when they were young, uses leg or shin of beef, which was a very popular cut and really delicious. It melted off the bone when properly cooked. The recipe was even costed—what wonderful training for young women!

Ingredients	Cost
3lbs of Leg or Shin of Beef, about 8d. per lb	2s 0d
2 Turnips and 2 Carrots, about 1½d	1½d
4 Onions	2d
Bunch of Mixed Herbs	
(i.e., Marjoram, Thyme and Parsley)	½d
1 Gill of Vinegar	½d
Pepper and Salt to taste	
Total	2s. 4½d

Cut the meat into neat slices, and dip each into the vinegar. Wash and scrape the carrots, and cut them into dice; also peel the turnips thickly, and cut into dice. Peel the onions and then parboil them. When the vegetables are prepared, put the meat into a saucepan with the vegetables, herbs, pepper and salt. Place the lid on tightly, and let the whole stew gently at the side of the fire for at least 3 hours.

Note: No water is required in cooking this stew, as the vinegar in addition to making the meat tender, draws out the gravy.

Stewed Stuffed Steak

This dish, using round steak, was also a great traditional favorite. It doesn't seem to feature as much nowadays, probably because it has to be watched over a period of a couple of hours. This is how Rosalie Dunne from Garryvoe remembers her mother making it in the 1950s.

"1–1½lb round steak in one piece was flattened out and a stuffing (made with breadcrumbs, chopped fresh herbs, sautéed onion, salt and pepper and a little butter, like a stuffing for chicken, see page 88) was laid on one half of it. The steak was then folded over and stitched around the edge. It was browned in beef fat in a heavy saucepan, a small amount of water added (some herbs could be added) and then braised for about 1½ to 2 hours on top of the cooker in a covered saucepan. It was necessary to turn and baste it occasionally to make sure it didn't dry out and stick to the pot. When cooked, the steak was removed and the liquid thickened a little with roux to make gravy. The thread was removed and the meat cut into thickish slices—the juices would have run into the stuffing. It was delicious."

Steak and Onions

Fried steak and onions with gravy has been a favorite in Ireland for many years. The delicious aroma could be smelt before one came in the door and, served with potatoes in their jackets, it made a delicious dinner. Sirloin or chump steak would have been used.

To Fry Beefsteak and Onions

I found this recipe in a wonderful little one-penny cookbook dated 1901 called *Lessons in Cookery and Housewifery for the use of Children* by Kathleen Ferguson. Published and printed at Athlone Printing Works, it would have been used in schools.

"Have the pan and dripping very hot; wipe the steak over with a damp cloth; put it on the pan and fry it for 15 minutes, or longer if very thick, turning it frequently so that the outside becomes sealed and the valuable juices are kept in. Peel and slice the onions; put them on the pan, and fry till a light brown color. Serve the steak on a very hot dish; put the onions on top and pour the gravy over all.

Gravy—Pour the dripping from the pan; pour boiling water, pepper and salt on the pan (and, if liked a little Ketchup or Worcester sauce); boil up the gravy and pour it over the meat."

The basic recipe hasn't changed much, except that nowadays people like their steak cooked to different degrees of "doneness." It is often broiled rather than fried and served with different accompaniments, such as fries, deep-fried onion rings, béarnaise sauce, pepper sauce, and so on. Different cuts are used, such as filet mignon, sirloin, or rib-eye.

Serves 4–6

2 tablespoons chopped onion
1 tablespoon oil
1lb raw ground steak
scant 1 cup breadcrumbs
salt and pepper
a pinch of dried herbs
1 tablespoon freshly chopped herbs
  (such as fresh parsley, thyme,
  and chives)
a little milk

Hamburgers

Monica Nevin also gave recipes for beef hamburgers using ground steak, so burgers are a more recent introduction to the Irish cook's repertoire than we might think. She gave this recipe at the request of "A constant Dublin reader."

First fry the chopped onion in the oil until soft. Put the meat into a bowl, add the other ingredients, and enough milk to moisten the mixture, but it should not be too moist to handle. Turn the mixture onto a floured board and shape into cakes about ¾-inch thick. Fry gently for 10 minutes or so and when nicely brown on both sides arrange on a hot dish and serve with brown gravy or tomato sauce.

Making Corned Beef

Order 5lb of topside, brisket, "housekeeper's cut" or silverside from your butcher. The latter is leanest and most expensive but, in my book, not necessarily the best (I favor a bit of brisket myself). Michael Cuddigan, who was our revered family butcher for many years, was emphatic that the piece of beef should hang for 5 days before going into the brine. In a large stainless-steel saucepan, prepare a brine with 3 quarts plus 1½ cups water and 3½ cups salt. Stir the brine to help the salt dissolve. (It'll be easier to cut the beef into perfect slices if you tie the beef into a neat shape with 3 pieces of white cotton string, but this is optional.)

Put the chosen cut of beef in the brine and sprinkle the top with another ½ cup salt. Put a cold sterilized plate on top of the beef and a weight on top of the plate so that none of the meat is exposed to the air (we use a Pyrex measure filled with water). Leave the meat in the brine for 5 days; after that, cook and serve as desired.

Serves 6–8

4lb corned beef
3 large carrots, cut into large chunks
6–8 small onions
1 teaspoon English mustard powder
large sprig of fresh thyme and some parsley stalks, tied together
1 cabbage
salt and freshly ground pepper

Corned Beef with Cabbage

Although this dish is eaten less frequently nowadays in Ireland, for Irish expatriates it conjures up powerful nostalgic images of a rural Irish past. Originally it was a traditional Easter Sunday dinner. The beef, killed before the winter, would have been salted and could now be eaten after the long Lenten fast, with fresh green cabbage and floury potatoes. Our local butcher corns beef in the slow, old-fashioned way that, alas, is nowadays more the exception than the norm.

Put the corned beef into a saucepan with the carrots, onions, mustard, and the herbs. Cover with cold water, and bring gently to a boil. Simmer, covered, for 2 hours. Discard the outer leaves of the cabbage, cut in quarters, and add to the pot. Cook for a further 1–2 hours or until the meat and vegetables are soft and tender. Season to taste.

Serve the corned beef in slices, surrounded by the vegetables and cooking liquid. Accompany with lots of floury potatoes and freshly made mustard.

7–10lb flank, breast (boned) or
   rump of beef

SPICE
1 tablespoon mixed spice:
   (¼oz each cloves, allspice, mace;
   ¼oz mixed ginger and cinnamon)
1 teaspoon thyme leaves, picked
   free of stalks
3 shallots
3 bay leaves
2 cups kitchen salt
½ cup plus 1 tablespoon brown
   sugar
½oz saltpeter
⅔ cup molasses

Spiced Beef

*This recipe came from a scrapbook cutting of a newspaper article by Mary
Frances Keating, who was a well-known food writer in the late 1940s and
early 1950s. Flank is a little fatty, but is usually tender when well hung,
and, when spiced, the fat is very good indeed.*

Mix the spices and thyme leaves together, and mince the shallots and bay leaves. Place
the mixture in a baking dish in a warm oven until the herbs can be crumbled to a powder.
Add the salt and sugar and mix again. Trim the meat so that it will make a neat roll for
cooking—but leave it flat for spicing. Rub the mixture into each side of the meat, working
it in well. Place in a large dish and leave the meat to marinate, covered, for 2 days in the
refrigerator. Remove and pour the molasses over the meat, rubbing it in well.

Marinate for a further 10 to 14 days, depending on whether you want the meat highly
or lightly spiced. Turn the meat every day and rub the mixture into the meat and leave to
rest for a few days, then roll it into a neat roll and tie firmly.

To cook the beef, place it in a casserole with a tightly fitting lid and pour over barely
enough warm water to cover. Bake in a moderate oven (350°F) until the meat is simmering
and then reduce the heat to (325°F). Allow 25 minutes to each 1lb meat and 25 minutes on
top. If this dish is cooked in the oven, the meat will be much more salty and spicy than if
boiled in the usual way, and it will be a nicer dish cold than hot.

6lb beef chuck, boned and rolled

SPICE
thyme, mixed herbs, mace,
   nutmeg, cloves, allspice,
   black pepper, bay leaf
   (6 teaspoons in total)
2 cups salt
½oz saltpeter
½ cup plus 1 tablespoon soft
   brown sugar
2 onions, 1 finely minced
3 carrots
1 small turnip
1 celery stick
a few parsley stalks
peppercorns

Aunt Lil's Spiced Beef

*Spiced beef was one of the many dainties served at dinner for "Little
Woman's Christmas" by Aunt Kate in James Joyce's short story* The Dead:

*While Gabriel and Miss Daly exchanged plates of goose and plates of
ham and spiced beef, Lily went from guest to guest with a dish of hot floury
potatoes wrapped in a white napkin … Mary Jane waited on her pupils
and saw that they got the best slices, and Aunt Kate and Aunt Julia opened
and carried across from the piano bottles of stout and ale for the gentlemen
and bottles of minerals for the ladies.*

Pound the herbs and spices together and mix well with the salt, sugar, and minced onion.
Tie the beef up well and place in an earthenware crock. Cover the meat with the spice
mixture, rubbing it in well by hand for several minutes. Replace the lid. Turn the meat
once a day, every day, for a fortnight, rubbing the spice mixture in each time.

To cook the spiced beef, dice the vegetables and place in the bottom of a pot with the
parsley stalks and black peppercorns. Place the meat on top and cover with cold water.
Simmer (for about 30 minutes per 1lb and then 30 minutes over). When tender, take out
the beef and press between 2 plates with a weight on top. Leave it overnight.

Serve with a warm potato salad containing lots of scallions and a hard-boiled egg.

Serves 4

8oz cooked meat
4 tablespoons mashed potatoes
1 tablespoon dripping
1 slice of onion
3 tablespoons all-purpose flour
⅔ cup stock or water
salt, pepper, and freshly grated
    nutmeg
1 teaspoon Worcestershire Sauce
    or Yorkshire Relish
1 egg
generous 1 cup breadcrumbs

Rissoles

This recipe came from the recipe notebooks of Lily O'Reilly, which date from around 1939, when she worked in the Civil Service in Dublin and attended cooking night classes before getting married in 1944. Lily was a great cook— at that time women had to retire from their jobs upon marrying, so home- making and cooking skills were very important and highly valued. Husbands often came home from work for lunch in the towns and cities, not just in farming households. Rissoles were often made on Monday with the meat saved from the Sunday roast, which would have been carefully kept in the "safe" on the north-facing wall of the house.

Remove any bones or gristle from the meat and put it through a grinder. Put it into a bowl, and mix with the mashed potatoes. Put the dripping into a saucepan and melt on a medium heat until smoking hot. Add the onion slice, fry until lightly browned in the dripping, and then lift out the onion and set aside.

Take the saucepan off the heat and blend the flour into the dripping, add in the stock or water a little at a time, bring to a boil, and boil for 3–4 minutes. Season to taste with pepper, salt, nutmeg, and Worcestershire Sauce or Yorkshire Relish. Pour over the meat and potatoes in the bowl, chop the onion, and mix well together.

Turn out onto a lightly floured board and shape the mixture into a roll. Divide into 8 pieces, form into balls with floured hands, brush with beaten egg, and toss in breadcrumbs. Shake off any loose crumbs and deep fry until golden brown.

Suet and Rendering Fat

Demanding physical labor meant that people needed fuel, and filling dishes made with suet were a good way of providing it. Suet was often used in pastries, puddings, dumplings, and mincemeat. Traditionally, people used rendered beef fat for cooking, as there were no oils 25 years ago. Chips were cooked in beef fat in a pan with a wire basket in it, using hand-cut potatoes.

I can still remember the smell in the house when my mother rendered fat. Rendering chopped beef suet from the local butcher to make beef fat provided a free source of fat for cooking, so it was well worth the effort. James Murphy from New Ross in Co. Wexford sent me several cuttings and recipes he came across while researching local history, including this piece from *For the Table*, 1907 on how to clarify fat:

"Cut up scraps of fat (cooked or uncooked), cover with cold water, cook slowly for three to four hours until all the water has evaporated. Strain and allow to cool."

However, we usually do it in a simpler way. We put it in a very low oven (300°F), and let the fat gradually render out over a period of a couple of hours, depending on the quantity being made.

Pork

The early Irish pig was thin, scrawny, and vicious in temperament. Until medieval times pigs were fattened on mast, the fruit of beech and oak, which was said to give the flesh a delicious flavor. After the widespread adoption of the potato, virtually every home could afford to rear a pig because the animal could be fed on surplus potatoes, potato skins, and sour milk.

Every scrap of the pig was used. The head was salted and boiled with cabbage or turnips or made into brawn. The feet, called "crubeens" in Ireland, were boiled and eaten on their own or with cabbage, or included in the brawn. The stomach was sometimes stuffed and roasted and was known as mock goose. In the days before footballs could be bought in every village shop the bladder or "padgin" was donated to the children, who pumped it up with air and had endless hours of fun with it.

Pork has suffered more than almost any other meat from modern intensive rearing methods. For many years I longed for the taste of the sweet juicy pork that we ate as children, so about ten years ago I bought two spirited saddlebacks and a black Berkshire boar. They range freely on the farm, and sometimes we let them into the apple orchards in autumn to feast on the windfalls, so that when we eat their delicious meat it comes with "built-in" apple sauce.

Traditional Roast Pork with Crackling and Applesauce

Serves 10–12

6lb loin of pork with the skin still on

STUFFING
1 tablespoon butter
¾ cup chopped onion
2 cups soft white breadcrumbs
2 tablespoons chopped herbs
   (parsley, thyme, chives,
   marjoram, savory, perhaps
   very little sage or rosemary)
salt and freshly ground pepper

GRAVY
2½ cups homemade chicken stock
roux (optional; see page 42)
fresh herbs (optional)

TO SERVE
roast potatoes
Applesauce (see page 91)

You can't have crackling without the pig skin, but sadly it has become quite difficult to buy a piece of pork with the rind still intact to make delicious crackling. It needs to be ordered ahead from the butcher, so do your bit and insist on getting it so that this essential part of the enjoyment of roast pork does not die out!

For really good crackling, score the skin at ¼-inch intervals running with the grain—let your butcher do this if possible, because the skin can be quite tough. (This will also make it easier to carve later.)

Next make the stuffing: sweat the onions gently in the butter for 5–6 minutes. When they are soft, stir in the breadcrumbs, freshly chopped herbs, and a little salt and pepper to taste. Cool.

Preheat the oven to 375°F. Put the joint, skin side down, on your work surface and sprinkle with salt and freshly ground pepper. Spread the stuffing over the meat, roll up tightly and tie with cotton string. Season the rind with salt. Roast on a rack, allowing 28–30 minutes per 1lb. Baste every now and then.

Just before the end of cooking time remove the pork to another roasting pan, return it to the oven and turn up the temperature to very hot—450°F, to get crisp crackling. When the roast is cooked the juices should run clear. (You should never eat pork pink.) Put the pork onto a hot carving dish and let rest in a very cool oven while you make the gravy in the original roasting pan.

Spoon off the fat from the original roasting pan and add the chicken stock. Whisk to dissolve the deposits on the pan. Bring to a boil. Season and thicken with a little roux, if desired. Freshly chopped herbs may be added to the gravy. Serve with crispy, roast potatoes and lots of applesauce.

4 slices pork tenderloin
lard or soft butter
all-purpose flour
1¼ cups chicken stock or water
fresh parsley sprigs, to garnish

**BASIC PARSLEY AND THYME
STUFFING**
4½ cups soft white breadcrumbs
1 teaspoon thyme
½ teaspoon marjoram (optional)
¼ teaspoon pepper
¼ cup (½ stick) melted butter
2 tablespoons chopped onion
1 tablespoon parsley
¾ teaspoon salt

Stuffed Pork Steak (or Mock Duck)

What is known in Britain as pork fillet (or tenderloin) is called pork steak in Ireland. It was the most highly-prized piece when the pig was killed. This is one of the ways my mother often used to cook it. It was also known as mock duck (see Mock Goose on page 115), because when stuffed and trussed it resembled the shape of a duck. Many dishes were named in this way when the ingredients to make the original dish were not available, for example Mock Turtle Soup—calves' head and cheaper ingredients were used as substitutes.

Irish food writer Maura Laverty writes about stuffings in her book Kind Cooking, *saying that "stuffing must do much more than improve a fowl's figure, or make a ration of meat for two serve four. It should, and can, improve flavour and add zest." I have been reading Maura's books again as her centenary was recently celebrated, so I give her recipe for Basic Parsley and Thyme Stuffing, which would be very suitable for stuffing a pork steak. For one pork steak, half the quantity would be plenty.*

First make the stuffing. Blend the melted butter with the other ingredients. This will stuff a bird or fish weighing 6lb. If you like your stuffing moist, add ½ cup stock, milk, or cream. If you like it cakey, add 1 well-beaten egg and ¼ cup milk. For variety add any of the following: 1 teaspoon grated lemon rind and ¼ teaspoon grated nutmeg, 1 cup chopped celery, ¼lb minced ham or bacon, ½lb sausagemeat. The marjoram maybe used in addition to, or instead of the thyme.

Trim the tenderloin of gristle. Unless they are very fat (which is most unlikely nowadays) leave what little fat there is. Split each slice down one side and open out flat. Season with salt and freshly ground pepper. Divide the stuffing between two slices. Lay the other slices on top and truss or sew all around the edge with cotton thread. Smear each with a little very good lard or soft butter.

Heat a heavy casserole, preferably oval. Brown the slices on each side. Cover with a butter wrapper and the lid of a saucepan.

Put in hot fat in a roasting pan and allow 25 minutes per lb and 25 minutes over. Put into a preheated moderate oven at 350°F for 45–60 minutes, cook until cooked through and nicely browned.

To serve, remove the stuffed tenderloin to a serving dish. Skim the fat from the cooking juices, return them to the roasting pan, add a little flour and stir well. Return to the heat and cook for a minute or two, then add the chicken stock or water, bring to a boil, stirring all the time with a little whisk to dissolve the caramelized sediment. Taste and correct seasoning. Strain into a gravy boat and serve with the pork tenderloin simply garnished with sprigs of fresh parsley. Cut the tenderloin into thick slices to serve.

A Christmas Feast

For Eamonn Mac Thomáis's childhood Christmas there was no goose or turkey but instead a "bit of roast," usually pork or a bit of ham or bacon (his father had died when he was 14). The pudding and iced cake were a present from the grocer they dealt with, and in a good year he would also include a big red candle and a bottle of sherry or port wine.

After the Christmas dinner the mother would douse herself in sherry and there would be great gas, she'd be half cocked for the afternoon. All the rest of the family were pioneers [total abstainers], so she'd have the bottle to herself.

Poor Man's Goose

Mary Conliffe from Naas, Co. Kildare sent me this recipe for Poor Man's Goose, taken from her mother's school domestic economy book. The book states that the recipe was given on the authority of Miss M.A.S. Tattersall, Gold Medalist and Cookery Superintendent.

Ingredients	Cost
1lb of Pig's Fry *	about 6d
2½ lbs of Potatoes	" 2d
1 Onion	" ¼d
Seasoning (i.e Sage, Pepper & Salt)	" ½ d
Dripping	" ¼d
Water	
Total	9d

"Scrub and wash the potatoes, then peel them thinly. Parboil the onion, and chop up with about three sage leaves, pepper, and salt. Cut the "Fry" into small pieces, and grease a quart dish with dripping. At the bottom of this dish place a layer of sliced potatoes, and sprinkle a little of the chopped onion, etc; then add a layer of the "Fry." Repeat this process until the whole of the prepared ingredients are used. Cover the whole with the skin of the "Fry", if obtainable, if not, use a piece of greased "kitchen paper" to put over the dish. Bake in a moderate oven for about an hour.

N.B.—1. Onions may be parboiled thus; Put the onions in to a basin with a piece of soda about the size of a hazel-nut. Nearly fill the basin with boiling water, and cover the top with a plate or saucer for about twenty minutes, or until the water becomes green.

N.B.—2. Grocery or drapery paper can be used as "kitchen paper" but newspaper or common printed paper should not be employed."

* Pig's fry consists of sweetbreads, heart, liver, lights (lungs), and melts (spleen).

Ciste

This wholesome, rib-sticking dish—which is perfect for a winter's day—came to me from North Tipperary. Císte is the Irish Gaelic word for cake, used here because this dish resembled a cake in the making.

Serves 4–6

2 pork kidneys
1 large onion
1 large carrot
6 pork chops
mixed herbs
salt and freshly ground pepper

PASTRY
1¾ cups all-purpose flour
generous 1 cup grated beef suet
½ teaspoon baking powder
salt
⅔ cup milk

Slice the kidneys and the vegetables, then place in a pot with the chops. Cover with water and add the herbs and seasonings. Cook on a low heat for about 30 minutes.

Make a pliable dough with the flour, suet, baking powder, salt, and enough milk to mix. Roll out onto a floured board, cut to fit inside the pot, and place on top of the meat. Cover with a lid, allowing the pie dough room to rise. Cook for 1½ hours on a low heat.

4 pork sausages
2 tomatoes
salt, pepper, and sugar
butter
4 × ¾-inch thick slices white
 pudding (see page 132)
4 × ¾-inch thick slices black
 pudding (see page 132)
8 bacon rashers, green or smoked
4 free-range eggs

An Irish Breakfast

Bacon and eggs is of Irish origin, according to a story told by the late Oscar Ashe, quoted by Florence Irwin in Irish Country Recipes:

"An old Irish peasant woman was frying the morning bacon for her good man in a pan over the peat fire. In the open chimney above roosted the fowls on the cross-beams from which the hams were hung to smoke. She turned to drive out of doors an old sow and her litter and the other domestic animals which shared the cabin at night with the rest of the family. As she was so occupied a hen dropped an egg from its roost. It struck the edge of the pan and its contents spilled into the sizzling fat. And so when the good woman came to take the pan from the fire, lo! for the first time she beheld an egg fried with bacon. She set the dish before her good man who consumed the lot, and he went forth to the monastery where he laboured, marvelling. And so the fame of the dish penetrated the monastery walls, and from monastery to monastery it spread, and from land to land, and from peoples to peoples, and was relished by rich and poor alike, and all by the grace of God and the irregular proclivities of the lazy old hen."

In 1957 the first course in Farm Guest House Management *was held at An Grianán, the Irish Countrywomens' Association Adult Education College in Termonfeckin, Co. Louth. This was a totally new idea in Ireland, but became a huge success story, bringing welcome income to farm women. Today Farm Guest Houses and Irish Bed and Breakfasts are a byword for a real Irish experience for visitors from at home and abroad, promoting tourism across the country. The Irish breakfast was the mainstay of all guesthouses, and when nicely prepared with good-quality ingredients, it is delicious and will, as the saying goes, "set you up for the day."*

Many families had the tradition of "fry" after Mass on Sunday, particularly when people went to an early Mass. A slice or two of fried soda bread was often added, cooked in the hot bacon fat that had rendered from the rashers while they were frying. It was filling and delicious and added another tasty item to the breakfast for hungry men. It was inexpensive and another way to use up slices of slightly stale bread.

Prick the sausages and fry on a medium heat until golden all over. Drain and keep hot. Cut the tomatoes in half, put onto a heat-proof plate and season with salt, pepper, and sugar. Place a little blob of butter on each tomato, cover loosely with a butter wrapper, and cook in a moderate oven at 350°F, for 5–10 minutes. Alternatively, fry gently in a skillet.

Fry the puddings gently on both sides and drain on paper towels. Cut the rinds off the bacon and fry until just crisp in a very hot pan. Finally heat a little bacon fat or butter in a clean pan, crack the eggs and cook on a gentle heat as desired. When cooked, divide the "spoils" between four hot plates and serve immediately with lots of fresh soda bread and hot toast.

Makes 4 breads

1 cup mashed floury potato
½ cup plus ½ tablespoon all-
  purpose flour
1 tablespoon melted butter or
  olive oil
a pinch of salt

Variation
Apple Potato Bread

Pin out the raw potato bread into
a round, place a large blob of
stewed apple in the center and
then fold the potato bread over
into a turnover shape. Bake on a
hot griddle until the potato bread
is cooked. Add ¼ cup steel-cut
oats or ½ cup cheese to the above
basic recipe for potato bread and
bake on a griddle. Alternatively, if
you are having a dinner party, cut
out the potato bread into 1-inch
circles approx ¾ inch thick, fry
off the potato bread and top with
bacon and relish, black pudding,
and homemade brown sauce
or scallops.

Robert Ditty's Potato Bread

*The Northern Irish equivalent of the Irish Breakfast is called The Ulster
Fry. The main difference is that in Ulster they also serve Potato Bread or
Farls with theirs. White all-purpose flour was scarce in the earlier part of
this century, so was considered a luxury. There were many recipes for potato
bread, potato pie dough etc. to help to "stretch" the flour. Paddy the "Cope"
Gallagher from Co. Donegal recalled that in the 1870s, when he was a child,
"flour bread was rare, we had oat bread and boxty instead. Boxty was looked
on as a rare treat, probably because there was white flour in it." Robert Ditty
of Ditty's Award winning artisan Bakery in Castledawson, Northern Ireland,
shared the recipe for Ditty's legendary potato bread with us.*

Boil potatoes, mash, and let cool. Sift flour and salt and add to potatoes with melted butter
or olive oil. Knead into a dough. Roll it out to an 8-inch round and then cut into quarters.
Bake on a preheated griddle or a heavy pan. Cook for 3–4 minutes on a medium heat until
speckled and pale golden in color on each side.

For the ultimate potato bread, serve as part of an Ulster Fry. Fry the potato bread in a
skillet straight after the bacon for extra flavor.

The Breakfast Roll

During the building boom in Ireland's "Celtic Tiger" years, the Breakfast Roll became an
institution and was sold to hungry builders in their high visibility jackets, from garage
forecourts, deli counters, fast food takeouts, and was even immortalized in a song by Pat
Shortt in 2006, "The Jumbo Breakfast Roll." It was basically a bread roll stuffed with as
many of the components of the Irish Breakfast as would fit or as desired!

"Well I wake up in the morning and I jump straight out of bed
Grab a hold of that luminous jacket and shake off me auld porter head
I don't have time for a fancy breakfast or put muesli in the bowl
I just head to the stat oil garage for the jumbo breakfast roll
Two eggs two sausage two rasher two bacon two puddings one black and white
All stacked like a tower on top of each other and then wrapped up good and
  tight."

To Cure Bacon

This recipe for a procedure that would have been common in many households up to the middle of this century is taken from the Receipt Book of Eliza Helena Odell, Odell Ville, Co. Limerick. It is dated 26 August 1851.

"450g (1lb) of English salt
110g (¼lb) of Irish or bay salt
50g (2oz) of saltpetre
110g (4oz) of black pepper (ground)
450g (1lb) of treacle

These proportions to every cut of bacon. Let the marrow be taken out of the bones of the Hams and Gammons and fill the holes with salt and saltpetre. When the pig is cut up sprinkle it with salt and leave it on a sloping flag or board to drain until next day. Then wipe each piece dry and rub the treacle well in at both sides. Put a layer of salt about an inch deep into the tub, then pack nicely a layer of meat (hams first), the skin side down, and sprinkle well the flesh side with pepper and saltpetre (which have first been mixed) then a layer of salt, then meat and so on to the top, press down the meat with stones and do no more till you hang it in four weeks, if the pickle don't rise in four weeks sprinkle salt over it to form some and also if the compliment of salt run short add more, for each layer must be thick enough to pickle out the meat—hams and bacon are treated the same way, but if heavy meat it is an improvement to give the hams and gammons slight hand rubbing, be sure to exclude all air and have the heads well cleaned from blood and the brains removed. Coarse brown sugar will do as well as treacle."

Bacon and Cabbage

Serves 12–15

4–5lb loin or shoulder of bacon with a nice covering of fat
1 head cabbage, Savoy, Greyhound, or spring cabbage, depending on the time of year
butter
white pepper
Parsley Sauce (see page 101), to serve

Without question Ireland's national dish—less widely known abroad but much more widely eaten, particularly in rural Ireland, than the legendary Irish stew.

Cover the bacon in cold water and bring slowly to a boil, discarding any white froth. Each time it forms, replace the water and reboil. Cover with hot water and simmer, allowing at least 20 minutes to every 1lb.

Meanwhile, remove the outer leaves from the cabbage. Cut the cabbage into quarters, remove the center core. Cut each quarter into thin strips across the grain. About 30 minutes before the bacon is cooked, add the cabbage. Continue to cook until the cabbage is soft and tender and the bacon fully cooked through. Remove the bacon to a hot plate and strain the water off the cabbage. Return the cabbage to the pan with a lump of butter; season with white pepper. Serve with the bacon and, traditionally, boiled potatoes and Parsley Sauce (see page 101).

Bacon

Flitches of home-cured bacon, stiff with salt, were hung from the rafters in virtually every kitchen in Ireland up to the early 1950s. Streaky bacon has fat in between the layers of meat, it can be smoked or "green" (unsmoked). It's a cheap, delicious cut, and a piece of streaky bacon is a most useful thing to have in the fridge: it can be used for lardons or added to a stew, a quiche, or a substantial soup. Patricia Murphy from Wexford sent me a recipe for Blind Stew (see page 178), which is a stew without meat, but she also added the variation of including some streaky bacon.

In Search of Dublin Coddle

For years I was intrigued by Dublin Coddle. It sounded utterly revolting and when I attempted to make it from the recipes I could find it looked and tasted revolting too. Every time I went to Dublin I would sound out a taxi driver about coddle. Most of them grew instantly nostalgic. Some talked of sneaking home to "the Mammy's" for a feed of coddle, but, interestingly, just as many talked about "the wife" or "herself" making it regularly. So there's no question that traditional Dublin Coddle is alive and well and still being made on a regular basis in Dublin.

As with Irish Stew, feelings run high on what a real coddle should be. One taxi driver had confided to me that his thoroughly modern wife put tomato and peas in to give it a bit of color. When I attempted to share this gem of information with the next taxi driver, however, he was so aghast that he turned right round in the seat to look me straight in the eye—and as a result nearly hit a bus.

"Not at all!" he declared emphatically, proceeding to give me a blow-by-blow account of how coddle should be made. "Put the rashers, sausages, potatoes and onions into a pot, cover them up with cold water and boil 'em up for an hour or so. Oh, and a nice bit of pepper," he added. Should I brown the sausages? I ventured to ask. "Not at all, amn't I after telling you how to make it?" What would you eat with it? "Tea and bread and butter, or maybe a bottle of stout if you had it."

Eventually one chap told me about the essential condiment that no cookery book had mentioned—the bottle of Chef or YR Sauce (bottled HP or brown sauce is the best alternative) to shake over the top. Several other people confirmed this—so there you are now!

8 good sized potatoes
4 good sized onions
8 bacon rashers (we left the rind on)
8 sausages
pepper

Winnie Dunne's Dublin Coddle

Well, it took Kevin Dunne, born and bred in the Liberties, in the heart of Dublin, to take the mystery out of coddle for me. Kevin showed me how to make his mother's coddle recipe, and also took many of the photographs for the first edition of this book in 1995. Kevin died a few years ago and is sadly missed. No one ever measures for Dublin Coddle but this is what we used to feed four people.

Kevin put the potatoes straight into a medium-sized pot, chopped up the onions into chunks, and added those, then laid the rashers and sausages on top. He put the pot under the cold tap until the ingredients were almost covered, then put the pot on the Aga and brought it to a boil. Then he added lots of pepper (no salt, as good Irish rashers will ensure that it is salty enough!). We covered the pot and simmered the mixture for an hour or so. I looked into the pot every now and then, and about half way through left the lid slightly ajar to reduce the liquid somewhat. The potatoes got a little fluffy but still kept their shape. It still looked distinctly unappetizing (lots of chopped parsley scattered over the top would take the harm out of the sausages which still appear to be raw) but surprise, surprise, it tasted absolutely delicious! (I'm not joking; delicious is not too strong a word for this dish.) I didn't have a bottle of YR Sauce to hand, but ate the coddle with lots of butter. Now I understand why this simple, good-humored dish is such a favorite—and why so many Dubs look forward to coming home to a plate of it after a night of liquid entertainment! It's comfort food at its best—although with all those salty rashers in it, it would give you a mighty thirst!

Wakes

Wakes, although primarily to mourn the dead, were important social occasions in Irish tradition, and have remained so until relatively recent times. During a wake, courtships might commence and marriages were sometimes arranged ("twas many a match was made at a wake"). Relatives, neighbors, and friends gathered in the house to pay their last respects to the dead. The corpse was laid out in the best bedroom or parlor, or even sometimes in the kitchen.

There was a strong tradition of feeding the mourners and even very poor families would virtually beggar themselves to provide a fine repast of funeral meats, cakes, tea, porter, whiskey and, of course, "poteen." John Dunton describes a Dublin wake in his 17th-century work, *Letters from Ireland*, 1698, edited by Edward MacLysaght (Dublin, 1982):

"About midnight, most of the company being then gathered that was expected to come, great platters of boiled flesh were brought into the barn, and an abundance of bread, all made in fine white cakes of wheat flour. I do not here mean small cakes, like our saffron ones or biscuits, but of size as large as a sieve and near three inches thick, portions of which with flesh were distributed to every one of the people and great tubs of drink which was brewed that day followed on hand-barrows … And now came tobacco, pipes and sneezing."

As a child in a country village I remember walking with some neighbors to a local woman's wake. The whole affair had a profound effect on me. We were ushered into the bedroom where the corpse was laid out in the bed. First we knelt beside the bed and I watched in horror as the older women kissed the corpse, then we joined other mourners who sat on chairs around the walls of the tiny bedroom. Every now and then I gathered up courage and stared in fascination at the corpse, so still and waxen with the rosary beads woven through her fingers. The blessed candles flickered at the four corners of the bed and the little Sacred Heart lamp under the holy picture illuminated the room in an eerie way. Even though we lived very close by, we were pressed to have tea and cold meats and sweet cake before we walked home in the dark.

Serves 12–15

1 × 10–12lb fresh or lightly smoked ham with a nice layer of fat raspings (fine dried breadcrumbs)

Raspings

Put the crusts, preferably of white bread, into a very cool oven to dry out (we put them into the coolest oven of the Aga) and allow them to become dry and crisp. They can then be crushed with the aid of a rolling pin and then sifted. Dried crumbs keep almost indefinitely in a sealed jar. Traditionally, they were used for sprinkling on the fat surface of cold ham or bacon, but they also make a perfect coating for croquettes or rissoles.

Funeral Ham

I came across many recipes specifically intended for wakes and funerals in my research for this book. Cold ham was a great traditional standby. The tradition of serving ham at a wake or funeral came about from convenience— it was something that people would often have cured themselves, or it might have been cured by a neighbor. There was great cutting in a ham, to serve as a cold plate or to make sandwiches for "soakage" when drink was being consumed. A nicely boiled piece of tasty ham is always a welcome item when one has a crowd to feed.

People who lived through "hard times" were very thrifty; not a scrap of food was wasted because they knew what it was like to be "without," hence the use of raspings in this recipe.

If the ham is salty, soak it in cold water overnight. Next day discard the water. Cover the ham with fresh cold water and bring it slowly to a boil. If the meat is still salty, there will be white froth on top of the water. If so, discard this water, cover the ham with fresh cold water again, and repeat the process. Finally, cover the ham with hot water and simmer until it is fully cooked, 1½ hours or more. Allow about 20 minutes to 1lb cooking time. Let the ham cool; remove the skin, which should peel off easily, then sprinkle the surface with fine dried breadcrumbs.

Bide Bodice

Salted pork ribs, bought and often cooked in a sheet, are a great Cork speciality, known as "bodice." This follows the Cork tradition of naming various bits of offal after items of women's clothing. We also eat skirts (see page 142)!

Cover with cold water, bring to a boil and simmer for an hour or more until soft and juicy. Divide into 3–4 pieces and eat with the fingers, seasoned with English mustard. Mashed potatoes, carrots, or swede are often served with bodice.

To Cook a Whole Ham

This method of cooking a whole ham was sent to me by Noreen Lehane of Cork City. It was given to her by an old lady from West Cork.

Steep the ham overnight (depending of course on the amount of salt, otherwise a few hours will do). Next day parboil it and leave the ham in the water overnight. Remove the ham from the water and dry it thoroughly. Make up a paste of all-purpose flour and water, then wrap the ham completely in the paste. Put it into a hot oven for about 30 minutes and reduce the heat to low. A large ham on the bone would take about 6 hours, a medium ham about 5 hours and a boned and rolled ham about 4 hours.

When cooked, remove from the oven. At this stage the paste will be very hard and you will need a hammer to break it.

Next skin the ham and remove some of the fat, if it needs it. Glaze in the oven until golden brown.

By this method the ham does not reduce and remains deliciously moist throughout the cooking process.

Curing a Ham

This recipe comes from the Annie Irwin 1910 manuscript and was credited to Mrs Warner.

"For a common sized ham take ¾ lb of bay (sea) salt, ½ lb of common salt, 2 ozs salt petre, 1oz black pepper, pound them all fine, and rub the ham well with it. Let it lay 14 days, turning and rubbing it every day—then take it out of the salt and pour over it a pound and half of treacle, turn it and baste it every day, for one month, then soak it 24 hours in soft water, lastly smoke it well, when dressed, which ought not to be before six months, it only requires scraping, but not soaking. It ought to be firm."

Killing a Pig

Killing the pig was a very important social occasion, planned several weeks ahead. Many of the neighbors would come to lend a hand. Each neighbor who came would bring a fist of salt for the curing, and when the work was done everyone would get a share of the fresh pork and the black and white puddings. In some cases the farmer himself killed the pig, but on my relatives' farm in Tipperary, a local man skilled in the killing of pigs would arrive on an ass's cart, bringing all the tools of his trade—a mallet, a knife, a saw, an apron, and a galvanized bath. He was highly thought of and had to be booked ahead.

As a child I loved all the excitement and wanted to be in on all the action with my brothers. I was highly indignant when I was barred from watching the actual killing simply because I was a girl—an early taste of male chauvinism!

As soon as the pig was stunned, its throat was cut and the precious blood was collected in a basin underneath for the puddings. Salt was added and the blood was stirred constantly to prevent coagulation. Then two or three fellas would rush off for buckets of almost boiling water from the black pot over the open fire. The pigs would be scalded in the big bath and then hiked up on to a table, or creel, which was balanced on top of the bath. Then three or four helpers would quickly shave off the hairs, being careful not to damage the skin. The intestines were removed and a few buckets of cold spring water from the pump were thrown over the carcase. The pig was then hung up by the back legs from the rafters in a cool, airy, white-washed outhouse, with two or three little pointed sticks propped into the centre to keep its inside open.

This accomplished, the laborious business of washing the intestines began, under the running water from the pump in the yard. The women usually did this and I was allowed to help. The large intestines were used for the white puddings and the small for the black. When the washing and scraping was complete, the intestines were put into salted water which was changed regularly until the puddings were made the following day or the day after. The morning after the pig was killed the butcher would come back and divide the pig in two lengthways; he would then extract the pork steaks, liver and kidneys. The pork steaks were the sweetest and most sought-after part of the pig.

Then the carcass was butchered. Spare ribs and loin were kept to be eaten fresh. The bacon curing got underway. Salt and saltpeter were rubbed vigorously into the meat which was then carefully packed between layers of salt in a wooden wine barrel from the distillery. The meat remained in the vat for three weeks, after which it was hung up on hooks from the rafters in the kitchen. Sometimes a ham was hung up inside the huge chimney over the open fire for smoking.

Most farmers killed a pig at certain times of the year (some of the most prosperous killed several pigs on the same day). There was a custom that pigs should be killed only when there was an 'R' in the month i.e. never in the summer—an eminently sensible precaution in the days before refrigeration. In some counties, such as Mayo and Galway, it was believed that the deed should be done under a full moon, but that was not the case in our area in the midlands of Ireland.

Pigs were kept somewhere close to the house where they could be fed easily on household scraps and grain. They were prized possessions, not only providing several months' supply of meat for the household, but also leaving enough over to share with neighbors, who would share their own meat in turn.

Up to the early 1960s, it was not unusual for people to keep a couple of pigs in cities as well as towns and villages. Our local post mistress kept a couple of pigs that were fattened on kitchen waste and slops of beer from the local pub. This was much sought after so the pigs would snooze more, and get fine and fat before slaughter.

Offal

Cork City has been an important trading port since the later medieval period. The provisioning of the ships involved thousands of people. The best cuts of meat were sold fresh and salted, other cuts were corned and spiced, and a great deal of offal was eaten by the Corkonians themselves. A certain weight of offal was allocated to each slaughterhouse worker as part of his weekly wage, hence the Cork people's great love for offal, which remains right up to the present day. The Cork Market, originally known as the English Market because when it was founded in 1788 the Irish were not allowed to trade inside its walls, still has many stalls which do a lively trade in pigs' heads, tails, offal bones, skirts, kidneys, bodices (salted spare ribs), crubeens (salted pigs' trotters), tripe, and drisheen (sheep's blood pudding).

Ironically, there has been a revival of interest in offal and all cheaper cuts, thanks in part to Fergus Henderson of St. John restaurant in London, who has piqued chefs' interest in offal and less expensive cuts of meat. In the current economic climate people are also keen to re-learn the skills of coaxing flavor and melting texture out of the cheaper cuts. The immigrants to our shores, the new Irish of recent years have these skills. If one walked through Cork's old English Market, you would see many of the cheaper cuts labeled in Polish and Russian, as well as in English. They too have many traditional recipe for things like pigs' tails.

Pig's Head

A boiled pig's head or half head was cooked in the same way as bacon. Butchers and grocery shops used to display pig's heads in the window. This is not a sight one sees much anymore, but they are still to be found in Cork's English Market. Pig's head has gone down in folklore but is not eaten frequently these days, although pig's cheek does appear on some fancier menus. Fergus Henderson, in his book *Nose to Tail Eating*, values all parts of the pig and gives recipes for their use.

James Murphy from New Ross in Co. Wexford sent me some interesting newspaper cuttings, including this one from the Kilkenny People dated 1938: a letter from James J. Healy, Carrick-on-Suir extolled the virtues of pig's head and he included a long poem entitled *The Irish Pig's Head*. Here is an excerpt:

'Twas the pride of our forefathers' table,
When each one was snug and content;
And, when came the call of the landlord
Sure 'twas always the pig paid the rent.
And still it's the pride of our country
For nought can against it be said;
'tis tender, not tough,
And you can't eat enough
Of a nice piece of Irish Pig's Head.

'Tis a dish that has ever proved wholesome,
And sure Irishmen showed it before;
When you taste it you'll eat till you're finished,
And then you'll be wanting for more.
Oh, if ever I've the luck to get married
I'll invite all the boys to 'a spread',
And we'll have lashin's galore,
But—I'll place to the fore
A nice piece of Irish Pig's Head.

Maura Laverty, in her book *Kind Cooking*, wrote about a character called Head Mooney, whose people were notorious throughout Co. Kildare for their passion for pig's head, and spent all the money they earned on them. "When the boy I'm talking about got married—Paddy, he was called then—his wife was full of a bride's eagerness to please." With her first week's wages, she bought the biggest pig's head she could find, thinking it would do them the week. She cooked it nicely and served it "bolstered on white cabbage" for Paddy when he came in from second Mass the next day. "Paddy sat down, blessed himself and started in. Wrapped up in it, he continued with the good work until his wife, who had a normally healthy appetite, could stand it no longer. 'What about me, Paddy?' she asked diffidently. 'Aren't you going to cut a little bit for me?' Paddy looked up in shocked amazement, 'And do you mean to tell me, girl,' he demanded, 'that you didn't cook e'er a one for yourself?' It was then she christened him Head, and the name never left him."

On the Blasket Islands it was customary for the islanders to fatten pigs for sale on the mainland. Tomás Ó Criomhthain, writing in *An tOileánach*, describes the house he grew up in, mentioning the animals that were kept there: "We lived in a small narrow house... There were two cows in it, two pigs, the hens and their eggs and a donkey." He writes that the animals were kept in the house at night and that the pigs were kept under the high bed; this was the norm at the time. Pigs were generally fed on potatoes and sometimes on meal. Unlike sheep and cattle, which grazed, pigs had to be fed on surplus foodstuffs. If there was no surplus—if potatoes were in short supply, for example—then pig-rearing would not be viable unless the islanders could improvise in some way. One of the reasons that the islanders gave up pig-rearing was the amount of time and expense involved in getting the pigs to market and then returning home. Half the price of a pig could be spent in An Daingean on the mainland, and some celebrating would also be involved.

There isn't any great recording of recipes for using pig meat on the island, but Máire Ní Ghuithín does mention that pickled pig's head was cooked along with cabbage or turnips. She said that pig's feet were good to eat, as long as they were well-cooked, "because they are full of sinews. Pig's feet were known as 'mouth organs' on the island"—a name I also heard in Cork. However, it is written by Tomás Mac Síthigh in *Paróiste an Fheirtéaraigh* that on the mainland "almost all of the farmers used to kill a pig every year." Pig's head was a popular food; blacksmiths, as well as being paid money, had to be given a pig's head for work done and, when people played cards, they might win a pickled pig's head as a prize.

Áine de Blacam said that on Inis Meáin island the occasional pig would be killed, mainly to sell for the market. They would share some too, but she doesn't remember puddings being made.

I came across many different recipes for curing ham in the manuscript cookbooks. It would have been common practice in country house kitchens to preserve ham for storage in this manner, as well as in farmhouses, when the pig was killed.

Pig's Head and Cabbage

Serves 4–6

half a pig's head
a head of cabbage

My eldest son reckons to be very cool; like many of his generation nothing seems to faze him. However, one day recently when he lifted the lid off a pot on the Aga, he shrieked and uttered some quite unprintable expletives when he caught sight of the pig's head bubbling in the pot. My daughters continually count my happy bonhams in the orchards to make sure that none of them end up in brawn. They were appalled at the unmentionable bits of this and that they occasionally glimpsed while I tested recipes for this book—pigs' tails, bodice, tripe, drisheen… such a lily-livered lot, this generation. I've become very partial to a bit of pig's head myself!

Remove the brain and discard. Wash the pig's head well. Put in a large saucepan, cover with cold water and bring to a boil. Discard the water, refill the pan with fresh water, and continue to cook, covered, for 3–4 hours, or until the meat is soft and tender and almost lifting off the bones.

Meanwhile, remove the outside leaves from the cabbage. Cut the cabbage into quarters and discard the center core. Cut each quarter into thin strips across the grain. About 30 minutes before the pig's head is cooked, add the cabbage, and continue to cook until the cabbage is soft and tender and the pig's head is fully cooked through.

Devotees of pig's head would simply surround the pig's head with cabbage on a plate and serve this. However, for a less dramatic presentation and ease of carving, the bones can be removed and the pig's head cut into slices. Don't forget to give each person a piece of tongue and ear. The pig's ear is a particular favorite.

Pigs' Tails with Rutabaga

Serves 6

6 pigs' tails
1 rutabaga, peeled and cut into
   1-inch cubes
a generous knob of butter
salt and freshly ground pepper

Pigs' tails are irreverently known in Cork as "slash farts" or "pigs' mud-guards," they are still available in Cork's English Market. Mrs Cullinane cooked these pigs' tails for me in her home in Ballymacoda and very tasty they were too.

Cover the pigs' tails with cold water, bring to a boil, then discard the water. Cover with fresh water and bring to a boil again.

Add the rutabaga to the pot, cover, and continue to cook until the pigs' tails are soft and tender and the rutabaga is fully cooked.

Remove the tails and keep aside. Mash the rutabaga with a generous lump of butter. Season. Put in a hot bowl and serve the pigs' tails on top.

Brawn

Serves 16–20

half a salted pig's head
1 free-range chicken
6 peppercorns
2 carrots, sliced
2 onions, sliced
1 rib of celery (optional)
a sprig of thyme
a few parsley stalks
3–4 tablespoons chopped fresh
   parsley and thyme
6 coriander seeds (optional)

2 ×1-quart pudding bowls

Making a brawn, head cheese, or collared head was a way of using up stray bits of pork and offal, and the wonderful gelatine that is extracted held the meat together. Brawn keeps well in the refrigerator for several weeks, and is delicious with a salad or in a sandwich. I came across several recipes for brawn during my research. Most use a brined pig head as the basis, some add the trotters (or crubeens), others include some ox tongue or boiled chicken. The cooking liquor is flavored with the addition of carrot, onion, celery, and a bouquet garni. Others added nutmeg and other spices.

Brawn was known by a variety of names in Ireland; it was also called collared head and pig's head cheese. The ingredients vary, with some including only pig's head, as in the 1810 recipe for "A Pretty Collar" from Mocollop Castle, outside Waterford (see opposite); others press pig's cheek and feet; while other recipes include pig's head, feet, and sheep's tongues. Our grandparents would be amused to note that brawn is making a comeback and now appears regularly on the menus of trendier restaurants.

Wash the pig's head, remove the brain, and discard. Put the head into a saucepan and cover with cold water. Bring to a boil then discard the water. Bring to a boil in fresh water and cook for 3–4 hours or until the meat is soft and tender and parting from the bones.

Meanwhile, put the chicken into another saucepan. Add the carrots and onions, celery (if you have it to spare), parsley stalks, and sprig of thyme. Add about 2½ inches cold water and a few peppercorns. Cover, bring to a boil, and cook until the bird is tender.

When both meats are cooked, remove them from the cooking liquid and take the meat from the bones. Skin the chicken and chop it and the pig's head into pieces. Mix the meats together and add the chopped parsley and thyme leaves. Taste and correct the seasoning.

Pack the meat into one large or two small pudding bowls and add a little of the cooking liquid from each pot. Press with a weight.

When cold, turn out and serve in slices with a salad. Brawn will keep for several weeks in the refrigerator.

This recipe was taken from the receipt book of Mrs Dot Drew from Ballyduff, Co. Waterford, dated 1810:

"The face and feet and ears of a pig put in salt a day or two wash them very clean and have them quite free from hairs and put them to boil in a little water. Slip out the bones and put em back in the water they were boil'd in and let em boil like in a good thick jelly. Cut up the meat in small pieces and season it with pepper salt and allspice. Cut some of gristle of the ear small. Have just warm some of the jelly and stir in some minced meat … Put it in a basin or mug to shape it."

The preparation of collared head is also recalled by Mary O'Brien in The Farm by Lough Gur:

"From pig's heads she made brawn or collared head … the little girls helped—hindered—her as she went about her preparations. We—and mother—made collared head, boiling part of the meat almost to jelly, then chopped the meat very small and spiced it with pepper, allspice and finely ground nutmeg. Then we put it in a mould which opened on a hinge and we kept shut with a skewer. Then it was set and turned out of the shape. It made a dish fit for a King."

Serves 15 (approximately)

1 whole pig's head (2 half-heads)
1 ox tongue
2 medium onions, finely chopped
1 level tablespoon salt
2 teaspoons pepper
1 level tablespoon allspice

Collared Head

Sister Bernadette from the Presentation Convent, Crosshaven, Co. Cork, sent me her favorite recipe for collared head.

Soak the heads in cold, salted water for 24 hours. Place in a large pan, cover with cold water and cook until very tender. Let cool in the water. They should be so well cooked that you will need to take them up with both hands. Leave overnight. Next day gather the pig's jelly around the heads and on the dish. You will need ⅔ cup, so if not sufficient get the remainder from the pot in which they were cooked. Skin the pig's head and remove the meat from the bone. Cut the meat into ¼-inch pieces, fat and lean as it comes.

On the same day as you cook the pig's heads, cook the ox tongue in a pan of simmering water until very tender and let cool in the water. Next day, skin and cut up in small pieces (do not use the fat). Mix with the pig's head meat.

Heat the reserved pig's jelly in a large pot and add the onion. Mix the salt, pepper, and spice with the meat and add to the pot. Bring to blood heat, but do not boil. Stir gently to prevent burning, but do not overstir.

As collared head containers are no longer sold, I got a handyman to prepare an empty pea or bean can (6lb) for me. He bored a circular row of holes around the base plus across and two rows of holes lengthwise down the sides. I kept the lid of the can. Put the mixture into the can, cover, and press with a half brick or old iron until all the fat has oozed out through the holes. Put on a dry dish and leave to drain for 24 hours.

To turn out, place the pan on the side of the cooker (low heat) for about 5 minutes and insert a flat knife around the sides of the can. Turn out onto a plate and store, covered. It will keep in the refrigerator for up to 10 days.

Collared head and brawn are good eaten with soda bread and butter and a simple salad. Nowadays, a variety of relish and chutneys are also served as an accompaniment.

Margaret Moriarty's Crubeens with Cabbage

Crubeens can still be bought around Cork City and I was delighted to hear that the stalls of the Old English Market in Cork often sell out of crubeens. O'Flynns of Marlboro Street, with true Cork wit, label the crubeens in the window of their butcher's shop "low mileage pig's trotters." This recipe for crubeens was supplied by Mrs Margaret Moriarty from Cahiracruttera, Inch, Co. Kerry:

"When I see the dry brown objects offered for sale in shops and vans, I realize they bear little resemblance in color, and I am sure in taste, to the crubeens that were dished up to us many years ago.

'Crubeens and cabbage' were 'on the menu' in our house when there was a plentiful supply of hard white cabbage heads in the haggard. Here's how my mother cooked them."

First the crubeens—six or seven were washed and scraped, put into a skillet, and covered with cold water to which a good drop of vinegar was added. The skillet was hung over the fire until the water boiled. Then it was removed—the water poured off—the crubeens taken out—and the nails (loosened then) were removed. They were washed again, put back in the skillet, covered with fresh cold water, and brought to a boil. After a few minutes boiling, the cabbage, crisp and washed, was ready to be put in. When the water was boiled up again, the skillet was removed, and put by the side of the fire—sitting on a few live coals where it simmered for at least 3 hours until dinner time (no fast cooking as we are told to do cabbage now). By dinner time the crubeens were beautifully soft, white pink, and juicy and flavored with the cabbage, which in turn was flavored and glazed with the gelatine off the crubeens.

At dinner we each had a crubeen lying on a bed of lovely cabbage (not a dry crubeen on one side of the plate and a heap of dry cabbage on the other), plus a dish of potatoes boiled in their jackets and bursting at the seams.

Crubeens

Salted pigs' trotters, known in many parts of the country as crubeens, became widely available with the establishment of the commercial bacon factories in Cork, Waterford, Limerick, Dublin, and Belfast in the latter half of the 19th century. Cork was a major provisioning port and crubeens were exported in huge quantities to the West Indies. Up to the 1940s it was commonplace to see women selling cooked crubeens from baskets in the city streets. According to the historian Eamonn Mac Thomáis, crubeens in Dublin were known as "Georges Street mouth organs," after the highly regarded pork butcher's shop located there.

Big pots of crubeens were cooked up and served in pubs, particularly on Saturday nights and fair days. Canny pub owners were not altogether unaware of the fierce thirst that these tasty little morsels provoked! Crubeens were eaten with the fingers—a thoroughly greasy and messy business—and washed down with copious quantities of beer or porter. The grease proved to be difficult to remove from the glasses, which was the primary reason why some of the classier pubs decided to discontinue this original Irish pub grub. Crubeens, though still available, are not now as widespread.

Roast Pork Hocks

Serves 4–6

2 tablespoons sea salt
4 whole cloves
4 juniper berries
10 black peppercorns
4 fresh pork hocks or knuckles

For this recipe you need to use fresh pork hocks, not brined. If you use brined pork it will be too salty when roasted.

Grind the salt, cloves, juniper berries, and peppercorns in a mortar and pestle until fairly fine. Put the hocks into a deep dish. Rub the salt and spice mixture over all the sides of the hocks; refrigerate for 24 hours.

Preheat the oven to 300°F. Cook the hocks until the outsides are golden, about 2½ hours. Increase the heat to 450°F for 10–15 minutes to crisp them up. Let rest before serving. Serve with red or white cabbage and champ.

Ham Hock and Split Pea Soup

Serves 8–10

1 x 1½lb ham hock
1 bay leaf
1 medium onion, halved
1 carrot, cut in two
2½ cups yellow split peas
generous ½ gallon (4¼ pints) water
    or light chicken stock
2 tablespoons extra-virgin olive oil
2 medium onions, chopped
4 ribs of celery, chopped into
    ½-inch dice
4 medium carrots, chopped
2 leeks, thinly sliced
2 garlic cloves, chopped
2 teaspoons thyme leaves
scant 1½ cups canned chopped
    tomatoes
freshly ground pepper
a good pinch of sugar
fresh parsley, chopped, to serve

For this recipe you can use green (unsmoked) or smoked ham hocks; there is lots of meat on them as well as rind and sweet fat. Eat everything; each element has a different flavor and texture.

Put the ham hock, bay leaf, halved onion, and carrot pieces into a saucepan, and cover with the water or light chicken stock. Bring to a boil and simmer for 1 hour. Add the split peas and simmer for a further 1½ hours until the meat and split peas are tender.

Meanwhile, heat the olive oil in a medium saucepan. Add the chopped onion, celery, carrots, leeks, garlic, and thyme leaves. Cover and sweat for 10–12 minutes on a gentle heat. Add the chopped tomatoes and juice, freshly ground pepper and sugar (it may not need salt), and continue to cook for a further 10 minutes.

When the ham hock and split peas are cooked, remove them from the cooking liquid and discard the bay leaf, onion, and carrot. Add the split peas and cooking liquid to the vegetable and tomato mixture.

Remove the skin from the ham hock and shred the meat and some of the succulent fat into bite-sized pieces. Add to the soup. Simmer for a further 5 minutes. Taste and add salt if necessary. Scatter lots of chopped parsley over the top, and serve.

Ham Hock with Colcannon and Parsley Sauce

One ham hock for just a few pence—a few dollars nowadays, but they are still inexpensive—would feed a hungry man.

Cook the ham hocks as above until the meat is almost falling off the bones. Serve with a generous helping of Colcannon (see page 152) and Parsley Sauce (see page 101).

Black Pudding

Ireland is still famous for its black and white puddings and sausages. Nowadays many butchers take great pride in producing their own specialties. The standard continues to rise, partly due to the National Competition in Black and White Pudding and Sausage Making, organized by the Irish Master Butchers' Federation every year. Black puddings may be stored in the refrigerator for 5–6 days. Black and white puddings were integral to the traditional Irish breakfast of pork sausages, tomatoes, bacon, and eggs (see page 119).

I found many recipes for black pudding, with countless regional and family variations on the basic theme. The main basic ingredient is the fresh blood from killing the pig. Some recipes use steel-cut oats, others whole wheat or breadcrumbs: these are all thickeners. Pearl barley is added to others, and chopped suet in some cases. Seasoning, spices, chopped onions, and herbs are also added in varying proportions. The mixture is stuffed into the small intestines.

At one point every butcher in villages and towns all over Ireland made black and white puddings, each one had his own secret recipe, which was closely guarded. Up to the late 1960s many still had their own abattoirs so the fresh blood and offal were readily available. However, once the stringent hygiene regulations began to be implemented in the 1970s, many abattoirs were closed so the butchers who persevered changed to using dried or frozen blood imported from Holland. This produced a less interesting product with a totally different and much less appealing texture. However, a few determined butchers battled on and continued to use fresh blood.

Jack McCarthy, a spirited butcher from Kanturk in North Co. Cork, the fourth in a five-generation family business, has a cult following for his puddings, some of which are totally traditional, others contain chocolate, chile, pistachio, honey... A special pudding to be served at the State Banquet in honor of Queen Elizabeth was created in Jack's shop from a recipe devised by chef Ross Lewis. Jack has also made a Boudin Bábóg, which has aphrodisiac properties attributed to the purity of the natural environment in the area, this is getting a lot of attention! A Christmas pudding with spices and fruit is also planned. Jack has won top prizes in national and international competitions. He could talk for Ireland about puddings and pork products, and explained to me about the regional differences. Kerry-style pudding is skinless and baked in a loaf pan and sold in squares, and within Kerry there are many distinct recipes from different parts of the county. Cork-style is a traditional horseshoe-shaped pudding made in the natural intestine casing that they call runners. In Kilkenny, cereal and onion are included in the pudding, but in Cork no visible cereal. Jack would like to gather together the myriad of recipes from traditional butcher shops, many of which are no longer in business, before they are lost forever.

The Confrérie des Chevaliers du Goûte-Boudin from France (Brotherhood of the Knights of the Black Pudding) visited Ireland for the first time in 2010 and knighted three Irish butchers, including Jack McCarthy who was awarded a gold medal for his cream and apple boudin. Willie Allshire, of Caherbeg Free Range Pork in West Cork, was the first Irish butcher to enter this competition. He won a gold medal in 2007 and a silver in 2010. Willie and his wife Avril rear free-range outdoor pigs on their farm. Sean Kelly from Newport, Co. Mayo, won a bronze medal for his traditional pudding made in his third-generation family butchers.

Drisheen, the famous Cork blood pudding made since medieval times, is just blood. Eileen Kenneally from Garryvoe and her brother Séamus O'Farrell recalled how their mother Johanna, now in her eighties, made drisheen and black pudding for their family's butcher shop O'Farrells in Midleton, Co. Cork. The drisheen was made with lamb's blood and sheep gut used for the casing, what their mother called "the bum gut." The blood was put into a spotless galvanized bucket she kept specially for the purpose. The top layer of blood had to be set like jelly, then she made a sign of the cross on top. Underneath the set layer was the liquid blood called the wine, which was strained into another bowl and used to make the drisheen. The gut was cleaned of any fat with the back of a knife so as not to tear it, then turned inside out. The blood was then filled into it, it was boiled and had to be carefully watched in case it burst. It was very pure with just natural ingredients.

Philip's Black Pudding

Makes 3 rings approximately

3 tablespoons sunflower oil
10oz fat bacon, cubed (approx.
    ¼ inch)
8oz onion (2 approx.), finely
    chopped
1 tablespoon finely chopped tansy
    or marjoram
5½oz pork fat, cut into ¼ inch dice
3¾ cups fresh pig's blood (see
    page 136)
1 teaspoon salt
½ teaspoon freshly ground pepper
generous 1¾ cups steel-cut oats
½ cup heavy cream
finely grated lemon zest from
    ½ organic lemon
1 teaspoon allspice
¼ teaspoon freshly grated nutmeg
¼ teaspoon cayenne pepper

This is Philip Dennhardt's delicious version, which he makes here at the school when we kill a pig. Many Irish people added the herb tansy to blood pudding and drisheen. Substitute marjoram if you can't source tansy.

Heat 1 tablespoon oil in a pan, add the cubed bacon, and cook on a medium heat until slightly crisp and golden. Transfer to a plate with a slotted spoon. Add the finely chopped onion to the pan and cook on a gentle heat until soft but not colored. Add the tansy or marjoram. Stir and pour into a strainer to let the fat drip off. Add the onion and tansy mixture to the bacon. Place the cubes of pork fat in the hot pan and toss for a minute or two, just until it starts to exude fat. Add to the bacon and onion.

Warm the blood gently in a heavy saucepan, just enough to bring it to room temperature. Add salt and freshly ground pepper. Stir and add the bacon, onion, fat, and oatmeal. Stir in the cream, lemon zest, and spices. Cook on a very low heat for 30–35 minutes. It must not boil or even approach a simmer. The oatmeal will plump up and expand and the texture will become firmer.

Have the prepared casings ready and tie the end of each length with cotton string. Put a plain piping tip into a pastry bag. Fill with the mixture and pipe into the casings. Be careful not to overfill the casings. Allow room for expansion, otherwise they will burst as they cook. Tie the end every 6–12 inches depending on the size you require. Prick each one in several places with a sterilized darning needle.

Put the rings in cold water. Bring very gently to a boil. The rings need to be poached gently for 30 minutes or more until they are firm to the touch. Handle gently, drain on kitchen paper. Cool quickly and let dry. Store in a refrigerator for 3–4 days.

To cook the black pudding, cut into thick slices and fry in a little butter or bacon fat on a gentle heat. Serve with applesauce made from dessert apples.

Casing

To prepare the casings for both black and white puddings, first separate the fat from the intestines. Cut the fat off with scissors (first removing the sweetbreads). Wash the intestines thoroughly under cold running water, let the water run through, then turn them inside out and repeat. Put into salt water until needed. Change the brine often, about 4 times a day. Drain and rinse before filling the casing. Cut up the fat that you remove from the intestines, wash it, and put it into salt water until needed. Change the water regularly as for the intestines to remove the blood. This fat is used for the black pudding.

White Pudding

Serves 10–12

pig's liver, lights (lungs), heart
    meat from belly of pig
scant 10½ cups whole wheat flour
about 18 cups breadcrumbs
    (about 4lb)
½ cup ground allspice
1 whole nutmeg, grated
2–3 teaspoons thyme
pinch of cayenne pepper
about ½ cup freshly ground pepper
    (to taste)
salt

White pudding does not use blood in the mixture. Traditionally the liver, lights (lungs), heart, and belly meat of the pig are used.

Boil the liver, lights, and heart until tender. Boil meat from the belly, and any other scraps left around when the pig is cut up, in about 1½ quarts water. Take up and keep water (for use in black puddings).

Grind all meat and boil together with the other spices. If you think the mixture is not dry enough, add more whole wheat flour and breadcrumbs. Fill into white pudding casings, cover with cold water, and boil gently for about 45 minutes. Put a tin plate in the bottom of the pot when boiling and add salt to water.

Blood

Blood is very nutritious and full of iron. All over the world there are examples of blood pudding in the traditional cooking lore of different countries, such as *boudin noir* in France, *morcilla* in Spain, and haggis in Scotland. People who may not have been able to afford meat could supplement their iron needs by eating blood pudding. In many parts of Ireland, Kerry, and Donegal in particular, during periods of famine when everything else had failed, the peasants had the habit of bleeding the cattle "which they had not the courage to steal." They sometimes added sorrel or steel-cut oats, or boiled it into a broth. "Kerry cows know Sunday" became a proverb, because it was to provide the Sunday dinner that they were bled.

In his Blasket Island's study, Malachy McKenna says that: "Pudding made from sheeps' blood was eaten along with a cup of tea in the morning." In general, this dish would have been eaten at Christmas, since this was when sheep were slaughtered on the Blaskets.

Duck Blood

Serves 6–8

scant 1½ cups duck or goose blood
salt and freshly ground pepper
⅓ cup finely chopped onion
⅔ cup fresh milk
2 tablespoons (¼ stick) butter

As soon as ducks were killed, their necks were cut and their blood collected in a bowl. This delicious mixture was made the next day.

Sprinkle the fresh blood with a little salt and leave in a cool place overnight. Next day put it into a heavy-bottomed saucepan with the onion, milk, and a lump of butter. Season with salt and freshly ground pepper. Cook on a low heat for about 20 minutes or until the mixture thickens and becomes similar to the texture of a soft scrambled egg. Do not boil.

Eat warm with fresh brown bread and butter. Spoon it up on top of the bread and eat it.

Goose Neck Pudding

Serves 6–8

scant 1 cup finely chopped onions
3 tablespoons (¼ stick plus
   1 tablespoon) butter
scant 1 cup breadcrumbs
⅔ cup rolled oats
¾ teaspoon salt
freshly ground pepper
1 flat teaspoon cinnamon
1 teaspoon mixed spice
1 level teaspoon ground nutmeg
blood from one goose (stir
   ½ teaspoon of salt into the
   blood as soon as it is taken
   from the goose; congealed blood
   can be kept in the fridge for
   a day or two)
1 goose liver, chopped
skin from the goose neck (optional)

Traditionally geese were killed around Michaelmas, Christmas, and the New Year. Jack O'Keeffe, whose mother came originally from the Sliabh Lúachra area on the borders of Cork and Kerry, showed me how to make this pudding, which has been passed down in his family for many generations.

Sweat the onions in the butter on a low heat. Put the breadcrumbs and oats into a bowl. Add salt, pepper, mixed spice, cinnamon, and nutmeg. Then add the onions and blood; mix and break up well. Stir in the chopped liver and mix again. Cook a tiny bit of the mixture and taste for seasoning.

If you are using the goose neck, turn it inside out and fill loosely with the mixture to allow for expansion. Knot the narrow end and sew the wide end to secure it tightly. Alternatively, fill the mixture into a pudding bowl, cover with a tight-fitting lid or a double thickness of parchment paper, and tie as for a steamed pudding.

Bring a saucepan of cold water to a boil and add 1 teaspoon salt. Prick the goose neck pudding with a darning needle and add to the saucepan of boiling water. Bring back to a boil and then reduce to a simmer. Cook for 1–1½ hours on a very low heat with the lid on, pricking during the cooking time also. If using a bowl, steam the pudding for 1½ hours in a covered saucepan.

The goose pudding will keep for a week or so in the refrigerator, or it may be frozen. Cut in thick slices and fry gently in a little butter—really delicious.

bag of lamb's intestines
1 gallon sheep's blood
1 ¼ cups half and half
1 ½ teaspoons salt
chopped tansy (optional)

Drisheen

Our local butcher Michael Cuddigan remembers when virtually every butcher in the Cork area made drisheen. He no longer sells it in his butcher's shop, but was delighted to come with a gallon of blood and a bag of intestines to show how he makes his much sought-after drisheen.

First we gave the casings a good rinse under the tap and Michael showed me how to turn them inside out. We then measured out 5 cups of the thin blood from the top and mixed it with the half and half and 1½ teaspoons of salt, adding a little chopped tansy. I tied the ends of the casings with cotton string and then, using a funnel, we filled them up and pressed out the air, allowing a little space for expansion during cooking.

The casings were then lowered into a saucepan of warm, well-salted water and brought gently to a boil. This process should not be hurried; it is necessary to keep the drisheen down in the water because they have a tendency to rise to the top. As soon as the water reaches boiling point, turn off the heat. The drisheen should feel firm to the touch. Carefully remove them to a large plate, let cool, then refrigerate and use as required.

To cook drisheen, put a ring of drisheen into warm salted water, and bring gently to almost boiling. Drain and cut into 3–4 inch lengths. Slit in half lengthwise and serve on very hot plates with melted butter and lots of white bread.

Drisheen in Cork Market

Hidden behind the city's main thoroughfare, Patrick Street, the former English Market in Cork is a bustling colorful hive of activity. Third- and fourth-generation traders sell vegetables, offal, and buttered eggs, side by side with "new age" sellers tempting their customers with a mélange of olives, sundried tomatoes, and exquisite Irish farmhouse cheeses. Just inside the huge archway at the Grand Parade end of the market is O'Reilly's stall, which sells tripe and drisheen—the famous Cork black pudding made from sheep's blood.

It is fascinating to observe the mix of customers. On a recent visit I noted not only Leeside natives, but also Chinese and German customers, devotees from Killarney and Macroom, and an elegantly dressed lady home on holidays from the United States after 50 years of absence from Cork. She was nostalgically buying drisheen to relive her childhood memories. In the background, 15lb of tripe and 10lb of drisheen were being packed for an exiled Cork man living in Dublin! He had sent a friend specially down by train to collect the precious order. There was much merriment around the stall when it was revealed that this man had "the misfortunate" to be married to a Dublin woman who refused point blank to cook him tripe or drisheen or to be in the house when it was cooked. However, the Corkman had hit on a solution. On "the wife's" night out, he would have a tripe and drisheen party for all his exiled Cork cronies.

I wonder whether he managed to find a bit of tansy in the Dublin suburbs, to spike the white sauce that is traditionally often served with drisheen? Mr Bell's stall in the Cork Market sells tansy, which originally was also added to the drisheen itself.

It is possible that drisheen has been available in Cork since the early medieval period, as a pudding called dressán is mentioned in the early 12th century tale *Aislinge Meic Con Glinne*. However, as Regina Sexton points out, it is more likely that the popularity of drisheen was established in the late 17th century. Between that time and 1825, the City of Cork was the largest center for the exportation of salted beef in the British Isles. Prior to shipment, the cattle were butchered in the City's slaughterhouses and the large quantities of blood were used in the preparation of puddings.

Tripe

Tripe is mentioned frequently in the early 12th century tale *Aislinge Meic Con Glinne* (*The Vision of Mac Conglinne*). It was a common and regularly available commodity in the shops of Cork City in 1649. Tripe also featured as an important item in the diet of the City's Franciscan friars throughout the 18th century. Traditionally the stomach tissue of sheep, pigs, and cows was consumed. Today, however, all tripe is invariably beef tripe. The most abundantly available comes from the first stomach, or rumen, and is termed "plain" or "blanket" tripe. More popular, but not always available, is the "honeycomb" which comes from the second stomach or reticulum. It is given its name because of its characteristic honeycombed texture. Tripe is an everyday dinner dish and is also served at Saturday tea-time. It is a very bland foodstuff and relies on the accompanying sauce for its flavor. Traditionally it was eaten with bread and butter and sherry, followed by tea and sweet cake.

Tripe and Onions

Serves 2–4

1lb tripe
1 small onion, peeled and sliced
cold milk—sufficient to cover
roux (see page 42)
salt and freshly ground pepper

This recipe was given to me by Michael Ryan of Isaacs Restaurant in Cork. This was how his father cooked tripe and onions.

Put the tripe into a saucepan, cover with a lid, and set aside for 5–10 minutes.
    Discard the liquid in the pot, add the sliced onion, and cover with cold milk. Simmer gently for about 1 hour until the tripe is tender. Strain off the milk into another pan and bring back to a boil. Whisk in the roux and season with salt and pepper. Pour back into the saucepan with the tripe and heat through. Check seasoning—it will take quite a bit of pepper.
    Serve on a slice of buttered white bread.

Variation
Tripe and Drisheen

After adding the thickened liquid back to the saucepan, you could if you wish add some drisheen to the tripe. Simply peel and slice some cooked drisheen, add it to the saucepan and heat through before serving. A generous sprinkling of parsley is a good, if not traditional, addition.

Tripe in Batter

Serves 4

8oz tripe
dripping
1 quantity batter (see page 63)

People who don't necessarily like the texture of boiled tripe enjoy it this way, cooked in crispy batter.

Wash the tripe very thoroughly in hot water. Put it into boiling water and simmer for 45–60 minutes or more, skimming well. When quite tender, remove the tripe, dry it, cut in pieces about 2 inches square, and cool. Heat the dripping in a skillet. When hot, dip the pieces of tripe into the batter and fry at once. Serve hot with a good mustard. Nowadays, tomato and chilli sauce is a great addition and perks it up.

PIE DOUGH
¾ cup plus 1½ tablespoons
   all-purpose flour
a pinch of salt
¼ cup (½ stick) butter, lard
   or dripping

PIE
1lb of beefsteak
a little flour
salt and freshly ground pepper
2 hard-boiled eggs
2oz bacon (cut thick if liked)
½ beef kidney
1¼ cups water or stock

Serves 6 (approximately)

1 beef heart
salt and freshly ground pepper
2½ cups beef stock
roux (see page 42)

STUFFING
⅓ cup (¾ stick) butter
1½ cups finely chopped onion
scant 3½ cups soft white
   breadcrumbs
1 tablespoon chopped chives
1 tablespoon thyme leaves
1 tablespoon annual marjoram
1 tablespoon chopped parsley
salt and freshly ground pepper

Variation
Sheeps' Hearts

Follow the same recipe. The
stuffing will be sufficient for
4–6 sheeps' hearts, but the
cooking time should be reduced
to about 1 hour. Sheeps' hearts
are more tender and juicy than
beef heart.

Steak and Kidney Pie

James Murphy from New Ross, Co. Wexford, sent me this 1907 recipe. It is interesting that eggs were used to make the meat in this pie go further.

"Cut the meat into thin strips, toss them in the flour adding pepper and salt on a plate. Roll them up with a lump of fat in the center, boil 2 eggs hard, then cut them up roughly. Cut the bacon into rough lumps, wash the kidney having removed the skin and core, and toss it also in the flour. Put all into a pie dish and pour over the stock, then cover the pie with pie dough.

   To make the pie dough, put the flour in a basin, mix in the salt and one-third of the butter, wet all to a light dough. Turn onto a floured board or table and knead into a round ball. Roll out, spread half of the pie dough with the remaining butter, fold over the other half. Then press the edges, turn the pie dough round so that the open edges are top and bottom, roll out the pie dough into a straight strip. Fold it in 3 and turn it, then roll it larger than the pie dish. Cut a strip from it all round, wet the edges of the pie dish, put on a strip cut side out, wet the strip all round, place the remaining pie dough over the pie and fasten it at the edges by pressing down on the strip already on. Make a hole at the other side to allow bad gases to escape. Decorate the top with some leaves and a pie dough rose. Put the pie into a moderate oven (350°F) and bake for 1 hour or longer according to size."

Stuffed Beef Heart

In former times fanciful names were created to disguise the true nature of the dish and to add a sense of intrigue. One such name for stuffed hearts was "Love in Disguise," which was sure to confuse the diner.

Trim the heart and cut away the "plumbing" to make a nice pocket. Wash thoroughly in cold salted water; dry well.

   Next make the stuffing. Sweat the onions in the butter for about 10 minutes until soft. Then stir in the breadcrumbs, herbs, and a little salt and pepper to taste. Let cool.

   Season the inside of the heart with salt and freshly ground pepper. Fill with the fresh herb stuffing, piling the extra on the top. Cover with a butter wrapper and tie with cotton string if necessary. Put into a deep roasting pan or casserole and add the beef stock. Season with salt and freshly ground pepper. Cover and bake in a moderate oven at 350°F for about 3–3½ hours or until the meat is cooked and tender.

   When the beef heart is fully cooked, remove carefully to a serving dish. Bring the cooking liquid to a boil, thicken with a very little roux, and correct the seasoning to taste. Strain into a sauceboat and serve with the sliced stuffed heart. Accompany with cabbage.

Stuffed Sheep's Heart

This recipe is based on one in Lessons in Cookery and Housewifery, *1901. This little book belonged to Rosalie Dunne's great-aunt, Bridget Hanlon, who lived in Courtwood, Co. Laois, in a lovely thatched cottage near the canal, with her brother Patrick who worked for the Grand Canal Company.*

"Wash the hearts well in salt and water; cut a hole in the centre of each; put in the stuffing; truss the hearts with cotton string; roast for 30–45 minutes in a moderate oven, basting frequently. For the gravy, skim the fat from the tin, leaving the juices. Pour boiling water on the tin, season with pepper and salt; boil up the gravy; pour it over the heart. For the stuffing you need 3 tablespoons bread crumbs; 1 tablespoon chopped parsley; pepper, salt (if liked); a little onion; some melted dripping; 1 tablespoon chopped suet. Mix all together; moisten with dripping; fill up the heart."

Fried Lamb's Liver

When butchers killed animals in their own abattoirs, there was a certain day to collect the liver, when a lamb would have been recently killed. When a lamb was killed, locals lined up to buy liver on the following day; freshness was considered to be of vital importance. It would be sliced in ½-inch thick slices, tossed in seasoned flour, and fried very briefly in butter or bacon fat. Delicious! Here is Doris Bewley's description of how to do it from her 1932 cookery notes:

"All internal organs must be thoroughly washed and sinews removed. Fry the bacon. Coat the liver with seasoned flour. Add sufficient dripping to the pan to come half way up the liver. Fry until a golden brown on one side and then turn to the other. Serve with brown sauce (if desired)."

Sheep's Liver

In parts of Ireland the liver of the newly killed sheep was put in one piece on the tongs over the embers of the open fire and roasted. Ellen O' Sullivan from Bantry, Co. Cork, told me that they used to fight over it as children. Her family lived about 10 miles from the nearest habitation, so they were virtually self-sufficient. They killed a sheep several times a year and every scrap was eaten.

lambs' tails (allow 2 per person)
salt

Lambs' Tails

I had never heard of lambs' tails being eaten until I began work on this book. However, Lil O' Connell from North Tipperary told me of how her husband Bob loved "a feed" of lambs' tails a few times a year. She remembers dreading it because there were so many lambs tails to be skinned and cooked—none were to be wasted. The lambs would have been about two months old. I mentioned this on a radio programme and several other people telephoned to say that they, too, had recollections of lambs' tails being eaten. Everybody assured me they were wonderful to eat, and smell sweet and delicious.

Peel the tails, wash, and cook in boiling salted water for about 45 minutes or until the meat is soft and tender. Serve with bread and butter.

Lil explained how the tails were traditionally eaten: "rub butter on both sides, sprinkle with salt and eat like corn on the cob; sweet and delicious."

Note: Ann Kennedy, of Rostrevor, tells me that friends of hers in Gloucestershire, who have many sheep, prepare lambs' tails by coating them with crumbs and deep-frying. She writes: "I've never tasted anything so delicious."

Baked Liver and Bacon

Serves 2–4

½lb lamb's liver
4 slices of bacon
¾–1 cup homemade stock,
    for cooking

STUFFING
2 tablespoons soft white
    breadcrumbs
1 teaspoon chopped parsley
1 teaspoon chopped onion
a pinch of mixed dried herbs
    (fresh herbs may of course be
    substituted)
2 teaspoons chopped suet (butter
    or margarine may be substituted)
salt and freshly ground pepper
stock or milk, to moisten

This dish was taught in the school cookery classes for many years, until the 1960s at least, and makes a very tasty supper dish. Here is Lily O'Reilly's recipe from her 1940s notebook.

To make the stuffing, put the breadcrumbs, parsley, onion, and herbs in a bowl. Add the suet, pepper, and salt, and moisten with a little stock or milk.

Cut the liver into strips about ½-inch thick, wash in cold water, and dry. Place on a greased baking dish and spoon the stuffing over it. Remove the rind from the bacon, thin out with a knife, and put on top of the stuffing. Pour on the stock, cover with parchment paper, and bake in a moderate oven (350°F) for about 30 minutes. When cooked, lift onto a hot dish and pour a little of the sauce around.

Roast Lamb Kidneys

Serves 4

4 lamb kidneys in suet
sea salt

Roast kidneys are moist and succulent. This is a traditional method of cooking them; I use our old Aga, but it works as well in a conventional oven.

Preheat the oven to 450°F. Put the kidneys on a rack in a roasting pan and cook for 30–40 minutes or until much of the fat has rendered and the outside is crisp and brown. Split in half, sprinkle with sea salt, and serve with soda bread or toast.

Skirts and Kidneys

Serves 2–4

3 onions
2lb pig's skirts (membrane
    separating the stomach from
    the heart and lungs)
2 pigs' kidneys
salt and freshly ground pepper
seasoned all-purpose flour
water
mashed potatoes and swede
    turnips, to serve

This recipe for a much-loved Cork dish was given to me by the late Eileen Aherne, a well-known fruit and vegetable stallholder in the Cork Market, who enjoyed it every week of her life.

Slice the onions thickly. Remove the membrane from the skirts, and cut each one into 2-inch pieces. Split the kidneys, remove the "plumbing," and cut into 1-inch pieces. Wash, dry well, and toss both skirts and kidneys in seasoned flour. Put the meat and sliced onions into a saucepan, cover with water, and bring to a boil. Simmer for 1–1½ hours or until soft. Serve with mashed potatoes and swede turnips.

1 pickled ox tongue
cold water

Pickled Ox Tongue

Amhlaoibh Uí Shúileabháin records in his diary for Shrove Tuesday, 1831, that he bought "six neats' tongues to preserve for Easter," and every country house sideboard would have featured pickled ox tongue occasionally. There's a great saying around Cork, often applied to someone out of favor (particularly after a night of liquid socializing!): "Ah, there'll be nothin' but hot tongue and cold shoulder for you for dinner!"

Cover the pickled tongue with cold water and bring to a boil. Cover the saucepan and simmer for 4–5 hours (depending on size), or until the skin will easily peel off the tip of the tongue. Remove from the pot and reserve the liquid. As soon as the tongue is cool enough to handle, peel off the skin, and remove all the little bones at the neck end. Sometimes I use a skewer to prod the meat to make sure that no bones are left behind. Curl the tongue and press it into a small plastic bowl. Pour a little of the cooking liquid over the tongue, put a side plate or saucer on top, and weigh it down. Serve it thinly sliced, with Horseradish Sauce (see page 106) and Pickled Beets (see page 183).

Note: pickled ox tongue will keep for up to a week in the refrigerator.

To Pickle Ox Tongue

Of course you can order a pickled ox tongue from your butcher, but it's easy and rewarding to do it yourself.

To pickle one or two fresh ox tongues, choose a stainless-steel saucepan. Put in 1½ gallons of water and 3½ cups salt. Stir the brine to dissolve the salt. Cut away any excess fat from the tongue and discard. If the forked bones that connect the root of the tongue to the rest of the animal are still attached to the tongue, carve them out and discard them too. Turn the tongue so that the underside faces up. Cut a 1-inch slit in the length of the tongue and pack it with salt. Put the tongue or tongues into the brine and let them cure for 5 days. Remove from the brine. (To cook the tongue, see below.)

Variation
Spiced Ox Tongue

Spiced tongue was a common 19th-century dish on the tables of the Irish middle classes. It was spiced with cloves and flavored with onion, thyme, parsley, salt and pepper.

In Cork, spiced ox tongue is available just before Christmas, when a few tongues are thrown into the spice barrel. Mr Bresnan in Cork Market spices tongues for me occasionally and they have been much enjoyed, not just at Christmas but on summer picnics also. Cook as for pickled ox tongue.

Potatoes

There is a long-established belief that Sir Walter Raleigh introduced the potato into Ireland in 1588, planting the first crop in his garden at Myrtle Grove in Youghal, Co. Cork. While Redcliffe Salaman, in his authoritative work *The History and Social Influence of the Potato*, suggests that potatoes may have been introduced into Ireland from plundered ships of the Spanish Armada, which were wrecked on the west coast. However, the historian Margaret Crawford tells us that the earliest reliable reference to potato cultivation in Ireland dates to a 1606 land deed from Co. Down. Within a century of its introduction, the potato was a common item in the Irish diet.

The potatoes beloved of the Irish are not the waxy varieties, but the dry ones, whose skins crack towards the end of cooking—referred to as "balls of flour" or "smiling spuds." Damp, waxy potatoes are still scorned in Ireland as being "wet" or "soapy." One of the finest sights in Ireland around the end of July and the beginning of August, is fields of potatoes in full bloom—a sea of pale purple and white blossom. The famous "Ballycotton potatoes" are much sought after in the English Market in Cork. The Irish Seed Savers Association has rescued some of the older traditional varieties, which suit the particular conditions in the part of the country where they originated.

The Potato and the Famine

Whatever its origin, the potato was certainly in Ireland by the early 17th century. It had already made its way to Europe and England at an earlier date, where it was viewed as a botanical curiosity for some time and was only slowly embraced as a novel vegetable. By contrast, the potato in Ireland quickly gained phenomenal popularity. The Irish climate is ideally suited to potato cultivation. The crop thrives in a cool damp environment and delights in the dark and crumbly soils of Ireland. Potato growing, when compared to cereal husbandry, was less laborious and infinitely more rewarding. Once set, the potato crop looked after itself and needed little attention until the harvest in August. It also returned greater yields per acre than grain crops. With only an acre or two of land a farmer could grow enough potatoes to support his whole family. A system of cultivation called the "lazy-bed" system developed—wide raised beds were cultivated by hand or with a distinctive spade known as a "loy" or "fack." They were enriched with manure from the milch cow or pig, and sometimes, in coastal regions, also with seaweed and shells.

The potato was also welcomed as a comforting crop offering food security after famine and plague had wreaked havoc throughout Ireland in the late 16th and 17th centuries. The clash of the Gaelic Irish with incoming settlers had seen the destruction of property, crops, and cattle. In addition, there had been catastrophic rains in the 1580s, which destroyed much of the corn harvest.

The insipid, abrasive oatencake was quickly usurped by the superior taste and texture of potatoes laced with buttermilk and melting butter. Such was the taste for potatoes that in preFamine Ireland the average cottier, or landless laborer, consumed anything between 7–14 pounds of potatoes per day. Arthur Young, writing his *Tour in Ireland* in the late 18th century, observed "six people, a man, his wife, and four children, will eat eighteen stone of potatoes a week or 252lb." The Poor Enquiry Commission recorded the following sentiment from a small Co. Down farmer in the 1830s: "a stone of potatoes is little enough for a man in a day and he'd want something with it to work upon."

Usually potatoes were simply boiled over the open fire and delivered to the table ungarnished. It is said that many peasants cultivated an extra long thumbnail with which to peel the potatoes. The potato could then be perched upon the nail point and conveniently dipped into buttermilk or other condiments. All the historical references highlight that potatoes were most commonly eaten with buttermilk or milk. Mustard was also popular and onion dip, a simply prepared sauce of onions, milk, flour, and butter, was served as an accompaniment to potatoes well into this century. For those who could afford it, a herring or piece of meat was boiled with the potatoes to stretch the dish and impart additional flavor. Pots of boiling meat and broth were nothing strange to the Irish, but once the potato was added, the country's most famous traditional dish, Irish stew, was born (see page 99). Similarly, introducing the potato to the iron griddle heralded the arrival of the equally traditional potato cakes, boxty, and fadge (see pages 158–160).

Potatoes were even recommended as a remedy against infertility. Reverend Maunsell, writing in his treatise *On the Culture of Potatoes from the Shoots* (1794) describes the potato as "the most fruitful root we have; its fructifying quality is visible in every cabbin you pass by… Doctor Lloyd… frequently recommended potatoes as a supper to those ladies whom providence had not yet blessed with children, and an heir has often been the consequence."

On a more serious note, the evidence strongly suggests that the potato was indeed responsible for the staggering expansion of the Irish population between the late 18th century and the 1840s. In 1780, the population was around four million. By the 1841 Census, the figure had risen to 8,175,125. This unprecedented growth in the population is attributed to improved diet; potatoes and buttermilk, though monotonous and bland, were an excellent source of protein, fat, and carbohydrate and also supplied most of the minerals and vitamins, particularly vitamin C, necessary for health and vigor.

The monotony of the potato diet was offset by the abundance of the crop. However, by the early 19th century, the demands of a swelling population, coupled with soil exhaustion and years of severe frost, resulted in poor potato yields and severe food shortages. By 1845 the people were accustomed to recurrent crop failures and when one-third of the crop was lost in that year, it was viewed as just another bad harvest. However, recognizing the impending crisis, Sir Robert Peel, the British Prime Minister, purchased £100,000 worth of maize in the autumn of 1845. The corn went on sale in March 1846 and those who could afford it could buy it for a penny a pound. Nicknamed "Peel's Brimstone," it was not popular. People did not know how to prepare it. Many people fell ill after eating improperly cooked corn and the Government was forced to issue pamphlets warning against these dangers.

In 1846, the people once again set their tubers and looked forward to an improved harvest. However, the fungal disease *Phytophthora infestans*, which had destroyed much of the crop in 1845, was to deliver its worst blow. By September 1846, over two-thirds of the entire crop was lost. Further bad harvests in 1847 and 1848 saw famine and disease sweep through the laboring and poorer classes.

Deprived of their sole means of existence, the peasantry were forced to exploit the food resources of the wild. Starving bands, if they had the energy to do so, migrated to coastal regions and picked the shores bare of shellfish and edible seaweeds. Others scavenged the woods and fields, collecting nuts, wild vegetation, and roots. Often the pulp of rotting potatoes was squeezed out and mixed with meal in a vain attempt to make boxty bread on the griddle. The cattle of wealthy farmers were stolen and slaughtered for food at night time, so that the smell of boiled meat would go undetected. Inland waterways were drained of all they could offer, but effective fishing, in particular deep-sea fishing, was impossible, for many people had been obliged to pawn or sell their boats and fishing tackle for cash, following the 1845 crisis.

In 1847 the Temporary Relief Act or Soup Kitchen Act saved many from starvation and death, but it was ill equipped to cope with the enormous numbers of distressed and destitute. Scenes of unprecedented suffering, like those described by Mr Nicholas Cummins, a leading Cork merchant, were nationwide. He describes his visit to West Cork in 1846:

"I entered some of the hovels… In the first, six famished and ghastly skeletons, to all appearance dead, were huddled in a corner in some filthy straw, their sole covering what seemed to be a ragged horsecloth and their wretched legs hanging about, naked above the knees. I approached with horror and found by a low moaning they were alive; they were in fever—four children, a woman and what once had been a man … in a few minutes I was surrounded by at least 200 of such phantoms, such frightful spectres as no words can describe. By far the greater number were delirious, either from famine or from fever."

The wretched famine years of 1847–48 are also recalled in Mary O'Brien's *The Farm by Lough Gur*:

"It was heart-breaking … to see poor people tottering to the door, half-fainting, swaying on their skeleton feet, as they held out little bags for the crust or a spoonful of flour—all we had to give them. One old man was found dead in the turnip garden: too weak to pull it up… little children died on the floor of the cabin where they slipped from the weak arms of their mother… it wasn't only starvation, more died from typhus and other diseases brought about by want, than lack of food. Corn, which came at last, and maize meal, sent from America, saved those who were still alive."

By the time of the 1851 Census the population of Ireland was reduced to six million. Over one million people had died as a direct result of famine and fever and a further two million had been forced to emigrate. The tragic consequences of dependence upon one key foodstuff had been realized only too graphically.

In the 18th, 19th, and even into the 20th century, potatoes were usually boiled, largely due to the scarcity of cooking utensils. Even prosperous farming households would have cooked over the fire, in a big black three-legged pot—a griddle, pot oven, a kettle, and skillet being the only other cooking implements. The potatoes were boiled in their jackets and served heaped up in the center of the table in a wooden frame or, more commonly, in a round shallow basket made from sally saplings (peeled osiers). Local names for this varied around the country, a *sciob* in Cork, a *sciath* in Kilkenny, a *ciseóg* in Galway, and a *scuttle* in Clare.

Olive Sharkey, in her book *Old Days, Old Ways*, recounts her father's memories of his potato dinners:

"The potato dinner was always the favourite meal in his home, years ago, with everyone reaching hungrily for the spuds the moment my grandmother placed them in their basket on the table. It was essential that everyone learn to peel their potatoes quickly or they might miss out, the greedy, skilful peelers hoarding up little caches of spuds on their plates before actually tucking in."

Champp

Like many other simple peasant dishes, champ has stood the test of time. It now features on the menus of fashionable restaurants in London, Paris, and New York. As with Ireland's other great potato dish, colcannon (see page 152), there are many regional variations. Ulster is a particularly rich source of recipes.

A huge quantity of potatoes were boiled for each meal in the big black pot over the open fire. The pounding of the potatoes, using a heavy wooden pounder called a beetle, was usually men's work. Florence Irwin, in *Irish Country Recipes* (1937), gives a wonderfully evocative picture of the laborious procedure:

"The man of the house was summoned when all was ready, and while he pounded this enormous potful of potatoes with a sturdy wooden beetle, his wife added the potful of milk and nettles, or scallions, or chives, or parsley and he beetled it 'till it was as smooth as butter, not a lump anywhere. Everyone got a large bowlful, made a hole in the centre, and into this put a large lump of butter. Then the champ was eaten from the outside with a spoon or fork, dipping it into the melted butter in the centre."

A common folk custom was to offer a bowl of champ to the fairies at Halloween. This would be left on field posts or under trees, such as hawthorns or whitethorns, which were particularly associated with fairies.

Serves 4

6–8 unpeeled russet or round
   white potatoes
4oz scallions (3–4 approx.),
   use the bulb and green stem,
   or 1½oz chives
1½ cups milk
¼–½ cup (½–1 stick) approx. butter
salt and freshly ground pepper

Champ

Potatoes could be relied on to satisfy hearty appetites, and in farming households, milk and butter would usually have been plentiful. One of the best-loved ways of cooking potatoes was (and is) to mash them with boiling milk, add chopped scallions or chives, and serve this creamy, green-flecked mixture with a lump of yellow butter melting in the center. Champ was economical as well as nutritious and tasty. Also, no shopping was required, since all the ingredients were to hand. I came across many regional variations on the champ theme, some called by different names. Champ is best made with the traditional main crop potato varieties, like Maris Piper and Desiree. Leeks, nettles, peas, and brown crispy onions are all delicious additions.

Scrub the potatoes and boil them in their jackets. Chop finely the scallions or chives. Cover the scallions/chives with cold milk and bring slowly to a boil. Simmer for about 3–4 minutes, then turn off the heat and let infuse. Peel and mash the freshly boiled potatoes and, while hot, mix with the boiling milk and onions. Beat in some of the butter. Season to taste with salt and freshly ground pepper. Serve in one large or 4 individual bowls with a generous knob of butter melting in the center.

Champ may be put aside and reheated later in a moderate oven at 350°F. Cover with aluminum foil while it reheats so that it doesn't get a skin.

Variations

Parsley Champ

Add 2–3 tablespoons freshly chopped parsley to the milk, bring to a boil for 2–3 minutes only, to preserve the fresh taste and color. Beat into the mashed potatoes and serve hot.

Dulse (Seaweed) Champ

Soak a couple of fists of the seaweed in cold water for 1 hour or more. Drain and stew in milk until tender, about 3 hours. Add a good knob of butter and some pepper and beat into the mashed potato. Taste and correct the seasoning. Serve hot.

Wild Garlic Champ

Add 2–3oz chopped wild garlic to the milk just as it comes to a boil. Beat into the mashed potatoes.

Parsnip Champ

Cook the parsnip separately in boiling salted water. Mash well and add to the mashed potato. Half and half is a good proportion, but it can be less or more.

Claragh Champ

I am indebted to Deborah Shorley for this recipe, which she calls Claragh Champ after the locality in which she first tasted it. We call it Ulster Champ down here.

When we were children, we were always told as we peeled our potatoes that Cork people ate their spuds "skin and all." As in this recipe, I prefer to cook the potatoes in their jackets rather then peeling them first.

Serves 8

4lb russet or round white
   potatoes, scrubbed
¼–½ cup (½–1 stick) butter
2½ cups milk
scant 3 cups young peas,
   shelled weight
8 tablespoons chopped parsley
salt and freshly ground pepper

Cook the potatoes in boiling salted water until tender; drain well and dry over the heat in the pan for a few minutes. Peel and mash with most of the butter while hot. Meanwhile bring the milk to a boil and simmer the peas until just cooked, about 8–10 minutes. Add the parsley for the final 2 minutes of cooking. Add the hot milk mixture to the potatoes. Season well and beat until creamy and smooth.

Serve piping hot with a lump of butter melting in the center.

1½lb russet or round white
   potatoes (3–4 approx)
1 teacup chopped nettle tops
1¼ cups milk
2–4 tablespoons (¼–½ stick) butter
salt and freshly ground pepper

Nettle Champ

Nettles have been valued in Ireland since ancient times, not only as a food, but also as a purifier of the blood. The belief is still strong, particularly among older people in the country, that one should have at least three dinners of nettles in April and May to clear the blood and keep away the "rheumatics" for the coming year. No doubt this was popular during April and May when the young nettles were at their best. It was a good way of getting the goodness of the nettles into the diet, as well as a seasonal treat.

Scrub the potatoes and cook in boiling salted water until tender. Meanwhile, chop the young nettle tops and cook in the milk for about 20 minutes. As soon as the potatoes are cooked, drain and peel immediately while they are still hot. Mash until soft and free of lumps. Pour in the boiling milk and the nettles and a good lump of butter. Beat the mixture until soft and creamy. Season with salt and freshly ground pepper.
   Serve hot with a lump of butter melting into the center.

Serves 4

1lb russet or round white potatoes
   (3 approx.)
12oz leeks (1–2 approx.)
2–4 tablespoons (¼–½ stick) butter
1 cup plus 1–3 tablespoons milk
salt and freshly ground pepper

Leek Champ

This is another really delicious version of champ—less well known than the others. I came across it in Ulster, but it is now also firmly entrenched in Cork.

Scrub the potatoes and cook in boiling salted water until cooked through. Meanwhile, wash and slice the leeks into thin rounds. Melt 2 tablespoons of the butter in a heavy pot, toss in the leeks, and season with salt and freshly ground pepper. Cover with a butter wrapper and the lid of the saucepan. Cook on a gentle heat until soft and tender.
   As soon as the potatoes are cooked, drain them thoroughly. Peel the potatoes and mash immediately. Bring the milk to boiling point. Beat the buttered leeks and their juices into the potatoes with enough boiling milk to make a soft texture. Season with salt and freshly ground pepper.
   Serve immediately with a lump of butter melting in the center.

Serves 4–6

beef dripping or butter
2–3 large onions cut into ¼-inch
   wide rings
1 quantity champ (see page 148)

Champ and Crispy Onions

My late mother Elizabeth O'Connell told me about this dish, which she remembered having as a child in Co. Kilkenny on Fridays, when eating meat was forbidden by the Church.

Melt the beef dripping or butter in a skillet and cook the onions until nicely browned. Put a good helping of champ on each plate, put some onions around the edge. Make a well in the center and put in a lump of butter. Dip a forkful of champ and onions into the butter, and enjoy.

Poundies

My late father-in-law, Ivan Allen, in his late eighties, spoke longingly of the Poundies he had as a child in Co. Tyrone. He remembers the potatoes being mashed with a big pounder (hence the name), after which lots of butter, salt and pepper, and gravy were added. The gravy would probably have been leftover from the Sunday roast of beef or lamb. He says that the potatoes were always quite soft and brown in color when they were served.

Thump

In her book *Kind Cooking*, Maura Laverty spoke of a dish called Thump, which is identical to champ.

Ceaile

Áine de Blacam described how they made Ceaile when they still had "old" potatoes. The potatoes would be boiled in their jackets and the children were often given the job of peeling them. The potatoes were mashed. They would heat up some of their own cow's milk with some shop butter and chopped onions. When it was melted they would make a hole in the center, pour in the hot liquid and mix. This was often served to the children for their dinner on its own or with fried mackerel in summer. The potatoes were always lovely and floury, having been grown in the shallow sandy soil of the island, with the addition of seaweed from the shore.

I asked Áine about the varieties of potato that were grown on Inis Meáin and she told me that Dates were the most common variety grown into the 1960s—I hadn't previously heard of this variety. She said that they kept well, right into July when the new season's crop would be ready. They were blight-resistant and suited the growing conditions on the island. Sadly the variety died out and has disappeared. They also had Banners (widely known as Aran Banners), an early variety. She also heard mention of a variety called Crows (*Preachán* in Irish), again this is an unfamiliar name to me.

Bruisy

An exiled Leitrim man who is now living in Dublin described to me a potato dish called bruisy from his childhood. The cooked potatoes were mashed together with butter and young nettles.

You could taste the iron—then you criss-crossed it with a knife and cut it into squares and made 'turf' out of it. You would drink milk with it. The game was to eat each sod of "turf."

Serves 6

2lb yellow potatoes (6 approx.),
   scrubbed
2 fat scallions or 1 finely chopped
   small onion
⅓ cup milk
salt and freshly ground pepper
¼ cup (½ stick) butter

Cally

This potato dish from Dublin is very similar to champ. It is a literal translation of the Irish "Ceaile" (see above).

Cook the potatoes in their jackets in boiling salted water. Meanwhile, slice the green and white parts of the scallions finely and put with the cold milk in a saucepan. Season with salt and pepper and bring slowly to a boil. Let simmer while the potatoes are cooking. Just as soon as the potatoes are done, peel and mash them, then quickly beat in the milk and scallions. Taste and add more seasoning if necessary. Serve immediately on hot plates. Make a well in the center of each helping and pour in some melted butter. Dip every forkful of cally into the melted butter and enjoy, as generations of Irish have done before you!

Colcannon

Colcannon was one of the festive dishes eaten at Hallowe'en, when a ring and a thimble would be hidden in the fluffy green-flecked mass. The ring denotes marriage, but the person who found the thimble would be a spinster for life. Poems have been written and songs sung about this much-loved dish:

Did you ever eat colcannon
When 'twas made with yellow cream
And the kale and praties blended
Like a picture in a dream?
Did you ever scoop a hole on top
To hold the melting lake
Of the clover-flavoured butter
Which your mother used to make?

Oh you did, so you did
so did he and so did I
And the more I think about it
sure the nearer I'm to cry
Oh weren't them the happy days
when troubles we knew not
And our mother made colcannon
in the little skillet pot.

Colcannon

Serves 8 (approximately)

2–3lb potatoes (6–9 approx.) e.g.
   Yukon Gold
1 small spring or Savoy cabbage
1 cup plus 1 tablespoon approx.
   boiling milk
salt and freshly ground pepper
¼ cup (½ stick) approx. butter

There are many regional variations of colcannon—Ireland's best-known traditional potato dish. In some areas green cabbage was added, in others kale was preferred. In parts of Dublin, Wicklow, and Wexford, parsnip was added, and onions or scallions are featured in several of the versions.

Scrub the potatoes. Put them into a saucepan of cold water, add a good pinch of salt, and bring to a boil. When the potatoes are about half cooked (about 15 minutes for old potatoes), strain off two-thirds of the water. Replace the lid on the saucepan, put on a gentle heat, and let the potatoes steam until they are fully cooked.

Remove the dark outer leaves from the cabbage. Wash the rest and cut into quarters, remove the core, and cut each quarter finely across the grain. Cook in a little boiling salted water until soft. Drain, season with salt, freshly ground pepper, and a little butter.

When the potatoes are just cooked, put on the milk and bring to a boil. Pull the skin off the potatoes, mash quickly while they are still warm, and beat in enough boiling milk to make a fluffy purée. (If you have a large quantity, put the potatoes in the bowl of a food mixer and beat with the paddle.) Then stir in about the same volume of cooked cabbage and taste for seasoning. Serve immediately in a hot dish, with a lump of butter melting in the center.

Note: Colcannon may be prepared ahead and reheated later in a moderate oven at 350°F, for about 20–25 minutes. Any leftover colcannon may be formed into potato cakes or farls and fried in bacon fat until crisp and brown on both sides—a cousin of bubble and squeak.

Dublin Parsnip Colcannon

Serves 8 (approximately)

1lb potatoes (3 approx.)
1lb parsnips (4 approx.)
1lb curly kale
1–1¼ cups half and half
2 tablespoons approx. chopped
    scallions
¼ cup (½ stick) approx. butter
salt and freshly ground pepper

Several Dubliners have spoken to me about a parsnip colcannon that "the Mammy used to make." Threepenny or sixpenny bits were sometimes hidden in the colcannon at Hallowe'en for the children to find. The proportion of parsnips to potato varied.

Scrub and peel the potatoes and parsnips, put them into a saucepan, cover with cold water, add a good pinch of salt, and bring to a boil. When the potatoes and parsnips are cooked, strain off the water, replace the lid on the saucepan, put on a gentle heat, and let steam for a few minutes, then mash.

While the potatoes and parsnips are cooking, bring a pot of well salted water to a boil, remove the central rib from the kale and cook the leaves until tender. Drain and chop finely.

When the potatoes are almost cooked, put on the milk and bring to a boil with the scallions. While the potatoes and parsnips are still warm, stir in the chopped kale, and beat in enough boiling milk to make a fluffy purée. (If you have a large quantity, use the bowl of a food mixer and beat with the paddle.) Add the butter and taste for seasoning. Stir over the heat and serve immediately in a hot dish with the butter melting in the center.

Colcannon may be prepared ahead and reheated later in a moderate oven at 350°F for about 20–25 minutes.

Pandy

Serves 4–6

2lb russet potatoes (6 approx.),
    scrubbed
¼ cup (½ stick) butter
1–1¼ cups half and half or
    single cream
salt

This light, fluffy mashed potato dish was often made for children or older people if they were feeling unwell. Alice Taylor gives this lyrical description of making pandy in her book Quench the Lamp:

"Pandy first required a big, soft, floury spud with a long smile across its face. Starting at the smile, the skin was eased off gently and the naked spud, almost too hot to handle, was transferred fast by hand into another plate, leaving its clothes in a heap behind it. Next a lump of yellow butter was placed on top, from where it ran in little yellow streams down the sides. A gentle little poke with the fork opened up a cavity into which went a drop of milk or a spoon of cream skimmed off the top of the bucket, followed by a shake of salt. Finally, the entire slushy combination was lightly whipped together and frequently tasted to ascertain that the correct balance was being achieved. It took great care and a discerning palate to make really good pandy; it had to be yellow, soft, delicately flavoured, and as light as thistledown on the tongue. When you were sick or not feeling happy you judged how much your mother and the world loved you by the quality of her pandy. It was our antibiotic, our tranquilizer and our sleeping potion."

Boil the potatoes in boiling salted water until just cooked, peel immediately, and mash with lots of butter. Season with salt and freshly ground pepper to taste and then whip in some cream. The texture should be light and fluffy. Eat while hot.

Lutóga

Lutóga was the name given to potatoes baked in the embers of the fire on the Blaskets and other islands off Cork and Kerry. In her book *Machnamh Sean-Mhná* (An Old Woman's Reflections) Peig Sayers wrote:

"There used to be ember-roasted potatoes at the foot of the fire and they were well roasted. My mother used to give me a little bit of butter and a drop of milk ... Nobody had white bread or tea at the time."

Deirdre Martin told me that when her father Donal (who came from Fanad in Co. Donegal) was in his teens, he used to put potatoes into the ash pit of the fire when he was going out to a dance. If his sister got home early she would smell the potatoes and eat them, then he'd be poking around in the ashes when he came home!

Strand Potatoes

A fisherman in the west of Ireland told me how they sometimes baked potatoes in the sand. They'd dig a shallow pit, lay the scrubbed potatoes in a single layer and cover them with sand. A fire would be lit on top, surrounded by a ring of stones. Water for the tea could be brought to the boil on top in a tin can or kettle and occasionally freshly caught fish was roasted over the fire or boiled in sea water. In Donegal, fishermen sometimes took "live" (smoldering) turf into their boats with them on calm days. This was used to bake potatoes and cook fish while they were out to sea.

Fries

old potatoes e.g. Atlantic, Superior etc. (allow ½lb/1 unpeeled potatoes per person)
beef dripping or good-quality oil
table salt

Homemade fries that start off with good Irish potatoes and end up in hot beef dripping or good-quality oil are still pretty sensational.

Fill a deep fryer with beef dripping, lard, or good-quality oil and preheat it to 325°F.

Scrub the potatoes, peel or leave unpeeled according to your taste. Cut into equal-sized fries so they will cook evenly. Dry meticulously in a dish towel or paper towel before cooking, otherwise they will splatter when they come in contact with the hot fat and will not brown so nicely.

Cook for a few minutes in the preheated fat or oil until they are soft and just beginning to brown, then drain. Increase the heat to 375°F and cook for 1–2 minutes more or until crisp and golden. Shake the basket, drain well, toss on paper towel, sprinkle with salt, and serve the fries immediately.

For how to render beef dripping, see page121.

Stovies

Serves 2–4

3 tablespoons beef dripping
4 medium onions, peeled and
    sliced
2lb potatoes (6 approx.), peeled and
    cut into thick slices
salt and freshly ground pepper
a little water

An ingenious traditional way of presenting the two basic ingredients, potatoes and onions, in a different guise. This recipe for stovies came from Co. Tyrone. Northern Ireland is an area particularly rich in potato variations.

Melt the dripping in a good hot pan and fry the onions until nearly tender, but not brown. Remove the onions, put in the potatoes, and toss them in the fat. Return the onions, placing them on top of the potatoes. Season well and cover the pan; cook on a gentle heat for 4–5 minutes, shaking the pan now and again to prevent sticking. Add a very little water if the mixture gets too dry. Do not try to keep the slices whole; as much of the surface as possible should brown. Serve hot with a mug of buttermilk.

Fried Potatoes

potatoes (allow ¼–½lb/1 per
    person)
lard, chicken fat, or butter, for frying
salt and freshly ground pepper
fried onions (optional)
chopped parsley

Potatoes were regularly fried to use up leftovers. A favorite way was to mix them with golden fried onions. The secret of really crispy fried potatoes is to have patience and not to attempt to turn them over until they have a nice crust. This can take 5–10 minutes, but it's well worth it.

Scrub the potatoes and boil until just cooked. When they are cool, peel and cut into ½-inch slices.

Heat a little lard, chicken fat, or butter in a heavy skillet. Put in the potatoes in a single layer, season with salt and freshly ground pepper. Fry on a medium heat until golden, then turn over to brown on the other side. Serve in a hot dish, mixed with fried onions if liked, and sprinkled with freshly chopped parsley.

Griddle Potatoes

cooked potatoes (allow ¼–½/1lb
    per person)
salt
butter, to serve

Co. Antrim is the source of this delicious, old-fashioned way of cooking potatoes.

Heat the griddle over the open fire, peel, and slice the potatoes thickly. Sprinkle some salt over the griddle pan and put the potatoes on top. Cook first on one side, then the other until crisp and tasty. Eat with country butter. This also works very well in a nonstick pan.

Potato Cake

Serves 4

2 tablespoons milk
2 tablespoons (¼ stick) butter
2 cups mashed potatoes
¾ cup plus 1½ tablespoons
   all-purpose flour
1 teaspoon salt

This is the potato cake recipe which is included in the little book Lessons in Cookery and Housewifery for the Use of Children, *1901, which belonged to Bridget Hanlon from Courtwood in Co. Laois. Bridget lived with her brother Patrick in a thatched cottage on the banks of the Grand Canal. Patrick had a lovely garden. Bridget used to bake in the pot-oven on the open fire.*

Melt the milk and butter in a saucepan and pour them over the potatoes, flour, and salt, mixed in a large bowl. Make into a light dough; knead into a round ball; roll out; cut into small cakes. Fry on a hot pan or griddle until a light brown color, turning from side to side.

Potato and Bacon Cakes

Serves 4

4 slices of bacon, rinds removed,
   chopped
2 cups mashed potatoes
3 tablespoons all-purpose flour
salt and freshly ground pepper
butter or dripping, for frying

Mollie Keane, the indomitable Irish writer, includes this recipe in her book Mollie Keane's Nursery Cooking.

Fry the bacon without any additional fat until crisp. Remove and drain on paper towels. Stir the bacon into the mashed potatoes with the flour, salt, and pepper. Form the mixture into four cakes. Heat the butter or dripping in a skillet, add the cakes, and fry for about 5 minutes on each side until golden and crisp.

Potato Oaten Cake

Makes 4–8

1 lb freshly cooked potatoes
   (3 approx.)
2–4 tablespoons (¼–½ stick) butter
⅔–¾ cup fine steel-cut oats
salt

Not surprisingly, steel-cut oats, another staple ingredient, was sometimes added to potato cakes. The result was generally known as Pratie Oaten— Prátaí *being the Irish word for potato.*

Mash the potatoes with the butter. Mix in the oats and season with salt. Roll out into a round and cut into rounds. Bake on a hot griddle for about 3–4 minutes on each side. Alternatively, cook in an iron pan in bacon fat. Eat hot with plenty of butter. Serve a few crispy slices of bacon with the potato oaten cakes.

Potato and Caraway Seed Cakes

Serves 6 (approximately)

1½lb yellow or round white
potatoes (4–5 large approx.),
scrubbed
3 tablespoons butter
2oz onion (½ an onion approx.),
finely chopped
1–2 teaspoons caraway seeds
1 tablespoon chopped parsley
salt and freshly ground pepper
heaping ⅓ cup flour
butter, for frying

The following description by Flurry Knox in Some Experiences of an Irish
R.M. *(Somerville and Ross, 1899) made my mouth water and inspired this
recipe, now one of our favorites.*

*"While I live I shall not forget her potato cakes. They came in hot and hot
from a pot-oven, they were speckled with caraway seeds, they swam in salt
butter, and we ate them shamelessly and greasily, and washed them down
with hot whiskey and water."*

Cook the potatoes in their jackets in boiling salted water. Meanwhile, melt the butter
and sweat the onion in it on a gentle heat until soft but not colored. Peel and mash the
potatoes while still hot. Add the onion and butter with the caraway seeds and chopped
parsley. Season with salt and freshly ground pepper, add the flour, and mix well. Knead a
little until smooth, roll out, and stamp into potato cakes with the top of a glass or a cutter.
Alternatively, divide the dough into 2 rounds and cut into cakes. Fry in melted butter on a
hot pan until golden on both sides. Serve hot.

Serves 4

1lb freshly cooked potatoes
(3 approx.), scrubbed
½ teaspoon salt
2 tablespoons (¼ stick) butter,
melted
½–¾ cup all-purpose flour

Fadge

These potato cakes are the way to an Ulsterman's heart, and often find their way into their suitcases on trips to friends and relatives far from home. One of my students from Belfast made them regularly in Cork to satisfy her craving for a taste of Ulster. Potato cakes, tatties, and parleys are other names for fadge.

Florence Irwin tells us that in olden days the peeled potatoes were placed on the bakeboard and a flat-bottomed mug or a pint can served to bruise them. This was then firmly grasped and pressed down on each potato in turn until no lumps remained.

Cook the potatoes in their skins in boiling salted water. As soon as the potatoes are cooked, peel them, put them into a bowl, and pound with a potato masher until free of lumps.

Sprinkle on the salt and gradually drizzle the melted butter over the mashed potatoes, then knead in enough flour to make a pliable dough. The potatoes I use take about ½ cup flour. Roll out the mixture into a round about ½ inch thick, and cut into cakes.

Heat a griddle and bake the potato cakes until golden brown on both sides for about 3–4 minutes (a nonstick pan, though less romantic, also works well). Eat hot, spread with butter or butter and superfine sugar. They are also very tasty fried in bacon fat and served for breakfast.

Note: A piece of fadge or potato bread added to the Traditional Irish Breakfast (see page 119) forms the delicious Ulster Fry.

Blasket Islands Potato Bread

To make this, leftover boiled potatoes were mashed with a wooden spoon. Salt and small quantities of butter, flour, and milk were added to make a dough. This was spread out by hand and cut into circles with the rim of a tea cup. The pot-oven was warmed over the fire, some butter was melted in it and then a little flour sprinkled in. The cakes were put in and cooked until brown on one side and then turned over. Máire Ní Ghuithín writes of them: "they had a delightful taste; they would melt in your mouth, they were so delicious." Máire also mentions that fried potatoes, cooked with butter, salt, and pepper in the pot-oven with the addition of some chopped onion, were eaten by children in the evening and "they would take the hunger away from us for the rest of the night."

Stampee or Stampy

May Fitzgerald from Ballycullane, Inch, Co. Kerry, sent me some recipes which her grandmother used to make with old potatoes in the spring. She had no scales or measures, but May vouches that the finished product tasted good.

"She peeled some potatoes, and grated them on a coarse grater into a colander. She left them for a while until the clear liquid dropped out (incidentally she used that to stiffen grandfather's hard collars). Before supper she mixed potatoes with sufficient flour, seasoning (pepper and salt) and an egg to make a dough, which in turn she shaped into cakes, and fried in the large iron griddle over the fire. Then she served them with a pat of homemade butter—delicious."

Boxty

Boxty vies with champ and colcannon as Ireland's best-known potato dish. It is particularly associated with the midland and northern counties, particularly Cavan, Tyrone, Fermanagh, and Derry. It may have originated in the late 18th and early 19th centuries, when potato harvests began to fail, as a way of using poor-quality potatoes that were useless for boiling. The watery, sometimes even rotting, potato flesh was put into a cloth and squeezed to remove as much liquid as possible. The remaining pulp was shaped into cakes and baked on a heated flagstone or griddle.

> Boxty on the griddle
> Boxty on the pan
> If you don't eat boxty
> You'll never get your man.

When eaten instead of bread for the evening meal, milk and salt might be added to the mixture, which was then known as dippity.

Boxty is particularly associated with the midland and northern counties, but it also turns up on the Blasket Islands according to Malachy McKenna—again I am indebted to Máire Ní Ghuithín, whose recordings of the food history of the islands is invaluable. She records that once she saw boxty being made on the Island, and she and a friend decided to try it for themselves. As they didn't have a grater, which was necessary for making boxty, they made one by hammering nails into a can to produce ragged edges. Six large, raw potatoes were peeled, washed, and dried, then grated and wrapped in clean white cloth. At this point two people were required; each one took an end of the cloth and both twisted it to squeeze the water out of the potatoes. The potatoes were then taken out of the cloth and any remaining water was squeezed out. They were placed in a dish to be mixed with a little salt and flour, and were then formed into a thin cake which was cut into four pieces. Next, some flour was sprinkled into the pot-oven, which had been heated until very hot. The boxty pieces were put into the pot without the lid on. Once they were cooked on one side they were turned over. After all that, Máire and her friend didn't like the boxty—they found it heavy and dense. It reminded Máire of bread that didn't have enough soda in it and didn't rise properly; the islanders would say of such bread "you've made a boxty of it!"

Seán Ó Dálaigh, writing in *Timcheall Chinn Sléibhe*, says that cream could be added to the mixture and this would make it "very crisp." It could be cooked on the griddle or in the pot-oven, but that melted butter should be used to prevent it sticking. It was eaten by the least well off. Yellow-meal bread was eaten by those who could afford the meal, and only "the very few" ate bread made from flour. He also says that poor fishermen would take a boxty-cake with them when they went on a day's fishing trip and, having eaten the boxty, were no more likely to be hungry at the end of the day than were those fishermen who took yellow-meal bread or flour bread with them. Some people found it too heavy altogether and it disagreed with them, but children were extremely fond of it and preferred to take it to school rather than yellow-meal bread. Children used to take it when herding cattle for a day. However, Seán adds that it was extremely laborious and "for that reason the people of Dún Chaoin haven't been making any boxty bread for many years."

Helen Faughnan from Mohill, Co. Leitrim sent me a recipe for Boxty Loaf, this is made in the same way as boiled boxty, but add a few chopped bacon slices and caraway when kneading. Form into a cake and bake in a moderate oven with a slice of bacon on top.

Pan Boxty

Serves 4

6 medium potatoes
a handful of all-purpose flour
salt
butter
fresh herbs (optional)

Whereas Leitrim and the Drumlin area seem to be the home of boxty, it crops up in many other places around the country under various names. In Co. Wexford and Co. Tipperary I was given recipes for "grated cakes in the pan," both of which were essentially pan boxty. Granny Toye from Clones, Co. Monaghan, now 88 years of age, gave the recipe to me. Granny Toye says that pan boxty may be eaten hot or cold and may be reheated. A tablespoon of fresh herbs provides a delicious, if untraditional, flavoring to the dish.

Scrub the potatoes well, but don't peel. Line a bowl with a cloth. Grate the potatoes into it, then squeeze out the liquid into the bowl and let it sit for about 20 minutes until the starch settles. Set the potatoes aside.

Drain off the water and leave the starch in the bottom of the bowl. Add the grated potato, a handful of flour and some salt.

Melt a nice bit of butter on a heavy iron pan and pour in the potato mixture. It should be ¾–1 inch thick. Cook on a medium heat. Let it brown nicely on one side before turning over and then on the other side, about 30 minutes in all depending on the heat. It's much better to cook it too slowly rather than too fast. It should be crisp and golden on the outside. Cut the boxty into four wedges and serve.

7lb raw potatoes (about 20), boiled
   in their skins
3lb 5oz boiled potatoes (about 10)
1¾ cups plus 2 tablespoons
   all-purpose flour
1½ tablespoons salt
butter or bacon fat, for frying

Boiled Boxty

Phyl O'Kelly, the late, much-admired cookery correspondent of the Cork
Examiner, *was reared in Leitrim. She gave me details of the three types of
boxty made in her area: pan boxty, boxty pancakes, and boiled boxty.*

   *This is her version of the famous Leitrim boiled boxty, which she
maintains is unique to Ireland, whereas versions of pan boxty can be
found in many countries. Note the large quantities because of the large
size of Irish families.*

Wash, peel, and grate the raw potatoes. Put them into a piece of cheesecloth or a clean flour
bag, squeeze out excess liquid into a bowl, and let settle. Peel and mash the freshly boiled
potatoes in a bowl. Add the grated raw potatoes, flour and starch that has separated out
from the potato liquid. Season well with salt and shape into 5-inch rounds, 2½–2 inches
high with slightly flattened tops.

   Bring a saucepan of water to a boil, add salt, gently drop in the boxty, and cook until
firm, about 45–60 minutes.

   They will be grayish in color and not wildly appetizing to look at. When cold, slice into
thick rounds and fry in butter or bacon fat until golden brown. Eat with country butter and
a slice of bacon if you fancy.

Mrs Mary B. Kelly's Boiled Boxty

*This recipe, also for boiled boxty, came from Mrs Mary B. Kelly from Carrick-
on-Shannon, Co. Leitrim.*

Peel and grate the raw potatoes, squeezing out all the moisture you can. Peel and mash
the boiled potatoes. Mix raw and mashed potatoes together, and add flour and salt. Mix all
well together and make into dumplings the size of an orange and slightly flattened. Have a
pot of boiling water ready and add the dumplings, bring back to a boil and simmer for
1 hour. Let cool for a few hours or until next day. Cut each dumpling into two half-moon
shaped pieces, then cut each piece carefully into 2–3 slices, to give 4 or 6 half-moon
shaped pieces. Fry these in butter until golden on both sides, eat as they are or with bacon
for breakfast.

Variation

Baked Boxty or
Boxty Loaf

Use one of the above recipes, then bake the boxty in 2 well-buttered loaf pans in a moderate oven
at 350°F for 1 hour.

Boxty Pancakes

Serves 4

8oz freshly cooked potatoes
  (1 approx.), boiled in their skins
8oz raw potatoes (1–2 approx.),
  peeled
1¾ cups all-purpose flour
½ teaspoon baking soda
a pinch of salt (optional)
1–1½ cups buttermilk
butter, for frying

Kat Clarke from Garbally, near Birr in Co. Offaly, suggests serving the pancakes with superfine sugar or corn syrup instead of the bacon or honey.

Peel the cooked potatoes while they are still hot. Drop them into a bowl and mash immediately. Grate the raw potatoes, add to the mash with the flour and sifted baking soda and salt. Mix well and add enough buttermilk to make a stiff batter.

Heat a griddle or skillet, grease with butter, and drop in tablespoons of the potato batter onto the pan. Make large or small pancakes according to your preference, using anything from 1 to 3–4 tablespoons of mixture. Cook for about 5 minutes on each side. Eat them straight from the pan with butter, crispy slices of bacon, or pure Irish honey.

Grated Cakes on the Griddle

Serves 4

1lb raw potatoes (3 approx.)
2 cups cooked mashed potatoes
1 teaspoon salt
¾ cup plus 1½ tablespoons
  all-purpose flour

I came across two different recipes for grated cakes, both based on the boxty tradition. In one recipe the mixture was made into a dough, which, when rolled out, was cut into pieces and baked on the griddle.

Peel the raw potatoes and grate them into a linen dish towel. Squeeze and collect the liquid in a bowl and let stand. Mix the grated and mashed potatoes. When the starch has separated from the liquid, pour off the water, and add the starch to the potatoes. Add the dry ingredients; mix well, adding enough flour to make a workable dough. Knead a little, then roll out and cut into 8 pieces. Bake on a hot griddle and serve the grated cakes warm with butter.

Grated Cakes in the Pan

Serves 6–8

1lb raw potatoes (3 approx.)
2 cups cooked mashed potatoes
1 teaspoon salt
1 teaspoon baking soda
scant 3½ cups all-purpose flour
½ cup buttermilk

The second recipe for grated cakes in the pan had the addition of baking soda and buttermilk, which was made to a dropping consistency—this was more like drop scones. Both were served warm with butter and sugar if desired: equally delicious!

Peel the raw potatoes and grate them into a linen dish towel. Squeeze and collect the liquid in a bowl and let stand. Mix the grated potatoes and mashed potatoes. When the starch has separated from the liquid, pour off the water, and add the starch to the potatoes. Add the dry ingredients and mix well, then add enough buttermilk to form a dropping consistency. Beat well and let stand a little before frying in spoonfuls in a greased skillet. Fry on both sides and serve with butter and sugar.

Baked Potatoes

This recipe from The Lough Rynn manuscript 1865 is not for baked potatoes as we know them, but it sounds quite tasty and easy to reproduce.

"Take about a dozen boiled potatoes. Peel and bruise them very fine with the back of a spoon. When they are in a sort of flour, make them into a paste with some sweet milk and a small bit of butter. Roll them in puffy round balls and flatten them a little. Put them on tin sheets and bake them in a moderate oven."

On the Blasket Islands, potatoes were also baked in the fire. Máire Ní Ghuithín reports that this was regarded as a healthy way of preparing them: "The old people used to say that these potatoes were very wholesome when cooked like this in the embers or live ashes because whatever water or moisture or starch was in them was drawn out by the heat of the fire." Such potatoes were often left in the turf ashes overnight and, without being added to or improved on in any way, were eaten in the morning by children on their way to school. Peig Sayers, referring to her youth on the mainland in Bheatha Pheig Sayers (1939), says, "Many's the morning I went to school relying [for food] on potatoes from the back of the fire. Five potatoes would be put at the edge of the fire so that they would be ready next morning for the child who would be going to school… Often we didn't even have milk to go with them." A family which had no fish and whose cow had gone dry would have nothing to accompany their potatoes except "pickle water," which Peig describes as water with some salt in it. The mainland author Tomás O'Cinnéide, in his book *Ar Seachrán* (Astray), notes "if you had a shed [full] of potatoes and two barrels of pickled fish you would have no fear of any winter, hard or mild. Alas, it's often we didn't have the fish, and the condiment we had then was the pickle or the 'dip' as those who spoke English used to say. If there was milk and a bit of salt in it, you would dip your potato in it—and it was good to taste—you filled your stomach."

Cottage Pudding

Ingenious cooks came up with many ways of using mashed potatoes, both freshly cooked or leftover, sometimes in sweet dishes. Even if there wasn't much in the pantry and flour was scarce, one could come up with a pudding. James Murphy from New Ross sent me this recipe dated 1907:

"Peel, boil and mash two pounds of floury potatoes adding a pinch of salt. Beat in thoroughly two ounces of oiled butter, two ounces of brown sugar and three quarters of a pint of milk. Put the mixture in a greased dish and bake for an hour."

Mary Ponsonby in her 1850 manuscript had something similar:

"Take some potatoes, boil and peel them, put them through a hair sieve, add the rind of a lemon, and four ounces of butter, beat up two eggs, and the juice of 2 lemons. Add all together and sweeten them to your taste, put them in a dish or bowl and bake them in a smart oven."

3 cups hot mashed potatoes
½ cup hot milk
1–2 eggs
salt and freshly ground pepper
parsley

Potato Drops

This little recipe appeared in the Biatas *magazine, which was sent to farmers growing sugar beet for the Irish Sugar Company. Lizzie Dunne cut it out and kept it, probably in the 1970s.*

Beat all the ingredients together. Add minced parsley or crushed herbs to taste. The mixture should be a thick batter. Drop in tablespoons, like pancake batter, into a skillet containing a little melted butter. Cook until brown below, and turn and brown on the other side. Fold in two.

Serves 4

2 cups mashed potatoes
salt and freshly ground pepper
1 tablespoon finely chopped parsley
2 tablespoons (¼ stick) melted
    butter
1 teaspoon finely chopped onion
¼ teaspoon finely chopped
    mixed herbs
1 beaten egg, to glaze

Potato Loaf

Potato Loaf appears in All in the Cooking: Book 1, *which was used as a school textbook during the 1960s. Rosalie Dunne remembers bringing the loaf home on the bus to the Curragh Camp from Newbridge in a bag: "the day we made it at school with our Domestic Science teacher Mrs Gibson, and I can still smell the White Vegetable soup that spilt in the bag!"*

Mix potatoes, seasonings, and flavorings together in a bowl. Add the melted butter and sufficient beaten egg to bind (reserving some for the glaze). Turn onto a lightly floured board, form into a cone. Brush over with the remaining beaten egg. Score with a fork. Place on a greased Yorkshire pan and bake in a hot oven (400°F) until nicely browned. Serve on a hot dish on a plain dish paper and garnish with parsley.

Variations
Potato Cones
Make the potato mixture as above, divide into 8 portions and shape each portion like a cone. Brush with beaten egg and bake as above.

Potato Nests
These were sometimes made in a similar fashion, and an egg could be baked in the potato nest.

Makes one 7-inch tart

1 cup plus 1 tablespoons
    all-purpose flour
a pinch of salt
generous ⅕ cup mashed
    potatoes
¼ cup (½ stick) butter
water, to mix

Potato Pie Dough

Helen Faughnan of Co. Leitrim sent this recipe, which is made in the same way as shortcrust pie dough, and can be used to make apple tart.

Sift the flour and salt and add to the mashed potato. Rub in the butter with your fingertips, and carefully add enough cold water just to bring the pie dough together, using a fork. Then collect the pie dough together into a ball with your hand. Wrap in plastic wrap and chill in the refrigerator for at least 15 minutes before use.

Vegetables

In pre-Norman Ireland, vegetables appear to have been used mainly as salads or condiments as accompaniments or relishes to more substantial meals of meat, cereals or dairy fooods. A number of vegetables were popular and although it is difficult to be certain of their identity, they seem to be of the cabbage and onion family. The early 12th century tale, *Aislinge Meic Con Glinne*, also mentions a root vegetable, *cerrbacán*, which may have been sweet to taste. In the Norman period and beyond, the cutlivation of vegetables may have been more organised with greater variety available. Certainly by the 17th century, Ireland was growing a wide variety of vegetables.

In 1605, for instance, Harry Holland agreed to cultivate part of the gardens at Trinity College Dublin (then known as the College of the Holy and Undivided Trinity) with turnips, parsnips, carrot, artichokes, onion and leeks. He provided vegetables for "thirty person and, eight messes as the cook hall think good." In the 18th century, a wide variety of vegetables and fruit—asparagus; seakale, salsify, and vegetable marrows—began to be cultivated in the walled gardens of the large country house estates. This wider choice of vegetables seems not to have been adopted by poorer people, however: John Dunton, writing in 1699, described a typical peasant's garden as containing "perhaps two or three hundred heaves of oats and as much pease, the rest of the ground is full of those dearly loved potatoes, and a few cabbages."

Cabbage

A variety of brassicas, including cabbage, grow wild in Ireland and were used from early times mainly as a condiment or salad. Cultivated cabbage did not become widespread until the 17th century. In *Trinity College Dublin and the Idea of a University*, Charles Nelson points out that during the early 17th century, the scholars of Trinity dined ceaselessly on cabbages, which "remained the constituent of the scholastic diet for a couple more centuries."

Cabbage is a relatively reliable crop and was therefore used extensively as an emergency food in the famine years of 1845–8. In many parts of Ireland, the waiting month of July between the end of the old stocks of potatoes and the harvesting wasknown as "July of the Cabbage." Even up to the present day, cabbage is probably the most widely grown vegetable, from cottage gardens to huge vegetable farmers. There was a tradition of growing cabbage plants to sell, often in a "cottage acre:" the piece of ground surrounding a cottage in the countryside. It was a way of making some extra money for someone who might be working as a farm laborer or a road worker. Certain people in every parish would be a good source for strong sturdy cabbage plants. They were sold in bundles tied with string and wrapped in damp newspaper. Farmers or their wives would buy them, often a hundred or more at a time, to plant in the haggard (garden). Other gardeners might buy a couple of dozen. It was common to see advertisements for cabbage plants in the newspaper, and sometimes they might even be sent by post. Sadly, the tradition of growing plants in this way has largely died out as that generation has passed on. Demand decreased gradually as people became more affluent. Growing one's own vegetables in many people's minds became associated with the "bad old times". A telling remark to illustrate this mindset comes from a Co. Tipperary man in the 1980s, who said: "Sure, if you grew the few vegetables yourself, 'tis how the neighbours would think you couldn't afford to buy them!"

Happily, however, there has been a resurgence of interest in growing your own. A whole new generation has been smitten by the self-sufficiency bug, and movements like the GIY (Grow it Yourself) have fired people with enthusiasm and set up a support system so people can sow and swap and share knowledge, labor, and the fruits of their endeavors with each other and the community.

Boiled Cabbage

The traditional way of cooking cabbage. Sometimes baking soda or even a lump of washing soda was added to keep the cabbage green.

Remove the stalks and shred the cabbage fairly finely. Boil in salted water or, better still, water in which bacon has been cooked, until done. The cooking time varies depending on the variety of cabbage, so keep a watchful eye and drain the cabbage as soon as it is cooked. Add a nice lump of butter and season with lots of freshly ground pepper, adding a little more salt if necessary.

Buttered Cabbage

Instead of boiling cabbage in the traditional way, this method may be used, which has converted many an ardent cabbage hater!

Cut the cabbage into quarters, remove the core, and slice thinly. Put 2–3 tablespoons of water into a wide saucepan together with 2–3 tablespoons butter and a pinch of salt. Bring to a boil, add the shredded cabbage, and toss over high heat, then cover the saucepan and cook for a few minutes. Toss again and add some salt, freshly ground pepper, and a pat of butter. Serve immediately.

Carrots

Traditionally carrots were cooked in the water in which bacon or corned beef had been boiled, which would give them a special flavor. On farms in the country, carrots and cabbage were pulled or cut just in time to be cooked for dinner. The clay was washed off in the barrel under the water pump in the yard and 5 minutes later they were in the pot. No wonder they tasted so good. It was a regular practice to store carrots and other root vegetables in a pit outside in the winter. Áine de Blacam said that this was also the practice on Inis Meáin on the Aran Islands. They also grew cabbage, onions, scallions, turnips, and potatoes.

During my childhood it was common practice to store both root vegetables and apples in pits for the winter. Pad, our gardener, dug down 5–6 inches, lined the pit first with sand and then with straw, perfect Bramley cooking apples were layered up, then covered with straw and earth and I think I remember tarpaulin or plastic. Carrots, parsnips, and beets were stored in a similar way. Potatoes were stored in the corner of a dark shed covered with Hessian sacks. It was, and still is, essential to exclude the light, otherwise they would go green and sprout.

Serves 4–6

1lb carrots (5–6 approx.), Chantenay and Nantes have particularly good flavor
⅓ cup plus 1 tablespoon cold water
a generous pinch of salt
a knob of butter
plenty of freshly ground pepper
a good pinch of sugar

GARNISH
chopped parsley or fresh mint

Boiled Carrots

As many people are growing their own vegetables again, cooking carrots straight from the garden is now an option, but if not, at least buy fresh unwashed carrots and cook them by this method to achieve maximum flavor. The leaves of tiny carrots can also be eaten or added to salads.

Cut off the tops and tips, scrub, and peel thinly if necessary. Cut into even slices ¼inch thick. Leave very young carrots whole. Bring the water to a boil, add the carrots and salt. Cover and boil until the carrots are tender. Drain off the water, (keep to add to the roasting pan for gravy), add a lump of butter, lots of pepper, and a sprinkling of sugar. Shake the saucepan so that the carrots become coated with the buttery glaze. Serve in a hot vegetable dish sprinkled with chopped parsley or mint.

Parsnips

The *cerrbacán* mentioned in early texts may refer to some sweet tuber like carrot or parsnip. Both grow wild in Ireland and both were known in Roman Britain so they may be early introductions. In their valiant efforts to help the poor during the potato famines of 1845–6, The Society of Friends encouraged the cultivation of parsnips, which may have been grown in Ireland since early Christian times. There are many references to *meacan* in early writings, which scholars believe may have meant parsnips. Traditionally, parsnips were boiled and mashed with country butter. They are also delicious mixed with carrots, or cut into chunks and roasted, either alone or around a beef roast. Crispy parsnip cakes also make an irresistible and inexpensive treat.

Carrot and Parsnip Mash

Serves 6–8

8oz carrots (3 approx.), peeled
and sliced
1lb parsnips (4 approx.), peeled
and sliced
salt
pinch of sugar
freshly ground pepper
2–4 tablespoons (¼–½ stick) butter
chopped parsley, to serve

"Green, White and Gold" and "Sunshine" are some of the evocative names given to this popular vegetable combination, still widely made in Ireland.

Cook the carrots in a little boiling salted water with a pinch of sugar until soft. Cook the parsnips separately in boiling salted water.

Strain both and mash or purée together. Add lots of butter, then the salt and freshly ground pepper. Sprinkle with chopped parsley.

Rutabaga Turnip

Probably because it was introduced to Ireland as cattle feed, the rutabaga turnip has humble connotations, which it is still struggling to overcome. Lieutenant Joseph Archer's Statistical Survey of County Dublin in 1801 specifically recommends the use of turnips for animal fodder rather than human consumption:

> "cabbages, potatoes or turnips would be better and more profitable for milch cows, than any, this is now used in Dublin."

However, it appears that turnip was unknown in many parts of Ireland up to the Famine period. During the famine years, turnip seed was distributed, thereby establishing the popularity of the vegetable. One account from Barnesmore, Co. Donegal, describes how in certain areas people ate so much of it that "their skin turned yellow from the eating of swedes [rutabaga]."

As a result of eating turnip through necessity in the famine period, many imaginative adaptations of potato dishes developed, such as turnip boxty and turnip champ. The unpretentious rutabaga turnip is now becoming increasingly popular. It is a key vegetable in the movement towards hearty, rustic food. Besides being incredibly good value, rutabaga turnip is much more versatile than many people suspect.

If you are going to serve it mashed in the usual way, you should perk it up with caramelized onions. Remember, too, that farmers say rutabaga turnips taste best after they have had a touch of frost.

Serves 6 (approximately)

2 x 3½ inch rutabagas (2lb approx.)
salt and freshly ground pepper
¼–½ cup (½–1 stick) butter
finely chopped parsley, to serve

CRISPY ONIONS
2–3 tablespoons olive oil or beef fat
4 onions (1lb approx.), sliced

Rutabaga Turnips with Crispy Onions

Some households preferred rutabaga turnips sliced, others cubed or mashed. This recipe gives an extra lift to mashed turnips. Rutabaga turnips were introduced to Ireland in the late 18th century. They were a very important crop because they could be eaten by both animals and humans and could stay in the ground until they were needed for use. They also had the appeal of being easy to cook for those with limited skills and equipment.

Heat the olive oil or beef fat in a heavy saucepan. Toss in the onions and cook on a medium heat until they are soft and caramelized to a golden brown (about 30–45 minutes). Stir regularly.

Meanwhile, peel the rutabagas thickly in order to remove the thick outside skin. Cut into ¾-inch cubes and cover with water. Add in a good pinch of salt, bring to a boil, and cook until soft. Strain off the excess water, mash the swede well, and then beat in the butter. Stir in the soft and caramelized onions. Taste and season with lots of freshly ground pepper and more salt if necessary. Garnish with parsley and serve piping hot.

Leeks

Leeks are frequently referred to in early Irish manuscripts. The 12th century tale *Aislinge Meic Con Glinne* speaks of "a forest tall of real leeks of onions and carrots stood behind the house." It is possible that the leek referred to may be the perennial Babington leek, which has a distinct garlic flavor and is still found growing wild at a number of locations on the west coast and the Aran Islands. It is thought to have been introduced to Ireland in pre-Christian times and now grows quite happily in my kitchen garden in Shanagarry. It tends to be rather tougher than modern varieties, so is perhaps best for flavoring broths and stews.

Leeks (*Allium babingtonii*) have been used since ancient times. There are many references in ancient manuscripts to pottages made by the monks, which included thinly sliced leeks. Wild leeks still grow in the west of Ireland—I also have some in my kitchen garden. They are very hardy and can be harvested every year, but they are definitely tougher and stronger in flavor than the annual varieties. I find them excellent to add to a stock.

Serves 4–6

6 medium leeks
3 tablespoons butter
salt and freshly ground pepper
1 tablespoon water, if necessary
chopped parsley or chervil

Leeks Stewed in Butter

Leeks were often just boiled and served with white sauce. The addition of parsley made this dish a bit tastier, but nonetheless they were a bit dull, so many people just didn't enjoy eating leeks as a result. This way of cooking buttered leeks makes them meltingly tender and mild in flavor. These melted leeks were often added to mashed potato to make a leek champ in winter.

Cut off the dark green leaves from the top of the leeks (wash and add to the stock pot or use for making green leek soup). Slit the leeks about halfway down the center and wash well under cold running water. Slice into ¼-inch rounds. Melt the butter in a heavy-bottomed saucepan; when it foams add the sliced leeks and toss gently to coat with butter. Season with salt and freshly ground pepper and add 1 tablespoon of water if necessary. Cover with a paper lid and a close-fitting saucepan lid. Reduce the heat and cook very gently for about 15–20 minutes, or until the leeks are soft and moist. Check and stir every now and then. Serve on a warm dish, sprinkled with chopped parsley or chervil.

Note: The pot of leeks may be cooked in a low oven (325°F) if that is more convenient.

Globe Artichokes

In my research for this book a particular surprise was the discovery that globe artichokes have been grown in Ireland since the Anglo-Norman Conquest. They were, and still are, widely cultivated in the walled kitchen gardens of country houses, including Ballymaloe—where a particularly good variety has been grown since 1835 or even earlier. One of the loveliest Irish sights is a whole field of globe artichokes in bloom down near Allihies on the Beara Peninsula in West Cork.

Globe Artichokes with Melted Butter

Serves 6

5 cups water
2 tablespoons white wine vinegar
2 teaspoons salt
6 globe artichokes
¾ cup (1½ sticks) butter
freshly squeezed juice of ¼ lemon

Some restaurants prepare globe artichokes very elaborately. However, I merely trim the base of the artichoke just before cooking so it will sit steadily on the plate, then rub the cut end with lemon juice or vinegar to prevent it from discoloring.

Have a large saucepan of boiling water ready. Add the white wine vinegar and salt to every scant 5 cups water. Pop in the artichokes and bring the water back to a boil. Simmer steadily for about 25 minutes. After about 20 minutes, test the artichokes to see if they are done by tugging off one of the larger leaves at the base. It should come away easily; if it doesn't, continue to cook the artichokes for another 5–10 minutes. When cooked, remove the artichokes from the water, and drain upside down on a hot serving plate.

While they are cooking, simply melt the butter and then add some lemon juice to taste. Serve the melted butter sauce in a little bowl beside the artichokes. Globe artichokes are eaten with the fingers, so you might like to provide a finger bowl. A spare plate to collect all the nibbled leaves would also be useful.

Braised Jerusalem Artichokes

Serves 4

1½lb Jerusalem artichokes
2 tablespoons (¼ stick) butter
salt and freshly ground pepper
2 teaspoons water
chopped parsley, to serve

Jerusalem artichokes are a perennial winter vegetable; once you plant them, they usually re-emerge every year and even spread if you are not careful. Their flavor matches particularly well with game, beef, or shellfish.

Peel the artichokes thinly and cut into ¼-inch slices. Melt the butter in a cast-iron casserole, toss the artichokes, and season with salt and freshly ground black papper. Add the water, and cover with a paper lid (to keep in the steam) and then the saucepan lid.

Cook on a low heat or put in a moderate oven (350°F) for 15–20 minutes, until the artichokes are soft but still keeping their shape. Toss every now and then during cooking.

Serve sprinkled with chopped parsley.

Note: If cooking on the stove top, turn off the heat after around 10 minutes—the artichokes will continue to cook in the heat while holding their shape.

Asparagus

Asparagus is a rare, native plant in Ireland. The Viceroy, Lord Clarendon, commenting on the standard of cultivation in Dublin in 1685, notes that "asparagus, here, is very good, large and green." Jonathan Swift praised the vegetable as an excellent kidney stimulant, which was also good for gout and rheumatism.

Food historian Regina Sexton, in an article in the *Irish Examiner* in June 2011, says that "Cork may once have been famed for its asparagus." She has been trying to trace the history of growing the crop in the county and discover why it is no longer a center for growing it. Regina says that "what is clear is that commercial nurserymen/seedsmen were operating in Cork from the mid-18th century, but most likely for some decades before."

Mary Forrest at the Agriculture and Food Science Centre, University College Dublin, notes in a recent study that the Library of the National Botanic Gardens in Glasnevin holds a collection of 120 nursery catalogs dating from the early 18th century to the present day. It notes 58 nurseries and seedsmen in the Dublin area during the 18th century. "The diversity, notes Sexton, is astonishing: Edward Bray is offering 19 types of peas, 12 beans, 10 French beans and 11 lettuces, thus dispelling the notion that Irish food of the 18th century lacked variety and character."

Interest in horticulture and gardening was no longer the prerogative of wealthy manor owners with their (sometimes vast) walled kitchen gardens. Cork seems to have redeveloped a reputation for asparagus growing. Asparagus likes sandy, loamy, moist, but well-drained soils. Areas of Cork fit the bill, according to Ultan Walsh, an organic vegetable grower from Nohoval, Co. Cork, and now the only commercial grower of asparagus in Cork. My late father-in-law, Ivan Allen, grew 5 acres of asparagus close to the sea near Shanagarry in East Cork, in the 1960s. The variety Martha Washington had a superb flavor, and we were all very sad when the field was eventually grubbed out.

Serves 4

16–20 spears of fresh asparagus
4 slices of bread
sprigs of chervil, to serve

Asparagus with Hollandaise Sauce

Both asparagus and seakale have long associations with country house cooking in Ireland, when they were grown in the kitchen gardens of the "big house." Hollandaise sauce or melted butter was the preferred accompaniment, rather than French dressing, which is a more recent accompaniment.

Trim the asparagus and cook in boiling salted water until a knife tip will pierce the root end easily. Meanwhile, make the Hollandaise Sauce (see below). Toast the bread, butter it, and remove the crusts. Place a piece of toast on a hot plate, place 4 or 5 pieces of asparagus on top, and spoon a little Hollandaise sauce over it. Garnish with a sprig of chervil and serve immediately.

2 egg yolks, free-range
2 teaspoons cold water
½ cup (1 stick) butter, cut into dice
1 teaspoon lemon juice (approx.)

Hollandaise Sauce

Put the egg yolks into a heavy stainless-steel saucepan on a low heat, or in a bowl over hot water. Add the water and whisk thoroughly. Add the butter bit by bit, whisking all the time. As soon as one piece melts, add the next. The mixture will gradually thicken, but if it shows signs of becoming too thick or of slightly "scrambling," remove from the heat immediately and add a little cold water if necessary. Do not leave the pan or stop whisking until the sauce is made. Finally add the lemon juice to taste. If the sauce is slow to thicken it may be because you are excessively cautious and the heat is too low. Increase the heat slightly and continue to whisk until the sauce thickens to a light coating consistency.

Seakale

One of the most exquisite of all vegetables, is known as strand cabbage (*praiseach trá*) in parts of Co. Donegal and Antrim. It grows wild on sandy, pebbly strands around the coast. Traditionally, devotees kept an eye out for the first leaves towards the end of February and into March. Knowing that seakale was best when the young stalks were excluded from the light, they would draw sand and pebbles over the plant as it grew. Weeks later, provided the same spot could be located, the pale yellow, tender stems were uncovered and harvested.

Seakale was a sought-after vegetable in country house gardens in the 18th and 19th centuries. It may not have been confined to the country houses. Lily O'Reilly in her night class notes in Dublin, c. 1940, had a recipe for seakale.

Seakale is rarely if ever seen for sale, but is relatively easy to grow, so is well worth cultivating. There is a seakale bed in the walled garden at Ballymaloe House. You can buy replicas of the old seakale blanching pots with lids, but a brick chimney liner covered by a slate works perfectly well. Even a simple black plastic bucket will suffice. Exclude the light from about November, then you will be rewarded with delicate shoots in the early part of April. Seakale is a perennial plant and is altogether beautiful, with white flowers in summer and lots of bobbly seed heads in autumn. It thrives with a mulch of cinders.

Kale on Toast with Shrimp and Hollandaise Sauce

Serves 4–6

2½ cups of water
½ teaspoon salt
1lb seakale or kale
2 tablespoons (¼ stick) butter, melted
18 shrimp, cooked and peeled
6 slices of toast, buttered
Hollandaise Sauce (see opposite)

GARNISH
a small bunch of chervil

Wash the seakale gently and trim into manageable lengths—about 4 inches. Bring the water to a fast boil and add the salt. Add the seakale, cover and boil until tender—about 15 minutes. Just as soon as a knife will pierce the seakale easily, drain it.

Meanwhile, melt the butter in a pan on a gentle heat and toss in the shrimp and warm through.

Serve the seakale with the shrimp on the hot buttered toast, and drizzle generously with Hollandaise sauce. Pop a little bunch of chervil on top of each toast and serve immediately.

Celery

Celery is thought to have been one of the earliest vegetables grown alongside leeks, onions, and kale in in the gardens of early medieval Ireland. It was probably used in pottages, with leeks, onion, and wild garlic. In early Ireland every provincial king was apparently entitled to have "three condiments supplied for his nursing; honey, fresh onions and an unlimited amount of celery."

Serves 4–6

1 head of celery
⅔ cup water
salt and freshly ground pepper
roux (see page 42)
½–¾ cup light cream

GARNISH
chopped parsley

Celery with Cream

For many people, celery was only eaten as an accompaniment to roast turkey at Christmas, and often not particularly enjoyed when served with white sauce. However, I think this version with a little cream is much more delicious. Celery, of course, has always made a wonderful soup and stock ingredient. Don't forget to remove the strings from the outside stalks.

Pull the stalks off the head of celery. If the outer stalks seem a bit tough, peel the strings off with a potato peeler or else use these tougher stalks in the stockpot. Cut the stalks into ½-inch chunks.

Bring the water to a boil and season with salt and freshly ground pepper. Add the chopped celery, cover, and cook for 15–20 minutes, or until a knife will go through the celery easily. Pour off most of the water into another pan. Add the cream to the pan of celery water and thicken with roux. Strain the celery from its remaining cooking water and add the celery to the sauce. Let the sauce bubble for a few minutes. Put into a hot serving dish, sprinkle with chopped parsley, and serve.

Onions

Onions have always been an essential ingredient in the Irish kitchen and they are a source of pride still in cottage gardens. Even people who would grow little else would buy a few sets (little bulbs) and grow them every year. Onion sets were always available at the hardware shop, the creamery or co-op. It was common to see onions spread out to dry on the roofs of galvanized sheds, before being stored for the winter.

Home-grown onions have a wonderful sweet flavor. Fried onions were and still are a favorite accompaniment to fried steak or lamb chops, sometimes incorporated into a rich gravy made on the pan. If the onion rings were tossed in flour before frying, this would thicken the gravy nicely. Onion sauce, or sauce soubise, was served with mutton, and with fish on Fridays.

Onion sandwiches were also a popular "feed" after a few pints, although not for the faint-hearted! Irish comedian Brendan Grace had a hilarious sketch where he described how his mother fed him onion sandwiches before going to a dance—the idea being to deter over-keen admirers. He was propelled around the dance floor by internal combustion!

Baked Onions

Baked or roast onions could be cooked long and slowly, either in the pot oven or in the embers of the open fire. Don't be alarmed by the thought of eating a whole onion! This cooking method makes them mild, sweet, and delicious. It is our very favorite way of eating onions and couldn't be simpler to prepare. You don't even have to peel them—just toss them into the oven.

Choose a number of small or medium-sized onions. Preheat the oven to 400°F. Place the unpeeled onions, on a baking sheet, in the oven and bake until soft; this can take anything from 10–30 minutes, depending on size. Serve the onions in their jackets. To eat, cut off the root end, squeeze out the onion and enjoy with butter and sea salt.

Jonathan Swift had a different recipe for ensuring against oniony breath:

> "There is in every cook's opinion
> No savoury dish without an onion
> But lest your kissing should be spoiled
> The onion must be thoroughly boiled."

Note: Stewed onions, eaten at night, were a folk remedy for constipation.

Serves 4 hungry men

1 rutabaga turnip, 1lb 15oz approx.
   when peeled
2 large onions (14oz approx.)
8 potatoes (3lb approx.)
salt and freshly ground pepper
2½ cups chicken or lamb stock
lump of lamb dripping
chopped parsley

Beggarman's Stew

This very simple dish of turnips, potatoes, and onions is quite delicious—comfort food at its best. It was sent to me by Queenie Endersen from Ballyellis, Mallow, Co. Cork. Her grandmother used to make it for the borders who lodged in her house. I came across several versions of this meatless stew, also mentioned by Patricia Murphy of Wexford as Blind Stew. It provided a filling, nutritious dinner even when meat could not be afforded.

Cut 1 small turnip into thick fingers, peel the onions, and slice into thick rings, peel the potatoes, and leave whole. Mix the onions with the turnips and put into the base of a saucepan. Place the potatoes on top and season well with salt and freshly ground pepper. Add the chicken or lamb stock, or failing that water. Bring to a boil, cover, and simmer until the vegetables are almost cooked (about 15 minutes).

Before the end of the cooking time, a nice piece of lamb dripping may be added. Watch carefully to ensure that the potatoes keep their shape and don't disintegrate. Add the chopped parsley and serve the stew in deep plates with lots of country butter.

Blind Stew

Serves 4–6

4–5 potatoes, peeled
1 medium carrot, peeled
1 parsnip, peeled
3 slices of turnip
a few slices of thick-cut bacon
 (optional)
2 large onions
salt and freshly ground pepper
chopped parsley
2 tablespoons all-purpose flour
2½ cups water

This is Patricia Murphy's recipe for Blind Stew, which is a stew without meat, but she also added the variation of including some bacon. Without the addition of meat, this was a hot nourishing meal for Fridays which was a "fast day"—no meat allowed. It had such a beautiful flavor, Patricia says.

Dice all the vegetables except the onion. Place in a saucepan. Cut the bacon slices into strips, if using, and fry until crisp. Add to the vegetables.

   To make the sauce, fry the onions in the bacon fat until caramelized. (Patricia told me that her mother would fry the onions until they were on the verge of burning, which gave a wonderful flavor.) Season well, adding some chopped parsley if available. Add the flour and slowly pour in the water, whisking well, and bring to a boil. Then pour the onion gravy over the vegetables. Cover and simmer until all the vegetables are cooked.

Peas

The Anglo-Normans Norse settlers may have introduced peas and beans to Ireland and they were a welcome addition to the Irish diet, which had relied heavily on milk products for protein since prehistoric times. Both peas and beans preserved well: we all here remember the packets of dried marrowfats, the forerunner to mushy peas! Fields of peas are grown around our area, so we feast on fresh peas for 2 or 3 weeks in July and August. At Ballymaloe, we offer guests freshly picked pea pods to nibble before dinner—a forgotten flavor for many.

Fresh Garden Peas

Serves 8–10

⅔ cup water
1 teaspoon salt
1 teaspoon sugar
1lb garden peas, freshly shelled
a sprig of mint
2 tablespoons (¼ stick) butter
1–2 teaspoons chopped fresh mint,
  to serve

Garden peas have a very short season, so feast on them when you can. Many of the peas in our garden don't even make it to the kitchen as my grandchildren eat them directly off the plant!

Bring the water to a boil. Add the salt, sugar, mint sprig, and the peas. Bring the water back to a boil and simmer until the peas are cooked, for approximately 4–5 minutes.

Strain the peas, reserving the water for soup or gravy. Add the butter. Garnish with a little chopped fresh mint and add a little extra seasoning if necessary. Eat immediately.

Marrowfat Peas

Serves 4–6

½ packet (8oz) dried split peas
½ teaspoon baking soda
4 cups boiling water
salt and freshly ground pepper
sugar
butter

Marrowfat peas were a traditional accompaniment to the Sunday roast in many households. The peas were soaked on Saturday night in a bowl of boiling water with the tablet of baking soda included in the packet. Next day they were cooked until they were soft and mushy. We didn't love them as children, but I now long for their almost-forgotten flavor.

Put the split peas into a bowl, add the baking soda and cover with the boiling water. Let soak overnight.

Next day, drain, and barely cover the peas with fresh boiling water. Bring to a boil and simmer for 15–20 minutes until tender.

When the peas are cooked, strain. Add salt, freshly ground pepper, sugar, and a big lump of butter to taste. Serve hot.

I found two recipes for cooking beans in the Lough Rynn manuscript of 1865. Lough Rynn in Co. Leitrim was one of Lord Leitrim's estates. Beans were a country house favorite, especially Scarlet Runner Beans which were grown in the walled gardens. Bean slicers were an essential gadget in country house kitchens. Beans are widely grown nowadays by keen home gardeners and there is a huge variety of seeds available for beans of varying size, color, and flavor.

This Lough Rynn recipe is particularly interesting in that it's the only reference to the use of the herb savory, a less well-known and under-used herb. Savory enhances the flavor of beans. There are two types: the annual summer savory, which is soft in texture; and the perennial winter savory, which has a more robust texture. The recipe didn't specify which beans, and, as ever, was not specific about the cooking time, so I suggest 5–6 minutes.

"Take a quart of beans. Blanch them and put them in a stewpan with a lump of butter, a bunch of parsley, green onions and savory. Strew a dust of flour over them. Toss them up. Moisten them with broth; season them with salt and pepper and let them be done enough. When done, thicken them with yolks of eggs beat up with cream, a little nutmeg and parsley cut very small. Dish them hot."

This recipe also from Lough Rynn is a very rich method of cooking French beans; the sauce seems to be similar to a Hollandaise sauce. Nowadays they would usually be cooked lightly and served more simply, maybe with a little butter.

"Take the tenderest French beans. Boil them in water, first breaking off their ends. When they are boiled, put in stewpan a piece of butter with them and parsley cut exceedingly small. When the butter is melted, put in the French beans. Give them two or three turns on the fire. Put in a little salt, a little flour and some good broth. Let them boil 'til the liquor is boiled almost away. And when you are ready to serve them up, beat up three yolks of eggs with a little milk. Put them to it and after put in a little dash of vinegar. Take care not to put it on the fire for fear of curdling."

Endive also features in the Lough Rynn manuscript in this recipe for dressed endive. It appears to have been a very sophisticated kitchen with a skilled cook.

"Trim and wash the endive. Boil it half an hour in water, then put it into cold water. Press out all the cold water until quite dry, then put it in a small stewpan with a little butter, a good broth and gravy. If you choose it with white sauce instead of gravy, put to it some yolks of egg beat up with a little cream. Serve it plain or under poached eggs."

Fresh Kale Salad

Serves 4–6

1lb curly kale, stalks removed
salt and freshly ground pepper
juice and zest of 2 lemons
½–¾ cup light cream
1 tablespoon sugar

Chop the kale very finely. Sprinkle with salt and the zest and juice of the lemons. Toss. Add the cream and sugar. Toss again. Taste and season.

Curly Kale

Serves 4–6

1lb curly kale, destalked (1lb 10oz with stalks)
salt, freshly ground pepper, and a little grated nutmeg
¼ cup (½ stick) butter
scant ½ cup light cream

Curly kale is a wonderfully nutritious vegetable, full of iron and trace elements. We grow many different varieties in the garden at the Cookery School, some with serrated leaves, some crinkly, others feathery. They come in a range of colors—purple, greeny-gray, creamy yellow.....

Bring a large saucepan of salted water to a boil, (3 quarts to 3 teaspoons salt). Add the curly kale, minus its stalks, and boil uncovered on a high heat until tender. This can vary from 5–10 minutes depending on how tough the kale is.

Drain off the water and purée the kale in a food processor. Return to the saucepan. Season with salt, freshly ground pepper, and a little nutmeg if you fancy.

Add a generous lump of butter and some cream, bubble, and taste.

Serve hot.

Cut and Come Kale

Serves 4

2lb winter kale
5 cups water
1 teaspoon salt
butter
salt and freshly ground pepper

*This type of kale (*Brassica oleracea*) is thought to be more than 2,000 years old and is of tremendous interest to botanists. It was unknown to me until I came across it in the 18th-century walled garden at Glin Castle in Co. Limerick. May Liston, one of the cooks at Glin, had originally brought slips of this vegetable from her home in Lower Athea and she gave me some to plant. The gardener, Tom Wall, called it "Cut and Come." Since I have begun to grow it myself in the kitchen garden several people have recognized it from their childhood and given it different names—Winter Kale, Winter Greens, Cut and Come, Cottier's Kale or Hungry Gap, because it was the only green available between the end of the winter and the arrival of the first spring vegetables. It is quite different from curly kale and is much more melting and tender when cooked.*

Wash and string the sprigs of kale. Bring the water to a boil, add the salt and kale. Cook the vegetable with the lid off, for about 25 minutes or until tender. Drain off all the water. Chop well, add a big lump of butter, and plenty of freshly ground pepper and salt.

Note: Cut and Come kale, like spinach, reduces a lot during cooking, so you need to start off with a large potful.

Cauliflower

Cauliflower was one of the later brassicas to be introduced to Ireland. It seems to have reached England during the 16th century from Spain and is likely to have reached Ireland soon afterwards. It is known that one Nicholas Shepherd sold cauliflower seeds in Dublin in 1685 to the gardener at Trinity College Dublin.

When I was a child, we grew cauliflowers in the garden. It was still considered a great treat. I remember helping Pad, our gardener, to bend the leaves up over the heads to protect the delicate white curds from the sharp midland frost.

I have failed to find the name of the old variety which we ate as children. Cauliflower varieties seem to have suffered more, flavorwise, than most other vegetables. The leaves are more flavorsome than the curd, so make sure not to discard them. Even a mediocre cauliflower can be made to taste delicious in a bubbling cheese sauce.

Cauliflower in Cheese Sauce

Serves 6–8

1 medium cauliflower with lots of
   fresh green leaves
table salt

CHEESE SAUCE
2½ cups milk with a dash of cream
slice of onion
3–4 slices carrot
6 peppercorns
a sprig of thyme or parsley
roux (see page 42)
1 heaping cup grated cheese,
   e.g. mature Irish Cheddar or a
   mixture of Gruyère, Parmesan
   and Cheddar
½ teaspoon English mustard
salt and freshly ground pepper
25g (1oz) grated mature Irish
   Cheddar cheese for the topping
chopped parsley, to serve

In the country house kitchen, cauliflower was often served with cheese sauce and gratinated in an oven. When cooking over the open fire this wasn't possible, so it was served boiled with white sauce. Grated cheese could be melted in the sauce: a simple grater was often made by punching holes in the base of a can with a nail from the inside.

Remove the outer leaves and wash both the cauliflower and the leaves well. Put not more than 1 inch water in a saucepan just large enough to take the cauliflower; add a little salt. Chop the leaves into small pieces and cut the cauliflower into quarters or eighths. Place the cauliflower on top of the green leaves in the saucepan, cover, and simmer until cooked (about 10–15 minutes). Test if the cauliflower is cooked by piercing the stalk with a knife: there should be just a little resistance. Remove the cauliflower and leaves to an ovenproof serving dish.

Meanwhile, make the cheese sauce. Put the cold milk into a saucepan with the onion, carrot, peppercorns, and thyme or parsley. Bring to a boil, simmer for 3–4 minutes, and remove from the heat; leave to infuse for 10 minutes. Strain out the vegetables, then bring the milk back to a boil, and thicken with roux to a light coating consistency. Add the grated cheese and a little mustard. Season with salt and freshly ground pepper, taste, and correct the seasoning if necessary. Spoon the sauce over the cauliflower and sprinkle with more grated cheese. The dish may be prepared ahead to this point.

Put into a hot oven (450°F) or under the broiler to brown. Serve sprinkled with parsley.

Note: If the cauliflower cheese is allowed to get completely cold, it will take 20–25 minutes to reheat in a moderate oven (350°F).

Beet

Beet was often grown along with potatoes, carrots, and onions in cottage plots. It appears to have lost popularity, partly, I imagine, because of the frightfully vinegary pickled variety on sale in jars. Some people ate it simply boiled as a vegetable, but typically it was pickled and served as part of a salad. It was also grown in kitchen gardens in country houses.

To prepare the beet, chop off the leaf stalks, leaving 2 inches of leaf stalk on the top and the whole root on the beet. Hold the beet under a running tap and wash off the mud with the palms of your hands, so that you don't damage the skin. Cover with cold water into which a little salt and sugar have been added. Cover the pot, bring to a boil, and simmer on top, or in an oven at 400°F, for 1–2 hours depending on size. They are cooked when the skin rubs off easily and if they dent when pressed with a finger.

Serves 5–6

2 cups water
1 cup plus 2 tablespoons superfine sugar
1 onion, peeled and thinly sliced
1 cup plus 1 tablespoon white wine vinegar
1lb cooked beet, peeled and sliced

Pickled Beet and Onion Salad

The onion may be omitted if desired. Malt instead of white wine vinegar would have originally been used. If using, let the beet mellow for a week or so before using.

Place the water and sugar in a pan and bring to a boil, stirring to dissolve. Add the sliced onion and simmer for 3–4 minutes. Add the vinegar. Place the beet in a bowl, pour over the pickling liquid and leave to cool.

Beet Salad

I came across a recipe for Beet Salad in the Bruen papers. Tarragon and chile vinegar sound thoroughly modern, but the papers actually date back to the 1800s.

"A little chopped shallot or onion
Also a little chopped parsley
1 tablespoonful of Tarragon and Chilli Vinegar
Also one of Salad oil
Pinch of pepper and salt"

Mix well together and pour over the beet (cooked), sliced thinly.

Pickled Beet

Annie Irwin's 1900 manuscript also included an intriguing recipe for pickled beet.
"Wash the beetroot [beet], but take care not to break the skin or the fibers which hang about it, else the color will fly. Boil softly for an hour or more if large, or bake them and as soon as they are cold enough to be handled, peel them, cut into slices, and place them in a jar, and have ready to pour over them cold vinegar in which black and Jamaica pepper, ginger, cloves and a little cayenne have been previously boiled. The slices when to be used, may be cut into the form of leaves, flowers or nicked around the edges—cochineal will improve the color."

Note: This pickle makes an elegant garnish, particularly if contrasted with the brilliant emerald green of pickled samphire (see page 201).

Radishes

Radishes were also grown as a salad component in summer, along with spring onions or scallions. The latter were often chopped up and added to hard-boiled egg and salad cream to make egg sandwiches. Egg sandwiches were a favorite for picnics, school lunches, and afternoon tea.

Traditional Irish Salad

This was often served for tea on Sunday with some cold meat sliced from the roast for lunch. It was also served as a summer treat with lettuce from the garden and slices of ham. Most village shops or bar and grocery establishments sold "cooked ham" which was sliced from a machine onto a sheet of parchment paper. This often had a scary bright yellow or orange crumb coating on the outside.

Sometimes on a "busy day" or when the new potatoes had just become available and the lettuce was ready in the garden, a dinner of salad and new potatoes with salad dressing was a delicious change. For tea, served with fresh crusty bread, it was often made into sandwiches at the table and was delicious with a cup of tea.

I came across many different salad dressings, soft, fresh, others boiled, which illustrates that salad was often eaten. There wasn't the wide variety of salad components we now expect, but when the main ingredients of lettuce, tomato, scallion, hard-cooked egg, beet, and meat were all of top quality, it was a tasty, deliciously fresh-tasting meal.

There is a reference in Malachy McKenna's writing on the Blasket Islands, *Putting Food on the Table*: "Gearóid O Catháin, who was born on the Island in 1947, was not fond of tomato and lettuce; an Island woman Mary Pheats Mhicí used to give Gearóid tomato and lettuce sandwiches, but these he just threw over the hedge once he had left her sight" (from *Oidhreacht an Bhlascaoid*/The Heritage of the Great Blasket Island).

Cookery Notes, published in 1949 and originally prepared for use in schools in Ireland, also includes directions for the preparation of salad: "Lettuce is often the only vegetable used. All or any of the following may be mixed with the lettuce: Mustard and cress, cucumber, celery, tomatoes, spring onions, radishes. The following cold cooked vegetables may also be used; beetroot [beet], potatoes, asparagus, peas and French beans. N.B. scraps of fowl, game, lamb, fish etc. may also be served to advantage in a salad."

Alice Taylor, writing *To School Through the Fields*, mentions having cold meat and salad as a "Tea Dinner" on Sunday at lunchtime. A "Tea Dinner" meant not cooking a meal with potatoes: it was an easy dinner, and could be a salad or a "fry," accompanied by tea and bread. It could be served on a busy day, such as a wash-day, or if one was going somewhere and trying to get away early.

My mother and Aunt Florence often spoke longingly of how my grandmother tossed crisp lettuce in a dressing of sour cream from the dairy with a little salt and sugar. Alternatively, she used fresh cream, sharpened with lemon juice, then balanced with sugar and salt.

2 free-range eggs
1 iceberg lettuce (the ordinary lettuce that one can buy everywhere)
4 tiny scallions
watercress sprigs
2–4 tomatoes, quartered
16 slices of cucumber
4 tablespoons Pickled Beet and Onion Salad (see page 183)
4 sliced radishes
chopped parsley

LYDIA STRANGMAN'S CREAM DRESSING
2 eggs, free-range if possible
4 teaspoons dark soft brown sugar
pinch of salt
1 level teaspoon dry mustard powder
1 tablespoon brown malt vinegar
3½–8 tablespoons cream

¼ tablespoon salt
1 tablespoon sugar
2 tablespoons mustard
3 tablespoons oil
3 eggs, beaten
8fl oz vinegar
8fl oz milk

Traditional Irish Salad

This simple old-fashioned salad is the sort of thing you would have had for tea on a visit to your Granny on a Sunday evening—perhaps with a slice of meat leftover from the Sunday roast. It is one of my absolute favorites.

It can be quite delicious made with a crisp lettuce, good home-grown tomatoes and cucumbers, free-range eggs, and home-preserved beet. If, on the other hand, you make it with pale battery eggs, watery tomatoes, tired lettuce and cucumber, and (worst of all) vinegary beets from a jar, you'll wonder why you bothered.

We serve this traditional salad as a starter in Ballymaloe, with an old-fashioned salad dressing which would have been popular before the days of mayonnaise. This recipe for salad dressing came from Lydia Strangman, the last occupant of our house.

Hard-boil the eggs for the salad and the dressing (4 in total). Bring a small saucepan of water to a boil, gently slide in the eggs, and boil for 10 minutes (12 if they are very fresh). Strain off the hot water and cover with cold water. Peel when cold.

Wash and dry the lettuce, scallions, and watercress.

Next make the cream dressing. Cut 2 of the eggs in half and sift the yolks into a bowl. Add the sugar, a pinch of salt, and the mustard. Blend in the vinegar and cream. Chop the egg whites and add some to the sauce. Keep the rest to scatter over the salad. Cover the dressing until needed.

To assemble the salads, first arrange a few lettuce leaves on each of 4 plates. Scatter with a few tomato quarters and 2 hard-cooked egg quarters, a few slices of cucumber, and a radish on each plate, and (preferably just before serving) add a slice of beet to each. Garnish with scallions and watercress. Scatter the remaining egg white (from the dressing) and some chopped parsley over the salad.

Put a tiny bowl of cream dressing in the center of each plate and serve immediately, while the salad is crisp and before the beet starts to run. Alternatively, serve the dressing from one large bowl.

Note: Nowadays we serve the hard-cooked eggs for the salad slightly soft in the center— cook for 7 minutes instead of 10. The eggs for the dressing, on the other hand, need to be hard-cooked as above.

Variation
Salad Dressing

This recipe was in a collection of hand-written recipes sent to me by Anne Mangan from Clonskeagh in Dublin,

Put the salt, sugar, mustard and oil into a bowl and stir into a smooth paste, then gradually whisk in the eggs, vinegar and milk. Put the bowl in a saucepan of boiling water over the fire and stir until it thickens like custard. Bottle when cold and cork tightly.

Food from the Wild

Our early ancestors, the hunter-gatherers, lived on the bounty of wild foods which were provided by the land and sea. They understood the pattern of the seasons, and moved from place to place in pursuit of different foods at different times of the year. In spring they camped around the estuaries and ate fish and shellfish, and the eggs of seabirds. Towards summer they moved inland, following the salmon up river, and in autumn there was a proliferation of nuts and berries to enjoy.

Nowadays, in times of relative plenty, many of these wild foods are neglected and often left to rot in the hedgerows. Fortunately it is now becoming wildly fashionable for restaurants to feature such things as wild garlic, bittercress, wild mushrooms, samphire, sorrel, damsons, and other free foods from nature on their menus. For years Ballymaloe House has encouraged local children to forage in the countryside and to bring their finds to the kitchen door for use in the restaurant. Here at the Cookery School we've been teaching a Foraging Course for almost 20 years and the demand gathers momentum as the interest in wild foods from the hedgerows, woods, and seashore continues to grow. There's now a deep craving to reconnect and relearn the innate skills of our hunter-gatherer ancestors.

Wild Garlic

Wild garlic has been used in Ireland as a condiment or as part of a relish since earliest times. In the heyday of many large Irish estates it was apparently quite common to plant it on the edges of woodland and pasture. In late spring, when the cattle and sheep were put out to grass after the long winter indoors, the garlic was thought to have a beneficial effect on them. There are two types: wild garlic (*Allium ursinum*), which grows in shady places along the banks of streams and in undisturbed mossy woodland, and snowbells (*Allium triquestrum*), which resemble white bluebells and usually grow along the sides of country lanes. Also delicious mixed with mashed potatoes or added to cooked greens or salads.

Serves 10 (approximately)

leg of young lamb (1.5–2kg approx.)
oil, butter, or lamb fat
salt and freshly ground pepper
3–6 wild garlic plants, picked preferably just before they flower
1lb scallions (18–22 approx.), peeled
3–4 small potatoes (1lb approx.), peeled

Lamb Braised with Wild Garlic

Myrtle Allen gave me this delicious recipe, which she serves at Ballymaloe when the wild garlic is just about to bloom in May. Later in the season, garlic cloves can be used with fresh herbs, such as thyme or marjoram, making a good substitute for garlic's own green leaves.

Brown the lamb in a little oil, butter, or lamb fat. Season with salt and freshly ground pepper. Chop up the wild garlic plants and press into the skin of the meat with the herbs (if using). Sauté the scallions and potatoes in the same fat and then put them around the meat and herbs in a heavy cast-iron casserole. Cover with a tight fitting lid.

Cook in a moderate oven at 350°F for 1½–2 hours or until cooked through. Strain off the juices and pour off the fat. Serve the juices separately as a gravy. A little good stock may be added if not enough juices are left in the pot. More chopped fresh wild garlic may be added to the gravy, if you wish.

Sorrel

Throughout the 16th and 17th centuries, a number of visitors to Ireland commented on the Irish practice of eating shamrock. These references to shamrock have been variously interpreted: one suggestion is that shamrock was, in fact, sorrel. One of the first to record the consumption of shamrock/sorrel was Edmund Campion in *A History of Ireland*, 1571, who observed that "shamrotes, watercresses, rootes and other herbes they feed upon."

In his Irish herbal of 1735, the *Botanalogia Universalis Hibernica*, the Reverend John K'Eogh makes the following entry for sorrel:

It is beneficial for the heart, mouth, and liver because it induces perspiration, it is also good against jaundice. It cleanses and heals rotten ulcers.

Sorrel Pie from Inis Mhic Uibhleáin

Serves 6–8

1lb all-purpose flour
1 level teaspoon baking soda
pinch of salt
½oz butter
1¼–1½ cups buttermilk
4–6oz sorrel leaves
2 heaping tablespoons brown sugar

baking dish, 9-inch x 2-inch

I first learned about the existence of this recipe from Jane Grigson. Charles J. Haughey tracked it down for me in the book Bean an Oileáin *by Máire Ní Ghuithín (1986) and had it translated from Irish. The author's aunt, who was born and reared on Inis Mhic Uibhleáin, was apparently the first and only woman to use this recipe. The pie was baked in a three-legged pot set over an open fire, with hot coals placed on top of the lid. According to* Bean an Oileáin *young children on the Great Blasket Island used to eat sorrel leaves, even though they found them very bitter.*

Place the flour in a bowl with the baking soda and salt. Rub in the butter and wet with buttermilk to form a soft, pliable dough. Knead lightly on a lightly floured work surface and cut in half. Flatten one half of the dough wwith your hand to form a circle the same size as your pot. Place the sorrel leaves on top of the pastry and sprinkle Flatten dough with hand. Place the sorrel leaves on one half of the flattened dough and prinkle with brown sugar. (We put some underneath and on top of the sorrel.) Flatten the second piece of dough to the same size and use to cover the sorrel mixture, pressing the edges to seal.

Butter and flour your cooking pot and place the pie inside. Put on the lid adn transfer to a hot oven at 450°F. Our pie took 1 hour to bake and cooked to a pale golden color in the covered pot. It had a bitter-sweet flavor and was quite delicious.

Nettles

Nettles have always been one of the most important and abundant wild foods in Ireland.

On Cape Clear, Oilean Cléire, an island off the West Cork coast, there was an annual feast on May 1st called *Féile na Neantóg*. On that day all the children would have great sport chasing each other with bundles of stinging nettles. If they wet the nettles beforehand it put "extra heat" in them. They stung every inch of each others' bodies. This was done with great glee and without a shred of remorse.

Older people also believed that nettle stings helped to cure "the pains." I have heard this in many parts of the country; on Cape Clear, Donncadh O'Drisceóil remembered how people would throw off their clothes and roll in a bed of nettles, not happy until their entire body was covered with the blisters. They were convinced that this would cure rheumatism. It would certainly divert your attention from the pain of the rheumatism for a while!

The tradition of eating nettles still lives on in many rural areas, particularly among the older generation. Many people still eat several "feeds" of nettles during May to clear the blood and "keep the rheumatics away" for the rest of the year.

Islanders also fed nettles to the pigs and hens. Donncadh O'Drisceóil described in his book *Aistí O Chleíre* how he would search around the edge of the house and sheds for young nettles. The nettles were scalded and mixed with yellowmeal to entice the pig to eat them, and it was highly prized as a cheap and healthy food. He also believed that the nettle supplement encouraged the hens to go broody and hatch bigger and healthier clutches of chickens—a very desirable thing in what was virtually a self-sufficient community.

Nettle Cheese

Nettle cheese was popular a few hundred years ago. It was made only about an inch thick to enable quick ripening. It was made with cow's or sheep's milk, and after a day or two it was laid on a bed of nettles and covered with nettles, which speeded up the ripening process. The nettles were changed once a day until the cheese was ready. This cheese was known sometimes as Slipcoat. Cornish Yarg cheese is also wrapped in nettle leaves.

Nettles may also be added to cheese in the same way as herbs: either dried and crumbled or cooked and finely chopped leaves. They can be added as the cheese is forming, or mixed into a soft cheese before eating. Nettle juice, or the liquid formed by boiling nettle leaves in a strong salt solution, can be used as rennet substitute in cheese-making.

Nettle soup is the most palatable way of serving nettles traditionally but it is likely that they would have been just cooked like spinach and eaten for their iron content and blood purifying properties. See page 19 for nettle soup recipes

In her book *To School through the Fields: an Irish Country Childhood*, Alice Taylor writes about growing up on a farm near Newmarket, Co. Cork, in the 1940s. She describes killing the pig and how every last scrap of the animal was put to use. "Gradually we ate our way down that barrel of bacon: we had bacon and cabbage, bacon and turnips, and once or twice a year—when my mother decided that the iron in nettles was very good for us—we had bacon and nettles, which we ate under loud protest."

To Cook Young Nettles

This recipe comes from Catherine Dowd-Rohan, from Annascaul, Co. Kerry:

"Fill a 2qt bowl with young nettles, just only the top of them, not more than 6 leaves, wash well and drain. Have ready an enamel saucepan and into it put about 1oz of fresh butter and a little seasoning of salt and pepper. Sometimes a tiny bit of spice of clove. pack in nettles. Put lid on saucepan for a few minutes over fire and then stir and chop vigorously with large wooden spoon. Put on lid again and in less than 10 mins this dish is ready and can be rubbed through a sieve and can be served with poached egg if liked."

Serves 4–6

1lb chanterelles
1–2 tablespoons butter
salt and freshly ground pepper
1 tablespoon chopped parsley
4–6 slices hot buttered toast

Chanterelles on Buttered Toast

Apart from field mushrooms, people are very wary and suspicious of other varieties of mushrooms. Those who traveled, particularly to France and Spain, became very familiar with late summer and autumn chanterelles, and searched for them in the woods and discovered how delicious they were, they then started to cook and serve them at home in a variety of ways. Chanterelles grow in woodlands of beech, birch, oak, and Scots pine and acid soil suits them.

Trim off the earthy part of the stems. Then wash the caps quickly but carefully, and drain them well. Slice or keep whole, depending on the size. Melt some butter in a skillet, add the mushrooms, and fry over high heat. The mushrooms will begin to exude their juice, but continue to cook on very high heat until the juices are reabsorbed. Season with salt and pepper, sprinkle with parsley, and serve immediately on hot buttered toast.

Field Mushrooms

The mere mention of wild mushrooms evokes nostalgic memories for most Irish people, who recall racing out at dawn with cookie pans to search for wild mushrooms in the dewy fields. Many remember cooking them over embers on the hearth, and on the cool plate of the range, with nothing more than a few grains of salt for seasoning. Sometimes the mushrooms were stewed in milk and occasionally, when there was a glut in warm humid autumn weather, we'd collect bucketfulls and make mushroom ketchup. See also the recipe for Field Mushroom Soup on page 21.

Nowadays the common field mushroom is scarcer than ever, because of modern intensive farming, but the Irish woods are peppered with wild mushrooms, chanterelles, morels, deceivers, hedgehog mushrooms, and many more. There is a deep suspicion of unusual wild mushrooms in Ireland, which may come from folk memories of cases of mushroom poisoning during famine times. However, people are now becoming much more adventurous and wild mushrooms are beginning to appear on the menus of more innovative restaurants. If you choose to pick wild mushrooms yourself, always be sure to have expert help with identification.

Alice Taylor also describes picking wild mushrooms: "When the sun had warmed the heart of the earth it thrust forth white garlands of little button mushrooms [...] Some fields were mushroom fields and others were not, and we knew where to look, but so did all the neighbouring children. Where mushrooms were concerned it was a free-for-all with farm boundaries of no consequence. So, if mushrooms were on your mind you rose early because as well as other early pickers there was the fact that cows and horses could trample them into the ground. Gathering mushrooms in the early summer morning, with the dew washing your toes and the thrill of discovery growing with each white cluster, was a lovely experience.

"Finally, gallon full, we skipped home through the sun-warmed fields to savour our collection. We cooked them for breakfast on red hot sods of turf beside the fire. Each white mushroom was placed on its back, in its pale pink cup a shake of salt which melted and mingled with the juices as it cooked. Picking it up, careful not to spill, first you drank it and then you ate it, a little chalice with the liquid and flavor of the open fields. Sometimes my mother boiled them in milk but somehow that was to reduce to the ordinary this food of the earth that needed no preparation as it was bathed in the morning dew and could be eaten as picked, such was its delicacy and freshness."

Máire Ní Ghuithín, writing about mushrooms in *Bean an Oileáin* (Women of the Island), describes how they cooked them in a similar way on the island. "We used to collect mushrooms and lay them on the embers of the fire. We sprinkled salt over them and when the juice was running out of them we would lift them off and eat them. They were very good. But we used to prepare them in a different way for the visitors who were staying with us— we took the stem off and peeled them. We fried them in fat from rashers or we cooked them in a drop of milk in a saucepan and added in onions and sauce. But we enjoyed them very much when they were roasted or cooked on the embers—that's how we ourselves ate them." Malachy McKenna writes that the sauce mentioned by Máire was probably made from milk and flour; the difference between the normal fare of the islanders and how they prepared food for visitors is again illustrated here, their own diet was simpler. Máire gives these mushrooms their Irish name of *púcaí peill*—they didn't pick any black ones as they were thought to be poisonous and shouldn't be eaten. The pale red or pink ones were the right ones to eat.

The late Monica Sheridan, Ireland's first television cook, writes in her 1963 book, *Monica's Kitchen*: "Towards the end of an Irish summer, when the air is still warm, a night of soft rain brings up crops of mushrooms in the fields. There is no commercially grown mushroom to compare with the wild fungus that grows, untended, in the open pasture, and city people who have never had the thrill of hunting for mushrooms on a dewy morning and cooking them for breakfast, have missed one of the great treats of life [...] Sometimes there is not a sign of them until September, and some years they hardly appear at all. But, in a good year, you can go out in the morning and fill a bucket in half-an-hour."

Wild Plum Gin

Makes 1.5 quarts approx.

4½ cups wild plums (about 1½lb)
1¾ cups granulated sugar
5 cups gin or poteen

Wild plums, the fruit of the blackthorn (Prunus spinosa) are very tart berries that resemble tiny purple plums in appearance. They grow on prickly bushes on top of stone walls and are in season in September and October. They make a wonderful drink, ready for consuming at Christmas. Delicious damson gin can be made in exactly the same way. A few fistfuls added to crab apples make a delicious wild plum and crab apple jelly, particularly good with cold pork or a coarse terrine.

Wash and dry the wild plums and prick in several places (we use a clean darning needle). Put them into a sterilized glass kilner jar and cover with sugar and gin. Cover and seal tightly. Shake during this time—initially every couple of days and then every so often for 3–4 months, by which time it will be ready to strain and bottle. It will improve on keeping, so try to resist drinking it for another few months!

Wild Damson Jam

Makes 6–8 jars

9 cups damsons (about 6lb)
9 cups granulated sugar
scant 4 cups water

Damson jam was a great favorite of mine as a child. My friends and I collected damsons every year in a field near the old castle in Cullohill, Co. Laois. First we ate so many we almost burst! The rest we brought home to be made into jam, fruit pies, or compotes.

Pick over the fruit carefully. Wash and drain well and discard any damaged damsons. Put the damsons and water into a greased stainless steel preserving kettle and stew them gently until the skins break. Heat the sugar in a low oven, add it to the fruit, and stir on low heat until the sugar is dissolved. Increase the heat and boil steadily, stirring frequently. Skim off the stones and scum as they rise to the top. A tedious but necessary job. Test for a set after 15 minutes' boiling. Pour a teaspoonful onto a cold plate and push the jam gently with your finger. It should wrinkle when the jam has set. Pour into hot sterilized jars and cover. Store in a cool dry place. Label and warn people to watch out for stray stones!

"Get the crabs fresh. Wash them well but do not peel them. Put them into a preserving pan, cover with spring water by two inches. Boil them quick they will fall in a few minutes. Put the whole into a flannel bag the juice will be got in a few minutes. Into a clean preserving pan put a pint of juice to a lb of sugar if a small quantity is made 20 minutes will make it, if a large lot it will take from 35–45 minutes but watch it and when it jellies dish it immediately if it stands two minutes after it is taken off the fire the jell will not be sound."

Makes 6–7 jars

9 cups crab apples (about 6lb) or cooking apples
scant 3 quarts water
juice and rind of 2 lemons
granulated sugar
chopped sweet geranium or mint leaves or cloves (optional)

Crab Apple and Sweet Geranium Jelly

We love this jelly flavored with sweet geranium to serve on scones or toast. Either sweet or savory; it can be flavored with cloves, rosemary, mint, sage or chile.

Wash the apples and cut into quarters. Do not remove the peel or core. Put the apples into a large saucepan with the water and the thinly pared rind of the lemons. Cook until reduced to a pulp (about 30 minutes).

Turn the pulp into a jelly bag. Let it drip until all the juice has been extracted (overnight is best). Measure the juice into a preserving kettle and measure out 2¼ cups sugar to each 2½ cups of juice. Warm the sugar.

Squeeze the lemons, strain the juice, and add to the preserving kettle. Bring to a boil, add the sugar (and the sweet geranium, mint or cloves if using). Stir over low heat until the sugar is dissolved. Increase the heat and boil rapidly without stirring for about 8–10 minutes. Skim and test to see if setting point has been reached by placing a teaspoonful on a cold plate and pushing it gently with your finger (if the jelly wrinkles, it is ready). Immediately pour into warm sterilized jars, cover, and seal.

Crab Apple Cake

Wild crab apple trees blossom and fruit all through the Irish countryside, year in, year out. I came across many recipes for crab apple jelly, and even wine, but this recipe, the only one for a crab apple cake, came from Mrs Carrow from Togher, near Drogheda in Co. Louth. She was given it by her mother. No doubt this would be delicious served with soft brown sugar and cream.

Serves 10 approx.

scant 5¼ cups all-purpose flour
1 cup plus 2 tablespoons superfine sugar
1 teaspoon baking soda
1 cup (2 sticks) butter
1 dozen crab apples
2 duck eggs
sour milk, to mix

Mix the flour, sugar, and baking soda together in a bowl and rub in the butter. Peel, core, and cut the crab apples in halves and put into the mixture. Beat the eggs well with a fork and add the sour milk to form a dropping consistency, then add the flour.

Knead the mixture into a round cake and bake in a well-buttered, covered sauté pan in a moderate oven (350°F) for 1 hour.

Medlars

The medlar, a type of wild apple tree, was probably introduced into Ireland in the 16th century. In the spring the trees are covered with pale pink flowers which produce the bizarre-looking fruit from which this jelly is made; in autumn they provide a feast of rich color. The fruit is similar to a crab apple and needs to be half-rotten (bletted) before it can be eaten.

Medlars are another fruit mentioned in John K'Eogh's 1735 work, *Botanalogia Universalis Hibernica*:

"Medlars have a cold dry astringent nature. When hard and green, they are useful in stopping diarrhoea. If the crushed stones of the Medlar are drunk in a solution, they break up bladder stones."

Medlar Jelly

ripe medlars—slightly soft (bletted)
granulated sugar
stick of cinnamon
2 cloves
2 strips of lemon peel

Don't let John K'Eogh's riveting description put you off, because medlar jelly is quite delicious! Serve it with game or pork, or with cream cheese.

Cut the fruit into quarters, put into a stainless steel saucepan. Cover with water, bring to a boil, and cook until soft. Pour into a jelly bag and leave to drip overnight. Don't squeeze the jelly through the bag or the juice will be cloudy. Next day measure the juice and allow 2¼ cups sugar to every 2½ cups juice. Warm the sugar and add to the hot juice. Add the spices and lemon peel and boil until setting point is reached. Pour into hot sterilized jars and cover immediately. Serve with game and terrines.

Clonbrock Medlar Jelly

This jelly was made from the medlars which grew in the walled garden at Clonbrock in Co. Galway, and the recipe is from the *Kitchen Book of Clonbrock*:

Take sufficient ripe medlars, they need not be yellow but must be quite ripe. Place in a preserving pan with the peel of a lemon and enough water to cover. Simmer very gently until the fruit is pulped. Pour the contents of the pan into a large sieve and allow the liquid to strain off gradually. Do not press the pulp through or the jelly will be cloudy. Measure the liquid and allow 350g (¾lb) of sugar to every pint. Pour the liquid into a clean pan and boil rapidly for thirty minutes, skimming off the scum if necessary. Heat the sugar in the oven and add to the contents of the pan, stir until the sugar is dissolved and continue boiling for ten minutes. Drop a little on a plate to see if it sets. If not, boil for a few minutes longer or until the syrup jellies when cold. Pour the jelly into small jars and stand in a sunny window for several hours. The next day put a round of white tissue paper dipped in the white of an egg on top of the jelly and cover with transparent paper in the usual way.

Note the interesting instruction to dip paper in the white of an egg before covering. In the *Birr Castle Manuscript Cookbook* papers were dipped in alcohol before being used to cover preserves.

Rowanberries

Rowan trees are native to Ireland. Rowans were not cultivated for their fruit, however, but for their powers to ward off evil spirits, often planting a rowan beside a house. Nevertheless, our ancestors clearly did not ignore the fruit of this magical tree. In a 12th-century Fenian poem it is said "I will eat good apples in the glen and fragrant berries of rowan tree."

Dr John Rutty, writing in his 1772 *An Essay towards a Natural History of the County of Dublin*, states that frost-bitten rowanberries possess a "sweet, acid, not an ungrateful taste."

Pickled Crab Apples

Makes 10 x 13oz jars

15 cloves
15 allspice berries
2 star anise
1-inch stick of cinnamon
5 cups white wine vinegar
2¼ cups granulated sugar
4½–6 cups small crab apples (about 3–4lb)

We use the ornamental crab apple "Red Sentinel" to make this delicious and pretty pickle. We love to serve them with a glazed ham, cold pork, or bacon.

Tie the spices in a little muslin bag. Put them into a stainless-steel saucepan with the vinegar and sugar, and bring to a boil, stirring until the sugar dissolves.

Wash the crab apples and trim their stalks to ¼inch. Put them into a perforated wire basket (like a chip basket) and carefully lower them into the boiling vinegar. Leave for 5 minutes and remove before the skins start to crack. Put the apples into small, sterilized bottling jars or jam pots.

Meanwhile, boil down the vinegar and sugar until very syrupy, then cover the apples in the jars with it and seal immediately. Leave for several months before using. In time the apples will leach their red color into the liquid, which makes a pretty pickle. Serve with pork or ham.

Monica Nevin's Rowanberry Jelly

Makes 3–4 jars

2lb rowanberries
1lb cooking apples (3 approx.) or crab apples (about 1½ cups)
2½ cups water
juice of 1 lemon
granulated sugar

If you know some secret place where there is still an "unrobbed" crab apple tree, now is the time to use your knowledge. Cooking apples are a good substitute, however.

Wash the berries and wash and cut up the apples without peeling or coring them. Put all the fruit into a preserving kettle with the water and lemon juice and stew gently for 1 hour. Strain the juice. Then finish in the same way as for apple jelly.

Blackberries

In the book *Ballycotton School Memories*, Bessie Mullane Walsh wrote about going to school in the 1930s (Bessie walked several miles to school). "We would have to be in school at half-nine and then it would be around four o'clock before we got back home—but if the blackberries were out, 'twould be later! We used to love the blackberries, and our mother would be out looking to see what was keeping us. She used to say, 'What kept ye this evening?' and we used to say we were kept in, but she'd say, 'Ye were not, weren't ye over there on the road for the last half hour!'"

Alice Taylor, in *To School through the Fields*, also remembers the blackberries. "Each blackberry was inspected on picking to see that the stem base was free from small tell-tale holes, the tracks of tiny snails that feasted on the blackberries, especially when the rain brought them forth in great numbers; any blackberries with these signs were returned to mother earth. First we ate what we could contain, developing purple-smudged mouths and fingers; then we filled gallons and buckets to the brim. My mother made large two pound pots of blackberry jam, most of which were consumed at a rapid rate, but some of which were stored to bring the taste of summer to the winter months." Two-pound pots of jam were once common, and jam covers came in two sizes for the one-pound and two-pound pots. They have since died out entirely.

"Blackberries were a great rarity on the Island, there was only one bush growing at the side of the glen beside a field that I had. As soon as the blackberries started to come out on the bush, they were eaten," writes Seán Pheats Tom Ó Cearnaigh about the Great Blasket Island, in *Fiolar an eireaball bháin* (The Whitetailed Eagle). "On visits to the mainland, where blackberries were in greater supply, islanders would pick them and bring them back to the Island." Áine de Blacam also remembers picking blackberries and wild strawberries on Inis Meáin.

"As well as blackberry jam, blackberry and apple tart was also made, in the bastible, or in more recent years in the oven."

Blackberry Jam

Makes 9lb (approximately)

7 cups blackberries (about 2lb)
11¼ cups sugar
12 cooking apples (about 4lb)

Rose Hanlon's recipe scrapbook, which she called The Joy of Good Eating, *dates from the late 1940s and early 1950s, and contains cuttings of many of Monica Nevin's recipes from the* Irish Independent. *Rose was great at preserving fruit, making jam, and bottling, using both the produce of the garden and wild fruit. In an article on windfalls, Monica Nevin gave detailed instructions on preserving and the secrets of potting and storing. She gave a recipe for blackberry jelly, and also a recipe for when blackberries are scarce: "If you do not want to go to the trouble of making blackberry jelly and would still like a preserve without seeds, you might like to try the following recipe." It is also a useful recipe when blackberries are in short supply.*

Take the stems from the blackberries and lay the berries in a dish. Sprinkle them with 2¼ cups sugar and let rest overnight. Next day, simmer them gently to extract the juice. Strain the juice. Peel, core, and slice the apples and put them in a preserving kettle with the blackberry juice and the rest of the sugar. Heat the contents of the kettle gently and stir the mixture until the sugar is dissolved, then bring the jam to a boil and boil rapidly until it sets when tested.

FOR THE PIE DOUGH

2½ cups all-purpose flour
¼ teaspoon salt
3 tablespoons superfine sugar
½ teaspoon baking soda
½ cup (1 stick) butter
1 organic egg, beaten
About ½ cup sour milk or buttermilk

3–4 cooking apples, e.g. Gala or
   Red Delicious
¾ cup blackberries
¾ cup–¾ cup plus 3 tablespoons
   granulated sugar (depending on
   sweetness of apples)
beaten egg to glaze

TO SERVE

fine superfine sugar, for sprinkling
soft brown sugar and softly
   whipped cream

10-inch enamel or Pyrex plate,
   lightly greased

Mummy's Country Blackberry and Apple Cake

This traditional Irish recipe is particularly interesting because it uses sour milk or buttermilk. This makes a softer pie dough, more cakey than other pie doughs. Made on a plate, it was a tart rather than a cake. Mummy made it throughout the year, according to what fruit was in season. Firm fruit such as apple, rhubarb, and gooseberries must be sliced thinly to ensure that it cooks properly.

Sift the flour, salt, sugar, and baking soda into a bowl. Rub in the butter. Add the beaten egg and enough sour milk or buttermilk to mix to a stiff dough. Turn out onto a floured board. Divide in two. Roll both pieces into rounds large enough to fit the plate and line the plate with one of the rounds. Peel and core the apples and cut into thin slices. Put a good layer of thinly sliced apple on the pie dough, put the blackberries on top, and sprinkle with sugar. Cover with another piece of dough. Pinch the edges together. Brush the top with egg wash. Bake in a moderate oven (350°F) for about 1 hour or until the pie dough is golden and the fruit is soft and juicy.
   Sprinkle with superfine sugar and serve warm with soft brown sugar and softly whipped cream.

Fraughans or Blueberries

Fraughans, blueberries, herts, or bilberries are the names used in different parts of Ireland for the intensely flavored wild blueberries that grow on the acid hilltops. Fraughans are inextricably linked with the festival of Lughnasa, the first Sunday in August, which came to be known as Garland Sunday or Fraughan Sunday. It was the tradition in many places for the whole community to take off to a chosen place in the mountains, or beside a lake or stream or holy well, for a carefree day of picnicking, singing, dancing, sports, and picking wild fraughans, which would either have been eaten crushed, with sugar and cream, as here, or baked into cakes. It was also a time for serious courting, as is clear from the maxim: "Many a lad met his wife on Blaeberry Sunday." Blueberries were also used to make a drink called *fraochán*.

fraughans or blueberries
superfine sugar, to taste
softly whipped cream, to serve

Crushed Blueberries

This is quite the most delicious way to eat these little wild berries!

Crush the berries with a pounder or potato masher and sweeten to taste with superfine sugar. Serve with softly whipped cream. Alternatively, fold in about half their volume of whipped cream to make a tasty blueberry fool.

Wild Food from the Seashore

"Poor people need never be hungry when you have the strand." Bridget Guerin, who lives in Ballyheighue, Co. Kerry, recalls how they picked *bairneachs* (limpets), winkles, and seaweeds, such as dilisk, *sliúháne,* and carrageen off the seashore and sold them. Enterprising and hardworking people all around the coast of Ireland collected what they could to feed themselves and to supplement what was often a meager income. They well knew their value in the diet, and the practice of chewing seaweeds is still very strong on the western and northern seaboard. Indeed there is currently a mini seaweed revival, now that the healthy properties of the seaweed that flourishes in Ireland's clean waters are recognized abroad.

On the Blasket Islands, seaweed was used mainly as a fertilizer and was greatly valued for the potatoes and cabbage. Some seaweed was eaten however. Máire Ní Ghuithín in *Bean an Oileáin* (Women of the Island) mentions a variety called *láir*, which was a brown seaweed that was washed up on the strand. There was another one that grew on stones: this had a hot taste and was known as *uisce beatha* (whiskey/water of life). *Duileasc* (dulse) was the other one she mentioned that was eaten.

Seagrass and sea lettuce were also mentioned as being eaten on the Blaskets. Máire Ní Ghuithín distinguished between *sleaidí dearg* (red sea lettuce) and *sleadí na trá* (strand sea lettuce). Red sea lettuce had the better taste of the two and it was used to make a sweet drink that the islanders drank. It was cooked in the pot-oven with salt water, and pressed against the side of the pot with a wooden spoon. The resulting liquid was poured into mugs and drunk, and the pieces of sea lettuce were eaten with a spoon.

Máire Ní Ghuithín records that limpets, dulse, and sea-lettuce were boiled together in salt water and eaten with boiled potatoes which were dipped in the juices.

Duileasc cloiche (lichen), literally meaning "stone dulse," was mostly picked at spring tide because it was possible to get to the stones on which it grew; it was mostly gathered by women, girls, and boys. Seán Ó Dálaigh, writing in *Timcheall Chinn Sléibhe* (Around Slea Head), says that some people ate fresh lichen, though they needed good teeth to do so. Usually it was treated before being eaten, and the most difficult part of this was drying it because it needed good sunshine. The best place for drying was on a thatched roof where it would get the sun as well as any breeze that blew. It had to be turned over for three or four days, and if it got enough sun during this period it would be properly dried and could be stored. If it got rain during the drying period it had to be thrown away because it was impossible to dry it, so it was only picked during sunny weather. As it dried a layer of salt formed on it—many people just licked the salt off it and didn't bother eating the lichen itself, as they believed that all the goodness was in the salt. Lichen was popular with visitors to Dún Chaoin and the island; if people came to visit their relatives they were delighted to be given some to take home. Emigrants in America were sent some in the post, and young girls when emigrating would take it with them for their relatives. Neilí Ui Bheaglaoich, writing in *Carraig a' Dúin* (The Fort Rock), relates that she brought dried dulse with her when she emigrated to America in the 1920s: "I took a white bag full of dulse over with me and it was tied to the outside of the case so that the smell of dulse wouldn't be on my clothes…The Customs didn't ask me about it—they knew what it was. They had got the smell of it."

Seán Ó Dálaigh also mentions that on the mainland not many people ate *clúimhín cait* (carrageen moss); they gathered lichen in preference to it. Máire Ní Ghuithín records that on the island people did gather the moss and brought it home in a tin. It was spread out on the ground to allow the dew to whiten it—it was ready to be cooked when it turned white. Máire describes how they cooked it: "we would wash some of it and then we would cook it in milk in a saucepan. When it had melted and thickened, we would pour it into a bowl and mix in half a spoon of coffee to take away the oily taste from it."

Sloke or Sliúháne *(Porphyra laciniata)*

Sliúháne is a short, thin ribbon seaweed that only grows on sloping rock flag—hence the name sliú *meaning slant. The flags are washed daily by the tide which makes them very slippery so the picking of* sliúháne *is highly dangerous.* Sliúháne *has a very short growing season from January to early March and old people say that it is best gathered after a spell of frost. This traditional recipe for* sliúháne *is supplied by John Francis Guerin of Ballyheigue, Co. Kerry. He tells me that* sliúháne *is reputed to be an aphrodisiac! It is certainly a particularly delicious seaweed.*

Cut the *sliúháne* into small pieces with scissors. Place in a pot of water and boil slowly for 1 hour. Then pound or knead the *sliúháne*, using a specially prepared stick with a pared, tapered end, until the whole lot becomes semi-liquid. Boil slowly for a further hour. Finally add a knob of butter and some pepper. Eat on its own or with fish, ham, or roast lamb.

Carrageen Moss

Carrageen moss is a seaweed which can be gathered off the south and west coasts of Ireland. It is rich in iodine and trace elements, and is also full of natural gelatin. *Carraigín* means "little rock" in Gaelic. Myrtle Allen writes in *The Ballymaloe Cookbook*:

"Ballyandreen is a tiny fishing village by a rocky inlet four miles south of Ballymaloe. For generations the inhabitants there have gathered and sold Carrageen Moss. It is picked from the farthest out rocks at low water during spring tides in June. This means that it is almost always covered by sea water. It is then laid out on the short grass on the cliff top to dry and bleach in the sun. It has the reputation of being a health giving food. It is a source of agar jelly. It certainly contains iron and minerals. Traditionally, it was fed to calves and made into cough syrups and milk puddings. I have used it all my life. I have thickened milk for babies with it at weaning time. For more sophisticated meals I serve it topped with whipped cream and coffee sauce strongly laced with whiskey."

Chocolate carrageen has nostalgic memories for me. I first encountered it at Sunday night supper in this house, long ago, when it was still clad in its Victorian décor and life was very different. A product that is hard to measure, however, is hard to market. This is so with carrageen moss. The success of this dish lies in using only just enough carrageen needed to get a set—so that you don't taste it in the pudding, as a less than enthusiastic friend pointed out! Carrageen makes a soothing drink for a sore throat and all our babies were weaned on it. Carrageen sometimes comes mixed with grass and other seaweeds, which should be carefully removed before use.

Myrtle Allen's Carrageen Moss Pudding

Serves 6

¼oz cleaned, well-dried carrageen moss (1 semi-closed fistful)
scant 4 cups milk
1 vanilla bean or ½ teaspoon pure vanilla extract
1 large egg, preferably free-range
1 tablespoon superfine sugar

TO SERVE
soft brown sugar and cream, or poached rhubarb

Many people have less than fond memories of Carrageen Moss, partly because so many recipes call for far too much carrageen. It is a very strong natural gelatin so the trick is to use little enough. Because it is so light; it is difficult to weigh, we use just enough to fit in my closed fist, a scant ¼oz. This recipe given to me by Myrtle Allen is by far the most delicious I know. Nowadays more chefs are using carrageen, but often they add stronger flavors, such as molasses or rosewater, which tend to mask the delicate flavor of the carrageen itself. Carrageen Moss is served at Ballymaloe House at least once a week.

Soak the carrageen in tepid water for 10 minutes. Strain off the water and put the carrageen into a saucepan with the milk and vanilla bean, if using. Bring to a boil and simmer very gently with the lid on for 20 minutes. At that point, and not before, separate the egg and put the yolk into a bowl. Add the sugar and vanilla extract (if you are using it) and whisk together for a few seconds. Pour the milk and carrageen moss through a strainer onto the egg yolk mixture, whisking all the time. The carrageen will now be swollen and exuding jelly. Rub all this jelly through the strainer and beat it into the liquid. Test for a set in a cold saucer: put it in the refrigerator—it should set in a couple of minutes. Rub a little more through the strainer if necessary. Whisk the egg white until stiff peaks form and fold it in gently; it will rise to make a fluffy top. Let cool.

Serve chilled with soft brown sugar and cream, or with poached rhubarb.

1 cup or ½oz cleaned, well-dried
carrageen (or 2 semi-closed
fistfuls)
scant 4 cups milk
1 vanilla bean or ½ teaspoon pure
vanilla extract
3 tablespoons cocoa powder
1 egg, separated
2 tablespoons superfine sugar

Ballymaloe Chocolate Carrageen

Myrtle Allen's recipe for Chocolate Carrageen from The Ballymaloe Cookbook *is lightly set and delicious. Note that twice the amount of carrageen is needed when cocoa is added.*

Soak the carrageen in tepid water for 10 minutes. Put in a saucepan with the milk and the vanilla bean, if using. Bring to a boil and simmer very gently for 20 minutes. Pour through a strainer into a mixing bowl. The carrageen will now be swollen and exuding jelly. Rub all this jelly through the strainer. Blend the cocoa with a little of the milk and add to the hot strained carrageen with the sugar, vanilla extract (if using), and the egg yolk. Test for a set in a saucer. Whisk the egg white until stiff peaks form and fold it in gently. It will rise to make a fluffy top. Spoon into serving dises and chill in the fridge until set. Best eaten next day.

Pickled Samphire Anne Kennedy from Rostrevor in Co. Down sent me this recipe:

Gather the samphire and soak for 3 hours in brine. Place in a pan, cover with a mixture of a little salt and 3 parts of white wine vinegar to 1 part of water. Cover and simmer for 30 minutes. Allow to cool and pack into jars. Carefully cover with liquid mixed with a little fresh vinegar. The samphire should remain a good green color.

Samphire

We gather two types of samphire, Rock Samphire (Crithmum maritimum) and Marsh Samphire (Salicornia europaea). Rock Samphire, which is also known as St Peter's Cress, is a fleshy-leaved plant that grows around the coast in little cracks between cliff rocks. It is still there free for the picking. A few years ago a group of us scrambled excitedly down the steep rocky slope to Goat Island near Ardmore in Co. Waterford, where rock samphire grew in abundance. Patricia Cockburn showed us how to cook the samphire, which we ate with a succulent salmon in cream. The other species is Marsh Samphire, which looks like a miniature cactus without the prickles and, as the name suggests, grows in salt marshes close to the sea. It is cooked in the same way but only takes 4–5 minutes to cook. To eat it, hold it by the stem end and pull through your teeth to separate the flesh from the stem inside.

Cover the samphire with cold water, bring to a boil and simmer for about 15–20 minutes until tender. Drain off the water, season with freshly ground pepper, and toss in lots of butter; no salt will be needed because samphire has a natural salty tang.

Dulse (*Rhodymenia palmata*)

This winey-brown seaweed—also called dillisk, dilisk, dillesk and *dilís*—is found all around the Irish coast, particularly on the western seaboard. It is mentioned in the 8th-century Brehon Laws, which describe a penalty for consuming another person's dulse without their permission. It is picked on the rocks at low tide and spread out on a tin roof or on the grass or shingle to dry in the sun. Once sold at fairs and markets all over the country, it is now found in shops close to the coast. Many people told me of sending little parcels of it to relatives who had emigrated and retained a craving for it. Dulse can be eaten raw or added to fish soups or stews. It was also mixed with potatoes for dulse champ (see page 149).

Dulse and yellowman (a homemade crunchy toffee) were and still are sold at stalls at the famous Ould Lammas Fair in Ballycastle, Co. Antrim, held on the last Tuesday of August every year.

At the auld Lammas Fair, were you ever there?
Were you ever at the fair of Ballycastle, oh?
Did you treat your Mary Anne to dulce and 'yallaman'?
At the auld Lammas Fair of Ballycastle, oh?

Pepper dulse (*Laurencia pinnatifida*) was also eaten on the Blaskets and Bere Island.

Shell Dilisk

Shell dilisk has a distinctive little mussel shell attached to the base. John Francis Guerin showed me how to identify the shell dilisk on the rocky Kerry coast. After the dilisk is picked, it should be spread out on the grass or on a flat tin roof to dry for a few days. Then store and chew a little whenever the fancy takes you.

Savins

These grew abundantly on the island and according to Máire "have a very bitter taste" and were used to make savin pies. Máire gave a recipe for savin pie in *Bean an Oileáin* (Women of the Island), which she says her aunt who was born and reared on Inis Mhic Fhaoileáin, one of the Blasket Islands, gave her. This recipe was unusual in that "no-one else on the Island" writes Máire, ever before then made a pie of green savins."

This is how she describes it: "the ingredients were one fairly large mugful of flour, half a teaspoonful of baking soda, a small piece of butter, sour milk, green savins and lots of brown sugar. The flour and baking soda were mixed in a bowl and the butter was worked into the flour; then the sour milk was added. The dough was formed into a small cake, kneaded and divided into two halves, each half being formed into a rounded shape. At this point, the pot-oven was hung over the fire to be heated. The savins were spread on one of the round cakes and brown sugar was sprinkled over them. The other cake was placed on top and the edges of the lower cake were folded up onto the top cake. The two were pressed together, so that, as Máire puts it: "you would think the pie had a hem around it." The pot-oven was removed from the fire, some butter was melted in it and flour sprinkled in. The pie was put carefully into the pot-oven which was then hung over the fire. The lid was put on and red embers were scattered around it. When the pie was ready, the lid was removed and the pot-oven was tilted on its edge so that the pie would slide out onto a plate.

Cowslip Wine

From the Mary Ponsonby Manuscript:

To 3 gallons of water 9 pound of fine sugar. Boil it one hour, when it begins to boil put in the whites of 2 eggs well beat, and keep it skimming, then strain it off, and about 2 hours after put in nine quarts of cowslip peeps, when your wine is new milk warm, put in 3 spoonfuls of Barm and 2 lemons sliced. Let it stand 2 days before you put it into the barrel then let it stand two or three months, before you bottle it rince the bottles with Brandy.

Damson Cheese

This recipe comes from Annie Irwin's 1900 manuscript:

Bake the fruit in a stone jar, and to every two pounds of fruit weigh half a pound of sugar—set the fruit over the fire—let it boil quickly till it begin to look dry, take out the stones and add the sugar; stir it well, and simmer it 2 hours slowly; then boil it quickly half an hour—pour the juice into potting pans or saucers, the fruit sh'd be pulped through a colander (the easiest way) and the stones cracked to boil in the kernels.

Plague Water

This recipe comes from a wonderful manuscript cookbook lent to me by Giana Ferguson who makes the award-winning Gubbeen Cheese in Schull, West Cork. The book was started in 1777 in Kings Bromley in England and has been in her family since. Giana says that the cooks in the Great Houses travelled and shared recipes. The housekeeper was also the apothecary in the house and the village and had many highly regarded cures. This plague water recipe uses many wild plants as well as spice seeds which would not have been available to most people outside the big house.

Take rue, egremony, wood sorrel, celandine, sage, angellico, tormentill, scabyous, mugweed, pimpernel, spearmint, scordis, cardis, dragons, feverfew, avens, burnett, motherwort, gatera, mary gold flowers, burrage flowers, cowslip flowers, pancy flowers, of each half a pound, rosemary one pound, a little root of alicompain, shred all small, fennel, aniseeds, coriander seeds, cardimony seeds, bruis the seeds, infuse all in 3 gallons of brandy. Lett it stand 6 days close stoped, then distill it in a common still pasted close. You may add 4 ounce of Mithrivate 6 ounce of Andronica treacle, mix this just before you still it.

Desserts

Most traditional Irish desserts (often known as the "sweet") are based on the fruits readily available in the garden or orchard, or on those found in the wild. Fruit pies, tarts, and crumbles, or simple stewed fruit, would have been prepared over the open fire, in the bastible, or, more recently, in the oven. The recipes vary slightly from one household to another, and would have been passed down orally in farmhouses across the country. My own mother taught me many of the recipes I still use; she would vary the fillings according to the season, from rhubarb to green gooseberries, blackberries, and apple.

Wild raspberries and strawberries have grown in Ireland since early times. In our garden there rarely seemed to be enough fruit for us children to have a real feast—I remember our gardener, Pad, chasing us any time he spied us in the strawberry patch. Not surprisingly, there never seemed to be a lot of fruit for the kitchen!

Steamed suet puddings are another great Irish tradition. They are the best kind of comfort food. By contrast, I have also included here some more elegant dishes from the great country house tradition, which we still serve at Ballymaloe. What they all have in common is their use of the fruits and dairy products for which Ireland is justly famous.

Fruit Desserts

People always used the native seasonal fruits before imported or frozen fruit became available. If someone had lots of apples they gave a bagful to a neighbor, who would share something else in return when they had "a plenty." Fruit tarts, and simple stewed fruit served with custard were, and perhaps still are, the best-loved family desserts. Fruit varied with the seasons, apple and rhubarb are top of the list, but in the old days anyone fortunate enough to have a kitchen garden would also have gooseberries and blackcurrants during their short summer season, whereas country houses with greenhouses grew peaches, melons, and even pineapples.

Rhubarb

Rhubarb, the first fruit to emerge after the long winter season, was eagerly anticipated, and was made into various tarts and pies, depending on the cooking facilities. Originally, desserts were made in the bastible over the open fire, and a type of scone dough might have been used—like that of the Country Rhubarb Pie (below)—or a sweet pie dough, like that of the Irish Apple Cake (see page 215). Later on, when ovens were more common and cookbooks came with them, shortcrust pie dough tarts would have been tried.

Stewed rhubarb was also very popular and was served with milk puddings or custard, often Bird's Custard, which was a great stock ingredient in many kitchens and was available in every village and local shop. Alfred Bird, a Birmingham chemist, invented it in 1849 because his wife was allergic to eggs, which were the main ingredient in homemade custard.

Country Rhubarb Cake

This delicious juicy rhubarb cake, based on an enriched bread dough, was made all over the country. Originally it would have been baked in the bastible or 'baker' beside an open fire. My mother, who taught me this recipe, varied the filling with the seasons.

Serves 8

2½ cups all-purpose flour, plus extra for dusting
pinch of salt
½ teaspoon baking soda
¼ cup superfine sugar, plus extra for sprinkling
⅓ cup (¾ stick) butter
1 egg, free-range if possible
generous ⅔ cup milk, buttermilk, or sour milk
1½lb rhubarb, finely chopped (about 6 cups)
¾–1 cup granulated sugar
beaten egg, to glaze
superfine sugar, for sprinkling

TO SERVE
softly whipped cream
soft brown sugar

10-inch enamel or Pyrex pie plate

Preheat the oven to 350°F.

Sift the flour, salt, baking soda and superfine sugar into a bowl and rub in the butter. Whisk the egg and mix with the milk, buttermilk or sour milk. Make a well in the center of the dry ingredients. Pour in most of the liquid and mix to a soft dough; add the remainder of the liquid if necessary.

Sprinkle a little flour on your work surface. Turn out the dough and pat gently into a round. Divide into 2 pieces: one should be slightly larger than the other; keep the larger one for the lid.

Dip your fingers in flour. Roll out the smaller piece of pastry to fit the pie plate. Scatter the finely chopped rhubarb all over the base and sprinkle with granulated sugar. Brush the edges of the pie dough with beaten egg. Roll out the other piece of dough until it is exactly the size to cover the plate, lift it on, and press the edges gently to seal them. Make a hole in the center for the steam to escape. Brush again with beaten egg and sprinkle with a very small amount of superfine sugar.

Bake in the oven for 45–60 minutes or until the rhubarb is soft and the crust is golden. Leave it to sit for 15–20 minutes before serving so that the juice can soak into the crust. Sprinkle with superfine sugar. Serve still warm, with a bowl of softly whipped cream and some moist, brown sugar.

2lb red rhubarb (about 6 stalks)
1¼–1½ cups granulated sugar

SCONE DOUGH
2¼ cups all-purpose flour, plus
   extra for dusting
1½ tablespoons superfine sugar
1 heaping teaspoon baking powder
a pinch of salt
¼ cup (½ stick) butter
1 egg
about ¾ cup whole milk

TO SERVE
soft brown sugar
softly whipped cream

one round 9 × 2-inch pan—we use
a heavy stainless-steel sauté pan
which works very well

Roscommon Rhubarb Pie

This is a perfect example of the way in which recipes originally cooked on an open fire can be adapted to produce the most delicious results today. Anna Dodd of Castlebaldwin in Co. Sligo, who gave it to me, remembers how her grandmother would strew the bastible with chopped rhubarb, sweeten it with a sprinkling of sugar, and cover it with an enriched bread dough. When the cake was baked, it was turned out so that it landed upside down, with the sweet juice soaking into the soft, golden crust. It was served warm, with soft brown sugar and lots of softly whipped cream.

Preheat the oven to 450°F.
   Trim the rhubarb, wipe with a damp cloth, and cut into pieces about 1 inch in length. Put into the base of your tin or sauté pan and sprinkle with the granulated sugar.
   Sift all the dry ingredients for the scone dough into a bowl. Cut the butter into cubes and rub into the flour until the mixture resembles coarse breadcrumbs. Whisk the egg with the milk. Make a well in the center of the dry ingredients, pour in the liquid all at once, and mix to a soft dough. Turn out onto a floured board and roll into a 9-inch round, about 1 inch thick. Place this round on top of the rhubarb and tuck in the edges neatly.
   Bake in the fully preheated oven for 15 minutes then reduce the temperature to 350°F for about a further 30 minutes, or until the top is crusty and golden and the rhubarb soft and juicy.
   Remove the pan from the oven and let it sit for a few minutes. Put a warm plate over the top of the pan and turn it upside down so that the pie comes out onto the plate. Be careful of the hot juices, they will be absorbed by the pie.
   Serve warm with soft brown sugar and cream.

   Note: This recipe may also be made with cooking apples, in which case Anna Dodd suggests adding a little cinnamon or mixed spice to the sugar.

Rhubarb Trifle

This came from a cutting of one of Monica Nevin's recipes in the Irish Independent *from the early 1950s.*
   "Rhubarb trifle is another nice sweet. Stew some rhubarb, (about a pound) in a very little water with a liberal amount of sugar and a little lemon peel. When cooked beat to a pulp with a fork.
   Place a layer of sponge cake in a dish. Pour over it the hot rhubarb pulp. Then cover with another layer of sponge cake. Press the top sponge cake well down. You can if you like put a plate on top of the sponge cake with a weight on top and leave for several hours. Then remove the weight and coat the top of the rhubarb sponge with a good custard. Decorate with whipped cream."

This simple recipe was included in Rose Hanlon's scrapbook from the 1950s. She writes: "In hot weather gooseberry fool is an excellent choice for sweet." Other fruits can be made into a fool in the same way. In the case of strawberries, uncooked fruit pulp is used.

"Cook 2lbs gooseberries with a little water, until reduced to a pulp, then rub through a sieve. Add sugar to taste—about ½lb—and fold in ½ pint thick custard. Serve in a glass dish or in individual dishes, and, if you wish, decorate with a few cooked whole berries. Serve very cold. A half-pint of softly whipped cream may be used instead of the custard and makes a nice fool."

This recipe came from Annie Irwin's 1900 manuscript and was credited to a Mrs Wilson. It is an interesting way of using gooseberries for slightly longer term keeping, and was probably served as a sweetmeat, perhaps like a lozenge.

"Drain the juice from the crushed fruit and to ½lb of thick pulp add an equal weight of fine powdered sugar and the whites of 5 eggs—heat the whole together for three hours. Drop it on paper and dry it thoroughly."

Serves 6–8

7¾ cups green gooseberries
2–3 elderflower heads
2¼ cups granulated sugar
2½ cups cold water

Gooseberry and Elderflower Compôte

"Gooseberries, currants and cherries for children, gingerbread for grown girls, strong beer and maddening whiskey for wranglers and busybodies," wrote Amhlaoibh Uí Shúilleabháin of the fare at a Pattern Day (a kind of fair) held near Callan in Co. Kilkenny in 1829.

Elder bushes, which grow freely in the hedges all around Ireland, produce a mass of blooms in May and early June. They smell strangely musty, but have the most magical muscat flavor when cooked with green gooseberries.

First top and tail the gooseberries. Tie the elderflower heads in a little square of cheesecloth and put in a stainless-steel or enamelled saucepan. Add the sugar and cover with cold water. Bring slowly to a boil and continue to boil for 2 minutes. Add the gooseberries and simmer just until the fruit bursts, for approximately 5–6 minutes. Let cool. Serve in a pretty bowl and decorate with fresh elderflowers.

Serves 6

3¾ cups green gooseberries
2 elderflower heads, tied in
   cheesecloth
1⅛ cups granulated sugar
1¼ cups cold water
softly whipped cream

Gooseberry and Elderflower Fool

Tart green gooseberries picked in May make the best gooseberry fool.

Poach the gooseberries with the elderflowers in the sugar and water as above, until the fruit bursts—about 5–6 minutes. Remove the elderflower heads. Liquefy or purée the fruit and measure the amount. When the purée has cooled, add up to an equal volume of softly whipped cream, according to taste. Pour into a glass serving dish and serve with sweet cookies.

Note: A little stiffly beaten egg white may be added to lighten the fool. The fool should not be very stiff, more the texture of softly whipped cream. If it is too stiff, stir in a little milk rather than more cream.

Raspberries and Strawberries

Raspberries and strawberries followed the gooseberries and blackcurrants in mid-summer. They were usually eaten with a sprinkling of sugar and fresh cream, often straight from the dairy. We enjoy them with Jersey cream from our tiny herd of three cows.

Makes 2 x 6-inch flans

FOR THE PASTRY CASE
1¾ cups all-purpose flour, plus extra for dusting
pinch of salt
½ cup (1 stick) butter—in the past a mixture of margarine and lard was sometimes used
1½ tablespoons superfine sugar
1 egg
cold water, to mix

two 6-inch flan rings

Fruit Flan

In the 1950s fruit flans came into vogue. Recipes were sent from America and special flan pans were often used. Canned fruit, such as peaches or fruit cocktail, were used if fresh fruit wasn't available, and the fruit was arranged in a neat pattern, sometimes topped with a jelly glaze and decorated with whipped cream. When fresh fruit was available, strawberries were often used, or blackberries later in the season. A glaze with fruit juice and gelatin could be made to top it, or there was a commercial gel which set in an instant and came in red or yellow, depending on which color fruit you wished to use as filling. A glaze made with thickened fruit juice could also be used: the juice from the canned fruit could be thickened with a little arrowroot or cornstarch (arrowroot gives a clearer syrup).

To make it, mix the arrowroot or cornstarch with the fruit juice and bring to a boil, stirring all the time. Cook for a few minutes. Let the syrup cool before pouring over the fruit in the flan.

A sweet pastry crust could also be used to make a flan case, which would be baked blind and filled later.

Sift the flour and salt into a bowl and rub in the fat with the fingertips. Add the sugar and mix thoroughly. Make a well in the center of the flour and add the egg and sufficient cold water (very little will be needed) to make a stiff dough. Turn out onto a lightly floured board and knead lightly until smooth. Roll out and use as required.

Note: Instead of using a whole egg, you can use 2 egg yolks. A little more water will then be needed. The egg whites can be used to make a meringue topping for the flan.

Monica Nevin gives suggestions for filling the flan.

Until the soft fruit comes into season you will have to depend largely on canned fruit for the filling of the flan. When using canned fruit, drain it well and arrange neatly in the flan case. Decorate with whipped cream or if you have used only the egg yolk to make the pastry crust, you can cover the top of the flan with meringue mixture and color the meringue delicately in the oven.

Alternatively, fill the flan with the drained fruit and then dissolve ¼oz gelatin in ⅔ cup of the juice. Add a few drops of food coloring, if liked, to the dissolved gelatin and juice. When the juice is on the point of setting (but not until then) pour over the fruit in the flan. When set, decorate with cream and serve.

Serves 8

butter, for greasing
2 eggs
¼ cup superfine sugar
heaping ⅓ cup all-purpose flour,
  plus extra for dusting

7-inch flan tin

Monica Nevin's Flan for a Special Occasion

Flans were made from a sweet pie dough or sponge. Monica Nevin guided her readers on how to make a Flan for a Special Occasion: she suggested having "a flan case or two in reserve for unexpected calls on your hospitality."

Grease the flan tin thoroughly and dust it with flour. Put the eggs and sugar in a bowl, stand this over a saucepan of hot water and whisk vigorously. When sufficiently beaten, the mixture should be pale in color and thick enough to retain the impression of the whisk or beater for a few seconds.

Remove the bowl from over the water and add the sifted flour, lightly folding it in with a metal spoon. (Nowadays the whisking of the eggs and sugar would usually be done in a mixer or with a hand-held electric whisk.)

Bake in a moderate oven (400°F) for 10 minutes approx. until a light golden brown. Remove carefully from the tin and let cool on a wire rack. When cold, fill with the desired filling. Sometimes a thin layer of jam was spread on the base of the flan to keep it from going soggy when the fruit is added.

Serves 8

3½ cups blackcurrants, strings
  removed
softly whipped cream

STOCK SYRUP
¼ cup superfine sugar
3½ tablespoons water

Blackcurrant Fool

Leftover stewed blackcurrants will make a delicious fruit fool. Years ago stiffly whipped cream was folded straight into the crushed blackcurrants, but nowadays they should be puréed and strained first.

To make the stock syrup, combine the sugar and water in a saucepan and heat, stirring continuously, until the sugar dissolves. Keep stirring until the syrup thickens slightly. Cover the blackcurrants with the stock syrup. Bring to a boil and cook until the fruit bursts—this will take about 4–5 minutes. Liquefy, strain the stewed fruit and measure how much purée there is. When the purée has cooled, swirl in up to an equal quantity of softly whipped cream, according to taste. Serve with Bessie's Shortbread Cookies (see below).

Makes 25

1⅓ cups all-purpose flour
¼ cup superfine sugar
½ cup (1 stick) butter

Bessie's Shortbread Cookies

These crisp little cookies are an essential accompaniment to fruit fools and compôtes. Watch them carefully in the oven as they can overcook easily because of their high sugar content. They should be a pale golden brown.

Put the flour and sugar into a bowl, rub in the butter as for shortcrust pie dough. Gather the mixture together and knead lightly. Roll out to ¼-inch thick. Cut into rounds with a 2½-inch cutter. Bake in a moderate oven (350°F) for 8–15 minutes (depending on the thickness of the cookies). Remove and let cool on a rack.

1 sponge cake (see recipe for
  Great-Grandmother's Sponge
  Cake, page 292)
scant 3 cups granulated sugar
scant 3 cups water
9 cups blackcurrants

3 pint pudding bowl

Blackcurrant Summer Pudding

Everyone seems to become wistful when you mention summer pudding. Bursting with soft fruit, served with lots of softly whipped cream, it's one of the very best puddings of summer. At Ballymaloe, summer pudding was, and still is, made with cake. We traditionally use blackcurrants, but you could use a mixture of summer fruits flavored with sweet geranium leaves. Cook the blackcurrants and redcurrants until they burst and then add the other soft fruit (raspberries, strawberries, loganberries etc.). Remember to pour the syrup and fruit into the sponge-lined bowl while still boiling hot, otherwise the syrup won't soak through the sponge properly.

Cut each sponge round in half, horizontally. Line your pudding bowl with the cake, crusty side inwards. It doesn't matter if it looks like patchwork as it will blend later. Reserve the rest of the cake for the top.

Dissolve the sugar in the water and boil for 2 minutes. Add the blackcurrants and boil until they burst—about 3–4 minutes. Immediately, ladle some of the hot liquid and fruit into the sponge-lined bowl. When it is about half full, if you have scraps of cake put them in the center. Then fill to the top with fruit and juice (save any leftover fruit and syrup). Cover the top with a final layer of sponge.

Put the bowl into a dish with sides. Put a plate on top and press down with a heavy weight. Let cool. If some of the juices escape, they will gather together in the dish and can be served spooned over the pudding as a delicious sauce.

Store the pudding in the refrigerator for a minimum of 24 hours before serving. It will keep for 4–5 days.

To serve, unmold the pudding onto a deep serving dish. Pour any leftover fruit and syrup around it, and serve with lots of softly whipped cream.

4–4½ cups strawberries or
  raspberries
superfine sugar, to taste
whipped cream, to taste

Strawberry or Raspberry Fluff

This very simple dessert uses two of summer's most delicious fruits.

Crush the berries roughly, sprinkle with the sugar and fold in the softly whipped cream. Serve with baby meringues or Bessie's Shortbread Cookies (see opposite).

Loganberry Tart

The walled garden at Timoleague House, the home of Robert and Laura Travers, was bursting with loganberries. Laura cooked us a delicious loganberry tart.

If you are lucky enough to have lots of loganberries, you can make a delicious loganberry tart using the pastry from the Cullohill Apple Pie on page 213. Simply fill with loganberries and plenty of sugar. You could also add raspberries.

Apples

Late summer and autumn brought apples, starting with the early cooking apples such as Grenadier in late August, Early Victoria, Bramley Seedling, Crimson Bramleys, Arthur Turner, Lane's Prince Albert, D'Arcy Spice, and other varieties which were native to these islands. Different parts of the country had apples local to a particular area where the soil and weather conditions suited them. Sadly, many of these have been lost in recent years, but some have been reinstated by the Irish Seed Savers Association. Many of these varieties were lost in overgrown gardens and orchards, but thankfully the Irish Seed Savers took cuttings from whatever trees remained, or that people sent to them, and propagated them so that some forgotten apple varieties are again becoming available.

Recipes for apple puddings abound, since most people had access to apples and came up with a myriad of ways to use them, both in simple ordinary households and sophisticated country house kitchens.

Apple Dumpling

Serves 6–8

7–9 cooking apples (about 3lb)
1 cup plus 2 tablespoons sugar
⅓ cup water
2–3 cloves, optional

TOPPING
½ cup (1 stick) butter
½ cup plus 1 tablespoon superfine sugar
2 eggs, free-range if possible
1⅓ cups all-purpose flour
1–2 tablespoons water or milk, if necessary
½ teaspoon baking powder

A Dublin taxi driver once told me about an apple dumpling that his mother used to make. The apples were peeled and put into the saucepan with some sugar, then a cake or scone mixture was put on top. The pot was covered, put directly onto the heat, and cooked on top of the stove until the apples were soft and fluffy and the topping had cooked in the steam. It was a wonderful way of producing a delicious apple dessert in homes that had no oven.

Peel and core the apples and cut into chunks. Put the apple pieces into a deep saucepan (we use a 9 × 4-inch stainless-steel saucepan). Add the sugar, water, and cloves, if you wish.

Cream the butter until really soft. Add the sugar and beat until white and creamy, using a wooden spoon. Beat the eggs and gradually add to the creamed butter and sugar. Beat well. If preferred, the eggs may be broken and beaten into the mixture one at a time. A little sifted flour may be added between each addition of egg if liked. Fold in the remainder of the flour, adding a little water or milk if necessary, to make to a dropping consistency. Add the baking powder mixed with the last addition of flour.

Spread the cake mixture as evenly as possible over the top of the apples. Put the lid on the saucepan and cook over a medium heat for 15 minutes then reduce the heat to the minimum for a further 15–20 minutes, by which time the apples should be soft and juicy and the topping cooked in the steam. Serve with soft brown sugar and cream or custard.

Apple Soufflé

This comes from the Clonbrock manuscript. It was attributed to Felicie and dated 1876.

"Pare 4 apples and cut them in quarters and put them in a saucepan with a little water, large piece of sugar and a small piece of vanilla. Let them stew slowly for 3 or 4 hours.

Take the whites of 3 eggs and beat them up till perfectly stiff. Put the stewed apples into the dish (to be sent up) and mix the white of eggs with them, put the dish (well buttered all round first) into the oven, which must be well heated, in ten minutes it ought to be done and have risen well."

Apple Fritters

Serves 6–8

3 cooking or eating apples
   (about 1lb)
good-quality oil, for deep-frying
superfine sugar

BATTER
¾ cup plus 1½ tablespoons all-
   purpose flour
pinch of salt
1 egg, free-range if possible
⅓ cup milk

Food memories are so evocative! Apple fritters were another delight, every bit as delicious today as they were when we all stood round as Mummy cooked them, excitedly guessing what each one looked like. The little wisps of batter at the edges cooked into legs, tails, ears, and horns as we let our imaginations run riot.

To make the batter, sift the flour and salt into a bowl. Make a well in the center and drop in the egg. Use a whisk to bring in the flour gradually from the edges, slowly adding in the milk at the same time. Leave the batter in a cool place for about an hour. Heat the oil in a deep fryer to 350°F.

Peel the apples and core with an apple corer. Cut into rings not more than ¼-inch thick. Holding each ring on a skewer, to dip into the batter then lift out with the skewer and allow any surplus batter to drain off. Drop the rings straight into the hot fat. Don't put too many fritters into the fat at the same time. Fry until golden brown. Drain well on kitchen paper and toss in superfine sugar. Serve immediately with softly whipped cream.

Note: The fritters can be shallow-fried in a pan if more convenient but use at least ½ inch of oil.

Cullohill Apple Pie

Serves 8–12

PIE DOUGH
1 cup (2 sticks) butter
¼ cup superfine sugar
2 eggs, free-range if possible
2½ cups all-purpose flour,
   preferably unbleached

FILLING
4–5 Granny Smith apples
   (about 1½lb)
scant ¾ cup sugar
2–3 cloves

egg wash
superfine sugar, for sprinkling

TO SERVE
softly whipped cream
Muscovado sugar

one rectangular 12 x 7-inch pan

For many years patrons of my family's pub, the Sportsman Inn in Cullohill, Co. Laois, enjoyed this apple tart made with my mother's famous pastry; she passed the recipe on to me. The pastry is made by the creaming method, so people who suffer from "hot hands" don't have to worry about rubbing in the butter.

Preheat the oven to 350°F.

First make the pie dough. Cream the butter and sugar together by hand or in a food mixer. Add the eggs and beat for several minutes. Reduce the speed and mix in the flour. This pie dough needs to be chilled for at least 1 hour otherwise it is difficult to handle.

To make the tart, first roll out the pie dough to about ⅛-inch thick and use about two-thirds of it to line your pan. Peel, quarter, and slice the apples into the tart. Sprinkle with sugar and add the cloves. Cover with a lid of the remaining pie dough, seal the edges, and decorate with pie dough leaves. Brush with egg wash and bake in the oven until the apples are tender, about 45–60 minutes. When cooked cut into squares, sprinkle lightly with superfine sugar, and serve with softly whipped cream and Muscovado sugar.

Serves 4

6 apples (about 2lb)
½ cup plus 1 tablespoon sugar
2–3 cloves (optional)

SHORTCRUST PIE DOUGH
½ cup (1 stick) butter
2½ tablespoons superfine sugar
1 egg, free-range if possible
1¼ cups all-purpose flour

beaten egg, to glaze

CUSTARD
1 large egg, free-range if possible
1 tablespoon superfine sugar
⅔ cup cream
½ teaspoon pure vanilla extract

1½ pint pie dish

Apple Custard Pie

The most delicious apple tart with a "built in" custard topping.

Preheat the oven to 350°F.

First make the shortcrust pie dough and set aside. Cream the butter and sugar together by hand or in a food mixer. Add the eggs and beat for several minutes. Reduce the speed and mix in the flour. This pie dough needs to be chilled for at least 1 hour, otherwise it is difficult to handle.

Peel and core the apples and chop into chunks. Put into the base of your pie dish, sprinkle over sugar and add the cloves, if using.

Roll the pie dough into a sheet ⅛-inch thick and cut several strips to fit onto the lip of your dish. Brush the top of the dish with cold water and press the strips of dough firmly on. Cut a circle of pie dough to form the lid, brush the pie dough rim with cold water and then press the dough lid firmly down onto the edges. Trim off the excess pie dough. Flute the edges and scallop with the back of a knife. Brush the pie with beaten egg. Cut some pie dough leaves from the excess and use to decorate the pie. Cut a hole in the center. Brush with eggwash again.

Bake in a preheated oven for 30 minutes until the apple is almost cooked (test with a skewer). Meanwhile, make the custard filling. Whisk the egg and sugar together in a bowl, then mix in the cream and vanilla extract. Open up the hole in the center of the pie if necessary and pour in the custard from a jug. Put the pie back into the oven for a further 25–30 minutes or until the custard has set. Sprinkle the top of the pie with a little sugar and serve.

Serves 4–6

6 large Granny Smith apples
    (about 2lb)
½ cup plus 1 tablespoon sugar
1 egg

TO SERVE
softly whipped cream
Barbados sugar

Apple Soufflé

This recipe comes from Anne Kennedy in Rostrevor, Co. Down.

Preheat the oven to 425°F.

Peel, core, and slice the apples and cook in a covered saucepan on a low heat with the sugar and about 2 tablespoons of water until tender. When the apples dissolve into a fluff, beat into a purée with a wooden spoon. Separate the egg and beat the yolk into the apple purée. Whisk the egg white until light and fluffy and fold into the apple. Pour into a buttered soufflé dish and bake in the preheated oven for 15–18 minutes. Serve immediately with softly whipped cream and Barbados sugar.

Serves 6

3 cooking apples (about 1lb)
½ cup water
¾ cup plus 1½ tablespoons sugar
2 egg whites

TO SERVE
Bessie's Shortbread Cookies (see
    page 210), soft brown sugar
    and softly whipped cream

Apple Fluff

This is a lovely light, fresh-tasting dessert, especially good made with new season's cooking apples, Grenadier, or Granny Smith.

Peel and core the apples, cut into thick chunks. Cook with the water and sugar on a low heat in a heavy-bottomed saucepan with the lid on. When soft strain or liquefy. Check for sweetness, if it needs more sugar, beat it in while the purée is still hot. Beat the egg whites until stiff peaks form and fold them in carefully. Serve well chilled, with soft brown sugar and cream and shortbread cookies.

Irish Apple Cake

Serves 6 (approximately)

1¾ cups all-purpose flour
¼ teaspoon baking powder
½ cup (1 stick) butter
scant ⅔ cup superfine sugar
1 egg, free-range if possible,
   beaten
3–8 tablespoons milk, approx.
1–2 cooking apples—we use
   Granny Smith or Grenadier
2–3 cloves (optional)
beaten egg, to glaze

TO SERVE
Barbados sugar
softly whipped cream

9-inch ovenproof plate

Apple cakes like this one are the traditional sweet in Ireland. The recipe varies from house to house and the individual technique has been passed from mother to daughter for generations. It would originally have been baked in a bastible or pot beside an open fire and later in the oven or stove on tin or enamel plates—much better than ovenproof glass because the heat travels through and cooks the pie dough base more readily.

Sift the flour and baking powder into a bowl. Rub in the butter with your fingertips until it resembles the texture of breadcrumbs. Add 7 tablespoons superfine sugar, then make a well in the center and mix together with the beaten egg and enough milk to form a soft dough. Divide in two. Put one half onto the greased ovenproof plate and pat it out to cover. Peel, core, and chop up the apples. Place them on the dough with the cloves, if using, and sprinkle over the remaining 3 tablespoons sugar—the amount you need will depend on the sweetness of the apples. Roll out the remaining pie dough and fit it on top. (This is easier said than done as this "pie dough" is very soft, like scone dough. You may need to do a bit of patchwork if it breaks.) Press the sides together and cut a slit through the lid. Brush with beaten egg and bake in a moderate oven (350°F) for about 40 minutes, or until cooked through and nicely browned. Dredge with superfine sugar and serve warm with Barbados sugar and softly whipped cream.

Blackberry and Apple Tart

Serves 6–8

1lb approx. puff pie dough (see opposite)
3–4 cooking apples e.g. Gala or Red Delicious
¾ cup blackberries
⅔–¾ cup superfine sugar (depending on the sweetness of the apples)
3–4 cloves
beaten egg, to glaze
superfine sugar, for dusting

TO SERVE
soft brown sugar
softly whipped cream

10 inch Pyrex plate

Blackberries and apples were referred to in glowing terms in the Irish medieval Fionn Mac Cumhaill legends. "Beautiful golden yellow apples" and "beautiful blackberries" are frequently mentioned in the 12th-century Fianna text Agallamh na Seanórach (The Colloquy of the Ancients).

Roll out half the pie dough and use to line your Pyrex plate. Trim the excess pie dough, but leave about ¾ inch overlapping the edge. Peel and quarter the apples, cut out the cores, and cut the quarters in half (the pieces of apple should be quite chunky). Put the apples onto the pie dough and pile them up in the center. Put the blackberries on top, leaving a border of 1 inch around the edge. Sprinkle with sugar, then add the cloves.

Roll out the remaining pie dough, a little thicker than the base. Wet the border of the pie dough base and press the pie dough lid firmly down on top. Trim the pie dough, leaving a ¼-inch edge. Crimp up the edges with a knife and then scallop them. Make a hole in the center to let steam escape. Brush with the beaten egg. Roll out the pie dough trimmings and cut into leaves to decorate the top of the tart. Brush with beaten egg.

Bake in a hot oven (475°F) for 15–20 minutes, then turn the heat to moderate (350°F) for a further 40–45 minutes, depending on how hard the apples are. Test the apples to see if they are cooked by inserting a skewer through the hole—they should be soft and fluffy. Sprinkle the tart with superfine sugar and serve hot with soft brown sugar and softly whipped cream.

Damson Tart

Damsons, or bullaces, are wild plums with dark blue-black skin. Wild damsons are much less sweet than the cultivated variety.

Substitute 5 cups damsons (do not remove stones) for the apple and blackberries. You may need more sugar, depending how ripe they are.

Worcesterberry Tart

Worcesterberries, once thought to be a cross between a gooseberry and a blackcurrant, are quite tart to eat raw but delicious in pies and tarts.

We first discovered worcesterberries in an old lady's garden when she replied to our advertisement in the local paper for fraughans (see page 197). She assured us that she had an abundance of them growing at the end of her garden, but they turned out to be quite a different fruit. These are, in fact, an old-fashioned species of black gooseberry. We used them for this tart and found them absolutely delicious.

Rhubarb Tart

Virtually every garden in Ireland had a few stools of rhubarb, a perennial plant which needs to be mulched in winter to crop in Spring.

Make the tart using 1lb of finely chopped red rhubarb and scant 1 cup sugar.

Puff Pie Dough

Makes about 2lb 10oz

scant 3½ cups chilled flour (use bread flour, if possible)
pinch of salt
1½ cups cold water
a squeeze of lemon juice
2 cups (4 sticks) butter, firm but pliable

Homemade puff pie dough takes a little time to make, but it is more than worth the effort for the wonderful flavor which bears no relation to the commercial equivalent. It is essential to use butter.

Sift the flour and salt into a bowl and mix to a firm dough (called detempre) with water and a squeeze of lemon juice. Cover with parchment paper and let rest for 30 minutes in the refrigerator.

Roll the chilled dough into a square about ½-inch thick. If the butter is very hard, beat it (still in the wrapper) with a rolling pin until pliable but not sticky. Unwrap the butter and shape into a slab about ⅛-inch thick. Place this in the center of the dough and fold the dough over the edges of the butter to make a neat parcel. Make sure your marble slab or pie dough board is well floured, then flatten the dough with a rolling pin, and roll it out into a rectangle about 18 inches long and 6½ inches wide (this is approximate, so don't worry if it's not exactly that measurement). Fold neatly into three, with the sides as accurately aligned as possible. Seal the edges with a rolling pin.

Give the dough a one-quarter turn (90°): it should now be on your pie dough bench as though it was a book with the open ends facing north/south. Roll out again, fold in three, and seal the edges with the rolling pin. Cover with plastic wrap or parchment paper and rest in the refrigerator for 30 minutes. The pie dough has now had two rolls or "turns." Repeat the rolling process another two times, giving the dough six rolls altogether, with a 30-minute rest in the refrigerator between every two turns.

Chill for at least 30 minutes before using.

Note: Each time you start to roll the pie dough, place it on your work surface with the open ends north/south as if it were a book. In hot weather it may be necessary to chill the pie dough slightly longer between rollings.

Rough Puff Pie Dough

Makes 14oz (approximately)

1¾ cups all-purpose flour
pinch of salt
⅔ cup (1½ sticks) butter
⅓–⅔ cup very cold water

Suitable for the tops of pies and tarts, this light and flaky pie dough was widely used by good cooks to cover game pies.

Sift the flour and salt into a cold bowl. Cut the butter into cubes about the size of a sugar lump and add to the flour. Do not rub in, but add just enough cold water to bind the pie dough together. Mix first with a fork and then bring together with your hand.

Wrap the pie dough in plastic wrap and leave to relax in the refrigerator for 10 minutes. Flour a board and roll the pie dough into a strip, this should be done carefully. The surface of the pie dough should not be over-stretched or broken. Fold the strip into three and turn so that the folded edge is to your left, like a closed book.

Roll out again into a strip, ½-inch thick. Fold in three again, cover, and leave in the refrigerator for a further 15 minutes. Roll and fold the pie dough twice as before then chill again for 15 minutes. Roll and fold again, by which time the pie dough should be ready for use, with no signs of streakiness. If the surface is still streaky, give it another roll immediately and rest for a further 15 minutes. Roll into the required shape. Chill again before using.

Lemons

Lemons seemed to have been readily available in country house kitchens, as illustrated by the number of lemon-based recipes contained in the archives. They featured both in cakes and puddings, and in my research I also found several recipes for pickling lemons.

Lemon Shape

This dessert is from the Marianne Armstrong manuscript from 1849. The manuscript doesn't say whether the dessert is served on its own, or with an accompaniment. A few summer berries would make a delicious accompaniment.

"2 tablespoons cornflour blend with a little cold water. Put in a little piece of butter as large as a bean. Pour as much boiling water as will clear it like starch. Put into a saucepan and boil for 2 mins stirring all the time. Have ready 2 yolks of eggs beaten up with sugar and juice of a lemon. Pour the cornflour on it, put into a shape to cook. Beat the whites stiff with a little sugar and when the shape is turned out put the whites over it and put in the oven for a minute or two."

Lemon Tart

This recipe, again from Marianne Armstrong, is very interesting. Lemon tarts have been very much in vogue in recent years, but they have been around for a while: this recipe dates back to the mid-1800s, and sounds like a lemon meringue tart. The pie dough would have been shortcrust.

"Line a flat dish with paste. 2 eggs beaten separately, the rind and juice of 2 lemons put to the yellows. Half pound sugar put to the whites. Spread on paste and bake half hour. "

Orange Pudding

The Lough Rynn papers (1865) contained several interesting pudding recipes that would indicate a skilled and confident cook. Here is one of them. See page 229 for the Lough Rynn Puff Pie Dough recipe.

"Boil the rind of a Seville Orange very soft and beat it very fine in a mortar. Add the juice and put to it two Naples biscuits or white bread grated very fine. Quarter of a pound of sugar, half a pound of butter and the yolks of six eggs. Mix them all well together. Lay a good puff paste around the dish and bake it half an hour."

Black Caps

Black Caps (also known as Black Cap Pudding) appear in a few sources. This is Mary Ponsonby's version, c.1850. I found a similar recipe among the 19th-century Bruen papers.

"Take as many apples as will fill a dish, cut them in two, cut out the cores, place one row of apples in the dish, over them some brown sugar, so on until the dish is as full as it will hold, sprinkle each layer of apples with a little water (one spoon full will be sufficient for the whole), then strew over a good deal of pounded superfine sugar and put them in a moderate oven."

Note: Half an hour in a moderate hot oven will bake them nicely, and grated lemon peel or the liquor of any preserves improves Black Caps.

Serves 4–6

2 tablespoons (¼ stick) butter
¾ cup plus 1½ tablespoons
    superfine sugar
1–2 lemons
2 eggs, free-range if possible
heaping ⅓ cup all-purpose flour
1 cup milk

TO SERVE
confectioners' sugar, for dredging
softly whipped cream

2½ cup pie dish

Fluffy Lemon Pudding

This is an old-fashioned family pudding which separates into two quite distinct layers when it cooks; it has a fluffy top and a creamy lemon base. If the lemons are very pale, use the zest of 1½ or 2 to give a sharper lemon flavor. In some manuscripts this recipe was called Lemon Soufflé, even though it was baked in a pie dish.

Cream the butter well. Add the superfine sugar and beat well. Grate the rind of the lemons and squeeze and strain the juice. Separate the eggs and add the yolks one by one, then stir in the flour, and gradually add the finely grated rind and juice of the lemons. Lastly add the milk. Whisk the egg whites in a bowl until stiff peaks form and fold gently into the lemon mixture. Pour into a 2½-cup pie dish and bake in a moderate oven (350°F) for about 40 minutes. Dredge with confectioners' sugar and serve immediately with softly whipped cream.

Serves about 6

2½ cups good-quality cream
rind of ½–1 lemon or orange, cut
    in strips
1½-inch piece of cinnamon stick
4 egg yolks, free-range if possible
3 tablespoons superfine sugar
2 teaspoons all-purpose flour
superfine sugar, to glaze

Burnt Cream

This rich custard pudding is very similar to crème brûlée. This delicious recipe comes from the recipe book of Mrs Dot Drew of Mocollop Castle near Ballyduff in Co. Waterford. It was lent to me by Diana Sandles.

"To 1.1litres of Cream, beat up the yolks of Eight Eggs a little Flour and some Sugar, put it over a fire with a little lemon or orange Peel and some Cinnamon, keep it stirring 'till it boils, then take it up and let it cool take out the cinnamon and peel and let it be put in the dish you intend to serve it up on grate a good deal of Sugar on it and brown it with a Salamander."

We tried this version and found it quite delicious:

Put the cream, lemon or orange rind and cinnamon into a saucepan and bring slowly almost to boiling point. Turn off the heat and let infuse for 15 minutes.

Meanwhile, whisk the egg yolks with the sugar and stir in the flour. Whisk in the infused cream and return the mixture to your saucepan. Bring back to a boil, stirring all the time (whisk occasionally if necessary). Pour immediately into a serving dish. Cool, cover, and chill well.

Several hours later or next day, sprinkle the top with a layer of superfine sugar and caramelize under a hot broiler (or cheat and use a blow torch!).

Serve as soon as the sheet of caramel solidifies. We like to serve a compôte of seasonal fruit with Burnt Cream.

Steamed Puddings

Steamed puddings were a great rib-sticking, winter stand-by, warming and energy-giving for people whose work was hard and physical. They were economical and filling and an essential part of the thrifty housewife's repertoire. Suet was used, which most butchers gave free to their customers, but for a lighter pudding one could substitute butter. A light steamed pudding would always have been a source of pride for the country house cook, served with a good custard sauce. Many of the older recipes mention putting pudding into a shape, which would have been a mold similar to a pudding bowl as we now know it. The copper, glass, or delph jelly molds that are now collectors' items, would have been used in all the country house kitchens.

Marmalade Pudding

Makes 2 puddings

scant 3½ cups all-purpose flour
4½ cups shredded beef suet
8½ cups soft white breadcrumbs
2¼ cups superfine sugar
4 teaspoons baking powder
4 eggs, free-range if possible
8 tablespoons homemade
   marmalade
milk, if needed

SAUCE
4 tablespoons water
1½ cups marmalade
juice of 1 lemon
sugar, to taste

2 lightly greased 7 inch pudding
   bowls

For almost a week during the cold January days the whole house smells of marmalade. My father-in-law looked forward to the final day when the last of the oranges had been turned into marmalade, because by tradition on that day there is marmalade pudding for lunch.

Mix the flour, suet, breadcrumbs, sugar, and baking powder together. Add the beaten eggs, marmalade, and a little milk to moisten if necessary (the mixture should have the consistency of plum pudding). Spoon into your greased pudding bowls and cover with a double sheet of parchment paper with a pleat in the center. Tie the paper firmly with string under the lip of the bowl. Place each bowl in a saucepan of boiling water. Cover and cook for 2–3 hours, topping up the water in the pan from time to time to make sure that it does not boil dry.

To make the sauce, put the water and marmalade into a saucepan. Warm them together for 15 minutes and then bring slowly to a boil. Continue to boil for 5 minutes. Add the lemon juice and sweeten with a little sugar to taste. When the pudding is cooked, turn it out onto a warm serving dish and pour the sauce around it.

Jam Roly-Poly

Serves 4

2 tablespoons chopped suet
4 tablespoons all-purpose flour
2 tablespoons sugar
pinch of salt
some cold water
jam

JAM SAUCE
2 tablespoons jam
2 tablespoons sugar
⅔ cup water

This pudding brings back memories to many people, and, made with homemade raspberry jam, it was delicious. It can be served with jam sauce or custard. This recipe is from the 1900 Lessons in Cookery and Housewifery. *It's interesting to note that all the measurements are in spoons: a weighing scale was not needed, and would not have been available in many kitchens. It is served with a jam sauce.*

Chop the suet very fine; mix it with the flour, sugar, and salt in a basin; wet to a light dough with cold water; turn onto a floured board; knead into a round ball; roll into a straight strip; spread with jam; wet round the edges; roll up the roll; tie into a wet floured cloth; put into boiling water, and boil from 1½–2 hours.

To make the jam sauce, place all the ingredients in a saucepan; boil for 4–5 minutes; pour round the roll when cooked.

Jam Pudding

Serves 4

½ cup (1 stick) butter, at room temperature
½ cup plus 1 tablespoon superfine sugar
2 eggs, free-range if possible
a few drops of pure pure vanilla extract
1¼ cups all-purpose flour
½ teaspoon baking powder
about 1 tablespoon milk or water
3–4 tablespoons homemade raspberry jam

RASPBERRY JAM SAUCE
4–6 tablespoons homemade raspberry jam
rind and juice of ½ a lemon
⅔ cup water
sugar, to taste

5 inch pudding bowl

This was one of our favorites, we raced home from school for lunch even faster when we knew Mummy was cooking a steamed jam pudding.

Cream the butter, add the superfine sugar, and beat until white and creamy. Whisk the eggs with the vanilla extract and beat, a little at a time, into the creamed mixture. Stir in the flour and baking powder, and add a little milk or water if necessary to make a dropping consistency.

Grease your pudding bowl. Spread raspberry jam over the bottom and sides. Carefully spoon the cake mixture into the bowl. Cover with pleated parchment paper, tied on firmly, and steam the pudding for about 1½ hours.

Meanwhile, make the raspberry jam sauce. Heat the jam with the water, add the lemon rind, and juice and sweeten with a little extra sugar if necessary.

Turn the pudding onto a hot dish and serve with the sauce and lots of softly whipped cream.

Apple Dumpling

Serves 6

1⅓ cup all-purpose flour
3oz suet (beef)
1 cup soft white breadcrumbs
½ teaspoon baking powder
cold water
3–4 apples, peeled and cut into
    chunks
1–2 cloves
1½ tablespoons sugar

Here is a recipe from Lily O'Reilly's early 1940s notebook. Suet gives a wonderful richness to the dough.

Chop the suet very finely using a little flour out of the amount for the pudding to prevent the suet from sticking to the knife. Put into a bowl with the other dry ingredients, mix well together and form into a stiff dough with cold water. Turn onto a lightly floured board.

Cut off a small piece to cover the top of the pudding. Roll out the remainder and use to line a greased pudding bowl, pressing it well around the sides. Fill up the center with apples (or any mixed fruit), sprinkle over the sugar and add the cloves, and a little water. Roll the small piece of pie dough into a round to fit the top of the bowl, damp the edges with cold water and place on top of the apples. Turn the edges of the large piece of pie dough over to seal. Press together with the fingers, cover with greased paper and steam for 1½–2 hours.

Note: A similar recipe appears in *Cookery Notes 1947*, which was used for teaching cooking in the schools. They suggest mixing a few blackberries or plums through the apples as a nice variation, or making a similar pudding with a rhubarb filling. One could add a little ground ginger to the rhubarb.

Currant and Apple Roly-Poly

Serves 6

1–2 apples (about 8oz)
⅓ cup currants
¼ cup sugar
nutmeg or mixed spice
2oz suet
1¼ cups all-purpose flour
pinch of salt
½ teaspoon baking powder
cold water

These seriously filling puddings were a great favorite in years gone by, before all the anxiety about cholesterol and the momentum of low-fat diets. They are beginning to find favor again among those who realize that a little of what you fancy every now and then doesn't do any harm!

Peel, core, and chop the apples, then wash the currants. Mix the fruits together with the sugar and spice. Chop the suet finely and put it into a bowl with the flour, salt, and baking powder. Mix well, then add cold water to make a stiff paste. Roll out to ¼-inch thick, spread the fruit mixture on the paste, wet the edges, and roll up neatly.

Scald a cloth in boiling water, wring it out, then sprinkle flour onto it. Wrap the pudding in the cloth and tie securely. Boil a large pan of water and lower the pudding in. Boil it gently for 1½ hours. Carefully unwrap the roly-poly. Serve on a very hot plate, with cream and soft brown sugar.

Fig Pudding

This richer version of the steamed pudding, from the Pope Papers (1823–1890), would serve 6 people.

"Quarter lb of figs, ¼ lb suet, a breakfast cup full of bread crumbs, same of milk and a little sugar. Boil the milk, and pour it over the suet, bread, figs and sugar. When you have mixed them, beat up four eggs and pour it over the other ingredients. Let the mixture stand a little time, then put it into a shape and boil for two hours. Serve with cream or sweet white sauce. Very good baked".

I also came across a Fig Pudding in one of Monica Nevin's Irish Independent articles and in Agnes Robins' school cookery copybook from her days in the St Mary's Dominican Convent in Cabra in Dublin around 1912.

Grandmother's Fierling

Serves 8

4 eggs, free-range if possible
4 tablespoons all-purpose flour
4 tablespoons milk
4 tablespoons superfine sugar
3–4 tablespoons butter

2 x 10-inch non-stick skillets

This recipe was given to Lucy Madden of Hilton Park, Co. Monaghan, by her grandmother, who suggested that it was a good pudding for a last-minute lunch in the kitchen. We found it absolutely delicious—certainly good enough to share with friends in the dining room.

Separate the eggs. Put the yolks into a bowl, add the flour and milk, and mix until you have achieved the consistency of thick cream. Whisk the egg whites stiffly with the superfine sugar and fold into the mixture.

Gently heat two skillets, adding half the butter to each. Divide the batter mixture between the pans and cook until the bottom is golden brown. Slide one of the "fierlings" onto a warmed serving dish, crispy side down and fluffy side uppermost. Gently place the other fierling on top, brown side upwards. Pour the pan juices over the top and serve immediately, just as it is or decorated with some summer berries.

Bread and Butter Pudding

Serves 6–8

3 tablespoons butter approx.
8 slices good-quality white bread, crusts removed
¼–½ cup raisins soaked in hot water and then drained
scant ⅔ cup superfine sugar
1 teaspoon ground cinnamon
5 eggs, free-range if possible
scant 5 cups milk
¼ cup cream
1 teaspoon freshly grated nutmeg
1 teaspoon ground ginger

The dish has been made in many homes over the years, and was originally a way for thrifty cooks to use up leftover bread: "what has become too stale for eating will answer excellently" (Cookery Notes, 1947). It comes in various degrees of richness. For many years it languished on the shelf of puddings we didn't care too much about; more glamorous puddings took its place, and then a few years ago it got a new life and started to appear on menus all over the place. Many versions were produced, but I love the richer version we make here at the school. We ring the changes depending on the time of year by adding rhubarb, gooseberry, marmalade, chocolate…

We find it much better to make it with cream and milk, and to put the fruit and nutmeg between the layers. We find golden raisins and raisins are preferable to currants.

Butter the bread. Break it up into smallish pieces and put into an ovenproof dish. Add the raisins. Mix one-quarter of the sugar with the cinnamon and sprinkle over the bread. Whisk the eggs with the remainder of the sugar and add the milk, cream, nutmeg, and ginger. Pour over the bread, put the dish in a water bath of hot water and bake in a moderate oven (350°F) for 1–1¼ hours.

Serve warm with lots of softly whipped cream.

Florence Bowe's Queen of Puddings

Serves 6

2½ cups milk
¼ cup (½ stick) butter
1 teaspoon pure vanilla extract
2¾ cups soft white breadcrumbs
grated zest of 1 lemon
1½ tablespoons superfine sugar
3 eggs, free range if possible,
 separated
½ cup superfine sugar, plus
 2 teaspoons for sprinkling
3 tablespoons raspberry jam

5-cup pie dish

Another pud that conjures up childhood memories. Interestingly, everybody seems to have a different opinion about what Queen of Puddings should both look and taste like. This recipe is a combination of several people's firmly held views. It's delicious, but as I've discovered, it's hard to please everyone! My Aunt Florence Bowe who is very fussy as far as Queen of Puddings is concerned has given this version her seal of approval!

Preheat the oven to 350°F and grease the pie dish.

Put the milk and butter into a saucepan, bring almost to boiling point, and add the vanilla extract. Mix the breadcrumbs with the lemon zest and 1½ tablespoons superfine sugar in a bowl. Stir in the hot milk; leave for about 10 minutes. Whisk in the egg yolks one by one. Pour into the buttered pie dish and bake for about 25 minutes or until just set.

Remove from the oven. Whisk the egg whites in a spotlessly clean, grease-free bowl. When they are just starting to become fluffy, add half the sugar. Continue to whisk until the mixture holds a stiffish peak. Fold in ½ cup superfine sugar. Warm the jam slightly and spread very gently over the surface of the custard. Pile the meringue on top in soft folds. Sprinkle the remaining 2 teaspoons of sugar over the top. Return to the oven and cook for 15 minutes or until the meringue is pale gold and crisp on top. Serve with pouring cream.

A Spoonful Pudding

This is another interestingly named little pudding from the Pope Papers.
 Take one spoonful of flour. 1 ounce of cream or milk. A little nutmeg, ginger and salt. Mix all together and boil it in a little wooden dish half an hour. You may add a few currants.

Balloons

Makes about 10

1 cup plus 1 tablespoon all-purpose
 flour
2 teaspoons superfine sugar, plus
 extra for rolling
pinch of salt
1 level teaspoon baking powder
milk
good-quality oil, for deep-frying

This cheap and simple donut recipe has been passed down for generations in my husband's family. Children adore these balloons because they cook into exciting shapes. Grown-ups hang about hoping they'll be allowed some too!

Sift the dry ingredients into a bowl. Mix to a thick batter (dropping consistency) with milk. Meanwhile, heat fat in a deep fryer to 385°F. Take 2 teaspoons of the mixture and push it gently off with your finger so that it drops in a round ball into the fat. Repeat with the rest of the mixture. Fry until golden, then remove and drain. Roll the balloons in superfine sugar and serve at once.

Hasty Pudding

I came across a few versions of Hasty Pudding—probably the cook's standby when it was announced at short notice that there would be guests for lunch or dinner. She would usually have the ingredients in the pantry. There was a version in The Receipt Book of Mrs Filgate, which commenced in September 1847 at Windsor and was stored in the Louth County Archives. Hasty Pudding in the 1947 Cookery Notes was a pudding requiring 2½ hours steaming, so actually quite far from hasty! Here is Annie Irwin's 1900 manuscript version:

¾ pint of milk
1½ oz flour
1½ oz butter
2 oz superfine sugar
3 eggs
a little wine or brandy
Mix the flour with the milk and boil 5 minutes, turn into a basin, add the other ingredients to it. Bake 20 minutes.

It doesn't say in the manuscript what it was served with, but I suggest that serving it with a little fruit and cream would make it much more palatable.

Philosophers' Pudding

This pudding from the Bruen papers would also have been a quick one to make, but you would need to be a philosopher to interpret the scant instructions!

Half pound butter beaten to a cream
Half pound flour
Half pound lump sugar powdered fine
Four eggs beaten
One glass of brandy
Bake for half an hour. Butter the dish well and the pudding will turn out.

Angel Pudding

This comes from Marianne Armstrong, Kiltoon Glebe, 1849, in the Harabrook House Receipt Book:

2oz powdered sugar
2oz flour
2oz butter
2 eggs without the whites
A little lemon
Divide into six small saucers and bake half an hour. Serve with a napkin and a little sugar over them.

German Puffs

Here is another similar type of baked pudding from the manuscript of Mrs Baker, Ballytobin, Co. Kilkenny. Dated 1810, this recipe was from Lady Anne Fitzgerald. It sounds delicious, though very rich.

"Four spoons full of flour and four eggs, mix them to a batter with two ounces of clarified butter, a little nutmeg and sugar and a pint of cream. Mix all together and put it in the cups you choose, bake them and turn them out of the cups, serve them with milled butter, brandy and sugar."

Milk Puddings

In farmhouse kitchens, the milk pudding was often left simmering in a double boiler saucepan at the side of the range, where it took care of itself while the woman got on with her chores. I remember a farmer's wife saying to me: "we had plenty of milk so that's what we made." Rice was the most popular, and semolina, tapioca, sago, and farola were the others most often cooked. A milk pudding was sustaining and provided energy for the men working hard on the land. It was economical when milk was readily available and the grains could be stored in the cupboard. For children, a milk pudding was easily digested, and served with a dollop of jam or apple jelly, it was delicious. It was often accompanied by stewed fruit. Sometimes an egg was added and it was baked in the oven with a sprinkling of nutmeg on top. The skin was delicious and everyone craved a little share.

Boiled Rice Pudding

Serves 4–6

scant ¼ cup whole or small grain (rice)
2½ teaspoons sugar
2½ cups milk

The 1952 edition of Good Housekeeping's Cookery Compendium *suggests using the following proportions for milk puddings:*

Add the washed grain (rice) and sugar to the milk and cook slowly in a double saucepan until the grain softens and absorbs the milk. This may take 2 hours or longer.

Tapioca or Sago Pudding

Serves 6

⅓ cup tapioca or sago
2½ cups milk
1 egg
2½ teaspoons superfine sugar
1 tablespoon butter
flavoring, such as vanilla extract or freshly grated nutmeg

Tapioca and sago were regularly used to make milk puddings in the 1940s and 1950s. This is how the pudding was made according to the recipe in All in the Cooking: Book 1, *which was used in schools in Ireland for many years.*

Wash the tapioca or sago by running cold water through it in a strainer, drain. Put into a double saucepan with the milk and cook until the grain becomes quite clear. Stir occasionally.

Add sugar, butter, and flavoring and mix well. Let cool for a short time. Beat up the egg and pour the tapioca or sago onto it, beating to prevent curdling. Pour into a well-greased pie dish.

Bake in a moderate oven (300°F) for 30 minutes or until set and nicely browned. Sprinkle a little superfine sugar on top and put on a dish with doyley underneath the pie dish.

Boiled Rice for a Black Fast Day

I couldn't resist this recipe from Annie Kiely's manuscript of 1908:
Wash ½lb rice in three waters, remove any black grains that are in it, then put into a quart of boiling water, boil for one hour, add one tablespoon of sugar, put into the shape, wet with cold water, allow it to set, turn out and serve with raspberry jam around it.

Eamonn Mac Thomáis described how his family would sometimes have a rice dinner during Lent that consisted of rice pudding made on water.

Christmas Pudding

The grand finale of the pudding year is the Plum Pudding or Christmas Pudding. Many families have their own special recipes, which have been handed down from generation to generation. John Young from Newbridge, Co. Kildare, sent me his grandmother Mary Jane Young's Christmas Pudding. This, he says, was passed down the line to him when his grandmother died in 1920. The Young family have been running Young's Medical Hall in Newbridge since 1888, started by his grandfather and now being run by his son.

Mary Jane Young's Christmas Pudding

This pudding does not include any flour or suet and is quite light, John says. It might be more to the taste of people who don't enjoy a heavier pudding.

Makes 2 x 7½-cup or 3 x 5-cup puddings

5 cups golden raisins
5 cups raisins
¾ cup mixed peel, chopped
4oz cherries, halved
scant 1 cup chopped almonds
½ glass brandy
2¼ cups brown sugar
8½ cups breadcrumbs
½ teaspoon salt
¼ teaspoon baking soda
1 teaspoon mixed spice
½ grated nutmeg
1½ cups (3 sticks) butter
9 eggs

Prepare the fruit and nuts and mix in the spices. Put into a large bowl, mix in the brandy, stir well, cover, and let soak overnight. Mix all the dry ingredients together. Add to the fruit and mix well. Melt the butter and stir into the mixture. Beat the eggs and add, mixing well.

Fill the pudding bowls and cover with a double thickness of parchment paper which has been pleated in the center. Tie lightly under the rim with cotton twine and make a twine handle for ease of lifting. Boil for 6 hours.

An Excellent Plum Pudding

Many of the manuscript cookbooks contain recipes for Plum Pudding. This is from the Bruen Papers:
*   1oz citron shred
*   A large wine glass of brandy
*   1 tablespoonful of flour
*   1lb best raisins well picked
*   1lb fresh beef suet cut small but not chopped
*   8 eggs, well beaten up, taking out 4 of the whites
*   The rind of 2 fresh lemons grated
*   A large nutmeg - ditto
*   2oz sweet almonds pounded to a paste
*   Boil 3 hours at least.

Elizabeth O'Connell's Plum Pudding

This recipe makes 2 large or 3 medium puddings. The large size will serve 10–12 people, the medium size will serve 6–8.

2½ cups raisins
2½ cups golden raisins
2½ cups currants
scant 1¾ cups brown sugar
6½ cups white breadcrumbs
3⅓ cups finely chopped suet
¾ cup candied peel (preferably homemade)
2 cooking apples, diced or grated
rind of 1 lemon
3 pounded cloves (½ teaspoon)
pinch of salt
6 eggs
¼ cup Jamaica rum
scant 1 cup chopped almonds

BRANDY BUTTER
⅓ cup (¾ stick) butter
⅔ cup confectioners' sugar
2–6 tablespoons brandy

It was always the tradition in our house to eat the first plum pudding on the evening it was made. As children we could hardly contain ourselves with excitement—somehow that plum pudding seemed all the more delicious because it was our first taste of Christmas. The plum pudding was usually made about mid-November and everyone in the family had to stir so they could make a wish! Mummy put silver plum pudding charms in the pudding destined to be eaten on Christmas Day.

Mix all the ingredients together very thoroughly and leave overnight. Don't forget, everyone in the family must stir and make a wish!

Next day, stir again for good measure. Fill into pudding bowls; cover with a double thickness of parchment paper which has been pleated in the center, and tie it tightly under the rim with cotton twine, making a twine handle also for ease of lifting.

Steam the puddings in covered saucepans of boiling water for 6 hours. The water should come halfway up the side of the bowl. Check every hour or so, and top up with boiling water if necessary. After 6 hours, remove the puddings. Allow to get cold and re-cover with fresh parchment paper. Store in a cool dry place until required.

On Christmas Day, or whenever you wish to serve the plum pudding, steam for a further 2 hours. Turn the plum pudding out of the bowl onto a very hot serving plate. Pour over some whiskey or brandy and ignite. Serve immediately on very hot plates with brandy butter (see below).

To make the brandy butter, cream the butter until very light. Add the confectioners' sugar and beat again. Then beat in the brandy, drop by drop. If you have a food processor, use it: you will get a wonderfully light and fluffy result.

Note: You might like to decorate the plum pudding with a sprig of holly; however take care, because the last time I did that I provided much merriment by setting the holly and my fringe on fire, as well as the pudding!

Sauce for Plum Pudding

This is Marianne Armstrong's sauce to accompany Plum Pudding from 1849:
    A lb of sugar either white or nice brown
    A glass of whiskey
    2 glasses of white wine
    One spoonful of flour
    A lump of butter about the size of a small egg
    Boil this for a few minutes.

Rose Hanlon's Mincemeat

1⅔ cups golden raisins
1⅔ cups currants
¾ cup raisins
¾ cup mixed peel
1-2 cooking apples (about ½lb),
   peeled and chopped
1 cup plus 2 tablespoons brown
   demerara sugar
¼lb suet, chopped
1 teaspoon mixed spice
½ teaspoon freshly grated nutmeg
¼ teaspoon ground ginger
¼ teaspoon ground cinnamon
grated rind and juice of
   1 orange and 1 lemon
½ wineglass of spirits (Irish
   whiskey or brandy)

This is a light fresh-tasting mincemeat, and is very quick to make. If you prefer a finer texture the dried fruit can be minced.

Mix all the ingredients except the spirits and let stand overnight. Next day, stir thoroughly and add spirits. Mix again. Pot and store in a cool dry place.

Lough Rynn Mincemeat

This mincemeat contains Naples cookie, which is similar to a macaroon, but made with ground pine nut kernels rather than almonds. It may have been flavored with rosewater.
   Take a quarter of a pound of Naples cookie, grate it fine. A pound of the sharpest apples and slice very small. Two pounds of pickled fruit, two pounds of currants and the yellow rind of two oranges, the juice of a large lemon, a quarter of a pound of sugar, spice and a little salt and a little brandy. Mix them together and put them pressed close into a crock for use.

Lough Rynn Puff Paste

This is similar to a rough puff pie dough and would have been used to make mince pies.
   Nearly the same quantity of butter and flour. Take less than the size of a walnut of butter and rub it well into the flour, then make a hole in the flour and wet it with water sufficient to roll out. When it is rolled out extremely thin and long, cover it with the remainder of the butter in pieces all over and take it up and roll it out twice only afterwards.

Lady Levinge's Mincemeat

Makes 8 jars (approximately)

8–9 Granny Smith apples (about
   3lb), peeled, cored, and chopped
grated rind and juice of 1 orange
   and 1 lemon
2½ cups cider
2¼ cups brown sugar
1 teaspoon ground cinnamon
1 teaspoon grated nutmeg
1 teaspoon ground cloves
3⅓ cups raisins
3⅓ cups currants (1⅔ cups currants
   and 1⅔ cups golden raisins)
2 cups maraschino cherries, halved
⅓ cup plus 1 tablespoon dark
   Jamaica rum

Originally mincemeat got its name because it included meat and later suet. Lady Maria Levinge of Clohamon House in Co. Wexford gave me this delicious recipe—which uses neither!

In a large saucepan bring the apples, juice and rinds of orange and lemon, and cider to the boil. Reduce the heat and simmer, stirring occasionally, for 10 minutes.
   Stir in the sugar, cinnamon, nutmeg, cloves, raisins, and currants. When the sugar has dissolved, simmer for a further 15 minutes.
   Remove the pan from the heat and stir in the cherries. Let the mixture cool and then stir in the rum. Spoon into clean jars, cover, and store in a cool, dark place.

Ballymaloe Mincemeat

Makes 7lb

2 cooking apples, e.g. Granny
  Smith
2 lemons
1lb beef suet
¾ cup mixed peel (preferably
  homemade, see page 317)
2 tablespoons orange marmalade
1⅔ cups currants
3⅓ cups raisins
1⅔ cups golden raisins
4½ cups Barbados sugar (moist,
  soft, dark brown sugar)
¼ cup Irish whiskey

This mincemeat recipe has been passed down through the Allen family and is the only one I know that keeps for literally years on end.

Core and bake the whole apples in a moderate oven (350°F) for about 45 minutes. When they are soft, remove the skin and mash the flesh into a pulp. Grate the rind from the lemons on the finest part of a stainless steel grater and squeeze out the juice. Add the other ingredients one by one, and as they are added, mix everything thoroughly together. Put into jars, cover with jam covers, and let mature for 3 weeks before using. This mincemeat will keep for months, or well over a year, in a cool, airy place.

Makes 20–24 mince pies

PASTRY
1¾ cups all-purpose flour
½–¾ cups (1–1½ sticks) butter
pinch of salt
2 teaspoons confectioners' sugar
a little beaten egg or egg yolk and
  water to bind

1lb Ballymaloe mincemeat
  (see above)
egg wash
superfine or confectioners' sugar,
  for sprinkling

IRISH WHISKEY CREAM
1 teaspoon confectioners' sugar
1½–3 tablespoons Irish whiskey
scant 1 cup whipped cream

Ballymaloe Mince Pies with Irish Whiskey Cream

Some people eat these delicious little pies just so they can have lots of whiskey cream. Myrtle Allen said that her mother used to measure the whiskey through a fork!

Make the shortcrust pie dough in the usual way (see page 305), and leave to relax for 1 hour in the refrigerator. Roll out the pie dough until quite thin and stamp out into rounds 3 inches in diameter. Line shallow bun pans with the pie dough rounds and put a good teaspoon of mincemeat into each hole. Damp the edges with water and put another round on top. Brush with eggwash and decorate each pie with holly leaves and berries made from the pie dough trimmings.

   Bake the mince pies in a moderate oven (350°F), for about 30 minutes. Let cool slightly, then dredge with confectioners' or superfine sugar.

   To make the Irish Whiskey Cream, fold the sugar and whiskey into the whipped cream.

Cold Puddings

Cold puddings and creams made in shapes and molds have always been popular because they could be made ahead and kept in the pantry, which was a help to the busy cook. Blancmange was made with milk and cornstarch, sometimes flavored with chocolate or other flavorings. Served with jelly, it was a much-loved combination.

Cornstarch Mold

This recipe was handwritten in Agnes Robins' school copy book. She also gave the costings for the recipe in pennies. It was a forerunner of blancmange. Blancmange was often served with jelly, or perhaps with jam.

½ pint milk	¾d
¾ oz cornflour	
1 dess'spoon sugar	½d
Flavouring	
Cost	1¼d

Boil the milk, reserving a little to blend cornflour, add flavouring, sugar, when boiling blend cornflour and add to the boiling milk, boil for about ten minutes, stirring constantly. Pour into a wetted mould and when set turn out. Serve with stewed fruit, or jam, or custard or cream.

Serves 4–6

¼ cup cornstarch
2½ cups milk
2 tablespoons (¼ cup) butter
4 teaspoons superfine sugar
¼oz gelatin
2 eggs
⅓ cup water
pure vanilla extract

Cornstarch Mousse

Mary Walsh from Woodsgift, Co. Tipperary, sent me her mother's recipe notebook, in which this recipe for Cornstarch Mousse was included. It is a lighter version of the Blancmange Pudding or Cornstarch Mold.

Mix the cornstarch to a smooth paste with a little of the milk. Put the remainder of the milk in a saucepan with the butter. When hot put it onto the cornstarch. Return to the saucepan and bring to a boil keeping it well stirred all the time. Simmer for 6 minutes.

Add the sugar, then draw off the fire and cool slightly. Separate the yolks from the whites of eggs. Beat up the yolks and stir them quickly into the cornstarch. Cook slowly at the side of the fire for a few minutes. Cool again slightly.

Dissolve the gelatin. Be careful not to boil it. Whisk the whites to a very stiff froth. Fold them into the cornstarch. Add a few drops of vanilla. Finally strain in the gelatin. Stir all lightly together. Pour into a wet mold and let set.

Very delicate and light, this is good served with poached seasonal fruit.

Jelly

In many households, making the jelly on Saturday night was as important as soaking the marrowfat peas for Sunday dinner. Alice Taylor, in *To School Through the Fields*, has a chapter called "The Jelly Jug," referring to a particular jug that was often used to make the jelly in.

Alice remembers that on Sundays they always had what was called a Tea Dinner: "nobody worked on a Sunday so there was no cooking done, and we usually had a cold meat salad with jelly and cream afterwards. My mother often made jelly the night before for this Sunday treat: I loved making jelly too, and watching it melting under the hot water always fascinated me. One day I put my jelly into an orange jug, not realizing that it was a family heirloom which my mother had got from my grandmother when she married. I poured the boiling water straight from the kettle onto the jelly and the jug split in two halves. I can still see the red jelly flooding out over the table as my mother's gasp of horror conveyed the enormity of my crime."

Hotel and restaurant menus also featured jelly and cream or jelly and ice cream as a sweet on their menus, it was a great treat. Sadly, in later years it was relegated to the children's menu, but we now make a variety of jellies from fresh fruit, which appeal to everyone.

Sherry Trifle

Sherry trifle was at the top of the list of cold desserts, and it featured on many hotel and restaurant menus. Most trifles never got a whiff of sherry, but, well made, it is a wonderful, still much-loved pudding. It is part of the Christmas tradition in Ireland, but is often over-shadowed by plum dessert. I think it deserves to be made much more often than it is.

Maura Laverty, in her book *Kind Cooking*, tells the story of a proposed match between an elderly spinster and a humorless farmer. The lady in question was well known for her cooking skills:

"on the evening the expected fiancé was invited to drop in for supper and a settlement, Miss Mary went beyond herself in the matter of food." There follows a detailed description of what she served. "But Miss Mary's chef d'oeuvre was the trifle, a sherry-soaked, cherry-sprinkled glory on which the whipped cream rose in Alpine peaks. All in all, that heavenly trifle should have been enough to make any normal man overlook such mundane trifles as small dowries and middle-age." However, it didn't work out like that: "He ate his bread, drank a cup of tea, stood up, broke off the match and walked out of the house. He said afterwards that it was the trifle which was mainly responsible. 'Three kinds of meat and six sorts of cake were bad enough,' he said. 'But a woman who would waste good cream on a pudden instead of churning it into butter would have a man in the workhouse inside a month.' Miss Mary had no regrets. She felt that she was well rid of a man who was so lacking in soul as to disrespect her lovely trifle."

Maura Lavery goes on to say that "A proper appreciation of the sweet course is of great importance in courtship and marriage." There are few men I know who don't enjoy a well-made sherry trifle!

2 layers of homemade sponge cake
(see page 292) or 1lb bought
trifle sponges (trifle sponges
are lighter so you will need
less custard)
¾ cup homemade raspberry jam
⅔–¾ cup best quality sweet or
medium sherry—don't spare the
sherry and don't waste your time
with cooking sherry

EGG CUSTARD
5 eggs, free-range if possible
1¼ tablespoons superfine sugar
¾ teaspoon pure vanilla extract
3¼ cups rich milk

DECORATION
2½ cups whipped cream
8 maraschino cherries or
crystallized violets
8 diamonds of angelica

Serves 8–10

SPONGE CAKE
4 eggs
½ cup plus 1 tablespoon superfine
sugar
¾ cup plus 1½ tablespoons all-
purpose flour

LEMON CURD
¼ cup (½ stick) butter
½ cup plus 1 tablespoon superfine
sugar
grated rind and juice of 2 lemons
2 eggs and 1 egg yolk, beaten

CUSTARD
4 egg yolks
1 tablespoon superfine sugar
grated rind of 1 lemon
scant 2 cups milk
⅔ cup cream

TOPPING
6 Granny Smith apples (about 2lb)
⅓ cup plus 2 teaspoons superfine
sugar
1–2 tablespoons water
2 egg whites
1¼ cups cream
½ cup toasted slivered almonds

Traditional Irish Sherry Trifle

There was always trifle as well as plum pudding for Christmas Day in our house. My mother's trifle was famous. She made two huge glass bowls of it, using trifle sponges and lashings of sherry. She used to hide it because my brothers would get up in the night to eat trifle. As each year passed she was forced to become more and more ingenious with her hiding place and eventually "hunt the trifle" became a traditional Christmas game.

Sandwich the rounds of sponge cake together with homemade raspberry jam. If you use trifle sponges, sandwich them in pairs. Next make the egg custard. Whisk the eggs with the sugar and vanilla extract. Heat the milk to the "shivery" stage and add it to the egg, whisking all the time. Put into a heavy saucepan and stir over low heat until the custard coats the back of the wooden spoon lightly. Don't let it boil or it will curdle.

Cut the sponge into ¾-inch slices and use these to line the bottom of a 7-cup glass bowl, sprinkling generously with sherry as you go along. Pour in some of the homemade egg custard and then add another layer of sponge. Sprinkle with the remainder of the sherry. Spread the rest of the custard over the top. Cover and leave for 5–6 hours, or preferably overnight, to mature.

Before serving, spread whipped cream over the top, pipe rosettes if you like, and decorate the trifle with cherries or crystallized violets and diamonds of angelica.

Apple Trifle

This delicious Apple Trifle is one I have adapted from a recipe that I believe originally came from Co. Armagh, which is famous for its orchards.

Make a whisked sponge in the usual way. Bake in a greased and lined 10 x 15-inch jelly roll pan for 15 minutes at 350°F.

While the sponge is cooking, make the lemon curd. Over very low heat melt the butter. Stir in the superfine sugar, lemon juice and rind, and then the well beaten eggs. Stir carefully over low heat until the mixture coats the back of a spoon. Draw off the heat and pour into a bowl (it will thicken as it cools).

Remove the sponge from the oven and transfer to a wire rack to cool. Divide the sponge into two pieces, spread one piece generously with lemon curd and top with the other piece. Cut into small squares and put half into a glass serving bowl.

Make the egg custard (see above), using milk and cream in place of rich milk, and lemon zest in place of vanilla. While it is still warm, pour half over the sponge. Top with the remainder of the sponge and the rest of the custard.

Peel and core the apples, cut into quarters, cover, and stew in a non-reactive saucepan with the sugar and water. When they are soft, beat into a fluff. Let cool. Whisk the egg whites and fold gently into the apple purée. Whip the 1¼ cups cream and fold most of it into the apple also, reserving some for decoration. Spread this on top of the custard, cover, and chill.

To serve, decorate with the remaining whipped cream, and sprinkle with toasted almonds.

Bread and Pancakes

The baking tradition is one of the richest and most varied aspects of Ireland's culinary heritage. From earliest times, breadmaking was an integral part of daily life in almost every home, and it is now undergoing a huge revival across Ireland.

For centuries, thin oatcakes were made on a bakestone or griddle over an open fire. Later, breads were leavened with sourdough and barm made from beer, sowans (the fermented juice of oat husks), and fermented potato juice. It was only in the first half of the 19th century that baking soda was introduced, enabling cooks to bake the wide range of soda breads for which Ireland is now so famous.

Even in the poorest country cabin, fresh soda bread would have been mixed on a wooden baking board and baked on the griddle, or in the pot oven or bastible, over the embers of the turf fire.

The traditional skills of breadmaking were passed on from mother to daughter, and were a great source of pride. It was a compliment of the highest order to be described as having "a light hand with baking." Try your own hand at griddle cakes, treacle, or potato bread, as well as the delicious soda breads!

Food of the Monasteries

Many monasteries were almost self-sufficient. The monks grew wheat which was stoneground on a mill wheel and then baked into bread to feed both the community and the poor. People flocked in their hundreds to the monasteries to be shrived and then to have bread and tea in the guesthouse. There was no charge, but it was understood that one should leave a donation according to one's means. The Cistercian Abbey at Mount St. Joseph in Roscrea keeps up this tradition to the present day.

There are many references in early literature to hermits and monks fasting on a meager diet of dry bread. Many of these holy men fasted on barley bread and water on weekdays and feasted on wheaten bread, salmon and ale on Sundays and feast days.

Flour

The flour, often ground from home-grown wheat, was traditionally stored in a wooden meal chest close to the fire. They were robustly built with a sloping lid and perhaps two or three divisions inside to store white flour, wheaten meal, and oatmeal, and on occasion some yellowmeal (corn meal). Many had a narrow shelf in the back near the top to store baking soda, cornstarch, and the precious, expensive sugar. The chest was kept locked in many households to guard against not only two-legged invaders, but also four-legged pests. Some good examples of these meal chests still survive.

This revealing account from Eric Cross's *The Tailor and Ansty* describes the goings on in a West Cork tailor's house in the early 20th century: "Upstairs are the bedroom, with the great box bed, and the small room beyond where Ansty keeps the meal and corn so that even at night when she is asleep, she can still guard it from the pilfering of the rats and the mice."

When times were hard, as they were more often than not, the woman of the house scrimped to try to ensure that the supply of meal lasted from one harvest to the next. The ability to produce freshly baked bread in the months of July and August was a source of great pride to a housewife.

Well-to-do households and farmers with several farm laborers to feed would have bought white flour by the sack. Originally farmers who grew their own wheat would have taken it to a local stone mill to be ground into flour. White flour was sold in white cotton flour bags. These were a great bonus and had a myriad of uses.

Thrifty housewives made them into tablecloths, sheets, pillow cases, nightdresses, tea towels... The Christmas plum pudding, for example, was boiled in one. Some more artistic housewives hand-painted them, or they embroidered the bags and transformed them into tablecloths or fancy cushion covers for use in the parlor.

On the Blasket Islands, cereals were ground to make meal until 1850. Tomás Ó Criomhthain associates this with Inis na Bró, of which he writes in *Dinnsheanchas na mBlaoscaoidí* (The Topography of the Blasket Islands). The island got its name from the querns which people used to grind corn there; oats, barley, and rye used to grow on the Blaskets. The meal was used to make bread, on the mainland the wheat was threshed and the women milled it using household querns.

Indian corn or yellowmeal is the cereal most frequently mentioned in the Blasket Island sources. It was bought in milled form and used to make bread and porridge. The bread was known as yellow bread. It was very nourishing: a mother and daughter living on Inis na Bró and cut off by the weather had only a stone of Indian meal and the milk of two goats, and they managed to survive on it. Tomás relates that when he was young, yellowmeal was used to make bread once the year's supply of potatoes had been used up. It was being eaten in the 1870s according to the sources, and the islanders were still buying it until the 1920s. By 1937, when Seán Ó Dálaigh's book *Timcheall Chinn Sléibhe* was published, yellowmeal was no longer being used to make bread on the mainland: "They say they wouldn't be able to knead it." There is no reference in the literature to the production of flour by the sieving of meal on the island. Flour was first brought in small quantities from the mainland for baking of Christmas loaves, and it was still a luxury item in the late 1800s, but by the 1920s it had become an established part of breadmaking on the island. However, it did not oust Indian meal altogether, even though there wasn't a great difference between them in price.

Tomás Mac Síthigh, writing in *Paróiste an Fheirtéaraigh* about life on the mainland at the time of the Great Famine, notes that around that time people on the mainland ate "wheat bread, barley bread and oat bread" but in general in the sources Indian meal bread is the most commonly mentioned. White bread was available on the mainland around the 1880s—Peig Sayers relates in *Beatha Pheig Sayers* that when it could be bought in An Daingean, the men from Dún Chaoin would dress up on Saturday night and walk to An Daingean to have white bread and tea. Later, a local woman named Siobhán Ní Argáin began to make it and sell it locally so the men no longer had to go to An Daingean for it. Peig says "it was no surprise that they had a liking for the bread: there was nothing but potatoes three times a day in every house at that time."

Bread was baked on a griddle or in a pot-oven. These became more plentiful as time passed; Máire Ní Ghuithín's family had two, a big one and a small one, the pot-oven was central to her way of cooking. She writes in *Bean an Oileáin* that the bread her mother made was known as hard yellow cake. The ingredients were two bowls of Indian meal, a little baking soda and boiling water. The meal was placed in a dish and the baking soda mixed in. Next, boiling water was added and the ingredients were mixed together. The dough was difficult to gather together because the yellowmeal was dry. The dough was turned out and formed into a thin cake of a size suitable for the griddle, approximately 14 inches. The griddle was heated over low fire, some flour was strewn over it, and the dough put on. To turn the cake, the griddle was taken off the fire, tilted on its side, and the cake flipped over.

The recipe for yellow bread to be baked in the pot oven was different. The ingredients were half a mug of yellowmeal, two and a half mugs of white flour, one teaspoon of baking soda, half a teaspoon of salt, and sour milk. The meal and flour were placed in a cake dish and mixed well. The bread soda and salt were added and mixed in. A hollow was made in the middle of the mixture, the sour milk was poured in gradually and at the same time the dough was gradually gathered together and care was taken to see that it wasn't too moist or too dry. When it had been kneaded, the dough was then spread out into a round shape that would fit the pot-oven and a cross was cut on it. The pot-oven was hung over a glowing turf fire and when the pot was quite hot, a little flour was sprinkled in and the dough was put in. The lid was put on and then covered with red embers from the fire. This meant that the bread baked from top downwards, as well as from the bottom upwards. Depending on the heat of the fire, the bread would be ready within 20–30 minutes. To lift the lid off the pot-oven, the handle on top was clasped using tongs, and the lid was lifted up carefully to avoid spilling embers or ash into the pot. While one loaf was baking, another would be prepared and put in as soon as the first one was baked. The second loaf was easier to bake than the first one because the pot-oven and the lid were already warm.

2 tablespoons (1oz) yeast
2½ tablespoons sugar
5 cups tepid milk and water

A Buttermilk Plant

Traditionally most farmers would have had their own cows and used buttermilk, leftover from churning the butter, in the breadmaking. Every year, we proudly teach hundreds of students from all over the world how to make our Irish soda breads, which soon become addictive. Many students worry about the difficulty of finding a regular supply of buttermilk back at home, so we now pass on this miraculous recipe, taken from Kind Cooking *by Maura Laverty. This buttermilk starter will increase and after a few weeks you will be in a position to pass some on to your friends.*

Cream the yeast with the sugar, gradually add the tepid milk and water. Put the mixture in some vessel that may easily be washed and scalded (delph or china, not stainless steel), cover it, and leave it in a warm place for a couple of days or until the milk smells and tastes like buttermilk. Put a piece of cheesecloth in the bottom of a strainer and strain the milk through this. The funny-looking thing like lumpy cornstarch which remains will be the plant. Rinse every drop of milk off it, by pouring a cup of tepid water over it. Let the water run through the strainer into the buttermilk—it will all make excellent liquid for mixing cake bread. To start a new lot, scrape the plant off the cheesecloth and put it back into the scalded and well-rinsed vessel. Add another 5 cups of tepid milk and water, cover, and leave it as before.

That first ounce of yeast will go on growing and multiplying, giving you buttermilk until the end of time. But the plant needs care.

It must be strained at least every 5 days. If you don't want the milk for baking, you can always drink it. I knew a woman so crippled with rheumatics that she couldn't kneel down to say the Rosary. After 6 months of drinking this buttermilk, she was able to do the Lough Derg Pilgrimage on her knees.

Make sure the milk and water is never more than lukewarm. Strong heat over 50°C kills yeast.

Cleanliness is very important. Careful rinsing after straining, and the scalding of the container must be done if the plant is to live.

2 mashed potatoes
2oz oatmeal
2oz flour
1 quart water

Steel-cut Oat Buttermilk

This buttermilk substitute, which has steel-cut oats as an ingredient, is from Cookery Notes 1947. *This recipe, and the one which follows, are in essence Irish sourdough starters—they give the bread a delicious slightly sour taste.*

Mix all together. Cover and leave in a warm place for a few days, stirring occasionally. When sour use as buttermilk for making soda bread if buttermilk cannot be obtained.

Winter Buttermilk

Yet another buttermilk substitute, which shows how inventive cooks were with the raw materials available to them. This one is from Kind Cooking *by Maura Laverty. This recipe makes about 10 cups, but you can keep it going for a while by topping it up with fresh water.*

The secret of good cake-bread is 3-day old buttermilk, a light hand for mixing and kneading and a brisk oven. Buttermilk is not always easy to come by. In the winter when the cows are not milking, some people use instead the water in which potatoes have been boiled. Far better is the 'winter buttermilk' which they use in Cork and Meath and this is how it is made.

Mix ¼lb flour to a smooth paste with 1 cup cold water. Put this in the bottom of a large jug or crock. Add 2 grated raw potatoes and 2 mashed cooked potatoes. Now mix in 7 cups cold water. Cover and leave on the kitchen mantelpiece or in some such warm place for 2 days. When you are baking, pour off carefully, and without disturbing the sediment, as much liquid as you require. This can be used in exactly the same way as buttermilk and will give you lovely light bread. Add fresh water to make up for what you have used. Stir up the contents of the vessel, cover it and put it by for the next baking.

One lot of potatoes and flour will give you a fortnight's supply of winter buttermilk.

Soda Bread

Baking soda, known in Ireland as bread soda, began to be used in Europe as a raising agent in the mid-19th century. Many years before that, native American Indians used soda or pearl ash as a leavening agent and soda breads or quick breads first appeared in an American cookbook in 1796. Baking soda is an alkali and the lactic acid in the buttermilk reacts with the baking soda to produce carbon dioxide, which raises the bread.

Áine de Blacam said that on Inis Meáin they saved up the cream to make butter. It would be beaten up and down in an old-fashioned dash churn. The buttermilk (the liquid left over after the butter forms) was used for making bread or for drinking—it had exceptional thirst quenching qualities. When the men were saving the hay—thirsty work—they welcomed a cup of buttermilk. Alice Taylor in *To School Through the Fields* also described buttermilk as "a grand drink on a hot summer day and a great favourite of the men coming in from the fields." At harvest time "the wheat was milled for flour. Some of the wheat was sold and more returned for our own use. My mother baked every day: big circles of brown and white bread baked in the bastibles over the fire. Shop bread rarely appeared on our table."

In her book *Full and Plenty*, Maura Laverty describes the wonderful soda bread made by Mrs Feeney: "When it came to making plain soda bread, there was no one in the County Kildare who could hold a candle to her. The dough of her bread was as light and as white as bog cotton. The crust was always brittle and richly brown, with never a crack or a seam. The shape had a symmetry usually to be seen only in advertisements, and the flavour was the true sweet nutty flavour of perfectly baked wheat."

Like many other children I began my cooking career at my mother's side while she made the daily soda bread. As soon as she reached for the mixing bowl, I'd don my apron and pester her for a little piece of dough to make a *cístín beag*. This was a tiny loaf shaped into a round just like my Mammy made. I'd solemnly cut a cross on top with a knife and my little *cístín* was baked beside her big loaf in the range. The result was often a bit tough and rather too crusty from over-enthusiastic handling, nonetheless I was delighted with it. Fortunately all the grown-ups who were invited to taste "my bread" were always careful to be encouraging and lavish in their praise as they sampled and chewed!

White Soda Bread

Originally baked in a pot oven or bastible beside the open fire, white soda bread is often referred to as cake bread. The word bastible seems to be a bastardization of the name Barnstaple, the town in Devon where these iron baking pots were made.

First preheat your oven to 450°F.

Sift the dry ingredients. Make a well in the center. Pour most of the milk in at once. Using one hand, stir in a full circle to mix in the flour from the sides of the bowl, adding more buttermilk if necessary. The absorption rate varies depending on the brand of flour. The dough should be softish, not too wet and sticky. When it all comes together, turn it out onto a floured board and knead lightly for a second, just enough to tidy it up. Pat the dough into a round about 2 inches deep and cut a cross on it to let the fairies out! Let the cuts go over the sides of the bread to make sure of this. Bake in the preheated oven for 15 minutes, then turn down the oven to 400°F for a further 20–30 minutes or until cooked. If in doubt, tap the bread bottom; it should sound hollow.

Let cool on a wire rack or on the windowsill in the time-honored way.

Note: Fresh crusty bread makes my mouth water, but some people prefer a soft crust. Years ago a clean flour bag would have been wrapped around the hot bread to soften the crust. A dish towel will produce the same result.

Bastible Bread

A bastible is an iron pot, usually with three little legs underneath and a slightly domed lid, that was used as a pot oven to cook over an open fire. Everything from breads and tarts to stews and even a goose was cooked in a bastible. Bread and tarts that were cooked in a bastible always had more tender crusts because the steam was trapped inside the pot, softening the crust. You can recreate a similar tender crust effect by cooking the soda bread in a covered casserole in the oven.

Preheat the oven to 425°F. Line the base of the casserole with silicon paper. Heat the lined casserole in the oven. Make the dough as in the recipe for White or Brown Soda bread. Pat the dough into a loaf about 1½-inch thick and just large enough to fit the casserole.

Cut a deep cross into the loaf and then prick the center of the four sections to let the fairies out.

Transfer to the hot casserole and cover with the lid. Bake for 40–50 minutes. Remove from the casserole and let cool on a wire rack. The crust will be soft and tender and the bread will be almost spongy in texture.

Makes 2 loaves

4½ cups whole wheat flour
 (preferably stone ground)
4½ cups all-purpose flour
2 rounded teaspoons salt
2 rounded teaspoons baking soda,
 sifted
3¼–4 cups sour milk or buttermilk

Variation

Brown Soda Scones

Makes 3 dozen (approx.) depending
 on size

Brown Soda Bread

The warm and comforting smell of brown soda bread wafting from the kitchen has cheered and nourished countless generations of Irish people after a hard day's work in the fields and bogs. It is the quintessential Irish bread.

Occasionally we add a small fist of fine stoneground oatmeal, 1 egg or 2 tablespoons butter to make a richer soda bread dough. Irish whole wheat flours are coarse and nutty with a rich wheaten flavor. The various textures will produce different types of bread.

First preheat the oven to 450°F.

Mix the dry ingredients together in a large bowl. Make a well in the center and add most of the sour milk or buttermilk all in one go. Working from the center, mix with your hand, and add more milk if necessary. The dough should be soft but not sticky. Turn out onto a floured board and knead lightly, just enough to shape into a round. Flatten slightly to about 2 inches deep. Put onto a floured baking sheet. Mark with a deep cross and bake in the hot oven for 15–20 minutes, then reduce the heat to 400°F for about 20–25 minutes, or until the bread is cooked and sounds hollow when tapped. Cool on a wire rack.

For scones, make the dough as above. Flatten the dough into a round about 1 inch deep. Cut into scones. Cook for about 20 minutes in a hot oven at 450°F.

Bocáire

Serves 4–8

1¾ cups whole wheat flour
1¾ cups all-purpose flour
1 level teaspoon salt
1 level teaspoon baking soda
1½ cups sour milk or buttermilk

Catherine O'Drisceóil from Cape Clear told us about this bread which was made from wheat grown on the island and milled on the mainland. Soda bread was called cake bread or just "a cake," not only on the islands, but also in many parts of the country. The term still lingers to this day.

Catherine explained that "bocáire was made when you'd find yourself running short of bread and you didn't have the time to make a big loaf of cake bread."

Bocáire was normal bread dough mixture "patted out very thin"—so thin that there was very little dough in the center between the two crusts. It was much thinner than normal griddle bread. It was cooked on a heavy-iron pan and was eaten immediately after it was cooked.

Áine de Blacam mentioned something similar on Inis Meáin. If her mother ran out of bread she would make some dough, roll it out thinly, and bake it on the griddle. She called it Cáca Tanaí (thin bread).

Heat a heavy iron pan over the fire.

Mix the dry ingredients together. Make a well in the center and add most of the sour milk or buttermilk. Working from the center, mix with your hand and add more milk if necessary. The dough should be soft but not sticky. Turn out onto a floured board and knead lightly, just enough to shape into a round. Roll out very thinly. Grease the pan with a butter wrapper. Bake for 20 minutes on one side, turn over, and cook on the other side. Cool on a wire rack. Eat freshly baked with country butter.

Nancy Ellis's Griddle Bread

Serves 4–8

2 fists all-purpose flour (approx.
   3 cups)
1 scant level teaspoon baking soda
no salt
fresh milk to bind (1¼–1½ cups)

Afternoon tea served in Madame Fitzgerald's kitchen at Glin Castle in Co. Limerick was a memorable experience for me. There was thinly sliced homemade bread, jam, a comb of honey from the beehive in the orchard, tiny scones with homemade raspberry jam and cream, a chocolate cake, and a moist plum cake. However, the pièce de résistance was Nancy Ellis's warm griddle bread, which she made on a heavy iron pan on the side of the Aga.

Nancy Ellis cooked at Glin for over 40 years and her food was legendary.

Nancy sifted the flour onto a tray rather than into a bowl. She then added a scant level teaspoon of baking soda, which she first rubbed between the palms of her hands to eliminate any lumps.

She mixed the dry ingredients well and then added enough fresh milk to make a softish but not sticky dough. This was flattened out to about 1½ inches thick and baked on a preheated pan on the cool plate of the Aga. It took about 30 minutes in total (approx. 15 minutes on each side). Originally it would have been baked on a griddle. Cool on a wire rack and serve while still warm

Note: a nonstick pan works very well for griddle bread.

Mrs McGillycuddy's Yellowmeal Bread

Serves 4–8

6oz Indian corn meal, sometimes
  referred to as yellowmeal
2 cups plus 2 tablespoons all-
  purpose flour
1 level teaspoon salt
1 level teaspoon baking soda
1½–1¾ cups sour milk or buttermilk

This bread tastes just as delicious today as it did over a hundred years ago and it deserves to be much better known. I've made it over and over again since Mrs McGillycuddy, from Caragh Lake in Co. Kerry, first showed me how to make it. I've also heard it referred to as Yalla Male *bread.*

    Other recipes from West Cork use equal quantities of yellowmeal and flour, which produces a slightly yellower bread with a grittier texture.

First preheat your oven to 450°F.

    Sift the dry ingredients. Make a well in the center. Pour most of the milk in at once. Using one hand, mix in the flour from the sides of the bowl, adding more milk if necessary. The dough should be softish, not too wet and sticky. When it all comes together, turn it out onto a floured board and knead lightly to tidy it up. Flip over the edges with a floured hand. Pat the dough into a round about 1½ inches deep and cut a cross on it to let the fairies out! Bake in the hot oven for 15 minutes, then turn down the oven to 400°F for 30 minutes or until cooked. If you are in doubt about this, tap the bottom of the bread—if it is cooked it will sound hollow.

Slim Bread

This old recipe was given to me by George McCartney of McCartney's family butchers in Moira, Co. Down:

It's one bread I remember well from my school days. My mother would have had the griddle on when we arrived home to cook slim bread which we ate warm with lots of butter and homemade strawberry jam. She lives next door to the shop, even yet when there is slim being made I slip round for some.

450g (1lb) plain white flour
1 level teaspoon bread soda (baking soda)
1 level teaspoon salt
55g (2oz) superfine sugar
55g (2oz) butter
1 egg, free-range if possible
250ml (8fl oz) buttermilk

Sieve the flour, soda and salt into a bowl. Add the sugar.

Rub in the butter and mix to a firm dough with the beaten egg and the buttermilk. Shape the mixture into two rounds and cut each one into four farls. Bake on a heated griddle for 6–10 minutes on each side, depending on the thickness. Eat hot or cold, split in half and spread with butter and homemade strawberry jam.

Fruit Slims

Add 1 cup sultanas to the dry ingredients before starting to mix in the liquid. Bake as above.

Slim Cakes

Makes about 10

scant 2½ cups all-purpose flour
a good pinch of salt
1 cup freshly rendered lard

Many recipes have turned up under this name. One version seems to have been made from freshly rendered lard, the week after the pig was killed. I'm not sure where the name comes from; perhaps it refers to the fact that the bread is rolled thinly. There's certainly nothing slimming about this recipe!

Sift the flour and salt into a bowl. Rub in the lard and continue to work until the mixture comes together. Roll out thinly. Bake on a hot griddle or nonstick pan until brown on both sides. Serve the cakes straight off the griddle, hot and buttered.

Co. Carlow Slim Cakes

Northern Ireland had its own special baking traditions. Slim Cakes, Fadge, and other potato cakes were a specialty here. This recipe for Slim Cakes comes from the Bruen papers, Co. Carlow, dating from the 1800s:

Rub ⅓ cup (¾ stick) butter in a quart of flour, make a hole in it and put in the yolks of 3 eggs, a little salt, and new milk. Work it to a stiff paste and roll it out as thin as you like. Cut into what form you please and bake them on a griddle.

Kerry Molasses Bread

1–2 tablespoons molasses
1 egg (optional), free-range if possible
1¼ cups approx. sour milk or buttermilk, to mix
scant 3½ cups all-purpose flour, preferably unbleached
1 level teaspoon salt
1 level teaspoon baking soda

This recipe was described to me by Mrs McGillycuddy from Glencar in Co. Kerry, who still makes it occasionally. A richer molasses bread, closer to gingerbread, was and still is widely made in Ulster.

First fully preheat your oven to 450°F.
   Heat the molasses until it begins to run. Whisk the egg, if you are using it, add to the molasses and mix well. Then add the buttermilk.
   Sift the dry ingredients. Make a well in the center. Pour in most of the liquid all at once. Using one hand, mix in the flour from the sides of the bowl, adding more liquid if necessary. The dough should be softish, not too wet and sticky. When it comes together, turn it out onto a floured board. Tidy it up and flip over the edges with a floured hand. Pat the dough into a round about 1 inch deep and cut a cross on it. The cuts should go over the sides of the bread. Bake in the hot oven for 15 minutes, then turn down the oven to 400°F for 30 minutes or until cooked. If you are in doubt, tap the bottom of the bread; it will sound hollow if cooked. Let cool on a wire rack.

Boston Brown Bread

1½ cups Graham flour (wheaten meal)
2 cups cornmeal (Indian meal)
½ teaspoon baking soda
a pinch of salt
½ cup molasses
2½ cups sweet milk

This comes from Nancy Elliott in Co. Fermanagh, and dates from the 1860s. Nancy's eldest daughter was married in America and probably sent some recipes home to her mother.

Put the flour and meal into a bowl, sift in the soda and salt. Mix the molasses with the milk and stir into the dry ingredients. Turn the mixture into a bowl, cover with parchment paper, and steam just like a steamed pudding for 3 hours.

Seedy Bread

scant 3½ cups all-purpose flour
1 level teaspoon salt
1 level teaspoon baking soda
1 tablespoon sugar
2 teaspoons caraway seeds
¼ cup (½ stick) butter (optional)
1¼ cups buttermilk

Many Americans are convinced that Irish soda bread traditionally contains caraway seeds. I was baffled by this assumption until I discovered that seedy bread was certainly made in Donegal and Leitrim. The tradition of putting caraway seeds in bread must have been taken to the United States by Irish emigrants.

First fully preheat your oven to 450°F.
   Sift all the dry ingredients and add the caraway seeds. Rub in the butter, if using. Make a well in the center and pour in most of the buttermilk at once. Using one hand, mix in the flour from the sides of the bowl, adding more milk if necessary. The dough should be softish, but not too wet and sticky. When it all comes together, turn it out onto a floured board and knead lightly for a second, just enough to tidy it up. Pat the dough into a round about 1 inch deep and cut a cross on it to let the fairies out! (Let the cuts go over the sides of the bread to make sure of this.) Bake in the hot oven for 15 minutes, then turn down the heat to 400°F for 30 minutes or until just cooked. If you are in doubt, tap the bottom of the bread: if it is cooked it will sound hollow.

Lady S. G. Bellew's Soda Cake

2 small teaspoons baking soda (2 level teaspoons is enough)
2 level teaspoons salt, to taste
1 teaspoon cream of tartar
2lbs of flour
scant 2 cups buttermilk

This comes from the Clonbrock manuscript of April 1910:

Mix soda and salt and cream of tartar well with dry flour, then add as much *buttermilk mixed with half a cup of sour cream to make a light dough. Roll out either thin, or round thick cake, and bake one hour, according to the heat of the oven. If you like you can make thin and bake half quantity on griddle or frying pan.
   *We used scant 2 cups buttermilk. We baked it at 425°F for 15 minutes and then reduced to 400°F for a further 40 minutes.

Oaten Bread

In Clones, Co. Monaghan, I talked to Granny Toye, whose memory, at 88, is crystal clear. "People going to America would always take a few cakes of oaten bread with them on the ship," she told me. "It sustained them and kept them from getting sick. Sure there's nothing in the making of it—use fine oatmeal and it must be well cooked." This is the method which she described to me.

Put oatmeal into a bowl, soak with water, add salt. Roll in a ball, then put on a bakeboard. Roll into a round approx. 10 inches across. Leave it to sit for an hour or so to dry out, by which time it will be possible to lift it. Put on to the harden griddle propped up by the fire and keep it turned as it browns. It will take about half an hour to cook, but the time depends on the heat of the fire. It should be dry and crisp. It keeps very well.

A beautiful iron "harden griddle" was part of the batterie de cuisine *in households where the cooking was done over the open fire. Country markets used the image as their logo, and still do.*

scant 2 cups fine stoneground oats
2 cups sour milk or buttermilk
2⅔ cups all-purpose flour
½ teaspoon salt
1 teaspoon baking soda

Oatmeal Soda Bread

For this early soda bread the oats were steeped in buttermilk overnight. It makes a light, pale bread with quite a different flavor—also absolutely delicious. This recipe was given to me by Honor Moore from Dublin.

Steep the oats in the buttermilk overnight.

Next day, preheat the oven to 350°F. Mix the flour, salt and baking soda together, then stir into the oats. If necessary add a little more milk, but don't make the dough too wet. Put into a large well greased loaf pan (we use one which is 5½ × 9½ × 2½ inches) and bake in a moderate oven for 1–1¼ hours.

Note: John Dunton, writing in 1698, recalls a meal he enjoyed in the west of Ireland:
"The oaten cake was sett next to me, at the lower end of our table was placed a greate roll of fresh butter of three pound at least, and a wodden vessell full of milk and water."

Makes 4

2 breakfast cups fine oats*
2 breakfast cups sour milk or
   buttermilk
2½ breakfast cups all-purpose flour
½ teaspoon salt—we thought it
   needed a little more salt, use a
   barely rounded teaspoon
1 teaspoon baking soda

* leftover porridge could also
   be used

Buttermilk Oatenbread

This recipe comes from Cookery Notes 1947.

Steep the oatmeal overnight in the buttermilk (we steeped it for 2 hours). Mix flour, salt, and soda together. Stir in oatmeal. If necessary add a little more milk but keep the mixture stiff. Knead until smooth. Roll out 2 inches thick. Cut in four. Bake in a moderate oven for 25 minutes.

Malt Wheaten Bread

3 large cups wheaten meal
1½ large cups flour
1 large cup Golden Drop (Yellow) meal
1 cup sugar (Demerara)
2 teaspoons baking soda
1 egg (if liked)

I came across a recipe for malt wheaten bread that includes yellowmeal in a little charity cookbook called Tried Favourites. *The book was undated, but I would guess it is from the 1940s or 1950s. This recipe is credited to a Mrs R.S. Boles, from Boyle, Co. Roscommon.*

Mix all ingredients together with sour milk till very moist and bake in a slowish oven 1¼ hours at 350°F.

Wheaten Bread

7 cups wheaten meal
7 cups all-purpose flour
1 teaspoon salt
6 teaspoons baking powder
water, to mix

This more modern recipe for wheaten bread is dated June 1948 and uses baking powder as a raising agent.

Mix all the dry ingredients in a warmed basin. Add water until the dough is fairly wet. Turn onto a board well floured with wheaten meal, and knead well. Bake as a whole cake in a moderate oven for 1 hour, 350°F.

Gemma Burke's Curney Cake

Makes 1 x 8-inch cake

¼–⅓ cup (½–¾ stick) butter (or more if you like—we used ½ cup (1 stick)
scant 3½ cups self-rising flour
a pinch of salt
½ cup plus 1 tablespoon superfine sugar
2½ cups golden raisins
1–2 eggs, beaten (Gemma uses 2 and keeps back a little to brush the top of the cake—so did we)
scant 1¼ cups milk—it took a full 1¼ cups when we tested it

Gemma Burke from Fethard, Co. Tipperary, sent me her recipe for Curney cake. This is a rich, sweet bread using eggs and fresh milk with self-rising flour.

Line an 8-inch round cake pan with parchment paper and preheat the oven to 350°F.
     Rub the butter into the flour until it is very fine. Add the rest of the dry ingredients. Add the beaten eggs (keeping back a little) then enough milk to make a soft dough. Put into the prepared pan, brush with some of the beaten egg, cut a cross on the top. Bake for approximately 1 hour. Turn out and let cool. Gemma wraps it in a dish towel when cooling, this would give a softer crust. You can butter if you wish.

Note: Bread soda and baking soda are colloquial names for bicarbonate of soda.

Barm

Barm comes from the old English word *beorma* meaning froth. The recipes for barm contain similar ingredients to the other breads, except that hops were also included. It appears to have been widely used until the introduction of baking soda as a raising agent, and before bakers started using fresh yeast. Barm is the foam or scum found on the top of liquor during fermentation. Various cultures which derived from barm are thought to be the ancestors of most forms of brewer's and baker's yeast available today. Using the term "barmy" to describe someone might indicate that they are of a "frothy" disposition!

Barm

I found several recipes for Barm in the manuscript cookbooks. This one dates back to 1869 and is initialled H.A.:

2oz of hops to 10 quarts of water boiled until all go to the bottom. Strain and leave it like it is milk warm (ie. as warm as fresh milk). Then whisk in ½lb brown sugar, 1lb flour, keep it in a warm place stirring it now and then. The next day have 2lbs potatoes mashed very fine, add them hot to the hops. Let it stand 2 days and nights. Then it is fit for you to make bread.

To make bread: Take a wine glass full to 2lb flour; ½ pint warm milk and salt to taste. The lightness of the bread depends on its being thoroughly kneaded after the ingredients are all mixed, the dough must then be left cold. Lay it before the fire to rise a short time before putting it in the oven. The milk must be warmed before adding it to the flour and the flour thoroughly dried before using.

Waterford Blaa

The *blaa*, a soft white saucer-shaped bread roll is synonymous with Waterford. It's made with strong baker's flour, salt, baker's yeast, and water. Originally made by hand it's now mixed by machine and thousands are baked every day in the city.

The origins of the *blaa* go back 300 years and are linked with the arrival of the French Huguenots in Ireland around 1572. Around 10,000 came to Ireland, mainly to the ports of Dublin and Waterford. They were skilled, industrious, honest people with a strong work ethic, and included lace makers and poplin makers in Dublin as well as bakers.

At that time all the bread here was made from brown flour and was quite heavy. It's likely that these French immigrants missed their own lighter French bread, so they started to import white flour into the port of Waterford and set up little bakeries making light white bread. The blaa was originally the by-product. When the larger pieces of dough were cut for a loaf, there were often small pieces left over which they cut into small pieces and baked on a tray as individual rolls and often gave away free or bartered for another product.

The blaa is about the size of a saucer. There are many theories about the origin of the name—it's possible that it came from the French *pain blanc*—white bread, or *blé*—flour. It gained in popularity and was eaten in many ways, just fresh with butter or as a sandwich with cheese and onion crisps and a slice of ham—a "hang blaa " Even more popular was a blaa filled with "red lead"—luncheon sausage—a by-product of the pork industry. Denny's had a bacon factory in Waterford and the sausage was made with pork off-cuts, flavored with herbs and spices and a pink coloring added. It comes in a round and fits the size of the blaa perfectly. Many of the workers in the famous Waterford Crystal factory ate blaas for lunch, the lead used in the crystal was a reddish color so that's where the name came from. The blaa is also used as a "container" for a breakfast roll.

No preservatives are used so it must be eaten on the day it is made, hence it doesn't often leave Waterford. The three main blaa makers in Waterford have come together and applied to have blaa formally recognised as a local food (with protected designation of origin) to protect the recipe and its local origins.

Rye Bread

Makes 1 or 2 loaves

½ tablespoon (¼oz) fresh yeast
warm water at blood temperature
2⅔ cups bread flour
1 cup plus 1 tablespoon dark rye
    flour
3 tablespoons caraway seeds
1 teaspoon salt
1 egg, free-range if possible,
    beaten
poppyseeds

Rye is mentioned in the 7th/8th-century Brehon Laws and there is substantial archaeological evidence for its cultivation in the 5th to 11th centuries. In her book, Land of Milk and Honey, *Brid Mahon says that rye bread continued to be part of the traditional Irish diet right up to the 19th century. A popular rhyme advises:*

Rye bread will do you good
Barley bread will do you no harm
Wheaten bread will sweeten your blood
Oaten bread will strengthen your arm.

Charles Etienne Coquebert de Montbret, on a visit to Cork in 1790, noted that "In the South of Ireland bread is made with oats, in Wicklow with rye and in Meath with a mixture of rye and wheat."

Rye straw was used for thatching, a use for which it is second only to wheat straw. It was grown specifically for this purpose in Donegal, and still is on the Aran Islands. Just last summer I watched rye being hand threshed against a stone on Inis Meáin.

Crumble the yeast and mix with 1¼ cups lukewarm water. Mix the flours, caraway seeds, and salt in a bowl. Add the yeast liquid, with extra warm water if necessary, to make a soft but not sticky dough. Knead until smooth (for about 10 minutes). Cover and let rise in a warm place until doubled in bulk. Punch down and knead again for 4–5 minutes. Shape into one or two loaves. Cover and let rise again.

Brush the loaves with beaten egg. Sprinkle with poppyseeds and slash the tops in a cross with a razor blade or sharp knife. Bake in a preheated oven at 450°F for about 25 minutes or until the bread sounds hollow when tapped underneath.

Seed Loaf

Makes 2 × 1lb loaves

1½ tablespoons fresh yeast
scant 2 cups warm water, or more
    as needed
scant 5¼ cups bread flour
2 level teaspoons salt
4 teaspoons sugar
2–4 tablespoons caraway seeds

In Cork city this bread was traditionally eaten on Christmas Eve. Paddy Ormond, whose family were bakers in Shandon Street for three generations, told me how people would eat seed loaf after Midnight Mass, presumably following "a feed of salted Ling" (see page 54), and also on Christmas Day. "A glass of port and seed cake after Christmas dinner and you were perfect." Caraway seeds are a splendid aid to digestion.

Recently I enquired about this bread in a local bakery, but the reply was "Yerra not at all girl, sure that's been discontinued. The modern housewife would have no meas on that, sure she'd think it was mouse droppings that was in it!"

Mix the yeast with ⅔ cup lukewarm water. When the yeast is dissolved, add a further 1¼ cups tepid water.

Sift the flour into a bowl and add the salt, sugar, and caraway seeds. Make a well in the center and pour in most of the lukewarm liquid. Mix to a loose dough, adding the remainder of the liquid or more flour if necessary. Turn the dough onto a floured board, cover and let relax for 5–10 minutes. Knead until smooth and springy (about 10 minutes). If using a food mixer with a dough hook, 5 minutes is usually long enough.

Put the dough to rise in the bowl covered with a damp cloth or tightly sealed with plastic wrap. Yeast dough rises best in a warm moist atmosphere, e.g. near your stove, on top of a radiator, or in a fan oven turned to minimum heat with the door open (use a thick pottery bowl if rising in a fan oven). Rising time depends on the temperature, but it is much better to err on the side of having it too cool rather than too hot. Remember that cold won't kill yeast, but heat over 110°F will.

When the dough has more than doubled in size, knead again for about 3–4 minutes until all the air has been forced out—this is known as "knocking back." Let the dough relax again for 10 minutes. Shape the bread into two loaves and place on a baking sheet. Let rise again in a warm place, this time for only 20–30 minutes. The dough is ready for baking when a small dent remains in it when pressed lightly with the finger.

Brush the loaves with water and sprinkle with flour. Bake in a preheated hot oven, 450°F for 30–35 minutes.

Note: You can also bake the loaves in pans. If so, brush the pans well with oil before putting in the dough. Use two 5 x 8 inch pans.

Cooking in a bastible

I was delighted to have an opportunity to watch an elderly Corkwoman cook in the traditional Irish way—in a bastible over an open fire. The late Joan Twomey, from Ballingrane near Shanagarry, was "80 years," as she says herself, in November 1994. She cooked absolutely everything on the fire: bread, apple cakes, geese, turkeys, chickens, stews, roast potatoes… often for large numbers of hungry men who helped with the haymaking or harvesting. Her house has always been known for "a warm welcome." Long ago, as Joan says, they played cards every night for tuppence and thruppence, and no one ever left her house without a cup of tea and a slice of sweet cake or apple tart.

When I first contacted Joan she was surprised to discover that I was interested in the old ways of cooking. However, when I explained my wish to pass on recipes and cooking methods to the next generation, she spoke excitedly about all the things she'd cooked through the years, and we set a date to cook bread and apple tarts.

When I arrived on the appointed day the fire was blazing in the big open fireplace in the old-fashioned, whitewashed kitchen. Joan already had the bastible, a heavy iron pot with three legs and a flat base, heating over the open fire. Nowadays Joan is troubled by arthritis in her hands so she instructed me on how to make her currant bread.

We put a round of brown paper and a round of buttered butter paper into the base of the bastible, which was hanging from a crane about 14 inches above the fire. Then the loaf of currant bread was laid on top. While we were making the bread the lid of the bastible had been heating on the open fire, so we lifted this onto the top of the bastible and then shovelled "spleece"—hot embers from the wood fire—over the lid. Joan showed me how to test the heat with my hand and how to lift off the lid carefully so that no hot embers dropped into the oven while I checked the bread. The bastible was held securely in position over the fire by a pronged stick called a *gaulóg* propped against the chimney's back wall.

In no time the currant bread was baked and we rested it on its side to cool. My first effort was a bit scorched on the base, but Joan assured me I'd get better at it with practice and she was right. While the kettle was coming to a boil for tea, we made an apple cake which Joan rightly said would take 10–15 minutes in the bastible. On my first attempt I cut the apple into chunks so it took longer to bake, but Joan explained to me that she would normally slice the apples and not pile them so high. The apple cake cooked amazingly quickly on a tin plate. Joan brushed the surface with milk and added a few dabs of butter. Both the bread and apple cake had soft and tender crusts, quite different from their oven-baked relatives.

The satisfaction of mastering this much more skilful way of cooking on the open fire was terrific. I am absolutely hooked, and have put an open fire into my house in Ballycotton specially to cook on!

Note: Mrs Bridget Guerin, of Ballyheigue, in North Kerry, described to me how she made yeast bread in the bastible back in the 1940s. This was an interesting discovery, as I had always associated the bastible with soda breads rather than yeast breads.

Makes 4

scant 5¼ cups all-purpose flour
1 level teaspoon baking soda
½ teaspoon salt
¼ cup superfine sugar
¼ cup (½ stick) butter
¾ cup currants
¾ cup golden raisins
⅓ cup chopped mixed peel
1 egg, optional; free-range if
    possible
2–2¼ cups buttermilk

Currant Squares

"The carts were big and box-like, filled with double rows of shallow trays on which rested row after row of steaming loaves, tuppence or tuppence-farthing each… Underneath a deep deep drawer, going the whole length of the cart, filled with lovely white an' brown squares, soda squares, currant squares, and brown loaves, covered with their shining golden crust."
(Sean O' Casey, *The Street Sings*)

Preheat the oven to 450°F.

Sift all the dry ingredients into a nice roomy bowl. Rub in the butter, then add the dried fruit and chopped peel and toss well in the flour. Whisk the egg if using and add the buttermilk. Make a well in the center and pour in the liquid all at once. Quickly mix to a soft dough. Turn out onto a floured board and tidy it around the edges with a floured hand. Flip the mixture over and flatten into a round, 2-inch thick. Cut into four wedges. Bake in the preheated oven for 15 minutes, then reduce the temperature to 350°F for a further 20–30 minutes or until golden brown. The bread should sound hollow when tapped on the base. Serve freshly baked with butter.

Spotted Dog

Makes 1 loaf

scant 3½ cups all-purpose flour
1–2 tablespoons sugar
1 level teaspoon salt
1 level teaspoon baking soda, sifted
½–¾ cup golden raisins, raisins
   or currants
1¼ cups sour milk or buttermilk
1 egg, free-range if possible
   (optional—you may not need all
   the milk if you use the egg)

At times of the year when the men were working particularly hard in the fields, the farmer's wife would go out of her way to reward them with a richer bread than usual for tea. According to her means she might throw in a fistful of currants or raisins, some sugar and an egg, if there was one to spare. The resulting bread, the traditional Irish "sweet cake," had different names in different parts of the country—spotted dog, curnie cake, railway cake, and so on. Currant bread was not just for haymaking and threshing, but was also a treat for Sundays and special occasions.

Preheat your oven to 450°F.

Sift the dry ingredients, add the fruit, and mix well. Make a well in the center and pour most of the milk in at once with the egg. Using one hand, mix in the flour from the sides of the bowl, adding more milk if necessary. The dough should be softish, not too wet and sticky. When it all comes together, turn it out onto a floured board and knead it lightly for a few seconds, just enough to tidy it up. Pat the dough into a round about 1½ inches deep and cut a deep cross on it. Bake for 15 minutes, then turn down the oven to 400°F and continue to cook for approximately 30 minutes. If you are in doubt, tap the bottom: if it is cooked, it will sound hollow.

Serve spotted dog freshly baked, cut into thick slices and generously slathered with butter. Simply delicious!

The Stations

"The Stations" is a lovely Irish tradition which dates back to Penal times, when religious persecution forbade Catholic priests to say Mass. They went into hiding, and Mass was often said rather furtively on Mass rocks in the woods or in people's houses.

The custom has lived on in country areas. People take turns every few years to have Mass said in their home for neighbors, friends and relatives—usually in the kitchen, with the kitchen table, covered with a starched linen cloth, serving as the altar. It is considered a great honor to be the chosen household. The woman of the house and one or two friends would traditionally be up at dawn, lighting fires, baking breads, making butter balls from freshly churned butter, and undertaking all the final preparations for the breakfast after the Mass. This feast would include porridge with thick cream followed by bacon, sausages, black and white puddings, tomatoes, fried farm eggs, and sometimes wild mushrooms. These were served with a mountain of buttered toast, soda bread, and copious cups of strong sweet tea. "Shop bread" or "priest's bread" (a buttered loaf from the local bakery) was bought for this special occasion.

When the priests left, the Stations were officially over, but in many parts of the country it was only then that the real party began. Often there would be a sing-song with music on a melodeon or even a few whistles. Stories were told and eventually people made their way home with a few sugar lumps as a treat for the children.

Makes 2 × 1lb loaves

1½ tablespoons fresh yeast
scant 2 cups water, more as
    needed
2 tablespoons (¼ stick) butter
2 level teaspoons salt
4 teapoons sugar
scant 5¼ cups bread flour or
    baker's flour

2 x 1lb loaf tins

Priest's Bread

White yeast bread became known as "priest's bread" in many parts of the country, as it was associated with these special occasions.

Mix the yeast with ⅓ cup lukewarm water until dissolved. Put the butter, salt, and sugar into a bowl with ⅓ cup of very hot water. Stir until the sugar and salt are dissolved and the butter has melted. Add ⅓ cup of cold water. By now, the liquid should be lukewarm, so combine it with the yeast.

Sift the flour into a bowl. Make a well in the center and pour in most of the lukewarm liquid. Mix to a loose dough, adding the remainder of the liquid, or more flour or liquid if necessary. Turn the dough onto a floured board, cover, and let relax for about 5 minutes. Then knead for about 10 minutes or until smooth and springy (if you use a food mixer with a dough hook, 5 minutes is usually long enough). Put the dough somewhere warm and moist to rise, in a pottery bowl sealed with plastic wrap.

When the dough has doubled in size, knead it again for about 4–5 minutes until all the air had been forced out. Let relax again for 10 minutes, shape into loaves, and put into 2 well-greased bread pans.

Cover with a dish towel and let rise again in a warm place for about 20 minutes. The loaves are ready for baking when they have doubled in size and a small dent remains in the dough if pressed lightly with a finger. Brush with warm water and dredge lightly with white flour.

Bake in a preheated hot oven at 450°F for 30–35 minutes. The bread should be crusty and sound hollow when tapped. Cool on a wire rack.

Buttered Loaf

Makes 1 x 2lb loaf

1½ tablespoons fresh yeast
scant 2 cups water, or more
    as needed
¼ cup (½ stick) butter
1 rounded teaspoon salt
1 heaping tablespoon sugar
scant 5¼ cups bread flour
light eggwash, made from beaten
    egg and water

Barry's Bakery in Midleton made this traditional bread as a special order for people having "the Stations" in their houses. Sadly they are gone.

Mix the yeast with ⅓ cup lukewarm water until dissolved. Put the butter, salt, and sugar into a bowl with ⅓ cup of very hot water. Stir until the sugar and salt are dissolved and the butter is melted. Add ⅓ cup of cold water. By now, the liquid should be lukewarm so combine it with the yeast.

Sift the flour into a bowl. Make a well in the center and pour in most of the lukewarm liquid. Mix to a loose dough, adding the remainder of the liquid, or more flour if necessary. Turn the dough onto a floured board, cover, and let relax for 5–10 minutes. Then knead for about 10 minutes or until smooth and springy (if you use a food mixer with a dough hook, 5 minutes is usually long enough). Put the dough to rise in a pottery bowl covered tightly with a damp cloth or plastic wrap (yeast dough rises best in a warm moist atmosphere, e.g. close to your stove or on top of a radiator). When the dough has doubled in size, knead it again for about 2–3 minutes until all the air has been forced out—this is called "knocking back." Let the dough relax again for 10 minutes.

Shape the bread into a loaf and put it into a well greased 2lb loaf pan. Cover with a dish towel and let rise again in a warm place. This rising period will be much shorter, only about 20–30 minutes. The loaf is ready for baking when a small dent remains in the loaf when the dough is pressed lightly with a finger.

Brush the surface of the loaf lightly with eggwash. Bake in a preheated hot oven at 450°F for 30–35 minutes.

Pancakes

As most cooking was traditionally done over the open fire, Ireland has a wide variety of recipes for pancakes and other griddle cakes. These are easily made from readily available ingredients—such as flour, yellowmeal, or potatoes mixed with milk or buttermilk and perhaps an egg.

Shrove Tuesday has always been seen as a last chance for merriment before the rigous of lenten fasting began. During Lent, Catholics were urged to abstain not only from meat, but also from eggs, milk, butter, and cheese—hence the tradition of using up these ingredients in pancakes on Shrove Tuesday. An early (decidedly lavish) recipe in Sheila Newcomen's manuscript book of 1717, from Co. Longford, includes eggs, flour, milk, brandy, nutmeg, ginger, butter, sugar, and salt.

It was a common folk belief that an unmarried girl's skill in tossing pancakes was an indication of her future prospects—if she dropped it, she had no hope of marriage during the coming year. As weddings were forbidden during Lent, there was a tremendous rush to the altar on Shrove Tuesday. A great deal of pressure was put on marriageable bachelors and spinsters as the day approached—with plenty of pranks and practical jokes!

Pancakes have really stood the test of time. During my research I found pancake recipes as far back as the Clonbrock manuscript dating from the 1730s. During the decades following, the Pope papers (1823) and all the editions of *Cookery Notes for Schools* from 1932 onwards had a pancake recipe, so every school child would have learned to make them.

In *Ballycotton School Memories*, Eileen O'Riordan Ryan (writing about the 1930s) recalls Brother de Sales, who spent his annual holidays in Ballycotton and regularly came to talk to the children in school. "Br de Sales set up competitions in art to see what we could produce, or he talked about cooking, which he loved. On one occasion we provided a primus stove so that he could demonstrate the art of making pancakes. When the pancakes were ready and rolled, he neatly cut and shared them between all the girls."

Most people had access to eggs, milk, and flour, and with a little imagination pancakes could be adapted to both sweet and savory recipes. They were the ultimate pantry fast food and a godsend to hungry children. Nowadays, every food market and festival boasts a crêpe van dishing up pancakes filled with chocolate spread and a variety of other fillings. Pancakes are still made in virtually every household in Ireland on Shrove Tuesday and are enjoyed by young and old alike. My children and grandchildren line up beside the Aga for theirs and eat them hot off the pan with a brush of melted butter, a squeeze of lemon juice, and a sprinking of sugar.

Buttermilk Pancakes

Makes about 20

scant 3½ cups all-purpose flour
1 teaspoon baking soda
a large pinch of salt
¼ cup sugar
1 egg, free-range if possible
2½ cups buttermilk

"Run round to the dairy and fetch me a jug of buttermilk and sure we'll make pancakes." My great aunt in Tipperary would put on the griddle to heat and within minutes she'd be mixing the batter. We would drop big spoonfuls of batter onto the hot griddle and watch the bubbles rise and burst. Then we'd carefully flip them over and wait impatiently for them to be cooked on the other side. We would eat them straight off the griddle with butter and homemade jam.

Mix the dry ingredients together in a bowl. Make a well in the center, add the egg and enough buttermilk to make batter of a dropping consistency (it usually takes the full amount). Drop spoonfuls of the mixture onto a lightly greased hot griddle and cook for 3–4 minutes on one side before turning over. The pancakes are ready to turn when the bubbles burst. Flip over gently and cook until golden on the other side. Serve warm with butter and jam or honey for tea.

The ABC of Making Pancakes

1¾ cups all-purpose flour
2 eggs
pinch of salt
2½ cups milk
lard, as required
1 lemon
superfine sugar

This comes from Mary Walsh, Woodsgift, Co. Kilkenny. There's no excuse for anyone not to be able to make pancakes with these clear directions!

Put the flour into a basin with a pinch of salt, make a well in the center, and pour in the eggs. Mix them with a small quantity of the flour until about the consistency of a thick custard. Then take about 1¼ cups of the milk and add gradually, and by degrees work in the remainder of the flour. When mixed smoothly beat well for a few minutes, then stir in the remainder of the milk and stand the batter aside for about an hour or so.

To fry the pancakes: Take a small skillet and put about a tablespoon of the melted lard into the pan—just sufficient to cover the bottom of it. Measure a half gill (¼ cup approximately) of batter and when the fat is hot in the skillet, pour in this batter and let it run all over the pan. When light brown turn it over with a knife or toss it onto the other side. When both sides are light brown turn the pancake onto a sugared paper, squeeze a little lemon juice on it, then roll the pancake and shake a small quantity of the sugar on top. Serve the pancakes at once on a dish with a lace paper. The latter absorbs the grease.

Currant or golden raisin fritters can be made from the same mixture—just throw a few currants or golden raisins into the mixture and fry as before. Fold them in half and serve.

Baked Pancakes

4 tablespoons fat or butter
¼ cup sugar
2 eggs
heaping ⅓ cup flour
about ¾–1 cup milk
a little lemon rind

This recipe comes from Doris Bewley's 1932 notebook. It shows a different way of making batter and cooking the pancakes.

Preheat the oven to 400°F. Cream the butter and sugar and add the eggs, flour, milk, and lemon rind, making a fairly thin batter. Let stand for about 1 hour, longer if possible. Pour into well greased saucers or pans and bake in a quick oven about 15 minutes. Turn out onto sugared paper and spread with jam between each pancake and serve hot.

Rolled Pancakes

This recipe, from the Clonbrock manuscript (1730s) seems very similar to Welsh Cakes, which illustrates the communication between cooks in country houses:

1 quart fine flour
¼lb sugar
6oz lard
6oz currants
4 eggs
a little salt and a little allspice

Roll the pancakes thin and round. Fry them in lard and divide them in quarters whilst frying. They should be as if baked. The ingredients must be well rubbed together.

Batter Pudding

This comes from Nancy Elliott's recipe collection (1860s). It is more like a soufflé pudding than a pancake.

Take a pint of milk and blend 2 tablespoonfuls of flour with a little of it. Put the remainder of the milk on the fire and when it comes to a boil stir in the blended flour, cook till it is done, then pour into a basin, add a piece of butter the size of a walnut a little sugar and flavoring. When sufficiently cold add the beaten yolks of 2 eggs and lastly the whites beaten to a stiff froth. Pour into a pudding dish and bake in a moderate oven for half an hour.

Maura Laverty's Irish Pancakes

Makes 6–8

scant 3½ cups all-purpose flour
1 teaspoon salt
1 teaspoon baking soda
2 eggs
buttermilk, to mix

In her book Full and Plenty *(1960), Maura Laverty gives a recipe for good old-fashioned Irish Pancakes.*

"It is Shrove Tuesday, and the men from the fields tread quickly coming in, because they know there will be pancakes for supper—real pancakes, none of your paper-thin rolled foolishness, but good substantial buttermilk pancakes. There's a clatter of them as high as your hip waiting on the hob, with melted butter and sugar trickling down the sides. What matter if the women of the house have developed thawlock from beating and mixing and turning pancakes for the past two hours? It's all in a good cause. Isn't it Pancake Night?"

Sift the flour with the salt and baking soda. Break the eggs into a well in the center of the flour and mix well. Beat in enough buttermilk to make a thick batter. Fry in spoonfuls on a greased pan. Butter them as they come from the pan and sprinkle thickly with sugar.

Snow Pancakes

Makes 6–8

3¾ cups milk
4¼ cups all-purpose flour
egg yolks (optional)

This unique recipe was sent to me by Elizabeth MacKevitt from Waterford. It originated with Miss Nancy McCoy who, with her sister Ursula, catered for large events and weddings in the Kilkenny region for many years. Nancy used to recommend putting a clean tray out in the garden to collect the snow so that it was not dirtied. This recipe would not necessarily be an annual event in Kilkenny, even though it is supposed to be the coldest city in the south—her words, not mine!

Beat up together. Add ¾lb of fresh light snow. Mix in gently and leave for some hours to melt, when the snow aerates the flour and milk. This makes a very light but very pale pancake. It can be made richer by adding some egg yolks, but the egg whites are not needed for the pancakes. They can be used for meringues.

Dairy

Milk and all milk products, known as *banbidh* or "white meats," were important features in the Irish diet. The Irish were incredibly innovative with their variations on this much loved food; there was fresh milk, sour milk, buttermilk, thick or ropy milk, cream, butter, curds, and cheese. Sheep's milk cheese was still made in Kilkenny up to the end of the 19th century. Goats' milk was always highly valued as being the most nutritious of all. Curds, eaten with cream and honey, were also very important.

Traditional cheeses ranged from simple curds, made by boiling sour and sweet milk together, to *tanach*—a hard-pressed skim milk cheese. A variation of this was known as *tanach torrach* ("pregnant" cheese). Other kinds included *tath*, a soft cheese made from warmed sour milk curds, *gruth* and *mulchan*, curd cheeses made from buttermilk, and *millsen*, made from sweet milk curds. Farmhouse cheesemaking has had an enormous revival during the past 30 years, and Ireland can once again take its place among the most important cheese makers in the world.

Before the establishment of rural creameries in the late 19th century, every farmhouse dairy had its own churn to make butter. The biggest butter market in the world between 1759 and 1870 was in Cork and Irish butter, under the name Kerrygold, is still exported widely today.

Cheeses and Cheesemaking

When people talk about the Irish food industry the same question always comes up: how did the artisan farmhouse cheeses earn their reputation, so much greater than the tonnage produced each year on small farms all around Ireland? For my mind the answer would primarily be the vivid flavors and strong identities, which make it easy for customers to go back again and again and ask for a particular dairy's produce by name.

Early pioneering roles played in this artisan cheeses revival were largely played by a few very determined families who understood the authenticity of cheese origins, either through travel or study, or from being from great European food cultures themselves. They brought these customs to their new Irish homes and seeded very sophisticated cheese practices, with roots going back 800 years. Traditions from Switzerland, France, Holland, and Spain were grafted onto the Irish grasslands and milk herds, which are certainly amongst the best in Europe. Add to this that when the first of us were developing our dairies and cheeses, we were self-policing in terms of regulation—that avalanche was yet to come!

So we established our original research and development on flavor, tradition and milk quality. We were rewarded with unique flavors and a skill base that translated the milk from our land into cheeses that we now recognize as having regional provenance, both microbiologically and in traditional curing methods. These ideals grew this new craft into a sibling of some of the greats of Europe, long lost but recognized and welcomed by the knowing food experts around the world.

In those early years, unharnessed by risk assessment, we worked with small herds grazing mostly on very clean pasture made up of varieties of native grasses and herbs, giving the milk so much of the non-specific cultures and influences that put great character in cheese. The research work that has been done in the interim years has proven the role of bio-diversity in the growth of great cheese varieties, not only the type of land grazed, but the flora of the air that flows through the curing rooms. These influences on taste and texture are the tools of the cheesemaker's trade.

Then there was education—we were very lucky to be supported by University College Cork and the food development agencies at Teagasc (Irish Dairy Development Agency) and An Bord Bia (Irish Food Board). In these areas we tapped directly into a huge stream of information and enthusiasm for a vital missing link in our food industry—Irishness!

Of real significance (and in our favor) is the emergence of local economies. In the last decade Irish farmers and country markets have re-emerged effortlessly, selling extremely high-quality foods from the local land and seas. This has brought people out with their shopping bags and, the mostly powerful of all economic tools, the purse.

This dawn of modern Irish food culture that many people attribute to the birth of farm cheeses has been supportive of so much in rural development and sustainability. Crucially it has also attracted tourists who are delighted to find not only Irish musicians, poets and painters, but very recognizable regional foods. For this we have to thank those smart, hard-working and fabulously inspired new Irish chefs, many of them were our dearest allies as we struggled into being through the duck shoot of closures, while regulator and food producers settled into a relationship of partnership rather than guerilla unrest! Chefs understand how fragile really great food is—it has to be fresh, seasonal, local, and edgy to be absolutely the best—they are prepared to battle for this, then, as now, they represent us and speak for us on their menus.

Like peer reviews in scholarship, winning prizes in International Cheese Awards has been hugely encouraging for new Irish dairies—in 2011/12 Ireland again won The Supreme Championship Trophy at the British Cheese Awards, no mean task as the growth and standard of artisan cheesemaking in Britain, Scotland and Wales is superb.

So looking to the future, will we still be at the forefront of cheesemaking? I am sure we will. And the reason—our children. So many of them have finished their education, traveled and dabbled and are now firmly back with us on our farms and in our dairies. They are bringing with them energy, plus new ideas for farm shops, new takes on cheeses or farming ideas with rare breed varieties and goat or sheep milk skills.

The real harvest, true sustainability, is the investment from the next generation coming home to work with us. Irish Artisan Cheeses are here to stay.

Giana Ferguson
Gubbeen Cheese
Schull
Co. Cork

For further information contact Cáis, The Irish Farmhouse Cheesemakers Association. www.irishcheese.ie

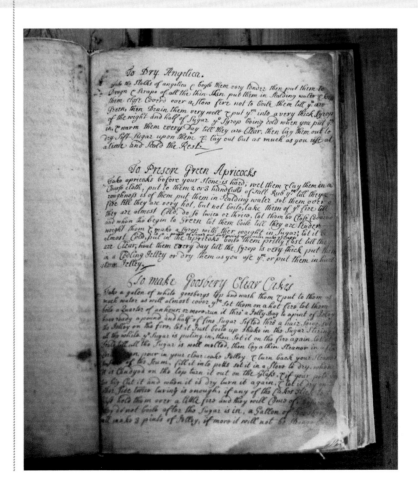

Quickly made cream cheeses seemed to have been popular in the countryhouse kitchens, where good cream was readily available. They were sometimes flavored with chopped herbs. The Clonbrock manuscript includes a recipe detailing the "Feed for Milch Cows" written by the Hay Steward, dated November 1888. This shows how seriously the job was taken.

Makes 1lb cheese (approximately)

9½ cups whole milk
¼–½ teaspoon liquid rennet
good-quality cheesecloth

Curd Cheese

The simplest of all cheeses made in the time-honored way.

Put the milk into a spotlessly clean, heavy-based stainless-steel saucepan. Heat it very gently on a low heat until barely tepid. Stir the rennet well into the milk, not more than ½ teaspoon—too much will result in a tough acid curd.

Cover the saucepan with a clean dish towel and the lid. The cloth prevents the steam from condensing on the lid of the pan and falling back onto the curd. Put the pan to one side and leave undisturbed in your kitchen for 2–4 hours. The milk should then have coagulated and will be solid.

Cut the curd with a long sterilized knife and heat gently on a low heat for a couple of minutes until the whey starts to run. It must not get too hot or the curd will tighten and toughen too much. Ladle into a cheesecloth-lined colander over a bowl. Tie the corners of the cheesecloth and let the curd drip overnight. Next day it can be eaten with soft brown sugar and cream, or freshly picked soft fruit from the garden.

Traditional Cream Cheese

The present Marquis of Waterford writes:

"The requirements are to have at least two cows in milk, preferably a Jersey and a Friesan. They must be hand milked into one container and the milk skimmed by hand, the resulting cream placed in a double muslin bag and left to hang until it stops dropping, which will probably be two days. It is then ready to eat. Salt, pepper, chives, etc. may subsequently be added according to personal taste, though in my opinion the pure cream cheese is the best. We used to have a cream cheese to the house twice a week in the days when we had cows in the dairy and a dairymaid to look after them."

Cream Cheese made with Rennet

This charming recipe appears on the very first page of the recipe book of Mrs Dot Drew from Mocollop Castle, Ballyduff, Co. Waterford, dated 1804. A pottle is half a gallon.

"Take a pottle of new milk, a quart of sweet cream and a quart of boiling water, put into a pan and when just milk warm put a teaspoon of rennet to it more or less according to the strength of the rennet, cover it with a napkin for about an hour. Put a napkin in hoop or vat or take up your junket with a saucer and lay it in a hoop or board with holes in it till 'tis about half full then throw spring water over it cover it with one part of the napkin and lay the saucer on it for a while to press it then put in more of your junket and spring water as before so until all is in let it lie till quite drained, then turn it out on another board with holes in it and put a swatch round it keep it in form, put nettles over it and under it. Next day put it on another board with fresh nettles, do this every day for eight or ten days when it will be fit for use."

Mrs Jackson's Cream Cheese

This comes from the Mary Ponsonby manuscript c.1850. Mary Ponsonby also gave this hint: to "keep cream sweet either for travelling or in hot weather" add "two tablespoonfuls of powdered white sugar to a pint of cream."

"A quart of thick sour cream.

Lay a napkin on a soup plate, throw some salt on it and pour your cream in. When the napkin is wet turn it on the other side and when that is wet put a clean one and so till ripe. It will be fit to use in three days."

Mrs Hay's Napkin Cream Cheese

This is from the Clonbrock manuscript and is dated September 1781:

"Take a napkin which has no starch in it. Dip it in pickle (salt and water) and lay it on a strainer (which should lay across a pan). Pour into the napkin (or ordinary glass cloth) a pint of thick cream—let it stand 12 hrs then change it into a clean (wet with pickle) napkin and lay it on a deep soup plate. Repeat this about 3 times—leaving a weight* to press it more firmly—it takes about 2 days before ready to send to table.
* ½ lb at first, increasing to 6lb."

A Cream Cheese

This recipe comes from Giana Ferguson's family manuscript dating from 1777:

"Take 3 pts of new milk and 2 of cream. Sett it with one spoonfull of rennett ye dish. Lay it into a sive with a cloth, there let it whay by degrees, now and then lifting up ye corners of ye cloth and ringing ye whay out as so let it stand 2 or 3 houres thus looking after it yn put it into a batt with a good weight as so let it be full night, yn take it out and & salt it & keep it in dry cloths for a week yn ripen it in wet cloths or nettles."

Milk

In *Ballycotton School Memories*, the late Sheila Egan recalls that when her children were born, Hydes farm used to provide her with the milk from one particular cow, as it was believed at the time that this was better for the child. She reared her three children from the milk of this one cow, which was thought to be the best one in the herd.

In the same book, Betty Murray (writing about the 1940s) relates that: "During the 'Emergency,' we had food rationing. Each one of the family had their own ration book. Each week we'd get our portion of butter from my mother, and my brothers used to hide their portions from one another in various hiding places in the house—this in the days before fridges! As I grew up, I used to do whatever work was needed on the farm. We had about twenty cows and I used to help milk them. Milking was a very social time: people would be humming a tune or swapping stories. Anybody coming to the door of the stall was in danger of getting a squirt of hot milk in the face! My brother, Mike, was a great milker and he could milk the crossest of cows. He just had a wonderful understanding of animals. We used to make our own butter and it was a slow process churning it." The family used to supply milk to the village, along with two other farming families, the Sloanes and Mannings. Each family had their own customers.

In *To School through the Fields*, Alice Taylor also recollects the 1940s with lovely descriptions of milking. She describes how a man named Dan who worked with them sometimes took the milk to the creamery. "This occasionally led to problems. These were the early days of hygiene inspectors and Dan resented inspectors in any form: he absolutely refused to allow any inspection of our tanks, demanding to know of them, 'What did you ever do for your country that entitled you to go around smelling our milk?'"

She also relates that "In early spring or late autumn, when milk production was at its lowest, we separated our own milk and made butter. We poured the milk, still warm from the cow, into the separator—a large iron dish with two pipes which was attached to a motor with a handle. It gave off a soft whine when the handle was turned, and out of one pipe came cream, out of the other skim milk. It was a simple but ingenious device and while my father manned it we young ones lined up with cups for drinks of cream." Alice also says that "Long churning makes bad butter." This country saying originates in the butter churning process: the faster it is accomplished, the better. It was a saying that was considered applicable to many situations in life.

Malachy McKenna, writing about the Blasket Islands, says that all the references in the literature point to cows' milk as being the most usual kind to be consumed on the island, although sheep and goats' milk was also consumed in the earlier part of the period he describes (1850–1950). "Since a cow in calf gives no milk, families who had only one cow would be without milk for a considerable part of the year. This was a cause of some hardship, given that milk was drunk at meal-times as well as being used for baking and putting in tea." In this regard, Máire Ní Ghuithín writes in *Bean an Oileáin*, 'The worst thing about the winter was the lack of milk when the cows went dry… We often drank bitter, black tea if the weather was bad and if the village had run out of sugar. The small children were given coffee when there was no milk."

Eileen Kenneally, from Garryvoe, grew up in the town of Midleton and remembers going for holidays to her uncle and aunt's farm in the country near Dungourney as a child in the 1960s. When they were approaching the house they always heard the sound of the transistor radio playing in the dairy. "The Streets of San Francisco" and "The Green, Green Grass of Home" will always be associated with those happy times: they believed that the cows milked better when they had the music playing.

I can milk a cow as good as anyone. It's like riding a bicycle—one never forgets. As a child in the little village of Cullohill in Co. Laois, I spent much of my time on summer evenings and at weekends on Bill Walsh's farm at the edge of the village, and often helped to milk the cows. We each had a three-legged stool and a bucket and I still remember the soft warmth of the cow's side against my forehead.

Oats and other Grains

From the time that Ireland became a society of farmers rather than hunter-gatherers, oatmeal has been a staple food. Oats grow well in parts of Ireland; the cool, damp conditions tend to suit it, and it doesn't suffer as much in wet weather as barley and wheat do. Oats also tolerate acidic soils better than many other cereals.

Early Irish literature contains many references to various kinds of porridge made, depending on the wealth of the household, with water, milk, or buttermilk. Oaten bread, or oatcakes, were also common fare. The oats were probably ground at home with a rotary quern, and the bread or cakes baked on a hot stone by the hearth.

A more recent introduction to Ireland was maize—imported from America to relieve starvation during the famine. Known as Indian corn, or yellowmeal, it still plays a part in some traditional Irish recipes, though as a "famine food" it fell into disrepute in the years of comparative plenty that followed. Recently these foods have been taken up again and their delicious and nutritious qualities recognized. Carefully made porridge, served with milk or cream and soft brown sugar, or crisp Donegal oatcakes with lashings of Irish butter and homemade jam, are hard to beat!

Porridge

Porridge is one of the oldest Irish foods. Eaten for breakfast and supper, it could be made not just from oats, but also from wheat or barley. It could be cooked in water, milk, or buttermilk and flavored with salt, butter, or honey and, in later years, sugar and eaten with milk or cream. The 7th/8th-century Brehon Laws regulate the types of porridge taken by the children of different classes who were being fostered:

"The children of inferior grades are to be fed on porridge or stirabout made of oatmeal on buttermilk or water taken with old butter and are to be given a bare sufficiency; the sons of chieftains are to be fed to satiety on porridge made of barley meal upon new milk, taken with fresh butter, while the sons of kings and princes are to be fed on porridge made of wheaten meal, upon new milk, taken with honey."

In the 11th-century tale *Aislinge Meic Con Glinne*, the hero dreamed of "fair white porridge made of sheeps' milk" and of "porridge the treasure that is smoothest and sweetest of all."

At one time porridge was the traditional breakfast, particularly during the winter months. When breakfast cereals such as Kelloggs Cornflakes, Rice Krispies, and Weetabix were introduced in the late 1920s and 1930s they became the breakfast of choice for many households—porridge had an old-fashioned frumpy image. Even the quick-cook versions needed some cooking at a time when convenience and fast food were the order of the day in the growing number of households with both partners working. However, there is a growing recognition once again that porridge is the best breakfast, its slow-release energy properties, and its value in reducing cholesterol, have brought it back to center stage. Oatmeal manufacturers have introduced many new versions of oatmeal breakfasts, to add to the slow cooking steel-cut oats and regular porridge. Now there's quick-cook, microwave porridge, lots of muesli, granola, and so on.

Steel-cut Oat Porridge

Serves 4

This was always made using a teacup as a measure

1 cup steel-cut oats
4 cups water
1 level teaspoon salt

Soak the oats in 1 cup of cold water. Meanwhile, bring 3 cups of water to a boil and pour onto the oats. Put into a saucepan on a low heat and stir until the water comes to a boil.

Cover and simmer for 15–20 minutes, stirring occasionally. Add the salt. Cover again and leave aside overnight. The oats will absorb all the water. Reheat and serve with light cream or milk and soft brown sugar.

Garnished Porridge

porridge
hundreds and thousands (sprinkles)
1 can of evaporated milk

An amusing recipe came from an Irish Times *newspaper cutting from the late 1920s, under the heading "Variety at Breakfast." "Why not make a resolution to give your family brighter breakfasts with more variety and so start them off well for the day? These recipes will help you." This would certainly cheer up a February morning!*

Cook the porridge in the usual manner; when ready to serve whisk or beat it to get rid of all lumps. Sprinkle hundreds and thousands over the top of each portion and serve with the evaporated milk. The gay appearance of colored sweets makes porridge attractive to the most difficult child.

Gruel

Gruel, which was strained oats, was mentioned in the 9th-century Monastery of Tallaght as part of the fasting fare of the Culdee monks. Their abbot, Maelruain, laid down a rule that "if a festival happened to fall on certain days the monks were given leave to make gruel of meal and water." Wow!

Oat Gruel

2 tablespoons steel-cut oats
2½ cups boiling water
1 tablespoon sugar

This recipe is suggested for invalids in Lessons in Cookery and Housewifery, *1901.*

Wash the oats, add it to the boiling water, boil for 10–15 minutes, or longer, strain, and use.

Sheep's Head Broth

This recipe for boiling a sheep's head to make broth is also from Lessons in Cookery and Housewifery, *and includes oatmeal. Again it is suggested for invalid cooking (it might be best not to let the invalid see the sheep's head beforehand!). Maura Laverty, in her version of this recipe, says that "preparing the head is a ghastly cannibalistic business, though the broth is so good that it's nearly worth it."*

Cut the head in two; steep it overnight in cold water; rub it with salt to remove the blood and rinse it before cooking; put it into a saucepan; cover with cold water. When the water boils, add some carrots, turnips, onion, chopped parsley, and 3 or 4 tablespoons of oatmeal blended in cold water; boil all slowly from 1½–2 hours.

Stirabout

I have always been baffled by the fact that the Irish never took to gruel made from the yellowmeal (maize meal) sent in to relieve hunger during the famine. In essence this is the same as polenta, so beloved of Italian peasants for generations.

According to Luke Dodd, curator of the Famine Museum at Strokestown Park, in Co. Roscommon, there were two factors responsible for this. Firstly, the Irish had been accustomed to cooking oats which cooked relatively quickly, so they frequently undercooked the yellowmeal and therefore it was indigestible and often sickened people. Secondly, Irish peasants of that period had become accustomed to eating 10–14lb of potatoes at a sitting, and so they were accustomed to bulk and were far from satisfied by the yellowmeal stirabout. In fact it is said that Irish men's stomachs were unusually large because of this factor.

An indication of the scale of yellowmeal imports during those times is given by the purchase of £100,000-worth of meal from America, ordered by Sir Robert Peel in 1845.

Rye porridge was also eaten extensively during the famine period.

Wheat Pudding

This recipe has been handed down from famine times. I found it in an undated booklet entitled Galway Homegrown Foodstuffs:

"Gather ears of wheat when turning ripe or better still quite ripe about late August. Rub them between the hands to remove the outside layer. Boil in water or milk for about 1 hour, stirring occasionally like porridge."

Use 2oz grain to 2½ cups liquid. Add sugar or salt according to taste and serve with milk or cream.

Próinsimín

Right up to the 1970s Diarmuid Ó'Drisceoil would be given próinsimín as a special treat when he went back to Cape Clear, an island off West Cork, to visit his relations. Home-grown whole wheat grains were roasted on a dry pan, almost like popcorn, except it didn't pop. (The pan was rubbed with a butter wrapper first.) As a special treat for the city kids, Diarmuid's great aunt would first melt some sugar in a little water, then she would toss the hot wheat straight off the pan in the syrup. This, according to Diarmuid, gave the mixture a sort of sweet "crystally" coating which they loved. Próinsimín was hard and crunchy, a challenge for the teeth even though the wheat grains were cooked into the center. It was always eagerly looked forward to and much enjoyed.

Ríobún

Another fascinating recipe from Cape Clear (Oileán Chléire)—an island located off Schull in West Cork.

Donncha Ó'Drisceoil spoke evocatively of ríobún in his book Aistí ó Chléire, *published by An Clóchombar, Dublin, 1987. Diarmuid Ó'Drisceoil described ríobún as "a sort of cold porridge with a delicious nutty flavor."*

To make ríobún, whole wheat grains were ground on a rotary quern on the table in the kitchen. This roughly ground wheat was called minbhró. This was eaten with milk and sometimes sprinkled with a little sugar as a special treat for the children.

Oatcakes

1 cup (2 sticks) butter
2½ cups rolled oats
scant ¾ cup superfine sugar
¾ cup plus 1½ tablespoons white
   all-purpose flour
a pinch of salt
1 level teaspoon baking powder

These delicious cookies keep for several weeks in a tin.

Melt the butter in a saucepan. Mix all the dry ingredients together. Take the saucepan off the heat and stir the dry ingredients into the melted butter. Roll out the mixture until it is about ¼ inch thick, and either cut into 2½-inch rounds or place in one piece in a jelly roll pan.

Bake in a preheated oven at 350°F for about 20 minutes. Cool on a wire rack.

Donegal Oatcakes

Serves 4

1 ½ cups fine oatmeal
1–2 tablespoons butter or lard
a pinch of salt
¾–1 cup boiling water

We use Macroom's fine stoneground oatmeal for this recipe.

Put the oatmeal into a bowl. Put the butter or lard and salt into a measuring cup, pour boiling water onto it, and stir until melted and dissolved. Pour this into the oatmeal and mix to a pliable dough. You may need a little more liquid to obtain the right consistency.

In Donegal the mixture was then left for several hours, or overnight, until it was dry enough to press out into a thin sheet. Press out with your fingers into a 10 × 9-inch pan. You may not manage to get it quite that thin on your first attempt, because the dough is rather difficult to handle.

Leave it to dry for another hour or two before you bake it. Bake in a very low oven at 250°F for 3–4 hours. The more slowly it cooks, the better the flavor will be. Oatcakes keep for ages in a tin and can be reheated. Eat with butter or butter and jam.

Mealie Greachie or Durgan

steel-cut oats
bacon fat

Armando Certuccelli, the Italian post-master in Ballycastle Post Office, on the North Antrim coast, told me about this dish which was one of the dinners expected by farm laborers at harvest time. It is still eaten in that area to this day. The problem nowadays, is where to buy a decent fatty bacon, so that there is some fat rather than nitrates left in the pan after you fry it.

Add some dry oats to the bacon fat in a skillet after you have cooked bacon in it. Fry, stirring, until the oats are nicely toasted. Serve with the bacon and potatoes. Fried onion is sometimes added to this meal also.

Crunchet

Makes 16

scant 1 cup steel-cut oats
a pinch of salt ½ cup (1 stick) butter
¼ cup soft brown sugar
2 teaspoon molasses

9-inch square baking pan

I came across this recipe in Doris Bewley's 1932 school notebook—it's a variation on the flapjack idea and deliciously treacly.

Preheat the oven to 1350°F. Put the oats in a bowl and add the salt. Melt the butter and sugar together with the molasses. When melted, pour onto the oats and mix together with a spoon. Press out into your greased pan and put in the preheated oven. Bake for 15–20 minutes. Cut into shapes and leave in the pan to cool.

Irish Shortbread

Makes 36 fingers

½ cup (1 stick) margarine or butter
⅓ cup plus 1 tablespoon superfine sugar
¾ cup plus 1½ tablespoons all-purpose flour
½ teaspoon salt
1 level teaspoon baking powder
1 egg
2 tablespoons cold water
½ teaspoon vanilla extract (optional)
1½ cups rolled oats

I found a little booklet with a lovely selection of recipes produced by the Flake Oatmeal Millers and compiled by the food writer Maura Laverty, who was Radio Eireann food expert at the time. It includes some illustrations of show kitchens from the Electricity Supply Board, and probably dates from the 1950s. This was rather misleadingly named Irish Shortbread, but tasted good. I think using butter instead of margarine makes it nicer, and a little vanilla extract is a good addition.

Preheat the oven to 400°F. Cream the butter and sugar. Sift the flour, salt, and baking powder. Beat the egg. Add the flour to the creamed mixture. Add the egg, water, and vanilla extract (if using). Work in the rolled oats. Roll out and cut into fingers. Place on a greased 12-inch square baking pan and put in the hot oven. After the first 5 minutes, reduce heat to 350°F and continue cooking until the shortbread is light brown in color, about 10 minutes.

Macaroons

Makes 21

¼ cup (½ stick) margarine or butter
¼ cup superfine sugar
1 egg
¼ teaspoon baking soda
½ teaspoon salt
1¼ cups rolled oats

Strictly speaking these are not macaroons as we know them. However, they are light and crunchy and lovely with a cup of tea.

Preheat the oven to 400°F. Cream the margarine or butter and gradually beat in the sugar. Add the well-beaten egg. Add the baking soda and salt to the rolled oats and work them into the butter and egg mixture. Form into ¾oz balls on a well-greased baking sheet. Cook for 20 minutes, or until nicely browned.

Flapjacks

Makes 16 or 32

¾ cup (1½ sticks) butter
¾ cup plus 2 tablespoons demerara sugar
2½ cups rolled oats
a pinch of salt

A very good simple recipe which has been a favorite in many Irish houses and children's lunchboxes since the early 1950s.

Melt the butter in a saucepan. Mix the sugar, oats, and salt together, then add the melted butter to the dry ingredients. Turn the mixture into a shallow jelly roll pan and spread it out evenly. Smooth the surface with an offset spatula. Stand the pan on a 8 x 12-inch baking sheet in the oven and bake for 30 minutes, at 375°F.

When cooked, let stand for a few minutes, then cut across into 16 squares, or 32 fingers. Leave in the pan until quite cold.

Potato and Oatmeal Rissoles

Makes 6

6 tablespoons fine oatmeal
   (or rolled oats), plus extra for
   coating
6 tablespoons mashed potatoes
½ cup grated cheese
¼ cup any kind of ground meat
   (or bacon)

Rationing was introduced during the Second World War in the 1940s, in what was known as the "Emergency" in Ireland. Tea, sugar, butter, flour, and bread were rationed, although not as severely as in the UK, where eggs and meat were also rationed. Many people depended on relatives in the country to supplement their diet. The government made allotments available in Dublin's Phoenix Park so that people could grow vegetables. The School Cookery Notes, 1943, includes "recipes specially adapted to these emergency conditions." Oats feature in several of them. It was home-grown and it would help stretch the flour supply. Potatoes were also used as a substitute for flour.

Mix all together with a wooden spoon until the mixture binds well. No liquid is required. Form into rissoles or flat cakes. Coat with fine oatmeal or dip in batter. Fry in hot fat.

Oatmeal Cookies

Makes 18

6 tablespoons fine oatmeal
   (or rolled oats)
Flahavans oatmeal
2 tablespoons flour
¼ cup (½ stick) butter or margarine
2 tablespoons superfine sugar
a pinch of salt
a pinch of baking soda
2 tablespoons hot water

This was the "Emergency" recipe. It reminded us of the oatmeal cookies we often made in the earlier days of the cookery school and had almost forgotten. Delicious eaten on the day they are made, they may also be stored in an airtight tin. The original recipe was given in tablespoons.

Mix together the meal, flour, soda, and salt. Rub in the butter roughly, add the sugar, then make into a stiff dough with the hot water. Roll out and cut into rounds with a 2½-inch cutter. Place on a baking sheet and bake in a moderate oven (350°F) until crisp and lightly browned, around 12–14 minutes. Cool on a wire rack and store in an airtight container.

Potato and Oat Scones

Makes 6–8

6oz cooked potatoes
2 tablespoons butter or dripping
1 tablespoon milk
2 tablespoons flour
½ teaspoon baking powder
⅓ cup steel-cut oats
½ teaspoon salt

In the advertisements from the war period there were many references to shortages and substitutes. A Royal Baking Powder advertisement suggested that, where eggs are omitted, "remember that for each egg omitted from your recipe use an extra level teaspoonful of baking powder and add a little extra milk." They suggested the following recipe:

Mash the potato and beat in the butter or dripping and milk. Sift the flour and baking powder. Work all the dry ingredients into the potato. Roll out to ¼-inch thick. Cut into triangles and cook on a hot greased griddle, or on a baking sheet in a hot oven for 12 minutes. When cooked, fold the scones into a clean cloth and serve hot with butter. They may also be fried with bacon.

Pearl Barley

Pearl barley is the name given to grains of barley that have been processed to remove the hull and outer bran layer, and then polished. It makes a very nutritious addition to soups and stews, and often features in the older cookbooks and in recipes for invalids. Pearl barley is often included in mutton and lamb stews, although some purists would not consider it an acceptable addition to an authentic Irish stew. It provides extra nutrition, is filling and economical, and adds body to stews and soups which might otherwise be a bit thin. It can also be added to the liquid when boiling a chicken to make a broth. Pearl barley has become very fashionable in recent years, and is sometimes included in recipes with lamb shanks, as well as in salads and vegetarian dishes.

Serves 5–6

1 tablespoon barley
1 quart stock or cold water
1 onion
1 white turnip
1 carrot
1 stick celery
8oz scrag of mutton
salt and freshly ground pepper
1 tablespoon chopped parsley

Mutton Broth

This is another recipe from Agnes Robins' Dominican Convent notebook. It is likely that the liquid used would have been lamb stock.

Wash the barley well and put in a pan with the stock or cold water. Peel the onion and turnip, scrape the carrot, and cut all into dice along with the celery. When the stock or water boils, add the vegetables, boil for 30 minutes. Then put in the meat and simmer for 1 hour. Add pepper and salt, 10 minutes before it's done. Remove the meat to a hot dish and cover with parsley sauce. Add 1 tablespoonful of chopped parsley to the broth before serving.

   Note: In another recipe for mutton broth, the mutton was served separately with melted butter and the broth was eaten with bread. It was suggested that in making mutton broth for an invalid the mutton is put into cold water so as to extract all the juice of the meat.

2 tablespoons barley
1 quart water or pot liquor
1 onion
1 turnip
1 potato
salt and freshly ground pepper
1 pint whole milk
2 teaspoons clarified fat
2 teaspoons brown sugar

Barley Soup

This soup, from the Cookery Notes of 1949, *would have been economical to make and nourishing. No need to cook for 2 hours, just until the barley is soft and the vegetables tender.*

Soak the barley overnight. Put it to cook in water. Let boil. Add vegetables peeled and sliced. Let it simmer 2 hours at least. Stir from time to time to prevent burning. Add pepper, salt, milk, fat, and sugar. Boil it up and serve.

Cakes and Cookies

The tradition of baking cakes for ceremonies and festivals—weddings, baptisms, funerals, harvest, Christmas, Easter, Mothering Sunday—is an important one in Ireland. Originally, no doubt, it arose from the practise of adding a few precious, luxury ingredients, such as a handful of dried fruit, to the daily bread to celebrate a special occasion. The traditional Irish barm brack, a fruited yeast bread or cake, is probably the direct descendant of these early celebration breads.

Having "a light hand with a sponge" used to be the highest compliment a woman could be paid. Indeed, her status in her village or community would virtually depend on how high her sponge cake rose! Some of the most delectable recipes I have collected in the course of writing this book have been for tea-time dainties that remind me of an almost forgotten era when women would have time to sit down together and chat, sip tea, and eat a slice of some featherlight homemade confection.

Children love helping with cake-making. I think it particularly appeals to them because of the magical way in which the raw runny ingredients puff up in the oven into delicious buns or cakes. I adored helping my mother when she baked and I have included some of her recipes, following the time-honored Irish tradition of passing the recipes down the generations.

Fruit Cakes

Irish people have always been partial to a bit of fruit cake, starting with the curney bread "cakes" (containing currants or golden raisins) made in the bastible or pot-oven over the open turf fire. From the early 1950s, as gas and electric ovens became more common, real fruit cakes were made using the creaming method, often from recipes accompanying the new oven, or from the cookery leaflets published by the ingredients producers, such as Odlums Flour, McDonnells Good Food Kitchen, Royal Baking Powder, or the Electricity Supply Board. More common were the lighter fruit cakes, which could be put together quickly and eaten fresh with a cup of tea after lunch or dinner. Richer fruit cakes made for weddings and special occasions required more skill and more expensive ingredients.

I was fascinated to learn that on Inis Meáin they only had cake at Christmas, and this would be a shop cake from the mainland. Áine de Blacam remembers that they had cookery classes on the island during the late 1960s, run by the Vocational Education Committee. Everybody made a Christmas cake, and that was the start of cake-making on the island.

Halloween Barmbrack

Everyone in Ireland loves a barmbrack, perhaps because it brings back lots of memories of excitement and games at Halloween. When the barmbrack was cut, everyone waited in anticipation to see what they'd find in their slice—a stick, a pea, a ring—and what it meant for their future. Now they're available in every Irish bakery, but here's a great recipe you can use to make one at home. It keeps in a pan for up to a week.

Makes 2 loaves

3¼ cups strong white bread flour
½ level teaspoon ground cinnamon
½ level teaspoon mixed spice
¼ teaspoon nutmeg
a pinch of salt
2 tablespoons (¼ stick) butter
1 heaping tablespoon (¾oz) fresh yeast, plus 1 teaspoon sugar and 1 teaspoon tepid milk
½ cup minus 1 tablespoon superfine sugar
1¼ cups tepid milk
1 organic egg, whisked
1⅔ cups golden raisins
¾ cup currants
⅓ cup candied peel, chopped
eggwash made with milk, sugar, and 1 egg yolk, to glaze

2 loaf pans, 5 x 8 inch, ring, stick, pea, piece of cloth, all wrapped in parchment paper

It's a help if all utenstils are warm before starting to make barmbrack. Sift the flour, cinnamon, mixed spice, nutmeg, and salt into a bowl. Rub in the butter. Mix the yeast with 1 teaspoon of sugar and 1 teaspoon of tepid milk and leave for 4–5 minutes until it becomes creamy and slightly bubbly. Add the superfine sugar to the flour mixture and mix well.

Pour the tepid milk and the egg into the yeast mixture, then add to the flour. Knead well either by hand or in the warmed bowl of an electric mixer at high speed for 5 minutes. The dough should be stiff but elastic. Fold in the dried fruit and peel, cover with a cloth, and leave in a warm place until the dough has doubled in size. Knock back again for 2–3 minutes. Grease the loaf pans and divide the dough between them.

Add the ring, stick, pea and piece of cloth, tucking them in well and ensuring they are hidden by the dough. Cover again and let rise for about 30–45 minutes until well puffed-up. Preheat the oven to 350°F.

Bake for about 1 hour or until golden and fully cooked. Glaze the top with eggwash and return to the oven for about 2–3 minutes. Turn out onto a wire rack. When cool, serve cut into thick slices with butter.

Barmbrack keeps well, but if it gets a little stale, try it toasted or in a bread and butter pudding.

This recipe, from Eliza Helena Odell's manuscript receipt book, is dated August 26th, 1851.

Take one ounce of hops with a plateful of malt and boil in two gallons of water for an hour and then strain them, when milk is warm add 2lbs of flour with a pint of old barm, jug it up well and set it in a warm place and it will be fit for use next day. 1 pint and about a wine glass will be sufficient for 4 quarts of flour.

Accounts from the 19th century show that barm bracks were associated with New Year's Eve festivities. Pieces of baked loaf were dashed against the back of the house door to ward off poverty in the coming year.

Makes 2 large or 3 small loaves

scant 3 cups raisins and golden raisins
scant 2 cups tea
⅓ cup maraschino cherries, halved
⅓ cup candied peel, chopped
½ cup plus 1 tablespoon soft brown sugar
½ cup plus 1 tablespoon granulated sugar
1 egg
3 cups all-purpose flour
¼ teaspoon baking powder

either 3 small 4 x 6-inch loaf pans, 2 large 10 x 15-inch loaf pans

Lana Pringle's Barmbrack

Lana Pringle came from Clydaville near Mallow in Co. Cork. She now lives in Shanagarry, where her breads, cakes, and cookies are legendary. Lana dislikes the din made by food processors, so all her cakes are creamed, beaten, and whisked by hand and baked in the temperamental Aga. Her recipe for barmbrack came from her husband Gerald's family who lived in Dublin.

Put the raisins and golden raisins into a bowl and cover with tea. (Lana occasionally uses a mixture of Indian and Lapsang Souchong, but any good strong tea will do.) Leave overnight to allow the fruit to plump up. Next day add the cherries, candied peel, both sugars, and egg; mix well. Sift the flour and baking powder and stir in thoroughly. The mixture should be softish; add a little more tea if necessary.

Grease the pans with melted butter. Lana uses old pans, of a heavier gauge than is available nowadays, so light modern pans may need to be lined with silicon paper for extra protection.

Divide the mixture between the pans and bake in a moderate oven at 350°F for about 40 minutes. Lana bakes her barmbracks in the Aga. After 40 minutes she turns the pans around and gives them a further 10 minutes. If you are using two pans the barmbracks will take about 1 hour. Leave in the pans for about 10 minutes and then remove and let cool on a wire rack.

Makes 2 loaves

3 medium cooking apples (about 1lb)
1 cup plus 2 tablespoons sugar
1 cup (2 sticks) butter
1 level teaspoon baking soda
2 large eggs, beaten
2⅔ cups all-purpose flour or half and half all-purpose and whole wheat flour (which is even nicer)
2 teaspoons mixed spice
1⅔ cups raisins
1⅔ cups golden raisins
½ cup crystallizd cherries
¾–1 cup chopped walnuts

2 loaf pans, 2lb

Apple Brack

This brack recipe is from Phyl O'Kelly who was a much-loved cookery writer in the Irish Examiner *newspaper for many years.*

Preheat the oven to 300°F. Grease and line the loaf pans. Peel, core, and slice the apples and stew them carefully with the sugar and a tiny drop of water, stirring frequently to make sure they are not sticking to the bottom of the saucepan. When cooked, add the butter and stir until melted. Set aside to get cold, then stir in the baking soda, eggs, and sifted flour and mixed spice. Stir in the remaining ingredients. Divide the mixture evenly between the 2 prepared pans and bake on the center shelf of the oven for 1¾–2 hours.

Raisin Cake from the Blasket Islands

On the Blaskets, Raisin Cake was the Christmas treat. Máire Ní Ghuithín gives the ingredients on her book Bean an Oileáin *(Women of the Islands). She doesn't say how long the cake should be allowed to rise if yeast is used, nor how long it took to bake the cake, but it would have been made in the pot-oven. Scales would not have been needed—the bag of raisins would be weighed in the shop. Every house had large mugs hanging on the dresser in the kitchen, they would hold 6oz of flour. I've included my adaptation of this recipe with weights of ingredients in brackets.*

3 mugfuls of white flour (18oz)
One spoonful of baking soda (1 teaspoon)
One spoonful of salt (1 teaspoon)
A small knob of butter (1oz)
One beaten egg
Half a cupful of sugar (4oz—I usd demerara)
Half a pound of big muscatel raisins with seeds removed (8oz)
Sour milk or yeast dissolved in warm water (I used 15fl oz buttermilk)

All the ingredients, except the sour milk or yeast liquid were mixed together. The mixture was then moistened with the milk/yeast liquid.

Here's my adaptation:

Sift the flour and baking soda into a bowl. Add salt and sugar, rub in the butter. Add raisins and mix well. Make a well in the center, add the egg and buttermilk. Mix to a softish dough. Turn into the lined pan. Bake for 1 hour approx. in the preheated oven.

Cool in the pan. Cut into wedges and serve buttered. This cake keeps well for a few days, but not for weeks like a traditional Christmas cake. We also enjoyed some toasted.

Sean Pheats Tom O Cearnaigh, also mentions in his 1992 book Fiolar an eireabaill bhain *(The Whitetailed Eagle) that milk or cream, and "yeast flour" were used to make a raisin cake, and that it was baked for an hour.*

Ballymaloe House Luncheon Cake

Serves 8 (approximately)

1¾ cups all-purpose flour
a pinch of salt
1 heaping teaspoon baking powder
⅔ cup (1¼ sticks) butter
¾ cup superfine sugar
½ cup golden raisins
⅓ cup mixed peel
grated rind of 1 orange
2 eggs, beaten
halved almonds, to decorate

one round 8-inch cake pan, greased and lined

Luncheon cake features in several of the manuscript cookbooks. It was a light fruit cake based on the rubbing-in method, which probably would have been baked fresh in the morning for lunch. It must be eaten on the day it's made as it stales quickly. It would have been eaten for lunch or with a cup of tea or coffee. We also have a favorite version at Ballymaloe House.

Preheat the oven to 350°F. Sift the flour, salt, and baking powder together. Rub in the butter very well. Add the sugar and rub in. Add the golden raisins, mixed peel, orange rind, and eggs and mix to make a stiff dough. Pour into the pan. Decorate the surface with a pattern of halved almonds. Bake for 50 minutes. Let cool on a wire rack and enjoy freshly baked.

Mixed Spice

1 tablespoon coriander seeds
1 cinnamon stick, crushed
1 teaspoon allspice berries
1 teaspoon whole cloves
1 tablespoon freshly grated nutmeg
2 teaspoons ground ginger

Little round cartons of mixed spice (a mixture of sweet spices) have been available in every village for the last one or two hundred years. If you cannot find it, here is a recipe from The Encyclopaedia of Herbs, Spices and Flavourings *by Elizabeth Lambert Ortiz.*

From the 17th century onward, cookery books began to list spices separately with each individual recipe, rather than as basic mixtures at the front, but a few popular blends are still in use. This traditional English blend of spices, also called pudding spice, is used in puddings, cakes, and cookies. Like all mixtures, the proportions and the ingredients vary according to personal taste.

Grind together the coriander seeds, cinnamon stick, allspice berries, and cloves. Stir in the freshly grated nutmeg and ground ginger. Store in an airtight container and keep in a cool place away from light.

Spiced Lunch Cake

Serves 8 (approximately)

2 cups self-rising flour
½ teaspoon salt
½ cup dripping or other fat (you can use butter)
½ cup minus 1 tablespoon sugar
1⅔ cup mixed peek
½ teaspoon mixed spice (see above)
grated nutmeg
1 egg, beaten
1 heaping tablespoon light corn syrup
⅔ cup milk or water
halved walnuts

This cake is on a similar theme to the Ballymaloe House Luncheon Cake (opposite), but is more recent. It is a lovely, easy recipe from the Good Housekeeping Cookery Compendium of 1952: *quick to make and a really useful cake to have in your repertoire. It's best eaten fresh. It's made with the rubbing-in method, which is great for beginners, but doesn't keep well.*

Put the flour and salt into a bowl and rub in the fat very lightly and thoroughly, until no lumps remain. Add the sugar, mixed fruit, mixed spice and nutmeg, and mix well. Add the egg and the syrup and stir in enough milk or water to give a stiff dropping consistency. Put the mixture into a greased loaf pan, decorate with the halved walnuts, and bake in a moderate oven, 375°F, for about 1¾ hours. Cool in the pan on a wire rack and store in a cake tin with an airtight lid.

Bachelor's Cake

½ cup (1 stick) butter
3½ cups flour
1⅔ cups currants
1⅔ cups raisins
1 cup plus 2 tablespoons brown sugar
2 teaspoons ground cinnamon
2 teaspoons ground ginger
2 level teaspoons baking soda
1⅓ cups buttermilk
sliced almonds or shredded coconut, to decorate (optional)

This interestingly-named light fruit cake comes from Nancy Elliott. The original recipe had 1oz cinnamon (7 tablespoons!); we reduced it to 2 teaspoons which still gave a good flavor. Nancy suggested ½oz ground ginger (9 teaspoons) so we also reduced that to 2 teaspoons.

Grease and line an 8-inch round cake pan. Rub the butter into the flour, add all the dry ingredients, stir in the buttermilk mixing thoroughly. Pour into the prepared pan and bake in a moderate oven, 350°F, for 1 hour 40 minutes. The top may be decorated with sliced almonds or coconut, if liked.

Cut and Come Cake

3¼ cups golden raisins
1 cup brown sugar
¾ cup cold black tea
2 cups flour
2 eggs
¼ cup crystallized cherries
⅓ cup Homemade Candied Peel
1 level teaspoon baking powder

5 x 8-inch loaf pan, lined with
greaseproof paper

A "cut and come" cake was a popular fruit cake to have in the tin to serve with a pot of tea in case anyone called. It was usually a big cake—you would cut some and go back for more. This recipe was sent to me by Mary Walsh from Woodsgift, Co. Kilkenny, and it comes from her mother's handwritten recipe book. The recipe is similar to the tea brack recipes that are still much loved in Ireland today.

Steep the golden raisins and sugar in the tea overnight. Next day add half the flour, beat in the eggs, and stir, then add cherries and peel and stir again. Add the remaining flour and the baking powder and stir again. Turn into the greased and floured pan and bake for 1½ hours.

Plum Cake

Plum cake features in several of the manuscript cookbooks and scrapbooks. "Plums" referred to dried fruit. It is a richer fruit cake than the luncheon cakes and would keep longer. Butter and sugar were often beaten using the hands: the warmth helped to speed up the creaming process.

Marianne Armstrong's Plum Cake

This is adapted from Marianne Armstrong's version from 1849, which is stated to be V.G. (very good). The method here is curious because the sugar is added after, rather than before, the eggs, but it seems to work.

1lb butter
1lb soft dark brown sugar
1lb currants
1¼lb flour
8 eggs
6oz orange and lemon candied peel
4 tablespoons Jamaica rum or other spirit to taste

9-inch round cake tin, base and sides lined with parchment paper

Beat the butter to a cream with the hand. Add the eggs well beaten two at a time, add to this the sugar which should be brown and then stir in the flour and currants. Flavor to taste, we used Jamaica rum.

Bake at 350°F for 1 hour, then turn down the oven to 325°F and bake for a further 1¼ hours.

Here is another lovely version of plum cake. This is from the 19th-century Bruen papers and is credited to Baroness de Robeck.

1lb flour
6oz butter, rubbed in the flour quite fine
6oz moist sugar
8oz [golden] raisins
3 whole eggs, broken
1 small teaspoon bicarbonate of soda [baking soda]

Put the soda into a ½ pint mug and foam a ½ pint of milk over it. Warm together till lukewarm and then mix them with the other ingredients, beat all together with the hand for 20 minutes and bake slowly for two hours—taking care not to open the oven for an hour at least. Line the tin with paper.

1 cup (2 sticks) butter
1 cup plus 2 tablespoons demerara sugar
1¾ cups flour
¼ teaspoon salt
¼ teaspoon ground cinnamon
¼ teaspoon ground ginger
4 eggs
1⅔ cups raisins
¾ cup golden raisins
¾ cup currants
¾ cup Homemade Candied Peel (see page 317)
1 tablespoon brandy

Rich Plum Cake

This recipe came to me from Valerie Kingston, who found it in an old family scrapbook which was compiled by her great-grandmother and grandmother between 1900 and 1940.

This piece on "Stand-by Cakes" was published in Home Notes *by Lydia Chatterton: "We have all experienced the disconcerting moment when visitors drop in and the cake supply is low, but this will never happen if we always make some good keeping cakes on cake baking days. Many kinds of cakes will keep for weeks and some for months, but you must have a good airtight tin. A full-sized biscuit [cookie] tin is as good as any kind, as the lid fits tightly."*

Beat the butter and sugar to very soft cream, then beat in the flour, to which has been added the salt and spices, then beat in the eggs and continue beating for 15 minutes with a wooden spoon. Now add the fruit, candied peel and brandy and, when thoroughly mixed, turn into a deep, 9-inch cake pan lined with parchment paper (when lining it allow the paper to rise an inch or two above the pan) and bake in a very moderate oven for 4½ hours*. Cover with parchment paper as soon as the cake begins to brown. To make a cake even when baked, put the mixture higher around the edges of the pan and low in the center, as they always have a tendency to rise in the center.

*We baked this cake at 300°F for 2¼ hours with excellent results.

2 cups (4 sticks) fresh butter, beaten to a cream
2¼ cups loaf sugar, finely powdered
rinds of 2 lemons, grated
scant 5¼ cups flour, well dried
scant 6½ cups currants
¾lb citron, cut into pieces
8–9 eggs, yolks and whites beaten together

Plum Cake

A recipe from Eliza Helena Odell's manuscript receipt book, dated August 26 1851: Mix all well and when ready for the pan add a large glass of whiskey—it will take two hours and a half in a brick oven to bake it well.

L. Croker

Bride Cake

The bride cake of former years was much less rich than the fruit cake of the present day. When white flour was still a luxury, bride cake was often just a simple wheaten cake or one made from honey and fruit. No matter how simple, it denoted prosperity and good fortune and was an important part of the wedding festivities.

When the bride entered her home after the wedding ceremony her mother broke the cake over her head for good luck. The pieces were then divided amongst the guests. In Irishtown and Ringsend in Dublin they broke cake over the bride's head up to recent times, for luck and fertility.

⅔ cup maraschino cherries
½ cup whole almonds
scant ½ cup best-quality golden raisins
scant ½ cup best-quality currants
1⅔ cups best-quality raisins
⅔ cup muscatel raisins, pitted
½ cup ground almonds
grated rind of 1 lemon
grated rind of 1 orange
⅔ cup Homemade Candied Peel (see page 317)
2¼ tablespoons Irish whiskey
1 cup (2 sticks) butter
1 cup plus 2 tablespoons pale, soft brown sugar
6 eggs, free-range if possible
1 teaspoon mixed spice
2 cups plus 2 tablespoons flour
1 large or 2 small Macintosh apples, grated

Christmas Cake

Recipes for Christmas cake abound, and most families have a favorite that has been passed down through the generations. It's not always appreciated if a new recipe is tried, as the family often don't like change at a traditional time like Christmas. For many people the Christmas cake was, and to a great extent still is, the most important cake of the year. For weeks thrifty women all over the country scrimped and saved to gather up enough dried fruit—golden raisins, currants, candied peel, crystallized cherries, perhaps even a few plump muscatel raisins—to make the cake of cakes. Eventually, when all the ingredients had been collected, a day toward the end of October or early November was chosen. Excitement was in the air. Making the cake was always a family affair and in our family there was no shortage of eager helpers. As children we pitted the muscatel raisins, washed and halved the jewel-like cherries, diced the chunks of candied peel and citron, and even helped with the laborious creaming of butter and soft Barbados sugar. Butter was always used for this traditional pièce de résistance—even by cooks who disapproved of such extravagance for the rest of the year.

The pan was lined with several layers of parchment paper and protected with a brown paper collar. Our old Aga was coaxed to the correct temperature and soon the seductive smells of home baking filled the house. We could all feel the tension as the cake was tested and rested—there was much examining the bottom of a magical skewer to determine whether it was "coming out clean." Then, with a sigh of relief, the cake was reverently carried to a shelf in the cool pantry, after a further blessing of Irish whiskey, or in some households a drop of the "hard stuff," to help it to mature.

By the time Christmas came round everyone was in a fever of anticipation. The cake was unwrapped, rich almond paste was applied, once more with the help of eager chattering children, and then the royal icing was lathered on to make a convincing snow scene. Finally the "plaster of Paris" snowmen and Santa were unwrapped from the tissue nests in which they had hidden since the previous Christmas and were placed on top. The cake then graduated to the parlor where it sat in state on the sideboard until Christmas Eve or Christmas Day.

Line the base and sides of a 9-inch round, or an 8-inch square pan with brown paper and parchment paper. Wash the maraschino cherries and dry them. Quarter or halve as desired. Blanch the whole almonds in boiling water for 1–2 minutes, rub off the skins, and chop them finely. Mix together the dried fruit, almonds, ground almonds, grated orange and lemon rind, and candied peel. Add the whiskey and then leave the mixture for 1 hour to macerate.

Preheat the oven to 325°F.

Cream the butter until very soft. Add the sugar and beat until light and fluffy. Whisk the eggs and add in bit by bit, beating well between each addition so that the mixture doesn't curdle. Mix the spice with the flour and stir in gently. Add the grated apple to the fruit and mix in gently but thoroughly. (Do not beat the mixture again or you will toughen the cake.)

Put the mixture into the prepared pan. Make a slight hollow in the center. Dip your hand in water and pat it over the surface of the cake: this will ensure that the top is smooth when cooked. Put into the preheated oven; reduce the heat to 300°F after 1 hour. Bake until cooked (about 3–3½ hours); test in the center with a skewer—it should come out completely clean. Pour a little whiskey over the cake and let cool in the pan.

Next day remove the cake from the pan. Do not remove the lining paper, but wrap in some extra parchment paper and aluminum foil until required.

To Ice the Cake

ALMOND PASTE
½ cup plus 1 tablespoon superfine sugar
¾ cup plus ½ tablespoon confectioners' sugar
2¼ cups ground almonds
2 small eggs
1 tablespoon Irish whiskey
pure almond essence

Sift the sugars and mix with the ground almonds. Beat the eggs, add the whiskey, and a drop of pure almond extract, then add to the other ingredients and mix to a stiff paste. (You may not need all the egg.) Sprinkle your work surface with confectioners' sugar, turn out the almond paste, and work lightly until the paste is smooth.

Remove the paper from the cake. Put a sheet of parchment paper onto the work top and dust it with some confectioners' sugar. Take about half the almond paste and roll it out on the paper: when rolled, it should be a little less than ½ inch thick. Paint the top of the cake with a lightly beaten egg white and put the cake, sticky side down, onto the almond paste. Give the cake a thump to make sure it sticks and then cut round the edge. If the cake is a little "round-shouldered," cut the almond paste a little larger and press it in against the cake with a palette knife. Then slide a knife underneath the cake or, better still, underneath the paper, and turn the cake the right way up. Gently peel off the parchment paper.

Next, measure the circumference of the cake with a piece of string. Roll out 2 long strips of almond paste and trim both edges to the height of the cake with a palette knife. Paint both the cake and the almond paste lightly with egg white. Press the strips against the side of the cake: do not overlap them or there will be a bulge. Roll a straight-sided water glass along the side of the cake to even the edges and smooth the join. Rub the cake well with your hand to ensure a nice flat surface.

Carefully lift the cake onto a cake board. Allow the almond paste to dry out for several days before applying the royal icing.

ROYAL ICING
2 egg whites
3¼ cups confectioners' sugar
2 teaspoons strained lemon juice
glycerin (optional)

To make the icing, whisk the egg whites in a large bowl until they just begin to froth; then add the sifted confectioners' sugar by the tablespoon, beating well between each addition. If you are making it in an electric mixer, use the lowest speed. When all the confectioners' sugar has been incorporated, add the lemon juice and add a few drops of glycerin if you would like a slightly soft icing. Beat until the icing reaches stiff peaks and scrape down the sides of the bowl. Cover the bowl with a damp cloth for 1 hour until ready to use the icing.

Smear the icing over the top and sides of the cake using a flexible palette knife. The simplest finish for a Christmas cake, most suitable for those of us not highly skilled in cake decoration, is the snow-scene effect. This is easily achieved by dabbing the palette knife onto the cake at irregular intervals, so the icing comes up in little peaks. While the icing is still wet, stick on some Christmas decorations, e.g. Santas, Christmas trees, and robins. If you want to be more ambitious, spread a thinner layer of icing onto the cake so that the top and sides are as smooth as possible. Cover the remainder of the icing with a damp cloth and leave the cake in a cool place or overnight to allow the first coat of icing to set.

With a small star nozzle, pipe rosettes or shell shapes around the base of the cake. Tie a red ribbon around the sides and tie in a flat bow. Decorate the top with rosettes in a star shape or in the shape of a Christmas tree. You could even try writing "Merry Christmas." Best of luck—have fun and a Merry Christmas to you too!

Aunt Louisa's Cake

scant 3½ cups flour
1 good teaspoon baking soda
½ cup (1 stick) butter
1⅔ cups raisins
2 teaspoons caraway seeds
1 cup soft dark brown sugar
3 eggs, beaten
1¼ cups sour milk
pinch of salt

one round 8-inch cake pan, base and sides lined with parchment paper

Mary Walsh said her mother didn't make a traditional Christmas cake— instead she made Aunt Louisa's cake, and as children they were always fascinated by the name. I came across Aunt Louisa's cake in the 1932 and 1943 editions of Cookery Notes. *History doesn't relate who Aunt Louisa was! It is unusual to have caraway seeds in a fruit cake; they are more often used on their own in a seed cake, but they are a delicious addition. Caraway seeds were available in any village shop, definitely a favourite cake ingredient.*

Sift the flour and soda into a bowl, rub in the butter, add the rasins, caraway seeds, and sugar. Add the beaten eggs and sufficient sour milk to make a fairly stiff dough. Put in a greased pan and bake at 350°F for 1 hour–1 hour 10 minutes.

Simnel Cake

½ cup maraschino cherries
scant ½ cup whole almonds
scant 2½ cups best-quality golden raisins
scant 2½ cups best-quality currants
scant 2½ cups best-quality raisins
⅔ cup Homemade Candied Peel (see page 317)
½ cup ground almonds
rind of 1 lemon
rind of 1 orange
4 tablespoons Irish whiskey
1 cup (2 sticks) butter
1 cup plus 2 tablespoons pale, soft brown sugar
6 eggs, free-range if possible
1 teaspoon mixed spice
2 cups plus 2 tablespoons all-purpose flour
1 large or 2 small Macintosh apples, grated

ALMOND PASTE
2¼ cups superfine sugar
4 cups ground almonds
2 small eggs
3 tablespoons Irish whiskey
a drop of pure almond extract

9-inch round or 8-inch square pan, base and sides lined with brown paper and parchment paper

Simnel was originally a spiced bread, most probably introduced by Elizabethan settlers in the 16th century.

Wash the cherries and dry them. Quarter or halve as desired. Blanch the almonds in boiling water for 1–2 minutes, rub off the skins, and chop them finely. Mix together the dried fruit, peel, cherries, almonds, ground almonds, and grated orange and lemon rind. Add about half of the whiskey and leave for 1 hour to macerate.

Next make the almond paste. Sift the superfine sugar and mix with the ground almonds. Beat the eggs, add the whiskey, and a drop of pure almond extract, then add to the other ingredients and mix to a stiff paste. (You may not need all the egg.) Sprinkle a work top with confectioners' sugar. Turn out the almond paste and work lightly until smooth.

Preheat the oven to 325°F. Cream the butter until very soft. Add the sugar and beat until light and fluffy. Whisk the eggs and add in bit by bit, beating well between each addition so that the mixture doesn't curdle. Mix the spice with the flour and stir in gently. Add the grated apple to the dried fruit, then mix it in gently but thoroughly to the cake batter (do not beat the mixture again or you will toughen the cake).

Put half of the cake mixture into the prepared pan. Roll out about half of the almond paste into an 8½-inch circle and place this on top of the cake mixture in the pan. Cover with the remaining mixture. Make a slight hollow in the center. Dip your hand in water and pat it over the surface of the cake: this will ensure that the top is smooth when cooked. Put into the preheated oven, reduce the heat to 300°F after 1 hour. Bake for about 3–3½ hours, until a skewer pushed into the center comes out completely clean. Pour the rest of the whiskey over the cake and let cool overnight in the pan.

Next day remove the cake from the pan. Do not remove the lining paper, but wrap the cake in parhcment paper and aluminum foil until required.

To ice the cake, roll out about two-thirds of the almond paste into a circle about 9-inch across. Brush the cake with a little lightly beaten egg white and top with the almond paste. Roll the remainder of the paste into 11 balls. The 11 balls represent 11 of the 12 apostles (Judas is absent, being in disgrace for having betrayed Jesus). Score the top of the cake into 1½-inch squares. Brush with beaten egg or egg yolk. Stick the "apostles" around the outer edge of the top and brush with beaten egg. Toast in a preheated oven (425°F) for 15–20 minutes or until the almond paste is slightly golden. Nowadays we decorate simnel cake with fluffy Easter chickens.

scant 3½ cups all-purpose flour
a pinch of salt
1 teaspoon baking powder
1 cup plus 2 tablespoons superfine
  or brown sugar
½ teaspoon freshly grated nutmeg
½ teaspoon mixed spice
1 cup (2 sticks) butter
3¼ cups golden raisins
⅓ cup chopped peel
⅓ cup maraschino cherries
1¼ cups porter or stout
2 eggs, free-range if possible

1½ cups (3 sticks) butter
scant 3½ cups flour
1¼ cups porter
1 tablespoon baking soda
3¼ cups currants
3¼ cups raisins
2¼ cups brown sugar
8oz citron
4 eggs, broken into the cake,
  not beaten
rind of 1 lemon
half 1 package of mixed spice and
  some nutmeg

1 cup (2 sticks) butter
1 cup plus 2 tablespoons soft
  brown sugar
4 eggs (lightly beaten)
2 cups all-purpose flour
2 level teaspoons mixed spice
1⅔ cups seedless raisins
1⅔ cups golden raisins
⅔ cup mixed peel
¾–1 cup chopped walnuts
8–12 tablespoons Guinness

Porter Cake

Porter cake, made with the black stout of Ireland, is now an established Irish cake, rich and moist with "plenty of cutting." Either Guinness, Murphy, Beamish, or some of the fine stouts from the growing number of new artisan breweries can be used, depending on where your loyalties lie.

Preheat the oven to 350°F. Line the bottom and sides of an 8-inch cake pan, 3 inches deep, with parchment paper.

Sift the flour, salt, and baking powder into a bowl. Add the sugar, freshly grated nutmeg, and mixed spice. Rub in the butter. Add the fruit, then mix the porter with the beaten eggs. Pour into the other ingredients and mix well. Turn into the lined pan and bake for about 2½ hours. Cool in the pan, then store in an airtight tin.

Traditional Porter Cake

This recipe is adapted from the manuscript cookbook of Eliza Helena Odell.

Rub the butter into the flour. Heat the porter and pour over the soda, then pour the porter mixure over the butter and flour. Add the remaining ingredients, mix by hand for 15 minutes, then transfer to a pan and bake as for the Christmas Cake on pages 284–285.

Mr Guinness's Cake

This recipe from Rose Hanlon's scrapbook appeared as part of a Guinness advertisement in a Sunday supplement many years ago: "Over the past couple of centuries, our beer has acquired a modest reputation, but our cake is still little known. This seems a pity, for one enthusiast has described it as like eating dreams." See what you think!

Preheat the oven to 325°F and grease and line a 7-inch round cake pan. Cream the butter and sugar together until light. Gradually beat in the eggs. Sift the flour and mixed spice together, then fold into the mixture. Add the raisins, golden raisins, mixed peel, and walnuts. Mix well together. Stir 4 tablespoons of the Guinness into the mixture and mix to a soft dropping consistency. Turn into the prepared pan and bake for 1 hour. Then reduce the heat to 300°F for another 1½ hours. Let cool.

Remove from cake pan. Prick the base of the cake with a skewer, and spoon over the remaining 4–8 tablespoons of Guinness. Keep cake for one week before eating.

Mrs Forde's Boiled Fruit Cake

3¼ cups golden raisins
1 cup (2 sticks) butter
1 cup plus 2 tablespoons soft light
  brown sugar
scant 1 cup water
2 eggs, beaten
2 cups flour
½ teaspoon mixed spice
½ teaspoon nutmeg
¼ teaspoon baking soda

9-inch round or 8-inch square pan,
base and sides lined with brown
paper and parchment paper

This is Mamie Forde's recipe for Boiled Fruit Cake, a great family favorite sent to me by her daughter Maeve. At Christmas her mother usually made a richer version of the cake by adding some cherries, mixed peel and a drop of whiskey. She gave cakes as presents to friends who were not so keen on the traditional rich Christmas cake. Mamie grew up in Dublin's Temple Bar and worked in the restaurant in the old Carlton Cinema on O'Connell Street before marrying into army life in the Curragh Camp in 1946. She was a wonderful cook and homemaker.

Boil the fruit, butter, sugar, and water together and simmer for 10 minutes. Let cool, stirring well while cooling. When cool stir in the beaten eggs. Then stir in the flour, spices, and baking soda. Put into a lined 8-inch round pan. Cover the top lightly with parchment paper while baking to prevent over-browning. Bake at 350°F for 1½ hours. Turn out and cool on a wire rack.

Slab Cake

scant 2½ cups golden raisins
½ cup maraschino cherries
1 cup candied orange and lemon
  peel
1 cup chopped almonds
grated rind of 1 orange and 1 lemon
2¼ cups (4½ sticks) softened
  butter
2½ cups superfine sugar
9 eggs, free-range if possible
6⅓–6½ cups all-purpose flour
2 teaspoons baking powder
a little milk

Slab cake was sold by weight in many grocers' shops. Recipes vary from plain cakes, such as Madeira or seed cakes, to rich fruit cakes. Men often used to bring home a piece of this slab cake after the fair, particularly if they were coming home a little late!

Preheat the oven to 325°F.
  Line the base and sides of a rectangular cake pan 10 × 14 × 3 inches with parchment paper. Mix the fruit, peel, and nuts with the grated orange and lemon rind. In another bowl cream the butter well, add the superfine sugar and continue to beat until light and pale. Whisk the eggs and beat in bit by bit, adding a little flour if it shows signs of curdling. Stir in the flour and baking powder and finally the mixture of fruit and almonds. If it appears too stiff, add a little milk. Pour into the pan and bake in the preheated oven for 1½–1¾ hours. Cool it in the pan. Store in an airtight tin.

Madeira Cake

2/3 cup (1 1/2 sticks) butter, softened
3/4 cup plus 2 tablespoons superfine
  sugar
3 eggs
1/2 teaspoon vanilla extract
1 3/4 cups all-purpose flour
1/2 teaspoon baking powder
1 tablespoon milk or water

one 7 x 3-inch cake pan lined with
  greaseproof paper

This was originally made to be nibbled by ladies as they sipped Madeira or port wine. It was also the basis for many other cakes, such as seed or marble cake. Occasionally it might have a piece of candied citron on top. A delicious cake if made with good eggs, fine butter, and pure vanilla extract.

Cream the butter, then add the sugar and beat until light and fluffy (this will give you a lighter, smoother cake than just dumping the sugar in with the butter at the beginning). Better still, cream the butter and sugar by hand in the time honored old-fashioned way—it will cream faster from the heat of your hand and produce a lighter cake.

Whisk the eggs with the vanilla extract and gradually add to the creamed butter and sugar. Beat well. If preferred, the eggs may be beaten into the mixture one at a time. A little sifted flour may be added between each addition of egg, if liked.

Mix the baking powder with the remainder of the flour and fold into the mixture. Add a little water or milk if necessary, to make a dropping consistency. Pour into the cake pan.

Bake in a moderate oven, 350°F, for 50–60 minutes. Cool in the pan.

Hot Cross Buns

2 tablespoons fresh yeast
1/2 cup minus 1 tablespoon
  superfine sugar
1–1 1/4 cups tepid milk
3 1/4 cups strong white flour
1/3 cup (3/4 stick) butter
1/4 teaspoon ground cinnamon
1/4 teaspoon nutmeg
2–3 teaspoons mixed spice
a pinch of salt
2 eggs
2/3 cup currants
1/3 cup golden raisins
1/4 cup chopped peel
2oz shortcrust pie dough or flour
  and water paste
egg wash made with milk, sugar
  and 1 egg yolk, to glaze

Today hot cross buns are traditionally eaten in Ireland on Ash Wednesday and on Good Friday. This practise would have been greatly frowned upon in the past when these were black fast days and people would scarcely have had enough to eat, let alone spicy, fruit-filled buns.

Dissolve the yeast with 1 tablespoon of the sugar in a little of the tepid milk.

Put the flour into a bowl. Rub in the butter and add the cinnamon, nutmeg, mixed spice, a pinch of salt, and the remainder of the sugar. Mix well.

Whisk the eggs and add to the milk. Make a well in the center of the flour. Add the yeast and most of the liquid and mix to a soft dough (add more milk if necessary).

Leave for 2–3 minutes, then knead until smooth. Add the currants, golden raisins, and chopped peel, and continue to knead until the dough is shiny. Cover the bowl and let the dough rise in a warm place until it doubles in size.

Knock back the dough by kneading for 3–4 minutes. Rest it for a few minutes, then shape it into 2oz buns. Put them onto a baking sheet and brush the tops with egg wash. Mark the top of each bun with a cross. Carefully put a cross made of thin strips of shortcrust pie dough on to each bun. Leave the buns to rise again to double their size, and brush again carefully with egg wash.

Bake in a preheated oven at 425°F for 5 minutes, then reduce the heat to 400°F for a further 10 minutes or until golden. Cool on a wire rack.

Protestant Cake

Makes 24

PIE DOUGH BASE
1 cup (2 sticks) butter
½ cup plus 1 tablespoon superfine
　sugar
2⅔ cups self-rising flour

TOFFEE FILLING
1 cup (2 sticks) butter
1 cup plus 2 tablespoons
　granulated sugar
4 tablespoons corn syrup
1 can sweetened condensed milk

CHOCOLATE TOP
8oz dark or milk chocolate

On a Saturday morning in the lobby of the famous old Dublin landmark, the Gresham Hotel, the Dublin folklorist Eamonn MacThomáis shared the food memories of his childhood with me. One of the dainties he spoke of with nostalgic longing was Protestant cake. His family were staunch Dublin Catholics, but he remembers this confection being dished out after Sunday School. "It was a layer of chocolate and a layer of icing and a layer of mushy stuff, it was very pleasant." His wife traced the recipe for me; I recognized it as a forerunner to caramel slices.

Make the shortcake base by rubbing the butter into the sugar and flour. Work until it comes together in a ball. Alternatively, blend the three ingredients in a food processor until the mixture comes together. Roll the mixture out evenly and place in a lightly greased jelly roll pan, 10 × 15 inches. Prick the base gently with a fork. Place in a preheated oven at 350°F for 15–20 minutes until golden.
　Next, make the filling. Melt the butter, over low heat in a heavy bottomed saucepan. Add the sugar, corn syrup and the condensed milk, stirring after each addition. Stir continuously for about 20 minutes over low heat as the toffee forms. The toffee burns very easily if not stirred. When the toffee is a golden brown color, test by placing a drop into a bowl of cold water. A firm ball of toffee indicates that it will make a firm toffee when set. A soft ball of toffee indicates a soft toffee. Pour the toffee mixture over the base, spreading evenly. Allow to cool.
　Melt the chocolate slowly in a bowl over hot water and spread evenly over the toffee. Decorate immediately by drawing wavy lines with the tines of a fork. Cut into squares when the chocolate is firm.

Caraway Seeds

Caraway seeds are another forgotten flavor that was very popular in cake-making. They have a very definite taste which one either loves or loathes! I came across one recipe in a handwritten cookbook which called for 4oz of caraway seeds.

Caraway Seed Cake

1½　sticks butter
¾ cup plus 1 tablespoon superfine
　sugar
3 eggs, free-range if possible
1¾ cups all-purpose flour
1 tablespoon ground almonds
　(optional)
1 tablespoon caraway seeds, plus
　extra for sprinkling
¼ teaspoon baking powder

one round 7 × 3-inch cake pan, lined
　with parchment paper

I hated seed cake as a child, but now it's one of my great favorites. My father had a passion for it, so it was always on offer when we went to visit our Tipperary relations on Sunday afternoons.

Cream the butter, add the sugar and beat until very soft and light. Whisk the eggs and gradually beat into the creamed mixture. Stir in the flour and ground almonds, if using. Add the caraway seeds and baking powder with the last of the flour. Turn the mixture into the prepared cake pan, scatter a few more caraway seeds on top and bake in a preheated moderate oven, 350°F, for 50–60 minutes. Cool on a wire rack. This cake keeps well in an airtight tin.

Rich Seed Cake

1 cup (2 sticks) butter
1 cup plus 2 tablespoons superfine sugar
2⅔ cups flour
4 eggs
1 tablespoon caraway seeds
grated rind of 1 lemon
1 teaspoon baking powder

8-inch round cake pan, lined with parchment paper

This recipe for Rich Seed Cake comes from Cookery Notes, *1943. I adore seed cake and can't resist trying any new recipe I come across. This version has a distinct lemony flavor—quite delicious.*

Cream the butter and sugar, then add flour and beaten egg alternately, a little at a time. Beat well and add the caraway seeds, lemon rind, and lastly the baking powder. Put in a lined pan and bake in a moderately hot oven, 350°F, until done — about 2 hours.

Caraway Angel Cake

1 cup plus 1 tablespoon self-rising flour
½ cup plus 1 tablespoon superfine sugar
½ stick butter
⅔ cup milk
2 egg whites
1 teaspoon baking powder
⅓ cup candied peel, chopped
1 large teaspoon caraway seeds

one round 7-inch cake pan, greased and lined

This is another of Lydia Chatterton's recipes from Home Notes, *included in the scrapbook lent to me by Valerie Kingston of Glenilen Farm in West Cork. She suggests this as a splendid recipe to make use of egg whites when you are making a custard with egg yolks—the same would apply to ice cream.*

Preheat the oven to 350°F. Beat the butter and sugar to a soft cream, stir in the milk gradually and when it is quite smooth add the stiffly-whipped whites of eggs. Mix the baking powder and a pinch of salt with the flour lightly, then the candied peel and the caraway seeds. Pour into a well-greased pan and bake for 50–60 minutes at 350°F. We loved this cake, the home-made candied peel gave a little extra edge and the egg whites lightened the texture. It could be served as a dessert with poached fruit or summer berries from the garden.

Granny Nicholson's Afternoon Tea

My mother came from just outside the village of Johnstown in Co. Kilkenny. Occasionally, she would receive an invitation from Granny Nicholson, mother of her childhood friends, to bring us all to tea. There was wild excitement when we heard this news, because Granny Nicholson lived in a much grander house than ours and we knew that she served the most sumptuous afternoon teas.

On the appointed day, we all dressed up in our best bib and tucker — quite a performance because we are a large Irish family. I wore my smocked dress and angora bolero; the boys wore long pants and ties and had their hair brushed back into a quiff.

On the car journey we were all warned to behave and instructed in the protocol of afternoon tea. (At this time, children were still more or less expected to be seen and not heard!) After we'd played for several hours with Granny Nicholson's grandchildren we were called to tea. We couldn't wait, but it was important not to appear too eager. We had to take our places quietly at the long table laid with pretty china and a white embroidered cloth.

We were then warned to wait patiently until one was offered first the thinly sliced bread and butter, then the tiny sandwiches with various fillings — egg and chive, cucumber, salmon, salad, or banana. You took the sandwich nearest to you rather than poke through them to find your favorite filling. Eventually we progressed to the buns, cookies, crumpets, delectable pastry shells, and finally the cake — usually coffee or chocolate. By this time we were in ecstasy, each morsel tasted more delicious than the previous one. These teas, and Granny Nicholson's warm indulgent smile, remain vividly in my memory.

Sponge Cake

A "light hand with a sponge" was always something to be proud of. Two main techniques were used, the whisking method and the creaming method. My favorite was always my great grandmother's cake. However, I came across some other sponge cake recipes in my research for this book. Lily O'Reilly's and a few others were made by a different technique.

1 stick plus 1 tablespoon butter
¾ cup plus 2 tablespoons superfine sugar, plus extra to sprinkle
3 eggs, free-range if possible
scant 1½ cups flour
1 teaspoon baking powder
1 tablespoon milk

FILLING
8oz homemade raspberry jam
1⅓ cups whipped cream

Great Grandmother's Cake

A buttery sponge cake was standard fare for afternoon tea at my grandmother's in Donoghmore, and a great many other Irish houses. When it was taken out of the Aga the cake was cooled on a wire rack by the window in the back kitchen. Thick yellow cream spooned off the top of the milk in the dairy was whipped, and as soon as the cake was cool it was sandwiched together with jam, homemade from newly-picked raspberries.

Preheat the oven to 375°F.
    Grease and flour two 7-inch sponge cake pans and line the base of each with a round of parchment paper. Cream the butter and gradually add the superfine sugar. Beat until soft and light and quite pale in color.
    Add the eggs one at a time and beat well after each addition. (If the butter and sugar are not creamed properly or if you add the eggs too fast, the mixture will curdle, resulting in a cake with a heavier texture.) Sieve the flour and baking powder and stir in gradually. Mix all together lightly and add 1 tablespoon of milk to moisten.
    Divide the mixture evenly between the two pans, hollowing slightly in the center. Bake for 20–25 minutes or until cooked. Turn out onto a wire rack and allow to cool.
    Sandwich the cakes together with homemade raspberry jam and whipped cream. Sprinkle with sieved superfine sugar and serve on an old-fashioned plate with a doyley.

¾ cup granulated sugar
⅓ cup water
3 eggs
scant 1 cup flour
½ teaspoon pure vanilla extract

one 7 x 3-inch cake pan, greased and dusted with sugar and flour

Lily O'Reilly's Sponge Cake

This recipe comes from the notebooks of Lily O'Reilly in Dublin, dating from 1939–1940. Lily worked in the Civil Service and attended night classes in cookery before getting married in the early 1940s. At that time women retired from their jobs when they married and homemaking and cookery skills were very important. This is an unconventional, but interesting method for making a sponge — the result is feather light. I use vanilla extract as flavoring, but you could use lemon or orange rind or coffee essence. One could serve it with poached fruit or berries, and softly whipped cream.

Put the sugar and water into saucepan and melt over the fire. Beat the eggs a little, then pour on the syrup beating at the same time—beat until thick and creamy (10–15 minutes). Sieve the flour lightly into the sponge but do not beat after adding flour. Add desired flavoring. (We used vanilla extract.) Turn into prepared cake pan. Bake at 350°F for 40 minutes. Cool on a wire rack.

Aunt Lil's Wild Strawberry Sponge

5 eggs, free-range if possible
¾ cup superfine sugar
1 cup plus 1 tablespoon
   all-purpose flour

FILLING
1½ cups cream
12oz–1lb wild strawberries or
   fraises du bois
superfine sugar, for sprinkling

one 9 x 12-inch jelly roll pan

When I was a little girl I spent a few weeks of my summer holiday each year on my great aunt and uncle's farm near Two-Mile-Borris in Co. Tipperary. Noard was a working farm. One of my favorite haunts was the long boreen down to the bog where I picked wild strawberries into a little tin "ponnie". I still remember the desperate inner struggle to prevent myself from eating too many of the exquisite wild berries so that Aunt Lil would have enough to sprinkle over her tender sheet of sponge.

Preheat the oven to 375°F. Line the bottom and sides of the pan with parchment paper. Brush the paper with melted butter and dust with flour and superfine sugar.

Put the eggs and superfine sugar into a bowl over a saucepan of simmering water. Whisk the mixture until it is light and fluffy. Take it off the heat and continue to whisk until the mixture is cool again. (If you use an electric mixer, no heat is required.) Sieve in about one-third of the flour at a time and fold it into the mousse using a large spatula or metal spoon.

Pour the mixture gently into the pan. Bake in the preheated oven for 12–15 minutes. It is cooked when it feels firm to the touch in the center. The edges will have shrunk in slightly from the sides of the pan. Lay a piece of parchment paper on your work surface and sprinkle it evenly with superfine sugar. Turn the sponge onto the sheet of parchment paper. Remove the pan and parchment paper from the bottom of the cake and allow to cool.

Meanwhile whisk the cold cream until softly whipped. When the cake is cold, spread whipped cream over the top, cover with wild strawberries, sprinkle with superfine sugar and serve.

Jam Sandwich

Serves 6–8

2 eggs
their weight in flour and butter and
   weight of one in sugar
1 teaspoon baking powder
jam

two round 7-inch cake pans,
   greased and dusted with flour
   and sugar

This is from Nancy Elliott's notebook, and is credited to M.C. Knight in 1865.

Beat the egg yolks and whites separately. To the yolks add sugar and butter which has previously been creamed. Sift in the flour, then the whites beaten to stiff and lastly the baking powder. Bake in a moderate oven, spread with jam when cool.

Cheese Cakes

The little buns commonly known in Ireland as cheese cakes don't actually include any cheese in the ingredients, but may have descended from Richmond Cheese Cakes or Maids of Honor made in Tudor times, and traditionally associated with Richmond-upon-Thames. In one of her articles in the *Irish Independent* newspaper, in the early 1950s, Monica Nevin mentions one legend associated with them: "When the English Court was due to leave London for Hampton Court, a party, including some Maids of Honor to the Queen, would be sent in advance to see that everything was in readiness at Hampton Court for the arrival of the Monarch. The Maids of Honor would break their journey at Richmond for refreshments. The little puff pastries filled with curds etc., which were always part of the refreshment, became known as Maids of Honor." They really were cheese cakes in those days, made with a mixture of curds flavored with almonds, sweetened with sugar, and lightened with eggs.

Citron Cheese Cakes

This recipe came from a very old Dublin newspaper cutting in Nancy Elliott's book, probably early 1900s. It sounds delicious.

Beat one pint of curds in a mortar until they are perfectly smooth; blanch and pound 4oz of sweet almonds, with a spoonful of orange water to prevent their oiling; well beat the yolks of four eggs, and mix them with curds and almonds; then add two Naples biscuits [cookies] (grated); 2½oz of loaf sugar (powdered small), all well together. Line some patty tins [cake pans] with the rich pastry, and fill with the mixture, put slips of citron on the top of each and bake them quickly.

To Macaroon Cheese Cakes

The Lough Rynn Manuscript (1865) had a recipe describing how to create a macaroon topping for cheesecakes.

Take two ounces of bitter almonds and analogous quantity of sweet syrup, a pound of loaf sugar well pounded and sifted with the whites of four eggs well beaten. The sugar and almonds must be pounded together in a mortar and wet with the eggs as they are pounding. The same baking as for tarts will be sufficient. They must be pasted over at the top of the tarts with the white of an egg laid on with a brush. This quantity will make twelve cheesecakes of a small size.

Almond Cheese Cake

This was included in the Pope papers (1823–1890).

Take half a pound of sweet almonds, and a few bitter pounded not very fine, half a pound of white sugar, pounded very fine and well dried. The whites of four eggs beaten to a froth. When the oven is ready, mix all together as quickly as possible and put it into the tins lined with paste. Put the white of one egg to the almonds when pounding.

Lemon Cheese Cakes

Cheese cakes were a great favorite for afternoon tea or a Sunday treat. This recipe is taken from Annie Kiely's manuscript book

Make some nice paste ½lb flour and ½lb butter, line some patty pans with it. Cream ¼lb butter and ¼lb caster sugar, 3 eggs, 6ozs flour, ½ teaspoon baking power, rind and juice of 1 lemon, put one teaspoon of the mixture in each patty pans and bake for ¼ hour.

This recipe comes from Giana Ferguson's family manuscript book of recipes and cures which was started in King's Bromley in 1777. Called Oringe Chees Cakes, this recipe comes from the earlier part of the book. The hand changes throughout the book as different people took over writing it. The recipe doesn't give baking instructions or how many cakes it makes.

Take ½ pd of almonds blanch and beat with orange flower water 2oz, 8 eggs, ½ ye whites, ½ pd of sugar. ye rine of an orange or lemon finely boil till tender and finely beat mix all together and when well beat altogether take 3pd of butter melted and almost cold, stir it well in and so fill ye cheesecakes dust some sugar over ym as you put in ye oven.

Makes 12 (approximately)

4oz rough puff or good shortcrust
  pastry (we used shortcrust)
1 egg
2oz superfine sugar
1oz ground almonds
1oz ground rice
1 teaspoon grated lemon rind
1–2 teaspoons of orange flower
  water (we used 2 teaspoons)
2 tablespoons (¼ stick) butter

Monica Nevin's Cheese Cakes

This delicious recipe is from Rose Hanlon's scrapbook. We couldn't stop eating them when they came out of the oven.

If a richer mixture is desired use 2oz ground almonds and omit the ground rice.
  Make the pastry and roll it out very thinly. Cut into rounds and line about 1 dozen patty pans. Beat the egg and sugar until thick and frothy. Add the ground almonds, rice, and flavorings and mix well. Lastly, stir in the butter, melted but not oiled.
  Put a good teaspoonful or so of this mixture in each of the paper baking cups and bake in a moderately hot oven, 350°F, for 15 minutes.

Makes 24

PASTRY
scant 1 cup flour
½ stick butter
cold water

FILLING
raspberry jam
½ stick butter
2oz sugar
1 egg, beaten
3oz flour
¼ oz baking powder

Welsh Cheese Cakes

These Welsh cheese cakes in Lily O'Reilly's 1940 notebook are more like what we now know as the cheese cakes that were baked at home. They are like mini Bakewell tarts, and often had a little cross of pastry or a halved blanched almond on top, or were sometimes iced with a little white glacé icing.

Make shortcrust pastry in the usual way. Turn onto a lightly floured board, roll out about ¼ inch thick. Cut into rounds with a 3-inch cutter and use to line lightly greased patty pans. Put a teaspoon of jam into each. Put butter and sugar into a bowl, beat to a cream, add beaten egg and sifted flour alternately, add baking powder with the last addition of flour. Put a teaspoon of the mixture on top of the jam and cook in a moderate oven for 20–30 minutes. When cooked, loosen with a skewer, remove from the pan and cool on a wire rack.

1lb cooked potatoes, mashed
¾–scant 1 cup all-purpose flour
½ teaspoon salt
1 or 2 Macintosh apples
2 tablespoons butter
sugar, for sprinkling

Potato Apple Cake

This was the highlight of a farmhouse tea in Ulster, particularly in Armagh in the apple growing season. For Halloween night, a ring would be hidden in one of the cakes. The late Monica Sheridan, the much loved television cook of the 1970s, associated this recipe with crisp autumn evenings when she was a child in Tyrone. She put a pinch of cinnamon over the apples, when adding the butter and sugar—a nice touch.

Mix together the potatoes, flour, and salt. Roll the potato mixture into a round about ¾ inch thick. Divide into four farls (shaped like pie wedges). Slice a couple of layers of raw apple onto two of the farls and put the other two farls on top. Pinch around the edges to seal. Heat a griddle or a non-stick skillet, or preheat the oven to 350°F.

Cook on both sides until the cake is brown on both sides and the apple is soft in the center (about 20 minutes). Slit each cake crossways with a knife. Cover the tender apples with slices of butter and sprinkle with sugar. Replace the tops and return to the griddle or oven until the butter and sugar have melted. This forms a delicious sauce. Remove carefully onto warm plates, and serve immediately. Fiddly to make—but delicious!

1 cup (2 sticks) butter
1 cup plus 2 tablespoons superfine
    sugar
rind of 1 orange
4 eggs, free-range if possible
1¾ cups all-purpose white flour
1 teaspoon baking powder
1 tablespoon of orange juice
candied orange peel, to decorate

ORANGE FILLING
½ cup (1 stick) butter
1½ cups plus 1 tablespoon
    confectioners' sugar
rind of 1 orange
1 tablespoon orange juice

ORANGE GLACÉ ICING
1¾ cups confectioners' sugar
juice of 1 orange

two round 8-inch cake pans, or one
    11 x 1½ inch pan

Aunt Florence's Orange Cake

When my Aunt Florence brings a present of this delicious cake in a tin, lots of people suddenly emerge out of the woodwork pleading for a slice. Without question it's the best orange cake any of us have ever eaten. In 2007 this cake and Porter Cake were chosen by the Irish government as Ireland's official birthday cakes to mark the 50th anniversary of the founding of the EU.

Line the base of each tin with parchment paper.

Cream the butter and gradually add the superfine sugar. Beat until soft and light and quite pale in color. Add the orange rind. Add the eggs one at a time, beating well between each addition. (If the butter and sugar are not creamed properly, or if you add the eggs too fast, the mixture will curdle, resulting in a cake with a heavier texture.) Sieve the flour and baking powder and stir in gradually. Mix all together lightly; stir in the orange juice.

Divide the mixture evenly between the two pans, hollowing it slightly in the center. Bake the cake in a moderate oven, 350°F, for 35 minutes. Turn out onto a wire rack and allow to cool.

Meanwhile, make the filling. Cream the butter; add the confectioners' sugar and orange rind. Beat in the orange juice a little at a time.

To make the icing, simply squeeze the juice from an orange and add enough to the confectioners' sugar to make a spreadable icing.

When the cakes are cold, split each one in two halves and spread with a little filling, then sandwich the pieces together. Spread icing over the top and sides and decorate the top, if you like, with candied peel. This cake keeps very well—if you can hide it!

Gur Cake

Gur Cake was "bought in the shops but seldom made in the home," according to the Dublin folklorist Eamonn MacThomís, who gave me this colorful description: "At the end of the day a shop would have excess bread, excess biscuits [cookies], excess cakes. They put them aside for a week, by which time the bread was rock hard and the biscuits were all soft and mushy, so they'd put the whole lot in a barrel, put a bucket of water in on top and stir it all up into a mush. Then they'd throw in a couple of tins of treacle [molasses], a bit of candied peel, a few currants or raisins or anything like that and mix it all in. Then they put all the mixture on top of a layer of pastry and then put another layer of pastry on top again. In fact there used to be a lovely marking on top and everyone was convinced in Inchicore that the woman in the shop used her false teeth to mark it, but she maintained that she did it with a fork! Then they'd paint it with egg to give it the shine and sprinkle it with a bit of sugar to give it a glisten. It only took about 10 minutes in the oven because it was all pre-cooked. The smell of that coming out of the oven on a big tray was gorgeous!"

Food Historian Regina Sexton wrote about the Cork version of Gur Cake in the *Irish Examiner* in November 1995: 'Throughout the 1920s, 30s, and 40s, stale bread puddings enjoyed immense popularity in Cork, especially with the city's children. So popular was the pudding with children, that they often delivered their own private batches of stale bread from home to the shops in the hope that this gesture would provoke the owners into making the tasty treat. On the day the pudding was prepared, excitement reached fever pitch, especially when the hordes of hungry children saw the shop window steam up; a clear signal that the pudding was made and ready for sale. Hot slices were devoured and wolfed down while sitting on the street kerbs. A more commonly known version of the bread pudding is the slab-shaped cake known variously as "Donkey's Gudge" or "Donkey's Wedding Cake." Given the cake's distinctive brown color and characteristic texture, the etymology of "gudge" is best left to the imagination. In Dublin, Donkey's Gudge is known as Gur Cake, and here again it has a particular affinity with children. Indeed, the term "gurrier" (meaning a tough street urchin) is said to derive from the fact that Dublin street children readily consumed Gur Cake on a regular basis. Over time the often derogatory terms for the cake and its association with poorer children led to its renaming. Posh labels such as Chester Cake, Fruit Slice, and Tipsy Cake (with added alcohol) have attempted to clean up the image of the cake, but unfortunately say nothing of its colorful past.'

Gur Cake

Makes 12

shortcrust pastry, enough to line and cover the pan
6oz stale cake, crumbled
3–4 tablespoons all-purpose flour
½ teaspoon baking powder
2 teaspoons mixed spice
3oz mixed dried fruit
¼oz candied peel
4–5 tablespoons milk
1 large egg, beaten; free-range if possible

one rectangular 8 x 12-inch pan, greased

Most bakeries made a version of these fruity slabs in an effort to recycle stale bread and cake scraps from the previous day's baking. The Dublin cookery writer Honor Moore tells me that they used to be known as "depth charges" around the docks area of Dublin in the 40s. Sold at one old penny for a slab between two and three inches square and about one inch or more thick, they were the school dinners of the day. One or two would sustain a pupil "mitching" from school—or "on the gur," as it was known in Dublin.

Preheat the oven to 375°F. Make the shortcrust pastry, cover and let it rest while you make the filling. Mix the cake crumbs, flour, baking powder, spice, fruit, and candied peel together. Gently heat the milk and mix well with the dry ingredients to make a soft mixture. Whisk the egg and stir in. Roll out half the pastry and line the pan with it. Spread the fruit mixture over the pastry. Roll out the remaining pastry to cover it and make a few slits in the top. Bake for 45 minutes–1 hour. When done, cool in the pan and cut into big squares.

Makes 9–12 squares

PASTRY
3¼ cups flour
small pinch salt
2½ sticks margarine (I use butter)
8 tablespoons very cold water

FILLING
1 pint stale bread, cut up small
¾ cup flour
1 teaspoon mixed spice
1 teaspoon baking powder
6 tablespoons (¾ stick) butter
1 cup plus 2 tablespoons brown
   sugar
⅔ cup currants
⅔ cup raisins
1 egg
¾ cup milk
grated rind of 1 lemon
superfine sugar, for sprinkling

one square 10 x 2-inch cake pan

Makes 35–40

2⅔ cups all-purpose flour
¾ cup plus 2 tablespoons superfine
   sugar
1½ sticks butter
2oz currants
2 teaspoons caraway seeds
½ teaspoon baking powder
1 egg, free-range if possible

Chester Cake

This recipe is from a newspaper cutting of Mary Frances Keating recipes from the early 1950s. This tasted supremely good despite the quantity of bread. This is the Cork version of Gur Cake—Scotland has Black Bun and canny bakers everywhere probably had their own recipe for using up stale cake.

Sieve flour and salt. Cut fat through flour till it resembles coarse breadcrumbs. Add water, carefully mixing in with knife to a fairly stiff dough. Gather and knead gently for a few seconds. Divide in two.

Soak bread in cold water and squeeze dry as possible. Sieve flour, spice, and baking powder, rub in fat, add sugar and fruit. Mix well. Beat up egg in milk and add lemon rind, and add to flour mixture. Add squeezed bread. Mixture should be soft but not sloppy, so squeeze bread as dry as possible.

Roll out the pastry, use one sheet to line the pan. Put filling on top of pastry in the pan. Place the other sheet of pastry on top and prick the top of pastry. Bake in moderate oven, 350°F, for 1½ hours. Cut into squares. Dust well with superfine sugar.

Wakes Cakes

Margaret O'Connor, an 88-year-old lady from Moyard in Co. Galway, tells me that these cookies were served at wakes (see page 123) in south Connemara years ago. They are thoroughly delicious.

Mix together the flour and sugar, then rub in the butter. Add the currants, caraway seeds, baking powder, and the egg to make a crumbly paste.

Roll out the paste thinly and cut into rounds (we use a 2½-inch cutter). Bake in a moderate oven, 350°F, for 20 minutes until the cakes are golden brown.

Funeral Buns

Mrs Marie Kelly of Ballon, Co. Carlow, believes that this recipe is over 150 years old. At that time funeral buns were a great favorite and were always given to the mourners at wakes and funerals. They were, of course, washed down with lashings of whiskey which was as easily given then as tea is now.

Take two stones of flour, 1lb of butter and 1lb of sugar rubbed together, 3lbs of currants, ginger, seeds, cinnamon to taste, and rosewater mixed with milk. This makes forty eight cakes each weighing 1lb before baking and costing three pence each. Make them round and bake them a fine brown. They will also take one pint of barm in the mixing.

Makes 12

½ cup (1 stick) butter
½ cup plus 1 tablespoon superfine
  sugar
2 eggs, free-range if possible
vanilla extract, orange or lemon rind
1 cup plus 1 tablespoon flour
¾ teaspoon baking powder
1 tablespoon milk or water

Queen Cakes and Other Dainties

Queen cakes, butterfly buns, and the like were often served for tea on Nollaig na mBan *(Women's Christmas) which was celebrated on the twelfth day of Christmas. This was the women's own feast day. There would be a splendid high tea when all the dainties that the women really enjoyed were served. Pretty little buns like these are often the first recipe that children attempt and they are still as adorable as ever.*

Cream the butter until really soft. Add the sugar and beat until white and creamy, either with your hand, as many of our ancestors did, or with a wooden spoon.

Beat the eggs and flavoring and add gradually to the creamed butter and sugar. Beat well. If preferred, the eggs may be broken and beaten into the mixture one at a time. A little sieved flour may be added between each addition of egg, if liked.

Stir in the remainder of the flour mixed with the baking powder, adding a little water, or milk, if necessary for a dropping consistency. Put the mixture in spoonfuls into well greased patty pans and bake for about 20 minutes at 400°F. Cool on a wire rack.

4 tablespoons (½ stick) butter
¾ cup confectioners' sugar
2 teaspoons cocoa powder

Chocolate Icing

Beat the butter, sugar, and cocoa together. Moisten with hot water to spreading consistency. Use to ice the cakes.

⅔ cup confectioners' sugar
finely grated rind of 1 lemon
1–2 tablespoons freshly squeezed
  lemon juice, strained

Lemon Icing

Sieve the confectioners' sugar into a mixing bowl and add the lemon rind. Add the lemon juice and stir to combine. Use to ice the cakes.

Fairy Cakes

Follow the recipe for Queen Cakes on page 299, adding 2oz plump golden raisin.

Cherry Cakes

Follow the recipe for Queen Cakes on page 299, adding 2oz chopped crystallized cherries.

Butterfly Buns

Follow the recipe for Queen Cakes on page 299. Cut the tops off each of the baked queen cakes. Cut these pieces in half and set aside. Put a little home-made raspberry jam and a blob of cream on to the bottom part of the cake. Replace the two little pieces, arranging them like butterfly wings. Dredge with confectioners' sugar. Serve on a pretty plate with a doyley underneath.

Coffee Cake

1 cup (2 sticks) butter
1 cup plus 1 tablespoon superfine sugar
4 eggs, free-range if possible
1¾ cups all-purpose flour
1 teaspoon baking powder
2–2½fl oz coffee essence (Irel or Camp)

COFFEE BUTTER CREAM FILLING
4 tablespoons (½ stick) butter
⅔ cup confectioners' sugar
1–2 teaspoons coffee essence

COFFEE GLACÉ ICING
1⅓ cups confectioners' sugar
scant 1 tablespoon coffee essence
2 tablespoons boiling water

DECORATION
hazelnuts or chocolate coffee beans

two round 8-inch cake pans, lined with greaseproof paper

Coffee cake made with Irel or Camp coffee essence has been popular for many years and I think it still makes the best coffee cake. The Johnson family began roasting coffee in Ireland in 1913. A liquid coffee essence with chicory and added sugar was manufactured and sold in bottle form under the brand name Irel (IRELand). This product has been used in households across Ireland ever since. During the sugar-rationed war years it was an ideal hot drink, as it was already sweetened. After World War II, demand fell as it was seen as a war-time product and the nation's trends moved to a pure ground coffee. Irel followed this trend and a ground coffee was produced, sold in a tin and available in both the food service and grocery sectors. Today, Irel is still roasted in Lisburn by fourth generation Johnson family and still used for making cakes. Camp Coffee is a Scottish product, which began production in 1876 by Paterson & Sons Ltd. in a plant on Charlotte Street, Glasgow, and it too is still being made.

Preheat the oven to 350°F. Brush the bottom and sides of the lined pans with melted butter and dust with flour.

Cream the butter until soft. Add the sugar and beat until pale and light in texture. Whisk the eggs and add to the mixture, bit by bit, beating well between each addition. Sieve the flour with the baking powder and stir gently into the cake mixture. Finally add the coffee essence. Spoon the mixture into the prepared pans and bake for about 30 minutes. Cool the cakes on a wire rack.

To make the filling, cream the butter with the sieved confectioners' sugar and add coffee essence to taste. To make the icing, sieve the confectioners' sugar into a bowl. Add coffee essence and enough boiling water to make icing the consistency of thick cream.

When the cakes are cold, sandwich them together with coffee butter cream. Ice the top and sides with coffee glacé icing. Decorate with hazelnuts or chocolate coffee beans.

Delicious Cakes for Afternoon Tea

This cutting came from a cookery column in a 1911 Dublin newspaper: "It is always useful to have a few cakes in the house which will retain their freshness if kept in tins. I know several women who make a point of making a large batch of cakes every weekend, and they tell me that new recipes are very acceptable. These which we have gathered together for today are especially reliable, cheap, tasty, and they will keep ten days if put into tightly packed tins." Here is a selection of the recipes.

Vanilla Buns makes 25

These cost about 6½d. This is a capital way of making them.

Ingredients: ½lb flour, 1 teaspoon baking powder, 3oz butter, 2oz superfine sugar, 2 eggs, essence of vanilla (we used vanilla extract).

Method: Mix together the flour, baking powder, and sugar, beat the eggs and stir into them 10 drops of pure vanilla extract. Cream the butter, add the dry ingredients, lastly the eggs. Divide into pieces about the size of a walnut, place on a greased baking sheet and bake for ten minutes in a quick oven. (We baked them for 15 minutes at 350°F.) Also good sandwiched with raspberry jam or melted chocolate.

Spice Buns makes 24

These are very popular with children, and they will like them at the school lunch hour. Cost about 6d. This recipe uses dripping.

Ingredients: 12oz flour, one teaspoon each of mixed spice and ground ginger, 1 teaspoon of baking powder, 3oz demerara sugar, 4½oz clarified dripping or lard.

Method: Rub dripping into the flour till no lumps are left; add the other ingredients and moisten with the beaten egg and a little milk; make them into small cakes and quickly put to bake in a moderate oven. (We baked them for 20 minutes at 350°F.)

Marmalade Buns makes 12

Cost 6d.

Ingredients: 6oz fine flour, 3oz superfine sugar, 2oz butter, 2½fl oz milk, 1 egg, 1 tablespoon marmalade (2 or 3 are better), 1 teaspoon of baking powder.

Method: Cream the butter and sugar, add the egg and the marmalade, the peel of which must be cut into small pieces, then add the milk and last the flour mixed with the baking powder; place the mixture in greased patty pans and bake in a sharp oven for about quarter of an hour. (We baked them in bun cases in a patty pan tray for 20 minutes at 350°F.)

Cake Dances

Irish country people were always happy to have an excuse for festivity, and the tradition of the cake dance goes back to medieval times or even earlier. It is still vivid in folk memory in many parts of the country.

On fine evenings from Easter Sunday onwards they would gather at crossroads and dance to the lively tunes of local musicians. The cake in question might have been a currant bread, barmbrack, or even a simple loaf of griddle bread, depending on the occasion. If it was a special feast — for example, Easter, Whitsun, or midsummer — the crust of the cake might be decorated with birds or animals. The cake was proudly laid out on a white linen cloth on top of a milk churn and decorated with wild flowers and whatever fruit was in season.

As soon as the musicians struck up, dancing began and the couples swirled for hours and hours. The winners might be the handsomest young couple who were lightest on their feet, or those who danced the longest, or a pair who announced their engagement. The winners who had the honor of "taking the cake" cheerfully shared it with their friends.

The earliest record of a cake dance was in Co. Westmeath in 1682: "On the patron day in most parishes, as also on the feasts of Easter and Whitsuntide, the more ordinary sort of people meet near the ale house in the afternoon at some convenient spot of ground and dance for a cake. The cake is provided at the charge of the ale wife and is advanced on a board on top of a pike about ten foot high; this board is round and from it rises a kind of garland, tied with meadow flowers if it be early summer. If later the garland has the addition of apples set in round pegs fastened into it. All dance in a large ring around the bushes they call the garland, and those who hold out the longest win the cake and the apples."

Makes 24–32, depending on size

2⅔ cups all-purpose flour
2½ sticks butter
1 cup plus 2 tablespoons superfine sugar
3oz ground rice
good pinch of salt
good pinch of baking powder
vanilla or superfine sugar, for sprinkling

10 x 15-inch jelly roll pan

Shortbread

It has become a tradition in Kinoith always to have shortbread in the Aga. Many years ago when I was attempting to hide the shortbread from the children, who seemed to devour it as fast as it was made, I discovered quite by accident that it keeps beautifully for days in the coolest oven of our ancient four-door Aga.

Sieve the dry ingredients into a bowl. Cut the butter into cubes and rub in until the whole mixture comes together. Spread evenly into the pan.

Our unorthodox but very effective way of doing this is to spread the shortbread mixture roughly in the pan, cover the whole tray with pure plastic wrap, then roll the mixture flat with a rolling pin. Remove the plastic wrap and prick with a fork. Bake the shortbread for 1–1½ hours in a low oven, 275–300°F. It should be pale golden but fully cooked through. Cut into squares or fingers while still hot. Sprinkle with superfine or vanilla sugar and allow to cool in the pan.

Makes 18 approx.

1 cup plus 1 tablespoon oatmeal
¾ cup plus 2 tablespoons superfine sugar
3oz shredded coconut
4 tablespoons (½ stick) butter
1 egg
1 teaspoon baking powder
a pinch of salt

Coconut Flapjacks

One of my best finds—very moreish.

Mix the dry ingredients together. Melt the butter and stir it into the dry ingredients, together with the beaten egg. Grease a baking sheet, or line with a sheet of parchment paper. Pile the mixture on it in small heaps of equal size, approximately 1oz in weight. Bake in a moderate oven until light brown, about 20 minutes.

2 tablespoons milk
½ teaspoon bread soda (baking soda)
1oz golden raisins
2oz ginger, preserved in syrup, chopped
½ cup butter
½ cup plus 1 tablespoon soft brown sugar
2 eggs, free-range if possible
8fl oz molasses
1¾ cups flour
1 teaspoon ground ginger
1oz raisins

Gingerbread

A much loved spicy bread, gingerbread was sold at fairs and markets, and given to children as a treat. There are many references in old cookery books to it—in fact ground ginger was almost as popular as caraway seeds. This recipe is particularly delicious.

Warm the milk gently with the bread soda and remove from the heat. Add the golden raisins and preserved ginger.

Cream the butter, add the sugar and beat until light and fluffy. Add in the eggs, one by one. Stir in the molasses and fruit mixture, then add the flour and ground ginger. Mix well. Pour into a large loaf pan which has been lined with parchment paper.

Bake at 325°F for 1–1½ hours. Cool on a wire rack. Gingerbread keeps well in an airtight tin.

Mrs Ray's Meringues

Makes about 20

4 egg whites
1 cup plus 2 tablespoons superfine sugar
pink and green food coloring (optional)
whipped cream

Florence Ray was one of my friends at the village school. She lived in a very grand house called Phillipsburg. Occasionally she asked me home to play. It was a more formal arrangement than with some of my other friends, for her mother would have afternoon tea spread out on the drawing-room table. It was here that I first tasted meringues, light, crisp little blobs, green, palest pink and white, deliciously chewy in the center and crisp on the outside. I longed to know how to make them so I could tell Mummy, but at that time was far too timid and overawed to ask.

Beat the egg whites until stiff but not yet dry. Fold in half the sugar. Beat again until the mixture will stand in a firm dry peak. Fold the remaining sugar in carefully. If you wish, divide the mixture into three bowls. Add a few drops of pink food coloring to one and a few drops of green to the second, leaving the third one white. Mix both to a delicate pale color. Line a baking sheet with parchment paper. Spoon blobs of mixture onto the sheet. Bake in a preheated oven at 200°F for about 4 hours. Allow to cool, then sandwich together in pairs with whipped cream.

Granny Nicholson's Pastry Shells

Makes about 30

1¾ cups all-purpose flour
a pinch of salt
1¼–1½ sticks butter
4–5fl oz very cold water
homemade raspberry jam
softly whipped cream

Nothing disappears so fast as these little cakes! They crackle in your mouth and taste utterly irresistible.

To make the pastry, sieve the flour and salt into a cold bowl. Cut the butter into knobs about the size of a sugar lump and add to the flour. Do not rub in, but add just enough cold water to bind the pastry together. Mix first with a fork then bring together with your hand.

Wrap the pastry in plastic wrap and leave it to relax in the fridge for 10 minutes. Flour a board and roll the pastry into a strip. This should be done carefully—do not over-stretch or break the pastry surface. Fold the strip into 3 and turn, so the folded edge is to your left, like a closed book.

Roll out again into a strip ½ inch thick. Fold in 3 again, cover and leave in the fridge for a further 15 minutes. Roll and fold the pastry twice as before, then chill again for 15 minutes. Roll and fold again, by which time the pastry should be ready for use, with no signs of streakiness. If it does still appear streaky, give it another roll immediately and rest for a further 15 minutes. Roll the pastry out thinly and stamp out 4-inch rounds, (this is most successfully done using the top of a glass). Fit the pastry circles into round-bottomed bun trays. Fill with little squares of paper towel (years ago we used the tissue paper that wrapped oranges) and dried peas or baking beans. Chill again before baking.

Bake in a preheated moderate oven at 350°F for about 15 minutes or until crispy and lightly browned. Remove the paper and beans and cool the pastry shells on a wire rack. They can then be piled into each other and kept in an airtight tin. Just before serving, fill each pastry shell with a teaspoonful of raspberry jam and put a blob of cream on top. Serve on a cake plate on a pretty paper doyley.

Jam Tarts

Doris Bewley describes how to make little jam tarts in the 1932 edition of School Notes. *Filling jam tarts was many a child's first introduction to baking, and they are still as appealing as ever. They would sometimes be made with pastry leftover from an apple tart.*

Shortcrust Pastry

Jam

Roll the pastry out very thinly. The pastry must fit exactly into the patty tins. Grease the tins. Put in the pastry. Add a little jam. Decorate as required with little strips of pastry. Bake for 7 minutes at 400°F.

Golden Syrup Tart

Golden syrup tart and little jam tarts were also very popular for home baking during the 1950s, and most cupboards contained a tin of Lyle's Golden Syrup (corn syrup) in the green and gold tin. This recipe is from Rose Hanlon's scrapbook. Sometimes the tart was divided into wedge-shaped sections divided by strips of pastry, and jam was put in some sections and syrup in the rest.

Line a 8-inch tart plate with shortcrust pastry. Mix together 2 tablespoons corn syrup and 2 tablespoons fine breadcrumbs. Add the juice of ½ lemon and mix well. Spread this mixture on the pastry and then arrange some thin strips of pastry trellis fashion on top of the tart. Bake in a hot oven 425°F for the first ten minutes, then reduce the heat and continue baking until the pastry is cooked, about half an hour in all. Bake for 7 minutes at 400°F.

Spiced Custard Tartlets

Makes 16

SHORTCRUST PASTRY
1¾ cups all-purpose flour
1½ sticks butter
pinch of salt
2 teaspoons confectioners' sugar
a little beaten egg or egg yolk and water to bind

FILLING
1¼ cups cream
2 tablespoons superfine sugar
2 eggs and 1 egg yolk
1 teaspoon grated nutmeg

This recipe came from an old newspaper cutting in Rose Hanlon's scrapbook. I'm not sure how traditional these are but they are delicious.

Make the pastry in the usual way and leave to relax in the fridge for 1 hour.

Cut out circles of pastry with a 3 inch cutter. Grease patty pans and line each pan with pastry. Chill for 15 minutes. Line each with parchment paper and fill with baking beans. Bake blind at 350°F for 15 minutes.

Whisk the filling ingredients together and spoon into the cooked pastry shells. Return to the oven and cook until set, 30 minutes approximately. Serve warm.

Red Cross Cookies

Makes 40

1lb flour
2 sticks butter
1 teaspoon baking soda
2 teaspoons ground ginger
1 tablespoon brown sugar
1 teaspoon mixed spice
a pinch of salt
½ cup molasses

This is another of Nancy Elliott's recipes. Don't know what the connection is to Red Cross, she doesn't relate where the name comes from. I wonder if this is the original Kimberley cookie?

Gently heat the molasses. Mix all the dry ingredients with the butter and make sufficiently moist to make a nice dough with the warm molasses. Roll out and cut into cookes, bake in a moderate oven at 350°F for 10–12 minutes.

These cookies can be sandwiched together with buttercream, you would then have 20 cookies. We tried this filling and they were delicious: 1 stick butter, 1¹/₃ cups confectioners' sugar, ½ teaspoon vanilla extract. Beat butter and icing sugar together and add vanilla extract. Sandwich cookies in pairs.

Drinks and Preserves

The more rural parts of Ireland did not get electricity until quite recently, and it is therefore only in the latter part of this century that such conveniences as refrigerators, never mind freezers, have been installed, in most houses. Perhaps for this reason, the traditional arts of preserving are still very much alive in Ireland, to keep food from a time when it is plentiful for consumption during the lean months of the year. Almost every household, whether a large country house or the cottage of a laborer's family, would have had its pantry of jams, preserves, bottled fruits, and cordials to provide a welcome touch of interest, and also some vitamins, to a monotonous winter diet.

Sugar is now used widely, but the traditional sweetening was honey, and beekeeping has a long and honorable history in Ireland—one I like to carry on, with my own hives of bees making Ballymaloe honey. I have included a recipe here for mead, made from honey, as drunk by the heroes of the early Irish legends. I cannot guarantee that your exploits will be as great as theirs!

No book about Irish food would be complete without mention of our other great traditional drinks—buttermilk, tea and, of course, whiskey. Many accounts from the 18th and 19th centuries attest not only to the quantities of food consumed in Ireland, but also to the prodigious drinking.

Marmalade

There was no shortage of marmalade recipes in the collections I studied, including Seville orange, sweet orange, grapefruit, lemon, and combinations of them. Our traditional Seville orange is my own favorite. John D. Sheridan, the Irish writer of humorous columns in the *Irish Independent* during the 1950s, wrote a great piece entitled "Marmalade Time." Here is an extract:

"This is marmalade time, it comes just a little ahead of the crocuses. This is marmalade time and no home is safe. During these steel-grey days women look through (a) cookery books (b) cookery notebooks (did you ever see a cookery notebook that wasn't wobbly-waisted from flour siftings and pasted clippings?) and (c) the daily papers, looking for marmalade recipes."

He continues: "All that is left now is the crisis, which is known officially as 'Test for jellying'—you put saucerfuls of the stuff on the window-sill and time its congealing. Then you let it cool, pour it into pots, and give most of it away. The Irish make each other's marmalade. That is why the making of marmalade is such a tense and wearying process—no woman can afford to let herself down before the neighbours. Everyone who calls at marmalade time gets a pot—'just to see what you think of it'—and then sends round a pot of her own in exchange. It's an old Irish custom—a sort of jammy fosterage. But it works out pretty well. You live on the neighbours, and they live on you."

Old Fashioned Marmalade

Makes about 7lb

2lb Seville oranges (about 3–4 oranges)
1 lemon
9½ cups water
9 cups granulated sugar

Seville and Malaga oranges give a distinctive flavor to the marmalade. They come into the shops after Christmas and are around for 4–5 weeks. The peel of the oranges must be absolutely soft before the sugar is added, otherwise it will become very hard at that point and impossible to soften.

Wash the fruit, cut in half, and squeeze out the juice. Remove the loose membrane but not the pith with a spoon, put with the seeds, tie them in a piece of cheesecloth and soak for 30 minutes in the cold water. Slice the peel finely or coarsely, depending on how you like your marmalade. Put the peel, orange and lemon juice, bag of seeds, and water into a nonreactive bowl or saucepan and leave overnight.

Next day, bring everything to a boil and simmer gently for about 2 hours until the peel is really soft and the liquid is reduced by half or even more. Squeeze all the liquid from the bag of seeds and remove it. Add the warmed sugar and stir until all the sugar has been dissolved. Increase the heat and bring to a full rolling boil, then cook rapidly, uncovered, until setting point is reached—about 5–10 minutes. Test for a set, either with a sugar thermometer (it should register 220°F), or on a saucer. To do this, put a little marmalade on a cold saucer and let it cool for a few minutes. If it wrinkles when you push it with your finger, it's done.

Stir well and pour immediately into hot sterilized jars. Cover right away and store in a cool, dry, dark place.

Orange Marmalade

This early version comes from the Lough Rynn manuscript dated about 1865. It's not unlike the method we use for Whole Orange Marmalade, which we also make here at the school. Cutting two dozen oranges into sufficiently small chips would take one person an entire day!

"To every pound of Seville oranges (weighed before they are boiled) take one pound and a half of loaf sugar. Steep them from the day before they are boiled. Wipe and dry them very well and put them into a preserving pan or brass skillet. Cover them with cold spring water and boil them until quite tender. They must be kept covered all the time and the water added after they begin to boil quite hot.*

When they are sufficiently done, cut them the cross-way; take out all the pulp, separate the seeds entirely from it and pour a little water on them. Put some of the water in which the oranges were boiled, which may be a pint to every pound of fruit, on the sugar and add that in which the seeds are steeped. Strain through a bit of muslin. Let none of the juice be lost or the pulp. Boil this syrup 'til clear and have the pots ready to put into it. They must be cut with nice small chips and boil all together for half an hour or 'til it comes to a jelly."

*When we make marmalade with whole oranges like this, we put a plate on top to keep the oranges submerged in the water.

Lemon Curd

Lemon curd has been a popular preserve for many years and appears in most of the older cookbooks. It's a short-term preserve and absolutely delicious, either just on bread or scones or as a filling for a light sponge, jelly roll, or lemon layer cake. It was sometimes used to fill little pastry tartlets and topped with meringue. Orange curd can be made in the same way. The method is always the same, but different proportions are given in different recipes. If one had a supply of eggs and butter it wasn't too expensive to make. This is a recipe from a 1930s newspaper cutting:

Allow one egg, one ounce of butter and three and a half ounces of caster sugar to each lemon. Grate the lemon rind, strain the juice, and place in a lined saucepan (or in a stone jam jar in a saucepan of water) with the butter and sugar. Stir over gentle heat until the butter and sugar are melted, then let cool before adding the beaten eggs. Replace in the pan, and cook over slow heat till thick, being careful that it does not boil. Pour into small pots and cover.

Lemon Marmalade

This was contributed by Mrs Johnstown, Newtowngore, to the Tried Favourites cookbook, a compilation of recipes that was probably collected for a Methodist Church fundraiser in Co. Leitrim or Sligo, and possibly published in the late 1940s or early 1950s.

Take seven ordinary sized lemons, slice the fruit quite thinly and take out the seeds. The seeds should be put in a tea cup two-thirds full of cold water, and allowed to stand. To every lb of fruit add three pints of cold water, let it stand for twenty-four hours, then boil until the peel is tender. Let it stand another twenty-four hours, measure, and to every pint add 1¼ lbs sugar. Strain the water from the seeds and add to the fruit, boil for an hour, or until it thickens and becomes transparent. When a little cool put into jars and cover.

Makes about 12 x 7oz jars

6lb apples
rind of 1 lemon, plus juice ½ lemon
water
6lb white sugar
2oz fresh ginger

Apple Cheese

Fruit butters and cheese were very popular and were made in the country house kitchens to serve as accompaniments to cheese or as sweetmeats.

Allow equal quantities of apples and sugar (cookers are best for this). Cut up the apples, but do not peel them. To 6lb apples, allow the juice of half a lemon and the grated rind of a whole one. Place in a jelly pan, almost cover with water, and boil, stirring frequently. When pulpy, rub through a strainer. Boil with the sugar for nearly an hour, adding some root ginger tied in a cheesecloth bag. When ready, remove the ginger and put into jars.

Makes about 7 x 7oz jars

4lb windfall apples (we used
   cooking apples)
2½ cups water
2-inch cinnamon stick
granulated sugar

Apple Conserve

These 1930 cuttings came from an old scrapbook.

Wipe the apples, cut them into quarters without peeling or coring them, put them into a pan with the water and cinnamon, and boil to a pulp. Remove the cinnamon and rub the apples through a strainer. Measure the purée and return it to the pan. (To each pint of apple pulp allow 1¾ cups sugar and cinnamon stick—we got 2 pints of pulp after sieving and used 3½ cup granulated sugar.) Add the requisite amount of sugar, stir until the sugar has melted, then boil fast for 10 minutes, stirring constantly. Put it into dry warm jars, and cover like jam.

Damson Cheese

This recipe was contributed by Mrs Henderson, Cavan, to the Tried Favourites *cookbook. Delicious served with cheese.*

Clean the fruit and put into a large jar or steampot, and cover closely. Cook in a low oven until soft, then rub through a strainer. (This is a labor of love!) Measure the pulp, and put into a preserving kettle with 1¾–2¼ cups sugar to every pint of pulp, according to taste. Boil until greater part of the syrup has evaporated and the pulp has become rather stiff. Stir frequently at first, and almost continually towards the end. Turn into jars, and cover closely. If desired, some of the stones may be cracked and the kernels added to the pulp with the sugar.

Marrow Butter

This is from a 1930 newspaper cutting.

Allow two pounds of sugar, three ounces of butter and 3 lemons for each 2 pounds of marrow. Peel the marrow, cut it into squares, boil until soft, then strain off all the water. Beat the marrow well with sugar, butter, and juice and grated rind of the lemons, then boil for 45 minutes. Pour into jars, leave until cold, then tie down. It will keep for a long time.

Pear Jam

Makes about 4 x 7oz jars

3lb pears
a lump of butter
5¼ cups white sugar
juice and rind of 1 lemon (optional)

One doesn't come across recipes for pear jam very often, so I thought it worth including, although it's actually more like a butter or conserve.

Take 1¾ cups sugar, or a little less (brown will serve quite well), to each 1lb pears. Peel, core, and chop the fruit small. Put a tiny lump of butter in the preserving kettle, add the fruit, and let it cook till soft, then put in the sugar, and boil for an hour, or until the pear is quite soft and the whole thick and rich. Lemon rind and juice are a good addition.

Green Gooseberry Jam

Makes about 5 x 7oz jars

14 cups green gooseberries
2½ cups water
5 or more (depending on size) elderflower heads, tied in cheesecloth (optional)
7¾ cups granulated sugar, warmed

For jam it's best to pick the gooseberries while they are still green and under-ripe. You can add elderflowers for a delicious variation.

Wash the gooseberries, then top and tail them and put them into a wide, stainless-steel preserving kettle with the water and the elderflowers, if using. Simmer for about 30 minutes, until the gooseberries are soft and the contents of the pan have reduced by one-third. Remove the elderflowers and add the warmed sugar, stirring until it has completely dissolved. Boil rapidly for about 10 minutes, until setting point is reached, at 220°F on a jam thermometer. Pour into hot, clean jars. Cover and store in a dry, airy cupboard.

Rhubarb and Ginger Jam

Makes about 8 x 1lb jars

4lb rhubarb (about 12 stalks), trimmed
9 cups granulated sugar
grated zest and juice of 2 organic lemons
2oz fresh ginger, bruised and tied in cheesecloth

This delicious jam should be made when rhubarb is in full season and is not yet thick and tough. I feel it's so worth planting a few stools of rhubarb—it's easy to grow and loves rich, fertile soil and lots of farmyard manure and will emerge every year for ever and ever if you feed it well.

Wipe the rhubarb and cut into 1-inch pieces. Put it into a large, stainless-steel or Pyrex bowl layered with the sugar. Add the lemon zest and juice and let stand overnight.
　　Next day, put the mixture into a preserving kettle, add the fresh, bruised ginger. Bring to a boil until it is a thick pulp, about 30–45 minutes, and test for a set. Remove the bag of ginger and then pour the jam into hot, sterilized jars. Cover and store in a cool, airy cupboard.
　　Note: If you like, 4 tablespoons chopped, candied ginger or preserved stem ginger can be added at the end.

Dried Apricot Jam

Makes about 2 x 7oz jars

3 cups dried apricots
a little flour
7½ cups water
juice of 1 lemon
6¾ cups sugar
½ cup blanched and shredded
almonds, blanched and shredded,
if liked

Jam made from dried apricots features in most of the scrapbooks and old cookbooks. It is a delicious and somewhat forgotten flavor! Sometimes chopped almonds were added. Good apricot jam is one of the main ingredients of almond fingers and it would have been a good pantry item for home bakers, and it would also have been enjoyed on scones and bread. Monica Nevin, in one of her early 1950s columns in Rose Hanlon's scrapbook headed "Shilling a Pound," recalls: "Before the war jam made from dried apricots was one of the cheapest jams to make, costing about fivepence a pound. That cost, of course, included the covers and fuel for cooking the jam. Today I do not think it could be made for less than a shilling a pound. However, it is an easy jam to make and as, by now, serious inroads have been made on the stocks of jam made during the summer, it is worth while making a few pounds to tide us over until the first of the soft fruits ripen." Here is Monica Nevin's recipe:

Wash the apricots thoroughly and cut them in 4 and put them in a basin with the water. Cover them and leave to soak for at least 24 hours. Then put the apricots into a preserving kettle or large saucepan with the water in which they were soaked and the lemon juice. Bring to a boil and simmer gently with the lid on for ½–¾ hour, stirring occasionally.

Add the sugar and the blanched and shredded almonds if using and stir until setting point is reached. Test by putting a teaspoonful of the jam on a cold saucer and cool as quickly as possible. If a skin is formed that wrinkles when a finger is drawn across the surface the jam is ready. If not, continue boiling the jam and test again. It is difficult to give the exact time it will take the jam to set, as much depends on whether a deep or shallow pan is used.

Jellies

Clear, sparkling jellies on a pantry shelf are a joy to behold. Some were made to be used like jam, and others as accompaniments to cold meats.

Elderberry Jelly

Makes 6–8 pots

4lb elderberries
2 quarts water
4lb crab apples or cooking apples,
e.g. Granny Smith or Grenadier
granulated sugar

Elderberries are in season in September and are a very valuable source of Vitamin C. They have long been used to make cordials and wine, as well as in medicine. Recent research indicates that they might be beneficial to the immune system in combating influenza. This recipe comes from Tried Favorites, *and was contributed by H.C. Drumshanbo.*

Put the berries, free from stalks, into half the water, and the apples cut into quarters into the other half of the water. (You can cook both together to save on saucepans.) Bring both to a boil, simmer gently for an hour, strain then mix juices, measure, adding 2¼ cups sugar to each 2½ cups of juice. Boil until a little sets on a cold plate.

Apple Jelly

This is from the Mary Ponsonby Manuscript. She notes that it is very good.

"Take golden or Lemon Pippins. Stew them as for an apple pye, put them into a pan with as much water as will cover them, let them boil till the water tastes very strong of the apple, then drain them through a jelly bag, to every pint of liquor put a pound of fine sugar, and the juice of a lemon, boil it till it jellies, skim it well and when nearly done throw in some lemon peel shred small, a hundred of apples will make three pounds of jelly."

Pickles, Chutneys and Catsups

There is a wealth of recipes for preserving fruit and vegetables in the country house manuscript cookbooks, as well as more recent books and scrapbooks that were lovingly assembled by keen cooks, mostly from newspaper cuttings and recipes which they swapped with friends. Having a "good recipe" for a particular preserve was a source of pride, particularly if it won a prize at a show or competition. It was then guarded carefully.

Lemon Catsup

This is from Mrs Pigott in the Mary Ponsonby manuscript. It was interesting to note that lemons seemed to be quite plentiful in the country house kitchens, judging by the number of recipes I came across.

"Take one dozen of the largest and fairest lemons you can get, quarter them the long way, so as to separate the quarters stuff them with salt and set them on a dish to dry either in the sun, or in an oven after the great heat is gone off, fix them in your pickling pot, boil two quarts of vinegar, let it stand till it is cold, pour it on the lemons and add to it four ounces of flower of Mustard, two ounces of Ginger, two cloves of Garlick, a quarter of an ounce of Mace, as much Allspice, a stick of Horse Radish scrap'd, 1oz pods of Capsicums, cover your pot close with a bladder let it stand a month before you use it, the longer it is kept the better. It will do as well without the Capsicums."

To Pickle Lemons

Pickled lemons have become very fashionable in recent years with the popularity of Moroccan and Middle Eastern cooking, but it seems that they are not that new in Ireland—they were preserving lemons in the Pope family kitchen in Co. Waterford in 1823–1890.

"Take six good lemons, bury them in salt taking care that they do not touch each other. At the end of six weeks take them out of the salt, rub them dry, and cut them in slices. Put them in a crock, and pour over vinegar in which has been boiled ½ oz of mustard seed and ¼ oz of whole white pepper, the mixture to be poured on luke warm—when quite cold cover the crock closely and at the end of a few months they will be fit for use. Eaten with veal."

Pontac Catsup for Fish

Another interesting recipe using elderberries from Mrs Ray in the Annie Irwin manuscript, 1900:

"Put ripe elderberries, picked from the stalk, into a stone pan with as much strong vinegar as will cover them. Bake it with your bread, or if you have not an oven, put the jar into a kettle of water on the fire, and while hot, strain it. Boil the liquor with a sufficient quantity of cloves, mace, peppercorns and shallots to give it a fine flavour. When that is obtained, put in half a pound of the finest anchovies to every quart of liquor, stir and boil only until dissolved. When cold, put it into pint bottles, and tie double bladders over each cork. The same method should be observed for preserving all catsups."

Nancy Elliott's Mustard Pickles

This recipe comes with the warning: "Appearances are deceitful else who would be brave enough to eat Mustard Pickles." As Nancy says: "This reads complicated and messy, but you have seen the result and it is worth trying. Takes about 1 hour of an evening to fix vegetables after they are all washed, make, cook peel the onions and about ½ hour next day to scald in brine, make mustard dressing, mix and put in jars." Don't be put off, they are delicious and worth making.

Cut up into small pieces:

 1 large cauliflower
 1 quart scarlet runner or string beans

Peel 1 quart button onions, pour boiling water over and as soon as cool enough to handle they can be easily peeled.
 1 quart of smallest cucumbers procurable, not peeled just cut in inch chunks and then across or 1 quart gherkins whole.
 If to be had, 4 green peppers cut up, taking out seeds carefully as they are too hot, or a scant handful of small sweet red peppers, which if not mild can be parboiled and then added to the rest.
 4 heads of celery stems cut up and 1 quart of green tomatoes cut up.
 Put all this cut up stuff in 1 gallon of water (4 quarts) with 1 medium cup of salt. Stand overnight. In the morning take granite saucepan, large and put in 2 quarts of good vinegar, put on fire to boil. Mix in bowl 1 small cup good flour, 1/8 lb mustard (2 tablespoonfuls big), same of turmeric, 4 tablespoons of sugar, 1 teaspoonful celery salt. Wet all with either ½ cup of vinegar or olive oil, add to hot vinegar and cook until thick stirring carefully. Put pickles and brine on fire, bring to a boil and boil for 5 minutes, dip out with a strainer, pressing gently to get rid of brine and add to boiling mustard dressing, as soon as all is dipped out and well mixed put into jars and seal or tie up securely will keep forever till the boys find it.

Sweet Chutney

Makes 1–2 jars

1lb sour apples or gooseberries
2½ cups vinegar
1⅔ cups golden raisins
3oz onions
1¾ cups sugar (demerara preferable)
1 egg
spoonful cayenne pepper (less if you do not like things hot)
2 teaspoons ground ginger
1oz garlic
3 tablespoons Indian sauce

It's possible that this is one of the recipes that Nancy Elliott's daughter sent her from America, as it's hand-written on notepaper and is not Nancy's own writing.

"Put the apples or gooseberries as the case may be on a fire in a saucepan with the vinegar, then pound all the other ingredients together in a mortar till they are in a regular pulp, put them and the sauce to what you have in the saucepan and give all a good boil for ¾ of an hour. Put in bottle and use."

Raspberry Vinegar

This recipe was given to me about 10 years ago by Mrs Mackey of Ringduffrin in Co. Down, as she presided over a wonderful afternoon tea on the long mahogany table in her dining room.

Put in crock or container and add same ratio for larger quantities fruit and vinegar. Stir occasionally and add more fruit etc. for 2–3 days if necessary. Strain through cloth bag. Boil juice for 30 minutes allowing 2¼ cups sugar to each 2½ cups of liquid.

Skim well until juice is fairly free of thick skim, (if you put the skimmings into a wide jug, this settles and can be used later). It is important to keep skimming and to take the thick part out of the juice, as it may thicken in bottles if too much is allowed to remain in the juice. It should keep indefinitely. Serve diluted with cold water as a refreshing sumer drink.

The recipe below is from Eliza Helena Odell's manuscript recipe book of 1851:

"Put the raspberries into a calico bag and let them strain till all the juice is gone, then put 1lb of sugar to 1 pint of juice, boil and skim it well, when nearly boiled put the vinegar to sour taste."

Cowslip Vinegar

Another recipe taken from Eliza Helena Odell's manuscript recipe book. It is dated 26 August 1851.

To 4 gallons of water with the chill just taken off add 6lb of sugar and half a peck of cowslips, flowers and stalks together, put all into a cask with 3 tablespoonfuls of barm put a piece of glass or slate over the bung hole an let it in a warm place till the vinegar turns sour when the bung hole may be fastened down. This is a cheap and excellent vinegar keeping pickles nice and crisp. If kept in a warm place it will be ready in 6 weeks for use ¼ ounce of Gelatine or Isinglas will help to clear it.

Gooseberry Vinegar

Another recipe from Nancy Elliott. Nancy doesn't give any clue as to how she used the vinegar, it would have been interesting to find out.

Gather the gooseberries when fully ripe, bruise them in a tub—to every quart of berries add 3 quarts of cold boiled water (spring), let them stand 10 hours, stirring frequently then strain through a hair sieve. To each gallon of vinegar add 1 ½ lbs of coarse brown sugar, stirring frequently all the time for 24 hours, then strain through a flannel bag in barrel. Place in the cellar with merely a bit of paper on the bung hole, in a year it is fit for use then bottle it.

Spiced Cherries

From Nancy Elliott, credited to Mrs Hubbard. Delicious with cold lamb, pork, or venison.

2.6kg (6lb) stoned red cherries (weigh after they are stoned)

Put on the fire 1.6kg (3½lb) of light brown sugar and 600ml (1 pint) of vinegar. When this boils skim it and put in the cherries and let it boil hard for five minutes. The next day drain off the juice and bring to the boil again and pour over the fruit, now add to the cherries a couple of sticks of cinnamon and two dozen of the kernels. They will keep in a crock if well covered.

Honey

Ireland has been described by many poets and storytellers as "the land of milk and honey," and there is little doubt that there was milk and honey in abundance from earliest times. Numerous references and legends refer to Ireland's sweet honey. Up to the end of the 12th century, when sugar was introduced by an Anglo-Norman baron, honey was the only sweetener in Ireland. However, it took until the 19th century before sugar was widely available to the poorer people.

Honey was so important in early Ireland that a whole section in the Brehon Laws was devoted to bees and beekeeping. Tributes were paid in honey, and no banquet was complete without honey and mead, the legendary drink made from it. Honey was used not just for cooking, but also for basting, and as a condiment to dip meat, fowl and fish in at the table.

I have always had a great love for bees and I keep a few hives in the apple orchard. My bees gather their pollen from the apple blossom and the flowers in the gardens nearby, and reward me with more than enough delicious comb honey for family and friends, even in a poor year. There's still a charming, if poignant, custom in many parts of Ireland that if a death occurs in the family, one must go down to the hive to "tell the bees," otherwise they would swarm or die in the hives.

Makes about 1lb 2oz

1 teaspoon sunflower oil
1½ cups plus 2 tablespoons superfine sugar
scant ¼ cup honey
½ cup glucose syrup (available from a chemist)
4 tablespoons water
1 tablespoon baking soda

1 baking tray—12 x 16 inch parchment paper or silpat mat

Honeycomb

This sweet crunchy confection that we now call honeycomb has always been associated with the Ould Lammas Fair of Ballycastle, which takes place in August. Like other favorite Irish foods it was celebrated in song:

> Did you treat your Mary Ann to dulse and yellowman,
> At the Ould Lammas Fair at Ballycastle—oh?

Dick Murray from Lurgan, a famous yellowman-maker of bygone days, sometimes hid a halfpenny or two in the mixture before it set, which generated a great deal of anticipation and excitement. The coin usually came back to him in exchange for more supplies of his yellowman! This is my daughter-in-law Rachel Allen's very addictive recipe.

Line a large baking sheet with parchment paper or silpat mat and grease lightly with the oil. Alternatively, line the sheet with a nonstick mat (there is no need to grease this).

Put the sugar, honey, and glucose syrup in a large saucepan with the water. Bring to a boil over high heat, stirring until the sugar dissolves. Remove the spoon, reduce the heat to medium and simmer without stirring for 5–10 minutes or until the syrup turns a light golden color and a sugar thermometer dipped into the mixture reads 300°F. Alternatively, check whether it has reached the hard-crack stage.

Immediately remove from the heat and quickly whisk in the baking soda. The mixture will grow, trebling in size very quickly, so be careful it doesn't spill over. Pour into the prepared baking sheet, swirling the sheet to spread the mixture evenly. Let cool completely and harden in a dry atmosphere before breaking into chunks. Cut with a knife or break with your hands and store in an airtight container.

This goes very well with ice cream.

Ballymaloe Fudge

Makes 96 pieces (approximately)

1 cup (2 sticks) butter
4½ cups light brown sugar or superfine sugar
1 can evaporated milk
¾–1 cup water
pure vanilla extract

1 jelly roll pan, 9 x 13 inch

Many people have a successful fudge recipe which doesn't always work for another person. It can be a bit bothersome, a lot depends on the diameter of the saucepan used.

Melt the butter in a heavy-bottomed saucepan on a low heat. Add the milk, water, sugar, and vanilla. Stir with a whisk until the sugar is dissolved. Turn up the heat and simmer, stirring constantly, until it reaches the soft-ball stage. To test, put a little of the fudge in a bowl of cold water. Pull the pan off the heat and stir until the fudge thickens and reaches the required consistency. Pour into the jelly roll pan and smooth out with a spatula.

Let cool and then cut into squares before completely cold.

Homemade Candied Peel

5 oranges
5 lemons
1 teaspoon salt
6¾ cups sugar
3¾ cups water

Elizabeth Murphy from Kenmare, Co. Kerry, recalled the ritual of making candied peel for the cakes and pudding in her childhood. Oranges and lemons were scarcer and more highly valued then.

Cut the fruit in half and squeeze out the juice. Reserve the juice for another use, perhaps homemade lemonade. Put the peel into a large bowl (not aluminum), add yhe salt, and cover with cold water. Let soak for 24 hours.

Next day, discard the soaking water, put the peel in a saucepan, and cover with fresh cold water. Bring to a boil. Cover and simmer very gently until the peel is soft, about 3 hours. Remove the peel and discard the water. Scrape out any remaining flesh and membranes from inside the cut fruit, leaving the white pith and rind intact. (You could do the next step the next day if that is more convenient.)

Dissolve the sugar in the water, bring to a boil, add the peel, and simmer gently until it becomes translucent, about 30 minutes. Remove the peel, drain, and leave it to cool. Boil down the remaining syrup until it becomes thick and syrupy, but don't stir or it will crystallize. Remove from the heat and put the peel in again to soak up the syrup. Leave for 30 minutes.

Pack the candied peel into sterilized glass jars and pour the syrup over. Cover and store in a cold place or in a refrigerator. Alternatively, cool the peel on a wire rack and pour any remaining syrup into the centers. Finally pack into sterilized glass jars and cover tightly. It should keep for 6–8 weeks, or longer under refrigeration.

Candied Peel for Petits Fours

Cut the freshly made candied peel into ¼–½ inch thin slices. Roll in superfine sugar and serve with coffee. Alternatively, dip one end of candied orange peel into melted dark chocolate. Let set and serve.

Drinks

In early times the Irish enjoyed many home-brewed beverages. St Brigid had the reputation for making the best ale in Ireland and St Patrick is said to have had his favorite brewer who traveled around the country with him as he converted the pagan Irish. We certainly got the message about the beer! Anyone could brew ale who wished to, but the Brehon Laws laid down regulations for the sale and the proper running of ale houses.

It has been suggested that the Irish also drank nenadmin, a cider made from wild or crab apples, fraochan made from fraughans or wild blueberries or blackberries, and bragget, made by fermenting ale and honey together. But of all the drinks mead, a wine made from honey and said to be both potent and delicious, was the favorite—the drink of celebration. It was served at every banquet. In Brid Mahon's book *Land of Milk and Honey*, there are vivid descriptions of two feasts which tell us of the kind of food and drink served at princely banquets. The first one concerns Bricriu, a wealthy and malicious chieftain who decided to give a feast and for that purpose built a house big enough to accommodate the Ulster heroes and their wives; the meal included "beef broth, roast boar, salmon, honey cakes and many other dishes; to drink the guests had the finest of ale, the choicest of mead and the rarest of wines…" In another story, "The Wooing of Etain," we read how King Eochaidh made a great feast at Tara, during which mead, fine wines, and barrels of ale were served.

The country house manuscripts contained some quite sophisticated recipes for drinks. The quality of one's cellar and drinks cabinet was very important when entertaining.

Sowans

Sowans is made from the husk and chaff residue (the "sids") of milled oatmeal, steeped in hot or cold water for any period between four days and three weeks. During that time the mixture ferments, and when this fermentation subsides it is strained to yield a whitish liquid, known as "bull's milk." This was used in baking and was drunk on church black fast days. It has a decidedly sour taste. Sowans were traditionally prepared at Hallowe'en for the returning dead, who, it was believed, visited their former homes at that time. It was customary to prepare a bed by the fire and to leave out tobacco and sowans for their visit.

In *Old Days, Old Ways*, Olive Sharkey recalls the popularity of sowans in her father's day: "Sowans were a drink made from the husks of oats, a widely acclaimed thirst-quencher when my father was a boy. It was made for the hay-making season when mouths were bone dry, if the weather was particularly dry. The husks were poured into a large earthenware pot, together with some whole oats and left to soak in water for up to a week. The liquid was then strained through a rush mat, ready for drinking."

Buttermilk

Since at least the 8th century, buttermilk (the thin milk left in the churn after buttermaking) has been a popular drink in Ireland. The Brehon Laws stipulate that it is a legal duty to provide hospitality to anyone who calls at one's door, and buttermilk is listed as an appropriate drink to offer. Centuries later, while touring Ireland in 1825, Sir Walter Scott found the same hospitable tradition: "perpetual kindness in the Irish cabin: buttermilk, potatoes, a stool is offered or a stone is rolled that your honour may sit down."

Buttermilk has remained one of the foundations of Irish cooking to this day. During the 18th and 19th centuries it was part of the staple diet of the peasantry. C. Valey, in *A New System of Husbandry* (1770), writes "at the time of the year when potatoes are out of season (May, June and July) their whole living is oat bread and buttermilk."

Buttermilk was believed to cure eczema. It was also common for girls and women to wash their faces with buttermilk to improve their complexions.

Tea

Tea was first introduced into Ireland in the late 17th century and quickly grew in popularity, though it was an expensive commodity. In September 1719 a duty of 12 pence per pound was imposed on tea imported from England. Household books from the prosperous Carew family of Castleboro estate in Co. Wexford show that in 1769 a pound of breakfast green tea cost 6s 6d. There was a major increase in tea-drinking in the rural communities in the late 19th century, as small grocery shops began to be established in small towns and villages. These grocers were willing to exchange tea and sugar for farm-produced butter and eggs.

There is a common belief that tea is useful as a cure for sore eyes, and in fact the Irish drink more per capita than any other nation—it has been a favorite drink down through the generations. Instructions on how to make tea were given in *Lessons in Cookery and Housewifery, 1901*:

1. Have the kettle boiling. 2. Heat the teapot. 3. Allow one teaspoonful of tea for every person, and one for the teapot. 4. Pour boiling water on the tea and draw it from 3 to 5 minutes, never longer.

It has always been an intrinsic part of country life and city life, and still is. Tea was taken to the bog for the turf-cutting and to the fields during the harvest; fishermen took it with them going out on the boat, children took it to school in bottles and later in flasks, and builders brought their flasks for the morning tea breaks before the advent of garage forecourt paper cups of tea.

In her book, *To School Through the Fields*, Alice Taylor includes a chapter called "Tea in the Meadow" with wonderfully evocative descriptions that will be familiar to those who grew up on farms or spent summer holidays there at harvest time. She writes: "Then somebody would call in a voice full of elation: 'The tea is coming!' My mother usually brought the tea in a white enamel bucket and maybe a tin sweet-gallon full as well. We made ourselves comfortable on various heaps of hay and passed around cups of tea with slices of homemade brown bread. We watched my mother's basket eagerly and usually she came up trumps with a big juicy apple cake. It is said that hunger is a good sauce but hunger and thirst certainly made the tea in the meadow a feast with a special flavour, like manna in the desert. The aroma of the sweet-smelling hay blended with the tea, funny stories and riddles made for great laughter and fun."

The much-loved television character Mrs Doyle in "Father Ted" of course reinforced the hospitality tradition by offering a cup of tea to all who called at the parochial house!

Dandelion Coffee

"Wash the root of the dandelion with a coarse brush and cut in small pieces. Roast it in the oven until it is crisp and dark brown. It will then go in powder when crushed. Use 1 teaspoon of this to each cup of coffee required. Brew or draw it like tea and then add boiled milk and sugar to taste. Dandelion has very valuable medicinal properties."

Florence Irwin, *Irish Country Recipes*

Ginger Beer

This recipe is from the Kitchen Book of Clonbrock:

"Put all ingredients into a pan which holds 6 gallons of water. Fill up with boiling water – be very careful that the water does boil – cover – when cold strain off – Take a large round of toast, on which put 2 teaspoonfuls of good yeast, cover, let it stand till next day – strain again, and bottle."

Protestant Lemonade

An old lady who did service in one of Ireland's big houses gave me this recipe which she called Protestant lemonade.

To make the stock syrup, dissolve the sugar in the water and bring to a boil. Boil for 2 minutes, then let cool. Measure ½ pint syrup for the lemonade; the rest can be stored in the refrigerator until needed.

To make the lemonade, squeeze the juice from the lemons and add ½ pint syrup and the water. Taste and add a little more water or syrup if necessary. Add ice, garnish with sprigs of fresh mint or lemon balm, and serve.

Doris Bewley's Lemonade

This was included in Doris Bewley's collection, written on a postcard addressed to Mrs Johnson in Rathgar, Dublin, dated 1954 and sent from Co. Galway.

Grate the rind and squeeze juice of oranges or lemons into a large bowl. Add the sugar and pour on boiling water: stir till dissolved and then add the acids and Epsom salts. Stir till dissolved. Fills about 3 orange bottles.

Mary Walsh's Lemonade

Mary Walsh from Woodsgift, Co. Kilkenny, sent me this recipe from her mother's scrapbook:

Peel the lemon thinly. Squeeze out the juice. Put into a jug. Add the sugar and citric acid. Pour on boiling water, stir well. Leave for about 12 hours, then strain. Use about one tablespoon lemonade to a tumbler of water.

Barley Water

Barley water is often included in recipes designed with cooking for invalids in mind, but is probably good for anyone feeling under the weather. It is very interesting to note that most old cookbooks and cookery textbooks included invalid cooking. Older family members often stayed at home when unwell rather than going into nursing homes and hospitals, which were not available except for the very wealthy, and people didn't go into hospital for lesser ailments. Feeding people nutritiously when they were ill took precedence over medicines before the advent of antibiotics. The food often wasn't terribly exciting, but was designed for nutrition and digestibility, and to avoid "upsetting the stomach." You would often hear of a person having a "bad stomach." Barley water was also sometimes given to infants, without the lemon flavoring.

Clear Barley Water

Makes about 18fl oz

1oz pearl barley
1 piece of lemon rind
juice of ½ lemon
1¼ cups boiling water

This is from Doris Bewley's 1932 notebook. To make thick barley water, double the quantities and cook the barley until the liquid has reduced by half.

Blanch the barley and put it into a tumbler with the lemon rind and juice. Pour on the boiling water and cover it; it is ready to serve when it is cold. Remove the lemon rind before serving.

Curaçao Egg

This is from the Clonbrock manuscript.

Beat up the yolk of an egg in a tumbler with a liqueur glass of orange curaçao (or with a dessert spoonful of brandy, and half a teaspoonful of powdered sugar), and then let out upon it from a siphon about a wineglass of soda water. In warm weather crushed ice may be added. Instead of soda water, milk may be added to the egg and curaçao; this makes the drink richer and more nourishing.

Whey

Makes about 1¼ pints

2½ cups whole milk
⅔ cup buttermilk

This was included in the Invalid Cookery section of Cookery Notes, 1947.

Bring the milk to a boil, add the buttermilk, boil up, and set beside the fire for 5 minutes. Strain and serve.

Flaxseed Tea

Makes about 1 pint

½oz flaxseed
2½ cups water
¼oz liquorice
¼oz of candy

Another invalid drink, probably to aid digestion.

Wash the flaxseed, put into a saucepan with the cold water, and simmer for 30 minutes, adding the liquorice and candy. Strain before using.

Tomato Juice

The Cookery Nook by Mary de R Swanton (a former dietician at the American Hospital, Paris), a little booklet that was probably published in around 1940 by the Dublin Catholic Truth Society of Ireland, contains lots of cooking advice, and included a recipe for tomato juice. It is now often served (iced, in a tall glass) as an alternative to grapefruit for breakfast in the big hotels and on liners. Tomato juice can, of course, be bought canned, but it is easy and far better to extract the juice from the fresh fruit. Cook them for a couple of minutes in boiling water, then pound them through a strainer and season with salt and pepper. Add a squeeze of lemon, if desired, and you have a marvelous drink.

Tanora

Tanora, a mineral (non-alcoholic drink) similar to red lemonade, is synonymous with Cork and was the staple of birthday parties, Christmas dinners, and other social occasions. The tangerine-flavored drink was introduced by John Daly & Co, a former tea, wine, and spirit merchants based on Cork's Kyrls Quay, as far back as the 1930s. The Daly's truck was a familiar sight on Cork roads. Many the Cork exile requested supplies of Tanora when anyone was visiting, and it's still a firm favorite, now being made by the Coca-Cola Co. Rosalie Dunne remembers going to Congress Guesthouse in Ballycotton with her father on Sunday mornings during the summer holidays, Tanora was the big treat! She still brings bottles to a Cork relative living in Dublin.

Mead

Boil 8 quarts water in a preserving kettle and dissolve in it 2lb honey. Add thin slices of lemon with skin, pith, and seeds removed. Remove pan from cooker and when the mixture is nearly cold, add 1 pint pale ale and quarter of a teaspoon of yeast dissolved in a little tepid water. Leave overnight. Strain into bottles, putting two washed raisins and a teaspoon of sugar in each bottle. Seal bottles and leave in a warm room for 4–5 hours. Store in a cool dark place. The mead is ready for drinking in a week.

Apple Wine

Recipes for apple wine regularly appear in old manuscripts and cookbooks. This recipe was given to Máire Ní Mhurchu by Nora Peter Paul O'Sullivan.

Wash the apples thoroughly. Cut them into slices or chunks, do not peel or core them. Allow a gallon of water to each gallon of cut-up apples. Leave them steeping for 10 days. Stir occasionally and strain through a clean cloth (fine nylon or a gauze). Add about 6¾ cups sugar to the strained juice and stir until dissolved. Cream ½oz yeast with a teaspoonful of sugar and add to the mixture.

Place this mixture in a large jar or big bottle. Keep in a moderately hot place while fermenting, covering the container with a one thickness of cloth.

It will take 10–15 days to finish and you will know when it is finished as soon as the liquid stops bubbling and hissing. Filter it through fine filter paper or use 3–4 thicknesses of nylon. Cork in sterilized bottles making sure that the corks have been boiled for 15 minutes. Cork tightly so that no air gets through.

Store on its side and keep the corks moist.

Note: apple wine takes about 3 months to mature; it will keep indefinitely.

Ginger Wine

Makes about 6 pints

15 cups water
3½ cups sugar
2 teaspoons ginger extract
1 teaspoonful capsicum
3 teaspoons browning
½oz tartaric acid

This handwritten recipe was included in Doris Bewley's collection. Capsicum, ginger essence and tartaric acid could all be bought online.

Heat water and dissolve sugar, when boiling add the ginger extract, capsicum, and browning, boil for 3 minutes, then add tartaric acid and boil for 10 minutes.

Blackberry Wine

Makes about 6 pints

10lb blackberries
2 gallons cold water
6lb loaf sugar

This recipe was given in a 1930s newspaper cutting in response to a reader's query—a reader called Nell.

Bruise the berries (which must be perfectly sound), and place them in a small tub, adding the water. Cover and set aside, in 3 days' time the wine will be ready for straining through cheesecloth. Press the berries well to extract all the juice. Put the juice back in the tub and add the sugar. Stir well, and when it has dissolved the wine must be covered, and left for 2 weeks before being poured into a dry cask. Push in the bung securely after pouring it in. The wine will be ready for use at the end of a year.

Green Gooseberry Wine

This recipe was with Annie Irwin's 1900 recipe collection and was credited to Mrs Pascell and Mrs Shuttlewood:

Gather the gooseberries when fully grown, just as they begin to turn, weigh them and pound them in a mortar and to every pound as before weighed add one quart of cold water, let them stand four or five days stirring them twice a day, then strain them into another vessel and to every gallon of liquor add three pounds of lump sugar, when the sugar is all dissolved run it all through a hair sieve into the cask which should be quite full and when all violent fermentation has subsided which should be in twenty-four hours bung it up tight, in a month or six weeks open the bung and take out of the cask by measure as much liquor as will make room for the brandy, one gallon of which will be sufficient for ten gallons of wine. Tie up isinglass the size of an egg in muslin, suspend it by a string from the bung then stop it up close. In 4 or 5 months it should be bottled but if to be drunk as champagne it should remain 12 months in the cask. When bottled, cork immediately.

Rhubarb Wine

Nancy Elliott's wonderful recipe collection included some preserves and cordials, which were made when the fruit came into season. Here is one of them, a recipe for rhubarb wine, credited rather interestingly to a Mrs Drought!

Peel and cut the rhubarb in small pieces, to every quart of rhubarb add 1 quart of boiling water, cover it up and let it stand 3 days stirring occasionally. Then strain and to every quart juice add 1 lb best loaf sugar and let it stand 24 hours, strain again and bottle it, do not cork it for 5 or 6 days. In about 6 months it is fit for use but the longer it is kept the better. To be kept in a cool place. June, July and August the fruit is fit for wine.

Whiskey

Ireland has a long and colorful history of distilling and Irish whiskey is now famous the world over. The earliest references to whiskey date to the 15th century; The Annals of Connaught, The Annals of Clonmacnoise, and The Annals of the Four Masters each record a tragic incident which occurred in 1405:

Risderd Mag Ragnaill, eligible for chieftainship of Muintir Eolais, entered into rest after drinking *usci bethad* [water of life—i.e. whiskey] to excess, it was a deadly water to him.

During the 18th century the first commercial distilleries were established; Kilbeggan Distillery was founded in 1757, followed by Jameson in 1780, Bushmills in 1784 and Powers in 1791. At the close of the century there are estimated to have been more than 2,000 whiskey stills in Ireland, most of them illegal!

Illegal poteen is still made in clandestine stills in remote country areas and distributed to eager customers by an underground network.

Blackcurrant Whiskey

This is from the Mary Ponsonby manuscript c.1850. It would have been made annually when the blackcurrants were in season and abundant in the kitchen garden. This also works well as a half quantity.

"To every gallon of spirits put five pounds of currants and two pounds of best lump sugar. The fruit must be well bruised with hands, putting by degrees half the quantity of whiskey, which must remain on them eight and forty hours, it then be strained through a flannel bag over the sugar, the other half of the spirits to be added the same way. Mix them together and when bottled rack it off, and bottle it for use."

Note: We used: 4 pints whiskey, 7 cups blackcurrants, 1lb lump sugar.

Adrienne Forbes' Hot Toddy

Serves 1

1 measure of Irish whiskey (everyone has their favorite brand!)
1 heaping teaspoon brown sugar (you can also use granulated sugar)
boiling water
a slice of lemon studded with cloves

A glass of hot whiskey or a hot toddy, as it's sometimes called, is a comforting drink on a winter night, or if one is coming down with a cold and needs an excuse! Adrienne Forbes has worked with me here at the Cookery School for the past 26 years. Having grown up in the Tower Bar in Cloyne, Adrienne watched her father Edmund Morrissey make many a hot toddy and she is a dab hand at it herself. Here is how she makes it.

Put a teaspoon into a glass and rinse the glass well with hot water. This heats the glass and the teaspoon prevents the glass from cracking. Pour the whiskey into the hot glass, add the sugar and boiling water, stir until the sugar is dissolved, then add the lemon studded with the cloves and enjoy!

Cordials

These three recipes are taken from Eliza Helena Odell's manuscript receipt book dated 26 August 1851:

Orange Cordial

To 1 quart of whiskey, put the peel cut very thin, and juice of 3 sweet oranges, 1oz of whole ginger sliced, the rind of 1 lemon and a little of the juices, put all into a crock with a close cover and let it stand for a week stirring it frequently, then strain it through a hair sieve, add 1lb of white sugar to each quart and filter it when ready.

Blackcurrant Cordial

Steep a gallon of blackcurrants in a gallon of whiskey, with 2oz of bitter almonds and 1oz of cloves (both pounded). Let them remain in a jar for three weeks shaking them occasionally then strain off the juice and to every quart put ½lb of loaf sugar. When the sugar is dissolved bottle for use.

Ginger Cordial

Pick bruise and strain 1lb of white currants and 1lb of white sugar and 3oz grated ginger, steep the rind of a lemon overnight in a quart of good whiskey or Brandy after which take out the lemon peel, add the whiskey to the above ingredients let them stand for a fortnight shaking the vessel daily then strain and filter, it must be closely corked.

White Currant Cordial

This is Mrs Alley's receipt, dated 1897, from Nancy Elliott's collection:

1lb white currants, fresh pulled
1 quart of whiskey
rind of a lemon

Let them stand 24 hours then strain whiskey and lemon off the currants pressing the latter gently.

1lb white sugar
½oz of ginger

The ginger goes in with the currants and the sugar when all is strained off, when the sugar is dissolved you bottle and strain thro' muslin.

Lemon Cordial

Makes about 2 pints

3 lemons
3½ cups sugar
1oz citric acid
1oz Epsom salts
1 quart boiling water

This recipe was contributed by Mrs J.T.H. Orr, Sligo from The Tried Favourites *cookbook.*

Grate lemon rind, squeeze out all the juice, add sugar, citric acid, Epsom salts, and water. Stir until sugar melts. Let sit quite cold and then strain.

Raspberry Syrup

Makes about 3½ pints

4oz tartaric acid
2 quarts hot water
6 cups raspberries
sugar

This is also from Tried Favourites *and came from a Mrs. G. Clarke, Roscommon. It would have been diluted as a drink, or possibly used in other recipes as raspberry flavoring.*

Dissolve tartaric acid in the hot water, pour over the raspberries in a crock, allow to remain at least 24 hours, stirring from time to time, strain. To each 2½ cups juice allow 3½ cups sugar, return to crock, stir often till sugar dissolves, which will be in 3–4 hours, bottle. Do not cork for 3 weeks

Punch

Visitors in the 16th and 17th centuries regularly comment on the Irish custom of flavoring and sweetening their whiskey. After the establishment of the distilling industry, whiskey became more widely available, at least to more affluent households, and several writers attest to the popularity of punch during the 19th century. Amhlaoibh Uí Shúileabháin (unsurprisingly) seems to have relished it, recording, for example, the night of October 19, 1830 as "a mild night which I passed happily at Michael Hickey's drinking sweet strong punch till midnight..." In his diary, he describes "a tumbler of punch, strong in whiskey and weak in hot water, sweetened with sugar and acid with lemon."

Thomas Carlyle, staying in the Imperial Hotel, Dublin in 1849, recounts in his *Reminiscences of my Irish Journey* how he enjoyed "punch... and after a silent pipe... tumbled into bed." Punch continues to have that effect!

Curaçao

This comes from the Lough Rynn manuscript:
"To a quart of French brandy put two ounces of curaçao orange peel (which may be procured at any chemist). Add a pound of sugar candy, finely pounded. Let it stand fourteen days, giving the bottle containing it a shake daily. Filter it and it is then fit for use."

(If your local chemist doesn't have orange peel use the thinly pared zest of a few organic oranges, believe me it will also be delicious.)

Cherry Brandy

This comes from the Lough Rynn manuscript:

"To be made of morelle cherries. One pound of cherries, one pint of brandy, a quarter pound of double refined sugar. Let all be infused in a crock and left for five or six days, stirring it with a stick every day. Then strain it through a jelly bag; then bottle it. The stones must be pounded. Cover the crock with a stone or slate."

Moselle Cup

This comes from the Lough Rynn manuscript. One can almost imagine this drink being served from a silver bowl in the garden on an early summer evening, or on the terrace before dinner. The use of woodruffe is a very interesting German influence.

"To each bottle of still or sparkling muscatel moselle, add one bottle of soda water, a glass of sherry or brandy, four or five thin slices of pineapple, the peel of half a lemon cut very thin and powdered sugar according to taste. Let the whole stand about an hour, and before serving add some lumps of clear ice. You may substitute a pint of fresh strawberries for the pineapple, or three or four peaches or nectarines. In place of fruit, add some sprigs of woodruffe, (Woodruffe is an herb much used on the Rhine for making May drink, its peculiar flavor being most powerful in May; it is to be found in forests in many parts of Ireland and England also.) When neither fruit nor woodruffe can be obtained, add instead of sherry or brandy a glass or two of milk punch or essence of punch and a little more of the lemon peel."

Claret Cup

Another Lough Rynn recipe, which sounds deliciously refreshing:

"To each bottle of ordinary claret, add a bottle of soda water, a glass of sherry or curaçao, the peel of a lemon cut very thin, powdered sugar according to taste. Let the whole remain an hour or two before serving. Then add some lumps of clear ice. To the above, can also be added a few slices of cucumber, or some sprigs of borage instead of the cucumber. In place of the lemon peel, you may substitute, when in season, a pint of ripe raspberries or four or five peaches or nectarines cut in slices. This is a most delicious beverage."

Orange Brandy

This is adapted from the Clonbrock manuscript. The recipe appeared on the same page of the manuscript as a recipe for gout cure! Too much of this brandy combined with a rich diet, and you might need it. It does sound deliciously extravagant, though, and the addition of saffron would give it a wonderful color.

"450g(1lb) sugar, 2.4l (4 pints) brandy, the peel of 2¼ oranges and 2¼ lemons, pinch of saffron. To be left in a large jar for a fortnight before bottling and in the cellar a year before drinking. (To be stirred and strained through muslin)."

Doreen Costine's Gaelic Coffee

Serves 1

2 teaspoons brown sugar
1 measure of Irish whiskey
strong black coffee
softly whipped cream

Gaelic coffee always reminds me of my late father-in-law, Ivan Allen, who always managed to end up with a white moustache as he carefully sipped it, much to the general hilarity of his grandchildren! Doreen Costine from Cloyne, who has worked here with me at the school for many years, makes a superb Irish Coffee. Sláinte agus saol agat—health and long life to you!

Warm a medium wine glass with hot water. Pour out the water and put the sugar and whiskey into the glass. Add the coffee and stir well. Pour the softly whipped cream out of a jug over the back of a spoon onto the top of the coffee. The cream should float on top so don't stir. Hot whiskey-flavored coffee drunk through cold cream is one of the very best Irish traditions!

Index

Bibliography

All in the Cooking, part 1 – Coláiste Mhuire Book of Household Cooking, published by The Educational Company of Ireland, 1950s
Allen, Myrtle, *The Ballymaloe Cookbook*, Agri Books, 1977
Andrews, Colman, *The Country Cooking of Ireland*, Chronicle Books, California, 2009
Bell, Jonathan & **Watson**, Mervyn, *Irish Farming Implements and Techniques 1750–1900*, John Donald, Edinburgh, 1986
Cambrensis, Giraldus, *The History and Topography of Ireland*, (trans. by John J. O'Meara), Penguin Books, London, 1982
Cambrensis, Giraldus, *Expugnatio Hibernica* (The Conquest of Ireland), edited with trans. by A. B. Scott & F. X. Martin, Royal Irish Academy, Dublin, 1978
Carberry, Mary, *The Farm by Lough Gur*,

Mercier Press, Cork and Dublin, 1973
Cosmopolite, A., *The Sportsman in Ireland*, vol. I & II, Henry Colburn, London, 1897
Crosbie, Paddy, *Your Dinner's Poured Out*, O'Brien Press, Dublin, 1991
Crohan, Tomas O, *The Islandman* (trans. by Robin Flower), Oxford University Press, Oxford, 1978
Cullen, L. M., *The Emergence of Modern Ireland*, 1600–1900, Gill & Macmillan, Dublin, 1983
Danaher, Kevin, *The Quarter Days in Irish Tradition*, Mercier Press, Cork and Dublin, 1959
Danaher, Kevin, *In Ireland Long Ago*, Mercier Press, Cork and Dublin, 1970
Danaher, Kevin, *The Pleasant Land of Ireland*, Mercier Press, Cork and Dublin, 1972
Danaher, Kevin, *The Year in Ireland*, Mercier Press, Cork and Dublin, 1972

De R. Swanton, Mary, *Cookery Nook*, published by Catholic Truth Society of Ireland, Dublin 1938
Derricke, John, *The Image of Ireland*, John Day, London, 1581
Donnelly, James S., Jr., 'Cork Market: Its Role in the Nineteenth Century Irish Butter Trade', *Studia Hibernica* No. II, 1971
Evans, E. Estyn, *Irish Folk Ways*, Routledge & Kegan, London, 1957
Ferguson, Kathleen, *Lessons in Cookery and Housewifery for the use of Children*, Book 1, printed and published at Athlone Printing Works, Westmeath Independent Office, 1901
Fitzgibbon, Theodora, *Irish Traditional Food*, Gill & Macmillan, Dublin, 1983
Fox, Robin, *The Tory Islanders*, Cambridge University Press, London, 1978
Flake Oatmeal Millers, *Flake Oatmeal Recipes*, compiled by Maura Laverty,

undated
Good Housekeeping Institute, *Good Housekeeping's Cookery Compendium*, The Waverley Book Company Limited, London 1952

Hall, Mr & Mrs C. S., Ireland, *Its Scenery and Character*, 3 vols, How and Parsons, London, 1841

Irish Countrywomen's Association, *Good Cooking*, 1965

Irwin, Florence, *The Cooking Woman*, Oliver & Boyd, Edinburgh, 1949

Jackson, Kenneth (trans. & ed.), *Aislinge Meic Con Glinne*, Dublin, 1991

Joyce P. W., *A Social History of Ancient Ireland*, vols I & II, M H Gill & Son, Dublin, 1920

Keane, J. B., *Strong Tea*, Mercier Press, Cork and Dublin, 1972

Laverty, Maura, *Maura Laverty's Cookery Book*, Longman, Green and Co, London, 1946, printed in Ireland by The Kerryman Ltd, Tralee.

Laverty, Maura, *Kind Cooking*, published by The Kerryman for Maura Laverty Miscellanies, 1955

Laverty, Maura, *Maura Laverty's Traditional Irish Cookbook, Full & Plenty, Part 1, Bread & Cakes*, Anvil Books, Dublin 1960

Lucas, A. T. 'Nettles and Charlock as Famine Food', *Breifne*, vol I, no. 2, Cumann Seanchais Bhreifne, 1958

Lucas, A. T., 'Irish Food Before the Potato', *Gwerin*, vol. iii, no. 3, Denbigh, Gee and Son, 1960–2

Lysaght, Patricia, 'When I makes Tea, I makes Tea, *Ulster Folk Life*, vol. 33, 1987

Mc Kenna, Malachy, Putting Food on the Table, The Story of the Blasket Islanders, 1850-1950, unpublished

McKinney, Jack, 'They came in Cars and Carts: A History of the Fairs and Markets of Ballyclare', Area Resource Centre, Antrim, 1989

MacLysaght, E., *Irish Life in the Seventeenth Century*, Cork University Press, Cork, 1939

Maguire, W. A., *Caught in Time*, Friars Bush Press, Belfast, 1986

Mahon, Brid, *Land of Milk and Honey*, Poolbeg, Dublin, 1991

Maxwell, Constantia, *The Stranger in Ireland*, Jonathan Cape, London, 1954

Maxwell, W. H., *Wild Sports of the West*, Richard Bentley, London, 1843

Meyer, Kuno (ed.), *The Vision of MacConglinne* (trans by Aisling MacConglinne), Lemma Publishing Corporation, New York, 1974

Mitchell, Frank, *The Shell Guide to Reading the Irish Landscape*, Country House, Dublin, 1986

Moryson, Fynes, *Itinerary*, 1605, John Beale, London, 1617

O'Donovan, John ed., *Annals of Ireland by the Four Masters*, 7 vols, Dublin, 1856

O'Drisceoil, Diarmuid, 'Fulachta Fiadh': the Value of Early Irish Literature', *Burnt Offerings; International Contributions to Burnt Mound Archaeology*, compiled by Victor Buckley, Dublin, 1990, 157–164

O Hógáin, Dáthí, *Myth, Legend and Romance*, London, 1990

O'Kelly, M. J., 'Excavations and experiments in ancient Irish cooking places', JRSAI 84, 1954, 105–155

O'Loan, J., 'A History of Early Irish Farming', *Journal of the Dept. of Agriculture and Fisheries* 62, Dublin, 1965, 131–98

O'Mara, Veronica & **O'Reilly**, Fionnuala, *An Irish Literary Cookbook*, Town House, Dublin, 1991

O'Neill, Timothy, *Merchants and Mariners in Medieval Ireland*, Irish Academic Press, Dublin, 1987

O'Sé, Micheál, 'Old Irish Buttermaking', *Journal of Cork Historical and Archaeological Society* 54, 1959, 61–67

O Shúileabháin, Amhlaoibh, *Cinnlae Amhlaoibh Uí Shúileabháin*, edited by Michael McGrath, Irish Texts Society, 4 vols., 1936

O Tuama, Sean & **Kinsella**, Thomas, *An Duannaire 1600–1900: Poems of the Dispossessed*, Dolmen Press, Portlaoise, 1981

Petty, Sir William, *The Political Anatomy of Ireland*, Irish University Press, 1691

Póirtear, Cathal (ed.), *The Great Irish Famine*, Mercier Press, Dublin, 1995.

Power, Catryn, 'Dental Anthropology', *Archaeology Ireland*, 4/3, 1990, 36–28

Proudfoot, V. B. 'The Economy of the Irish Rath', *Medieval Archaeology 5*, 1966, 94–122

Regulo New World Gas Cookers, *Radiation Cookery Book*,1952 edition

Ryan, Michael (ed.), *Treasures of Ireland*, Royal Irish Academy, Dublin, 1983

Salaman, Redcliffe, *The History and Social Influence of the Potato*, Cambridge University Press, Cambridge, 1949

Sayers, Peig, *Machnamh Sean-Mhna (An Old Woman's Reflections)*, Oxford University Press, Oxford, 1962

Sexton, Regina, *Cereals and Cereal Foodstuff of the Early Historic Period in Ireland*, Unpublished Thesis, Cork, 1992

Sexton, Regina, ' "I'd ate it like Chocolate": The Disappearing Offal Food Traditions of Cork City' in *Proceedings of the Oxford Symposium on Food and Cookery 1994*, Oxford, 1995

Sharkey, Olive, *Old Days Old Ways*, O Brien Press, Dublin, 1985

Sheridan, Monica, *Monica's Kitchen*, Castle Publications Ltd, Dublin 1963

Stationery Office, Dublin, *Cookery Notes – originally prepared for use in Schools and Classes for Girls, working under the Schemes of the Department of Agriculture*, editions 1932, 1943, 1947,1949

Taylor, Alice, *To School Through the Fields*, An Irish Country Childhood, Brandon Book Publishers, Dingle, Co Kerry 1988

Thackeray, William Makepeace, *The Irish Sketch Book*, vol. XVIII, Smith Elder & Co. London, 1879

Tried Favourites (no publication details), charity cookery booklet

Wakefield, Edward, *An Account of Ireland*, Statistical and Political, vols & II, London, 1812

Watson, Mervyn, 'Standardisation of Pig Production: The Case of the Large White Ulster', *Ulster Folk Life*, vol. 34, 1988

Went, Arthur E.J., 'The Irish Hake Fishery 1504–1824', *Journal of The Cork Historical and Archaeological Society*, vol. 51, 1946

Wilson, Anne, *Food and Drink in Britain*, Constable, London, 1973

Wilson, Anne C. (ed) *Traditional Country House Cooking*, Weidenfeld and Nicolson, London 1993

Young, Arthur, *A Tour in Ireland*, vols 1 & II, Cadell, London

Manuscripts

National Library of Ireland:
Ms 5606 Mary Ponsonby
Ms 27,969 Marianne Armstrong
Ms 34,932/1-3 Pope
Ms 29,785/3 and Ms 29,785/11 Bruen of Oakpark

Birr Castle Manuscript Cookbooks – Lord and Lady Rosse, Birr Castle Archives

Kitchen Book of Clonbrock

History of Lough Rynn - Fiona Slevin, www.loughrynn.net

Mary Lee Heathfield 1823 and Annie Irwin 1900 – both courtesy of Lynne Hoare

Author's Acknowledgments

The research for both the revised and original editions of this book has taken many years and brought me into contact with countless wonderful people who have generously shared their memories and their recipes with me. I would never have been able to complete the task without their support, and am delighted to have made many new and lasting friendships in the process.

I also owe a special debt of gratitude to the many people who welcomed me into their homes and showed me, so willingly, how to make the dishes of their childhood. Lana Pringle who gave me the secret of her family Barm Brack; the late Jo Twomey who painstakingly taught me how to cook on an open fire and took the mystery out of baking in the pot oven or bastible; Bridget Guerin who showed me how to make Bairneach Soup; Jack O'Keeffe whose family originally came from Sliabh Luachra, and who specially drove all the way to Shanagarry to pass on his family recipe for goose blood pudding. A big thank you to these and the many, many more who are mentioned in the introductions to the individual recipes.

Thank you to the countless people who wrote to me with recipes, especially Queenie Endersen of Mallow, Co. Cork who wrote wonderfully evocative letters in her own sweeping hand, each of which I treasure; and Margaret Breen of Beaufort, Co. Kerry, who even sent me slips of Cottiers Kale through the post. I was greatly helped by friends in *Bord Iascaigh Mhara* (The Irish Sea Fisheries Board), by the Government Publications Office and the Ulster Folk Museum.

I also want to thank the people who posted me old recipe books, especially early manuscripts and precious recipe books handed down through generations. They include a manuscript collection begun in the 1730's by the Dillon family of Clonbrock in Co. Galway, the Ballyduff manuscript book from Mocollop Castle, dated 1801, Eliza Helena Odell's recipe book dated 1851, Alice d'Olier's recipes collected from 1893, and Annie Kiely's manuscript, dated Cork 1908. Thank you to Lord and Lady Rosse who allowed me access to the Birr Castle Manuscript Cookbooks started in the mid 17th Century by the Parsons Family, Giana Ferguson who lent me her family manuscript book dating from 1777, Lynne Hoare who lent me the manuscripts of Mary Lee Heathfield 1823 and Annie Irwin 1900. I also had access to the wonderful manuscript collection in the National Library of Ireland in Dublin. All of these and many others proved to be an extraordinarily rich source of information.

For this revised edition I am particularly indebted to Malachy McKenna for sharing his research and fascinating insights into the diet of the Blasket Islanders, Áine de Blacam for many illuminating conversations about the food and culture of Inis Meáin.

A very special extra dimension to this book is the insightful introduction to the food of the aristocracy and the country houses provided by Dorothy Cashman. Thank you also to Dorothy for sharing her knowledge of the manuscript collections.

Regina Sexton supplied her expert historical advice both for the original and this revised edition. She authenticated my own research and provided many additional insights of her own. Her exemplary foreword anchors the book firmly in its historical context.

I am grateful to Alice Taylor and the family of the late Maura Laverty for graciously allowing me to reproduce some of their work. Thanks also to Brendan Grace and Pat Shortt for permission to share some of their material.

Rosalie Dunne for her meticulous help with the research and for typing the manuscript. Emer Fitzgerald and Florrie Cullinane who tested and re-tested recipes, in many cases venturing into previously unknown territory to taste such unfamiliar items such as pig's head, lamb's tails, tripe and drisheen and beggarman's stew.

Very special thanks to editors Jenny Wheatley and Emma Bastow for their generous help and encouragement, who remained smiling to the end even though tired and battle weary from trying to extract the final manuscript.

I am especially grateful to the late Kevin Dunne, Michelle Garrett and Kristin Perers, for the beautiful photographs which have brought my book to life and have captured that elusive Irish feeling, often so difficult to portray.

Heartfelt thanks also goes to my late Aunt Lil, my mother the late Elizabeth O'Connell, and my mother-in-law Myrtle Allen of Ballymaloe House, this book is dedicated to all three. They all kindled my interest in traditional Irish food and were good enough to share their rich store of fascinating old recipes with me.